Fighting to Leave

Fighting to Leave

The Final Years of America's War in Vietnam, 1972–1973

Colonel Robert E. Stoffey

ZENITH PRESS

To Cpl. Thomas J. Murphy, a retired U.S. Marine who survived a penetrating gunshot wound through the head in combat during the 1972 counteroffensive against the large-scale Vietnamese invasion into South Vietnam. Even to this day, Cpl. Tom Murphy suffers from the effects of traumatic brain injury (TBI).

•

Also, equally, to U.S. Marine Master Sgt. Kenneth W. Sargent, shot in the head during an ambush in Iraq in August 2004. His wife, Tonia, continues to help him with his daily physical therapy. He is also supported emotionally by his two daughters, Tasha and Alishia, as he continues to work for maximum recovery from TBI.

First published in 2008 by Zenith Press, an imprint of
MBI Publishing Company, 400 First Avenue North, Suite 300,
Minneapolis, MN 55401 USA

Zenith Press titles are also available at discounts in bulk quantity for
industrial or sales-promotional use. For details write to Special Sales
Manager at MBI Publishing Company, 400 First Avenue North, Suite 300,
Minneapolis, MN 55401 USA.

To find out more about our books, join us online at www.zenithpress.com.

Library of Congress Cataloging-in-Publication Data

Stoffey, Robert E., 1934–
   Fighting to leave : the final years of America's War in Vietnam,
1972–1973 / Robert E. Stoffey. — 1st ed.
       p. cm.
   Includes bibliographical references and index.
   ISBN 978-0-7603-3310-5 (hb w/ jkt)
   1. Vietnam War, 1961–1975—Naval operations, American. 2. Vietnam
War, 1961–1975—Aerial operations, American. 3. Vietnam War,
1961–1975—Personal narratives, American. 4. Stoffey, Robert E., 1934–
I. Title.
   DS558.7.S76 2008
   959.704'3—dc22

                                             2008015728

Designer: Chris Fayers

Printed in the United States of America

On the cover: Three Fighter Squadron 161 (VF-161) F-4D Phantom II fighter
aircraft from the USS Midway (CVA-41) and three Corsair II attack aircraft from
the USS America (CVA 66) drop Loran Bombs during a strike mission in March
1973. National Archives

Contents

• • • • • • • •

Appendixes

Foreword

• • • • • • • • •

This is a book that needed to be written, and Robert E. Stoffey was the man to write it. Vietnam was the most intensely reported war in the American experience. The daily headlines, the continuing editorials, and the grim scenes on the living room TVs of millions of Americans every night during the evening news exerted an influence on national policy that determined the strategic direction of the war. So powerful was this influence, and so profound was its impact, that in the future our military may have to accept a new criteria for defining a "winnable" war. A successful outcome must be assured in the first six weeks or so. Vietnam conclusively demonstrated that the American people will no longer support an inconclusive conflict of continuing carnage.

In spite of the most comprehensive, real-time coverage that saturated the American public, the history of the Vietnam War is far from complete. Historians are still struggling to put the Vietnam years into a national perspective, although both ends of the spectrum are being addressed. There are excellent accounts of the individual in combat by battle experienced infantrymen such as Webb and Puller. At the other extreme, the political side of the Vietnam War is becoming better documented as national policy makers such as Clark Clifford and Henry Kissinger publish their memoirs.

What has been missing until now is the view of the man in the middle, the military commander in the field—this is an aspect of special interest and importance in the history of the Vietnam War that has gone undiscussed. Until Vietnam, the role of the National Command Authority was one of strategic direction, succinctly expressed in broad objectives such as strike, invade, seize, or defend. During Vietnam a new term had to be invented to describe the function of the White House and the Pentagon—*micromanagement.* From the earliest days of our involvement in Southeast Asia, the office of the Secretary of Defense generated a suffocating mass of rules of engagement that had been dutifully accepted by the operating forces in military operations. In Vietnam, not only were sanctions established and military installations prescribed, but the control of friendly fire became so detailed that for many targets the directions of approach and pullout for attacking aircraft were specified by compass headings.

It became the job of the senior on-scene commander, such as the Commander, Seventh Fleet, to develop the tactics and conduct the operations to pursue the military objectives in Vietnam in spite of the complex web of well-meant but almost paralyzing restrictions constantly flowing from Washington, D.C. It was the responsibility of the local area commanders to see that the Washington rules of engagement were implemented and enforced. But it was also their responsibility to continue to try to "win" that war.

For the first time, with Colonel Stoffey's book, we have an account that focuses on the Vietnam War at the level of the field commander. It is not only exciting reading, but fascinating as a seminal element of Vietnam military history.

The Seventh Fleet, at the time, included all U.S. Navy ships and aircraft, U.S. Marines, and allied forces operating off the coast of Vietnam in the Gulf of Tonkin. The extent of the participation of the navy and the Marines in Vietnam was remarkable for what must have seemed to many to be an army–air force theater. The first air strikes against North Vietnam came from the Seventh Fleet carriers. In the course of the war, half of the sorties flown into North Vietnam were by U.S. Navy and Marine Corps aircraft. And the majority of the maneuver battalions actually engaged in combat with the enemy ground troops were Marines. The mines laid in North Vietnamese waters were emplaced by navy tactical aircraft, and all the minesweeping done in conformance with the terms of the ceasefire agreement was accomplished by U.S. Navy and Marine helicopters.

During 1972 and 1973, the period covered by *Fighting to Leave,* the operations of the Seventh Fleet were especially significant. U.S. ground forces were no longer engaged with the enemy, but carrier planes continued to strike targets inside of Vietnam. Cruisers and destroyers conducted gunfire shore bombardments to support the friendly forces on land, and the amphibious ships with their Marine helicopters moved South Vietnamese troops over the beach and around the battlefield to outflank the attack of the North Vietnamese Army. Seventh Fleet sailors, airmen, and Marines were heavily engaged in combat operations.

Robert E. Stoffey is admirably qualified to write this book. His is the narrative of a trusted staff officer, who was often the point man for the combat direction of the Seventh Fleet military operations. His unique contribution in his staff capacity, as well as his special qualifications to author this book, are due to his previous tours of duty in combat as a Marine pilot, and because Robert E. Stoffey was a damn fine professional officer: smart, articulate, with a can-do attitude. Stoffey earned the confidence of the fleet commander and as a consequence was intimately involved in the concept, planning, and conduct of the fleet's operations during 1972 and 1973, our final two years in Vietnam.

Fighting to Leave is more than just a thoroughly readable book. It is important history, as a firsthand account of a special part of a major epoch in our country's Vietnam experience, the wind down of American combat operations. It is important because Robert E. Stoffey was one of the young planners who parlayed his professional competence and combat experience into the sharpened perceptions, skillful planning, and superior staff work that have become a tangible part of the story he tells.

James L. Holloway III
Admiral, U.S. Navy (Ret.)
Chief of Naval Operations (1974–1978)
Commander Seventh Fleet (1972–1973)
President, Naval Historical Foundation, Washington, D.C.

Preface
• • • • • • •

As a result of review of this narrative by John Sherwood, PhD, Naval Historical Center, Washington Navy Yard, Washington, D.C., several continuing controversies are noted. Dr. Sherwood brought to this author's attention that some historians differ as to what really happened during events described by the author in Chapter 8. On May 10, 1972, during the start of Operation Linebacker, navy pilot Lt. Randy Cunningham and his radar intercept officer (RIO), Lt. j.g. Willie Driscoll, in their F-4J Phantom engaged several North Vietnamese MiG fighters. This author wrote that during the encounters, and while shooting down their third MiG, they had shot down a Colonel Tomb. Shortly after the shootdown, U.S. Air Force Intelligence officers at the Seventh Air Force Command Center, code name Blue Chip, confirmed Cunningham's and Driscoll's third kill of May 10, 1972. They also revealed that the third MiG shot down was a North Vietnamese pilot named Colonel Tomb or Toon, who had been credited with thirteen American kills.

Dr. John Sherwood's review reported that Dr. Istvan Toperczer, a Hungarian air force medical officer, had conducted extensive research on the Vietnamese People's Air Force (VPAF) in Hanoi and claims in his book *Air War over North Vietnam* that he could not find any record of a pilot named Tomb. Additionally, Toperczer stated that official Hanoi archives indicated that no pilot in the VPAF achieved thirteen aerial victories and no active VPAF pilot in 1972 held the rank of colonel. The thirteen kills on MiG-21 No. 4326 apparently refer to the number of claims made by all the pilots who flew that specific aircraft.

Dr. John Sherwood, in reviewing this manuscript, contacted colleagues who work at the National Security Agency (NSA). NSA had routinely monitored radio transmissions between VPAF ground controllers and pilots. Interestingly, the NSA sources corroborated the existence of a Tomb-like pilot named, Maj. Dinh Ton. According to NSA documents, Maj. Dinh Ton downed ten American aircraft, making him the top VPAF ace. Dr. Sherwood further reported to this writer that Major Ton apparently survived the war but then fell out of favor with the Democratic Republic of Vietnam (DRV) regime in the 1980s over alleged "Chinese affiliations." Dr. Sherwood expressed that this may explain why Ton's name did not come up in Dr. Toperczer's research in the Vietnamese archives. Ton's name may have been literally expunged from the official records. In another twist of irony, while NSA did not confirm the existence of a top Vietnamese ace with a name similar to Tomb, Toon, or Ton, no NSA records could be found that confirm the Cunningham-Driscoll third kill on May 10, 1972. Dr. Sherwood states that "This does not mean it did not happen. The story of their third kill is well documented in numerous official sources, including the air force Red Baron study of air-to-air combat during the Vietnam War, Cunningham and Driscoll's Navy Cross citations, the Chief of Naval Operations' briefing notes of May 10, 1972, and numerous navy and air force messages from that period. What it does mean is that the identity of this third shot-down MiG pilot remains a mystery today."

That third kill on May 10, 1972, by Cunningham and Driscoll, after having previously shot down a MiG-17 and MiG-21, made them the first American flight crew to down five enemy aircraft — and the first Aces of the Vietnam War.

With the foregoing controversy expressed, I wish to inform you that this is not a history book, nor simply a memoir. It is a book containing anecdotal material culled from the author's personal experience as a field-grade officer on the Seventh Fleet staff, calling it as he saw it during the confusing closing years, 1972 and 1973, of our war in Vietnam. If you were there at that time and saw it differently, write your own book and present your documents to the National Archives.

The reader must keep in mind the Vietnam War was the longest in U.S. history. American fighting lasted from July 1959 to January 1973, with continuing economic support until the fall of Saigon in May 1975. This book covers the period just after American ground-fighting troops withdrew from Vietnam in 1971. It also discusses the response of American advisers and U.S. Marine Corps and Army helicopter support, which were brought in after the invasion of the North Vietnamese Army in South Vietnam during 1972. The narrative then follows with the details of the full U.S. Navy and Air Force support rendered, leading to the end of American fighting in Vietnam and the end of the war with the cease-fire directed by President Nixon on January 15, 1973. The conclusion of the American political support came during 1975, when Saigon fell to the North Vietnamese, two years after American fighting forces left Vietnam, in accordance with the Paris Peace Accord of 1973. During this lengthy war, about 2.7 million Americans served in the war zone; 58,000 Americans were killed, 300,000 were wounded, and approximately 75,000 were permanently disabled.

Acknowledgments

I gratefully acknowledge the help I received from the Headquarters Marine Corps History and Museums Division, Washington, D.C., for reviewing the manuscript and confirming the dates of my described actions of the ASHORE perspective of the ground battles in Quang Tri Province, South Vietnam, in the spring of 1972. Particularly, I thank retired Marine Corps officers Charles Melson, chief historian, Marine Corps Historical Center, and Curtis G. Arnold. They both researched and wrote the narrative *U.S. Marines in Vietnam: The War that Would Not End: 1971–1973* for the History and Museums Division. Charles Melson thoroughly reviewed my manuscript and I am grateful for his professional contributions.

I am thankful to John Sherwood, PhD, historian at the U.S. Naval Historical Center, Washington, D.C., for his professional and detailed review of the manuscript. Dr. Sherwood's review revealed that some historians have surmised and claimed some differences of opinion as to what happened on several events described in this book. Some of those differences remain controversial in several military and historical circles to this day (and are discussed briefly in the preface).

Appreciation is expressed to David M. Brahms, Brigadier General, USMC (Ret.) and attorney at law, for technical advice.

I thank Darrel D. Whitcomb, air force forward air controller (FAC), who flew combat missions in Vietnam with the call sign Nail 25 and is the author of the book *The Rescue of Bat 21*; I am grateful that he gave me permission to extract from his narrative the complex attempts to rescue air force crewmember call sign Bat 21 Bravo for incorporation into one chapter of my story. Both the attempts and the successful rescue are relevant to my narrative and were supported by our naval gunfire ships of the Seventh Fleet. The rescue was accomplished by U.S. Navy SEAL Lt. Tom Norris and coordinated by Marine Corps Lt. Col. Andy Anderson.

I am extremely thankful to Gary Murphy, who gave me permission to mention his heroic Marine Corps brother, Tom Murphy. Tom suffered a serious head wound while flying in a helicopter during one of the many Marine Corps helicopter missions flown supporting South Vietnamese Marines during the Lam Son Counteroffensive Operation of 1972.

Special acknowledgment is also due to Vice Adm. Edward S. Briggs, USN (ret.); Capt. John T. "Jack" Beaver, USN (ret.); Gen. Walter E. Boomer, USMC (ret.); Fred H. Cherrick, former Navy Lt., j.g. (1972); Capt. James C. Froid, USN (ret.); and Capt. Stuart D. "Stu" Landersman, USN (ret.), who all reviewed the manuscript at various points.

Without the professional editorial assistance of my wife, Eleanor, this story could not have made it to the completed manuscript stage.

Introduction
· · · · · · · · · ·

As a personal combat participant in the Vietnam War for more than four years, I experienced and witnessed three distinctly different ways both sides fought that war. Therefore, I have categorized these different periods into what I term *phases of conflict.* I happened to participate in all three phases. Phase One consisted of the American counterattacks against the local Viet Cong cadres in South Vietnam. Phase Two was when the Americans fielded large numbers of troops to counter the arrival of North Vietnamese Army troops in South Vietnam. Phase Three took place when the Americans rendered assistance to the South Vietnamese to counter the North Vietnamese invasion in South Vietnam a year after the United States removed their major ground-fighting units in 1971.

This is the story of a specific period in American military history, the closing years of the Vietnam War, 1972 and 1973. It is the period that commenced a year after our ground forces retrograded out of Vietnam. Much of this important phase of that war is not known by most of the American public.

This phase of our longest, most misunderstood war became the third and final phase of more than a decade of American sacrifices and involvement in this Vietnam debacle and political— not military—defeat.

You could say Phase One commenced as far back as 1950, when a U.S. National Security Council (NSC) study recommended "close attention to communist aggression in Asia, particularly in French Indo China." In 1953, NSC reported, "Loss of Indo China to Communism would be critical to the security of the U.S. and any negotiated settlement with Ho Chi Min in the North would mean losing Indo China and the whole of Southeast Asia."

In June 1954, CIA Agent Col. Francis G. Lansdale arrived in Saigon to set up a team of agents to commence paramilitary and political psychological operations against North Vietnam. By 1958, the United States had sent 350 military personnel to Saigon.

During John F. Kennedy's years as president, 1961 to 1963, Eisenhower's "limited risk" period of dealing with communism's expansion in Vietnam moved into a "commitment" to stop a communist takeover of South Vietnam.

President Kennedy resisted pressures to introduce American ground-fighting units into South Vietnam, but he expanded the military and political involvement significantly. In the spring of 1961, JFK made commitments to South Vietnam by ordering four hundred troops of Special Forces and one hundred American military advisers to South Vietnam, without public announcements. In January 1963, the United States had 2,650 servicemen in South Vietnam; by October 1963, there were 16,732.

Civilian and military advisers to JFK expressed that sending American servicemen would "spark" the South Vietnamese Army to defend itself against the Viet Cong. In 1963, the Joint Chiefs of Staff (JCS) estimated that if the Democratic Republic of Vietnam (DRV), referred to as North Vietnam, invaded the Republic of Vietnam (RVN), referred to as South Vietnam, approximately 205,000 American troops would be adequate to stop them from taking control of South Vietnam. JCS agreed that number (about six divisions) of American defenders would do the job, even if communist China joined the invasion into the South.

JFK's civilian and military advisers felt that the DRV, or North Vietnam, along with Red China, would have logistical difficulties in maintaining forces in the field, particularly if our U.S. airpower were given a "free hand against logistical targets."

Phase One continued into the early sixties with a buildup of advisers and ground units to assist the South Vietnamese Army (ARVN) to fight the local Viet Cong (VC) guerrillas.

This dilemma of using "limited means" to stop the communists was then inherited by President Lyndon B. Johnson.

By 1965, the conflict evolved into Phase Two with the U.S. and ARVN troops inflicting massive casualties upon the rural-based VC cadres. The North Vietnamese Army (NVA) then introduced regular army troops into South Vietnam during 1965 and increased NVA troops into the South in 1966. The opposing troops increased in numbers in South Vietnam by both the United States and the North Vietnamese.

President Johnson, in his last major decision in attempting to get out of Vietnam, directed a complete halt of bombing North Vietnam on November 1, 1968. The last mission flown north of the DMZ was by the navy commander of Air Wing Fourteen dropping his bombs on a bridge from a VA-97 Corsair II aircraft.

The massive antiwar demonstrations across the United States had prevented the Johnson administration from exercising capable, decisive military actions for a military solution to the long war. President Johnson, dismayed by the long war, decided not to seek reelection.

In January 1969, President Richard M. Nixon, promising the American public a "secret plan" to end the war, entered the White House with few options for ending the war. Nixon chose the option of large-scale withdrawal of Americans from Vietnam.

Because President Johnson, in a goodwill gesture to North Vietnam, had stopped all bombing of North Vietnam in 1968, during 1969, U.S. military air operations concentrated in South Vietnam as well as the Ho Chi Minh trail in Laos and Cambodia.

It had been more than a decade, and three American presidents (Kennedy, Johnson, and Nixon) had been involved in South Vietnam by the time the United States hit maximum troop levels of 549,000 in South Vietnam during 1969.

On June 8, 1969, President Nixon met with South Vietnamese President Thieu and announced that he had ordered a phased withdrawal of American troops from Vietnam. The Nixon Doctrine of 1969, the Vietnamization of the war, began the U.S. disengagement from Vietnam. The United States planned for, and expected, the South Vietnamese to transition to fully defending their country through the Vietnamization doctrine.

In 1970, more than one hundred thousand American troops were pulled out of Vietnam. By July 1971, the major ground-fighting units of U.S. Army and Marines had been retrograded from South Vietnam.

The commander, U.S. Military Assistance Command Vietnam (MACV), Gen. Creighton Abrams, was delegated the mission to transition the South Vietnamese to assume total defensive responsibilities for their country. General Abrams would execute this mission while his forces were rapidly being removed from Vietnam due to domestic political pressure.

The U.S. Navy's Seventh Fleet kept carriers and gunships in the Gulf of Tonkin, off the coast of Vietnam. The carrier-based aircraft and U.S. Seventh Air Force aircraft gave support to the withdrawing U.S. Marines and Army ground units.

The major battles of the 1968 NVA Tet Offensive resulted in a devastated, defeated North Vietnamese Army in South Vietnam. The NVA-VC suffered major losses from the American-ARVN forces. NVA-VC losses were 32,000 dead and 5,800 captured. No territory temporarily gained by the communist attacks was held, and even more importantly, the communists failed to rally the South Vietnamese people to their side. NVA General Giap, who defeated the French at Dienbienphu in 1954, had to withdraw his battered army back across the borders into North Vietnam and Laos.

Between 1968 and 1971, North Vietnamese General Giap reevaluated his plans and shifted to building a strong force of tanks, artillery, antiair artillery, and surface-to-air missiles (SAMs). General Giap not only rebuilt his army, but he planned a large-scale invasion into South Vietnam with a superior force, to be executed when the American ground forces left South Vietnam. This invasion plan included a fully conventional infantry with massive artillery and tanks, protected overhead by massed antiaircraft guns and sophisticated radar-guided and heat-seeking SAMs.

In the spring of 1972, the majority of the U.S. Army and all U.S. Marines, except for advisers, had been withdrawn from South Vietnam. It had been a full year since the 1971 massive American pullouts associated with Nixon's Vietnamization program. The United States had left only a few ground forces with limited defensive orders as well as advisers assigned to the South Vietnamese Army and South Vietnamese Marine Corps.

The U.S. Air Force, with the Seventh Air Force in command at Tan Son Nhut AFB outside of Saigon, had reduced its support size during the 1968–71 withdrawals.

The U.S. Army had only the ground unit, 196th Brigade, located near Da Nang Air Force Base. It had ground detachment elements north of Da Nang at Hue City and nearby Phu Bai airfield. The brigade's orders were to "execute defensive perimeter patrols only."

The 196th Brigade also had assigned to it F Troop, 8th Cavalry. F Troop consisted of twenty-five helicopters and a platoon of forty infantry troops. F Troop's primary mission was to perform reconnaissance to locate enemy units and report their locations to intelligence for passing on to the ARVN troop commanders to take action against the NVA-VC units in the area.

U.S. Air Force units remaining in South Vietnam consisted of approximately sixty F-4 Phantoms and five AC-119 gunships at Da Nang AFB, and twenty-three A-37 light bombers at Bien Hoa airfield, near Saigon.

All U.S. Air Force units in Vietnam and those flying combat missions into Vietnam from Thailand and Guam remained under the control of the Seventh Air Force located at Tan Son Nhut Air Force Base near Saigon.

The F Troop helicopters under command of Army Maj. Jack Kennedy were still based at Marble Mountain Airfield, two miles east of Da Nang. I had previously spent two thirteen-month combat tours as a Marine helicopter pilot (1965–66) and then as a fixed-wing pilot and forward air controller flying OV-10A Bronco aircraft (1969–70) in Marine Air Group 16 located at Marble Mountain Airfield.

Having flown 440 combat missions and been shot down twice, I had personally experienced two phases of that war. Soon, unexpectedly, I would be thrust into Phase Three of the Vietnam War. I would rapidly become personally involved in the day-to-day actions and operations of this new change in direction of an old war.

Phase Three was initiated by the Politburo of the Democratic Republic of Vietnam, known as the North Vietnamese government. They directed their North Vietnamese Army to commence a large-scale, blitzkrieg attack across the demilitarized zone (DMZ) and from bases in Laos into South Vietnam with three reinforced divisions. The three divisions attacked the northern area of the South Vietnamese I Corps area of responsibility. At the same time, the NVA unleashed another multidivision attack in the II Corps area of Kontum in the central highlands of South Vietnam and into the III Corps area just north of Saigon at An Loc.

Nothing of such large-scale, heavily equipped NVA attacks like this had ever been executed before.

On March 30, 1972, the Thursday before Easter Sunday, Phase Three began. The NVA, now very well equipped, invaded South Vietnam.

Three months prior to this massive North Vietnamese invasion, on December 23, 1971, I had reported to my new assignment on the staff of the Commander, Seventh Fleet, on board the guided missile cruiser USS *Oklahoma City* (CLG-5), afloat in the Gulf of Tonkin off Vietnam. During this, my third tour of duty, I was assigned as the assistant amphibious warfare and Marine Corps air officer of Vice Adm. William P. Mack.

This is the story of how the South Vietnamese and the residual American military still in Vietnam after Nixon's Vietnamization program responded to the NVA invasion of March 30, 1972 (often called the Easter Offensive). Thus, Phase Three, 1972 and 1973, ended the American participation in the war in Vietnam.

On January 15, 1973, offensive actions against North Vietnam were suspended by Nixon. This was followed by Henry Kissinger and Le Duc Tho, who had been engaged in secret talks on behalf of their governments for years, signing a treaty on January 23. Finally, on January 27, a ceasefire agreement was signed by the leaders of the official delegations at the Paris peace talks. North Vietnam had agreed to stop the fighting in South Vietnam and return the American prisoners of war. The Americans agreed to stop bombing North Vietnam and clear the North Vietnamese harbors and rivers of mines laid by the Americans in 1972.

The American mine sweeping operation, code name End Sweep, commenced on February 27, 1973, and concluded on July 27, 1973.

The North Vietnamese released the first American POWs on February 12, 1973, and the POW exchanges ended when all 566 American POWs were finally released on March 29, 1973.

Although the American participation in the Vietnam War was technically over, several incidents occurred causing some military actions until the end of the End Sweep mine sweeping operation on July 27, 1973.

Finally, Americans left the war-torn country of Vietnam, with the exception of only a few Americans in the U.S. Embassy in Saigon and at the nearby Tan Son Nhut airfield. South Vietnam was on its own.

This narrative details only the time of 1972 to 1973, the period of America's last military actions involved in Vietnam. It does not cover the fall of Vietnam, in 1975, after all American support forces had left. The 1975 fall of South Vietnam should be expounded upon by someone who was there and can relate exact events to the historians regarding what happened after the Americans abandoned their ally in 1973 to extract themselves from the conflict.

This following story reflects the war as seen from the Seventh Fleet perspective. It depicts what the Seventh Fleet's Navy and Marine personnel sacrificed to assist South Vietnam to fight for their freedom against the determined communist North Vietnamese invasion force that invaded South Vietnam on March 30, 1972.

The Vietnam War was not only our longest war, it was a very costly war in lives, resources, and money. The cost, or impact, of the psychological trauma experienced by many American combatants due to the lack of support by the American people is immeasurable.

One thing certain about this factual story is that it records, for history, that the U.S. Navy and Marine Corps units, within the Seventh Fleet, suffered substantial losses. With military professionalism, however, these brave Americans carried out their assigned missions, despite the restrictive constraints dictated by our elected civilian leadership in Washington, D.C., which quite often endangered and cost lives.

Chapter 1

• • • • • • •

Afloat with the Seventh Fleet

On March 30, 1972, afloat the Seventh Fleet, we watched, in shock, from the bridge of the Commander, Seventh Fleet, on board the Seventh Fleet flagship, the guided-missile cruiser USS *Oklahoma City*. We saw numerous North Vietnamese Army (NVA) tanks driving south and crossing the Ben Hai River, the separation line between North Vietnam and South Vietnam. The NVA tanks continued rolling from the demilitarized zone (DMZ), charging for the bridge at the South Vietnamese town of Dong Ha. I picked up a pair of binoculars and saw NVA tanks to the northeast of Dong Ha, much closer to us. NVA troops were following behind the fast-moving tanks. Some NVA amphibious tanks plunged into the Cau Viet River and began to move to the south side. Our ship sat almost straight east from the Cau Viet River. The NVA were obviously on the attack; many tanks were headed south toward the South Vietnamese Army and Marine Corps (VNMC) defensive positions farther inland to the west.

As members of the staff of the Commander, Seventh Fleet, we all expected this to happen. At noon, March 30, 1972, the North Vietnamese launched a blitzkrieg attack upon South Vietnam. Between the first assault waves on March 30 and April 2, the NVA crossed the DMZ and the Cau Viet River with thirty thousand troops, substantial artillery, and hundreds of tanks.

What made this invasion so incredible was the fact that the NVA had a protective umbrella of surface-to-air missiles inside the DMZ.

In March and April 1972, both the Seventh Fleet and Seventh Air Force commanders had requested permission through the chain of command to execute preemptive strikes upon the large buildup of antiaircraft artillery and SAM sites being placed inside the DMZ by the NVA. All preemptive-strike requests were denied by higher authority. But shortly after, some of the SAMs in the DMZ were destroyed by U.S. Air Force F-4 Phantoms. General John D. Lavelle, Commander, Seventh Air Force, located at Tan Son Nhut AFB outside of Saigon, had assumed that because these SAMs could easily hit any of his Seventh Air Force aircraft flying just south of the DMZ, they should be destroyed. An air force enlisted man working in the intelligence section of the 432d Tactical Reconnaissance Wing at Udorn, Thailand, wrote a letter to his senator questioning these U.S. strikes into the DMZ. General John Ryan, U.S. Air Force chief of staff, who was based at the Pentagon, ordered an inquiry. The investigation revealed that the Seventh Air Force had indeed launched strikes into the DMZ and that General Lavelle had exceeded his authority. General Ryan quickly recommended to the secretary of defense that General Lavelle be immediately relieved of command of the Seventh Air Force and brought back to the United States. General Lavelle was reduced from four-star general to major general (two stars) and retired.

Those of us on the Seventh Fleet staff had been watching the air force message traffic and—along with our own immediate boss, Vice Adm. William P. Mack, Commander, Seventh Fleet—observed the dismissal of his counterpart, General Lavelle, from command.

General John Vogt replaced General Lavelle as commander, Seventh Air Force.

The Seventh Fleet, Seventh Air Force, and other intelligence units had been reporting an enormous buildup of North Vietnamese military supplies and SAM sites in the DMZ. Despite the intelligence reports of this massive buildup that were continually moving up the chain of command—all the way to Washington, D.C.—the staffs of the U.S. military command, Vietnam, in Saigon had a false sense of security. They did not believe a direct full-scale attack would come from the north across the DMZ. Planners in Saigon still felt that any attacks, large or small, would continue from the Ho Chi Minh trail areas from the west. Since the removal of U.S. ground combat units from Vietnam in 1971, there were only a few Americans up near the DMZ. The Americans were the U.S. Army and Marine Corps advisers and Air Naval Gunfire Liaison Company units supporting the South Vietnamese Army and South Vietnamese Marine Corps units in Quang Tri Province. The U.S. Marines consisted of sixty officers and eleven enlisted men located just below the DMZ to train and advise the South Vietnamese Army and Marine Corps units. These were identical to the adviser roles played by Americans supporting South Vietnam ten years earlier, in 1962.

South Vietnamese Lt. Gen. Hoang Xuan Lam, commander of the northernmost 1st Corps of South Vietnam, referred to as I Corps, had his hands full. General Lam had his headquarters in Da Nang, well south of the DMZ. His troops were suddenly confronting three reinforced North Vietnamese divisions (thirty thousand troops) with three artillery regiments and, for the first time in South Vietnam, antiaircraft units. The antiaircraft units had also brought with them handheld, Russian-built SA-7 Strella heat-seeking missiles and surface-to-air missile launchers. To make matters worse, these swift NVA attacks were reinforced by hundreds of Soviet-built T-34, T-54, and PT-76 amphibious tanks.

The false sense of security that the ARVN and MACV planners in Saigon had felt, with U.S. ground forces gone from South Vietnam, was now chaotically disrupted. Even though intelligence reports of a large-scale military buildup in the DMZ had been circulating for months, the South Vietnamese 3d ARVN Division outposts hadn't heard anything about it from Saigon.

Later, I would learn that one of those U.S. Marine advisers to the South Vietnamese Marine Corps was Maj. Walter E. Boomer. Major Boomer was, at the time, with a lone VNMC battalion at Outpost Sarge. Earlier, Major Boomer had contacted Gen. Vu Van Giai, 3d ARVN Division commander. Major Boomer had been watching the NVA buildup in the DMZ through his binoculars. He reported the heavy activity of the NVA in the DMZ and stated to General Giai, "I suggest we commence some patrolling out there to see what is going on."

General Giai, apparently not adequately warned by the South Vietnamese general staff in Saigon about the massive NVA buildup, responded, "Major, I don't have the manpower to send out patrols." General Giai didn't seem too concerned. Why should he? He had no worrisome intelligence reports from Saigon. But for days he had been receiving reports from his forward ARVN and VNMC outposts about sightings of the North Vietnamese Army stockpiling ammunition in the DMZ.

Marine Corps Lt. Col. Gerald H. "Gerry" Turley, assigned in Saigon, was in command of the seventy-one U.S. Marine advisers. He happened to be up from Saigon visiting his advisers to the Vietnamese Marines along outposts north of the 3d ARVN Division when the NVA began their probes at about 1000 that morning, March 30, 1972. The probes were followed by the lead elements of the NVA as they crossed the DMZ into South Vietnam, along Highway 9. Suddenly, the NVA were in South Vietnam, attacking the ARVN.

Since the Marine Corps ground units had left a year earlier, the U.S. Army and Marine advisers had no well-established fire-support coordination system to function with the U.S. Navy's gunfire ships in the Gulf of Tonkin. They also had no way to request U.S. Navy, Marine Corps, or Air Force attack aircraft. The reason for this serious shortcoming was that the advisers were part of the 3d ARVN Division, which was not in the U.S. chain of command. As the NVA struck with force, the advisers were immediately isolated on the forward edge of the battle area.

Because the Marine Corps advisers to the VNMC were not in our Seventh Fleet's Navy–Marine Corps chain of command, we didn't know, personally, who these advisers were. But, as the action progressed we began to hear some advisers' names through contacts in Saigon. Later, we heard that Major Boomer was with the VNMC battalion commander, Maj. Tran Zuan Quang, at Fire Support Base Sarge as it came under intense ground and heavy artillery attack.

U.S. Marine Capt. John W. Ripley was an adviser to the 3d Vietnamese Marine Corps Battalion as they rapidly moved north to Dong Ha to attempt to repulse the invading NVA, not imagining the massive size of the NVA force. Captain Ripley was able to contact U.S. Seventh Fleet Task Group 70.8's cruisers and destroyers, and they gave him some much-needed naval gunfire support (NGFS) as he made contact with lead elements of the attacking NVA supported by tanks. The NGFS stopped the NVA tanks and troops from reaching the Dong Ha Bridge, for the time being.

Admiral Mack shook his head, as we watched the stream of enemy forces heading south from the DMZ area. He turned to his chief of staff, Capt. Earl F. Godfrey, and said, "Well, Earl, just like we've been reporting up the chain of command to Washington. They certainly were building up to something very big inside the DMZ. Now, here it is. This is one helluva invasion. It's bigger than I envisioned."

"Yes, sir, Admiral. But, we weren't allowed to knock out those SAMs in the DMZ. Also, we weren't authorized to hit the trucks coming down along the North Vietnamese coast, loaded with ammunition. Now, the NVA has a helluva protective SAM umbrella over their attacking troops. We'll have to see what Washington allows us to do about this big one."

Admiral Mack's message traffic continued to report the situation to CincPacFlt, with copies sent to CincPac, MACV, Seventh Air Force, and JCS. We continued to wait to see just what we would be authorized to do.

The Joint Chiefs of Staff in Washington finally directed that we respond with "limited force," which we immediately did with our Task Group 70.8 ships, including our ship, shooting at the NVA tanks. But the low cloud coverage over the invading NVA troops kept our Task Force 77 carrier aircraft from attacking the NVA troops. It was catch-up time, yet the U.S. Navy and Air Force on-site commanders simply were not authorized to strike back at the NVA in North Vietnam. At this juncture, we were still in a defensive posture that was limited by Washington's orders to refrain from launching any U.S. surface or air strikes north of the DMZ.

On the next day, March 31, a preponderance of NVA continued to stream from the DMZ into Quang Tri Province.

On April 1 and 2, 1972, we staff members would find time to leave the war room and dash out to the admiral's bridge to physically observe some of the closer-to-the-shore ground action. You couldn't miss the B-52 arc-light raids to the northeast of Quang Tri City. The smoke rose hundreds of feet into the air.

On April 2, Easter Sunday, I stood next to Admiral Mack and his chief of staff, Capt. Earl Godfrey, on the bridge of the USS *Oklahoma City*. There were about ten other staff officers out on the bridge observing as well. We all watched in awe as hundreds of NVA tanks continued crossing the Cau Viet River, heading south for Dong Ha and Quang Tri City. Every now and then, staff members would run back into the war room from the bridge to read our message traffic, hoping that Admiral Mack would, after repeated requests, be authorized to execute swift retaliation raids into the DMZ as well as into North Vietnam. After all, it was from North Vietnam that the enemy continually came, visiting all this bloodshed upon their southern neighbors. His requests were not answered by the chain of command in Washington.

As we floated in the Gulf of Tonkin, very close to shore and off the Cau Viet River, the *Oklahoma City*'s 5- and 6-inch guns fired heavy volumes at NVA Soviet-built T-54 tanks and amphibious T-76 tanks on both sides of the Cau Viet River. I saw six NVA tanks destroyed by the *Oklahoma City* guns in just a few minutes, before I had to get back to my staff desk to monitor the big picture.

The *Oklahoma City*'s executive officer, Cmdr. Joe Fairchild, was down in the ship's combat information center (CIC)—the combat brain of the ship responsible for operating the ship's air- and surface-search radar and for maintaining voice communications with other ships and aircraft. During these heavy shore bombardments, particularly those aimed at the enemy tanks and troops crossing the Cau Viet River well south of the DMZ, CIC was the active focal point for naval gunfire support operations. CIC also coordinated antiair warfare by rapidly and accurately collecting, processing, displaying, evaluating, and disseminating tactical information throughout the ship. Joe Fairchild stayed very busy in CIC, looking at radar scopes, listening to reports, and managing and coordinating weapons firing with navigation and engine room crews.

Commander Fairchild called up to the ship's bridge, "Captain Tice, this is Commander Fairchild in CIC. Our radar screens indicate we are making many hits on what appear to be fast-moving vehicles heading south."

"You sure as hell are, Joe! We, on the bridge, can easily see it from up here. Your hits upon NVA tanks, as they emerge from the river on the south side, are fantastic. Tell your personnel they are doing one helluva job! Tell them the captain is most impressed with their rapidity of fire and accuracy."

"Aye, aye, Captain. Glad to see all systems operating so well. I'll pass your words on to the crews," responded a very busy Joe Fairchild.

At about 2200, April 2, we, the staff aboard the *Oklahoma City*, began hearing radio reports about a U.S. Air Force EB-66 radar electronics-jamming aircraft, call sign Bat 21, having been shot down just south of the DMZ. Some of the radio chatter was apparently from U.S. Air Force fixed-wing and helicopter crews in Bat 21's area. A couple of radio transmissions indicated that only one of the crew of six, Bat 21 Bravo, was a survivor on the ground. We then heard radio discussions from air force forward air controllers stating that Bat 21 was down in the middle of a very large, advancing enemy force.

At that time, none of us realized that the advancing enemy force consisted of thirty thousand NVA troops attacking the 3d ARVN Division and its attached VNMC battalions. We occasionally could hear U.S. Air Force helicopter rescue crews chattering. It all sounded like they were experiencing severe difficulties in attempting to get Bat 21 Bravo out from the midst of the large NVA force, where he had apparently parachuted into.

Poor weather continued to preclude our carrier strike aircraft from attacking NVA ground and artillery units, which were pushing rapidly toward Dong Ha and Quang Tri City. Finally, when the weather cleared enough to allow launching aircraft from the carriers, SAM-2 missile sites inside the DMZ shot down twelve of our navy carrier aircraft operating north of Quang Tri City, which was just below the DMZ. Navy search-and-rescue units were busy. These were SAM sites that the Seventh Air Force and Seventh Fleet were not authorized to strike several weeks before, when both had requested permission to do so.

Finally, after the third day of the NVA invasion, higher authority authorized the Seventh Air Force and Seventh Fleet to run air strikes into the DMZ.

On April 3, Task Force 77 carriers launched anti-SAM missile site attacks within the DMZ to attempt to neutralize the antiair protection that the three NVA divisions enjoyed. Again, heavy cloud cover effectively hampered the U.S. Air Force and Navy bombers from knocking out the numerous SAM-2 sites in the DMZ, but the overcast skies did not hamper the U.S. Army helicopter crews from offering much support to the 3d ARVN Division. We also continued to hear a lot of radio chatter from U.S. Air Force and Army helicopter crews still attempting to rescue Bat 21 Bravo in the midst of all the confusion, but we couldn't determine Bat 21 Bravo's location or if he was still alive from the monitored radio transmissions. There was quite a battle going on in that area.

We did hear radio calls from U.S. Army helicopter crews; their call signs indicated they were from Marble Mountain Airfield, two miles east of Da Nang. Then we started to hear radio communications decribing some serious, very dangerous enemy fire that these army helicopter pilots were braving in their heroic attempt to rescue our U.S. advisers to the 3d ARVN Division and Vietnamese Marines. We heard someone report that one U.S. Marine lieutenant died while being helo-lifted out of the Quang Tri City area and that three U.S. advisers were still in the town of Cam Lo when it was reported overrun by the NVA infantry. We never did hear what their fate was over the radio transmissions received in the war room. Because we were not in their chain of command, we were receiving much of our information by scanning the radio nets to try to determine the ground situation our advisers were confronting.

Because the U.S. ground forces had pulled out of Vietnam in 1971, there were no news correspondents in the field up in the NVA invasion areas, but UPI correspondent Stewart Kellerman reported from Da Nang, which was well to the south of the battlefield. He stated, "The U.S. Army chopper pilots returning to Da Nang from their missions up north reported every hill up near the DMZ looked like a Christmas tree from the numerous sparkles of NVA machine-gun fire at them. There were muzzles blazing all over the place."

Occasionally, we'd hear radio chatter from an air force Jolly Green rescue helicopter checking in with air force forward air controllers (FACs) below the DMZ. They'd be discussing extremely difficult attempts to rescue Bat 21.

General Frederick Weyand, deputy U.S. commander, Vietnam, flew up to Da Nang from Saigon to confer with ARVN General Lam, who reported, "The NVA are thrusting directly at Quang Tri City."

We received reports that the NVA were attacking Quang Tri City with massive artillery fire and tanks followed by commandos using recoilless rifles as a heavy base of fire. We also heard reports over the radio transmitted by FACs that as civilians were fleeing Quang Tri City, North Vietnamese gunners, located on top of tanks, were shooting at the civilians as they fled the burning city. Most of these reports came from U.S. Air Force FACs flying very slow O-1 Bird Dog aircraft and swifter-moving, but still dangerously slow, OV-10 Bronco aircraft over the battlefield.

Because there had been no news reporters in the combat area since the U.S. Marines left a year earlier, there was no one to report the North Vietnamese atrocities against the South Vietnamese civilians. If our press and TV media had been there, would they have reported the NVA atrocities? In all previous years that the U.S. press was in-country, they continuously reported the negatives of the U.S. troops and consistently wrote news articles that depicted the invading North Vietnamese and their local Viet Cong counterparts as the good guys. That continual slanted news coverage, without a doubt, significantly contributed to and fueled the anti–Vietnam War demonstrations back home.

The U.S. press offered little coverage in 1968 when invading NVA troops killed hundreds of civilians and monks at Hue City. The press offered more coverage of those atrocities when the U.S. Marines, after a tough battle, recaptured Hue City and mass graves of South Vietnamese civilians butchered by the invading NVA were discovered. Somehow, though, it never became big news back in the United States.

While the hell on earth created by the North Vietnamese Invasion raged in South Vietnam, life in the real world continued. After all, it was Easter.

I assumed that my three children were enjoying a traditional Easter egg hunt somewhere on Yokosuka Naval Base in Japan. It seemed like such a long time since Christmas week of 1971, when I had left my wife, Eleanor, and our children in Yokosuka.

While Easter was being celebrated by Christians worldwide, the North Vietnamese continued their invasion thrust toward Quang Tri City. The North Vietnamese felt they would soon prove that President Nixon's Vietnamization of the war, with the American withdrawals commencing back in 1968, would not work. The North must surely have felt that the South could not defend their country alone.

And so it was that on April 2, at 1520, Camp Carroll surrendered to the 24th NVA Regiment, resulting in Mai Loc being exposed on the flank, as these were mutually supporting camps.

The 3d VNMC Battalion at Dong Ha knew the NVA were rapidly advancing with many tanks on April 3. A heavy NVA artillery barrage hit the South Vietnamese Marines near the Dong Ha Bridge. Our Seventh Fleet ships, USS *Buchanan* (DDG-14), USS *Joseph Strauss* (DDG-16), USS *Waddell* (DDG-24), USS *Hamner* (DD-718), and USS *Richard B. Anderson* (DD-786) began responding to air naval gunfire company (ANGLICO) calls for naval gunfire support. With the help of the Seventh Fleet's gunfire, the 3d VNMC Battalion established defensive positions on the south side of the Dong Ha Bridge. However, the NVA continued coming at Dong Ha with many more tanks supported by heavy fire from NVA artillery units to the north.

As Easter day slowly passed with ferocious attacks by the NVA from the North, the North Vietnamese, with three more divisions, struck from the Ho Chi Minh trail and the central highlands in an obvious effort to cut South Vietnam in half. Then, we received reports that three additional reinforced divisions were attacking into South Vietnam from the Parrots Peak area of Cambodia, thrusting straight toward Saigon.

Communists worldwide would blame this massive invasion for not getting what they wanted at the on-again-off-again Paris peace talks, which President Johnson had called only five days before the presidential election in 1968. As a goodwill gesture, Johnson halted all bombing in North Vietnam in 1968. As we now stood on the bridge of the *Oklahoma City* on April 2, 1972, President Johnson's directive against bombing North Vietnam was still in effect. Johnson's stopping the bombing of North Vietnam right before the elections didn't help his party's presidential candidate, Vice President Hubert Humphrey, at all, and so, Richard M. Nixon won the election. Several weeks later, the Paris peace talks began. For all these years, the peace talks had been mired down with wide disagreements.

The North Vietnamese knew a year before, in 1971, that most U.S. ground-fighting forces had withdrawn under Nixon's Vietnamization plan. The North chose this period, with continual overcast skies greatly in their favor, to invade South Vietnam.

The whole world wondered just how much support the

Americans would give their ally South Vietnam during this massive invasion from the North. Looking from the bridge of the ship and seeing the raging fires ashore, I also pondered the same question.

The official directives finally reached our staff off the coast near the Cau Viet River in South Vietnam: "Give air cover and naval gunfire support to the South Vietnamese . . . no landing of U.S. Marines ashore . . . repeat . . . no landing of U.S. Marines ashore . . . strike only in South Vietnam."

During the turmoil ashore and our confusion about if, when, and how Washington would allow retaliative action, I received hand-carry mail from my wife, Eleanor, who was in Yokosuka, Japan. She wrote something to the effect of, "Living in Nagai, eleven miles from the Yokosuka Navy Base until now; we finally obtained a nice home right on the Yokosuka base, where the children are going to school."

The hand-carry mail was the second most important activity onboard the ship, following running the war. Whenever the ship's loudspeaker announced "hand-carry," everybody aboard came alive. Each time an officer or enlisted man would join or leave the ship or staff, going to or from Yokosuka, he would be assigned to hand-carry a large bag of mail. The officers' wives' club at Yokosuka would then distribute the mail received from the ship and would gather mail for someone to hand-carry back to the ship. Sometimes, I'd receive a letter from my wife in three days. The regular mail system would take about three weeks because it was carried by helicopters and planes, via Da Nang, RVN.

Back in Washington, President Nixon ordered his top advisers to prepare recommendations for U.S. action to counter this rapid, full-scale invasion thrust by communist forces into South Vietnam. The president's press secretary, Ronald L. Ziegler, refused, under questioning by newsmen, to rule out the possibility of resuming U.S. air attacks on North Vietnam, or even the use of U.S. ground forces. Ziegler stated, "All options are open."

The U.S. State Department released a statement that branded the communist invasion a violation of the 1968 secret agreement that led President Johnson to suspend bombing attacks upon North Vietnam. And it was a direct violation of agreements made in those secret meetings.

During this invasion period, the Seventh Fleet had two aircraft carriers in the South China Sea, the *Coral Sea* (CVA-43) and the *Hancock* (CV-19). The Joint Chiefs of Staff had previously directed that the Seventh Fleet be ready to respond to any set of circumstances, including a direct invasion from the north. However, JCS never did spell out what the on-site commanders of the Seventh Fleet and Seventh Air Force should do, other than await higher-level direction, if something big happened. Basically, the on-site commanders were not authorized latitude or military response decision-making in the combat zone.

By Monday, April 3, the NVA had pushed the South Vietnamese ARVN and VNMC ten miles from the outposts just below the DMZ and they were attacking Cam Lo. As Cam Lo fell, fifty thousand civilian inhabitants fled from the attacked city.

Also on April 3, as we attended a war room meeting, Admiral Mack said to Cmdr. George Boaz, our Task Force 77 aircraft carriers' cognizant staff officer, "Commander, recall two additional carriers to report on station off of Vietnam."

George Boaz sent a message to Commander, Task Force 77, Adm. Damon Cooper. The message directed that the *Kitty Hawk* (CVA-63) and the *Constellation* (CVA-64) return to the gunline from the Philippines and Japan, respectively.

Upon these two carriers' return, the Seventh Fleet had 275 attack aircraft on four carriers, combined with the limited number of air force attack aircraft still in Da Nang and other bases in South Vietnam, with more in Thailand. B-52 bombers were still in Guam and Thailand. These, combined with many navy destroyers, would support twenty thousand South Vietnamese Army and Marine troops who were fighting to stave off the ferocious NVA attack on northern Quang Tri Province.

From my vantage point on Admiral Mack's bridge, floating off the Cau Viet River, I could see only the volumes of smoke rising from a burning Quang Tri City, as the NVA long-range artillery slammed hundreds of shells into the city. I could not see, from my distance, the hundreds of civilians who were trying to escape from the attacked city, as reported by U.S. Air Force forward air controllers flying over Quang Tri. I took movies of the B-52 arc lights and the large volumes of fire and rising smoke from Quang Tri City. I also took movies of our *Oklahoma City*'s 5- and 6-inch guns firing at the NVA and their tanks.

It was reported by air force FACs that many of the NVA were located northeast of Quang Tri, supported by their artillery units. It was obvious the NVA were continuing to push for capture of Dong Ha and then Quang Tri City.

While these land battles continued ashore, our daily unclassified message traffic brought us up to speed on what was happening worldwide in the "real world." Some press releases offered a little information about the apparent large-scale invasion by the North Vietnamese into the northern areas of South Vietnam.

From the first large-scale invasion crossings of the DMZ that initially began on March 30, with the NVA's three divisions of 30,000 troops, the NVA forces grew to 120,000 troops in the thirteen divisions that invaded into three major areas of South Vietnam. This almost impossibly large force of NVA arrived inside of South Vietnam on Easter weekend.

North Vietnamese planners wisely selected this time of year for the invasion because the skies in that area are generally thickly overcast. This adverse weather severely impacted the South Vietnamese Air Force and the U.S. military's air attempts to try to blunt the NVA ground attacks. By Wednesday, April 5, though, we knew that firebases once occupied by the U.S. Marines as late as a year ago, in 1971, had been overrun by the NVA. Areas where U.S. Marines bravely held off NVA attacks until they were ordered out of Vietnam under Nixon's Vietnamization program had been captured by the NVA. Places with familiar names like Fuller, Hollcomb, Rockpile, Con Thien, Camp Carroll, and Mai Loc had been overrun by the NVA in the northern area of Quang Tri Province. Things appeared very grim. Even if Washington, D.C., were to order the Seventh Fleet and the Seventh Air Force to adequately respond to the invasion and prevent the entire loss of South Vietnam, the task would be enormous.

Chapter 2

• • • • • • •

The NVA Invades

At 1030 on March 30, 1972, on shore just below the DMZ, a platoon patrol from the 1st Vietnamese Marine Corps Company on Ba Ho East made contact with a North Vietnamese Army platoon one thousand meters northwest of Nui Ba Ho. Almost simultaneously, the 8th VNMC Battalion made contact with NVA units. Immediately, NVA 120mm and 130mm artillery fire began impacting from the west, striking Mai Loc and Camp Carroll. While NVA artillery pounded the fixed South Vietnamese Marine Corps bases, the NVA infantry aggressively attacked VNMC positions.

By 1100, three NVA companies were seen boldly marching in the open toward the base at Nui Ba Ho. Apparently, due to the unexpected attacks by the NVA and poor fire-support coordination among the South Vietnamese defenders, no VNMC artillery fired upon the NVA advancing in the open. Heavy cloud cover precluded any attack-aircraft bombing support.

Lieutenant Colonel Gerald H. Turley, recently assigned as assistant senior Marine adviser with the Naval Advisory Group Vietnam in Saigon, had been visiting the South Vietnamese Marines of the 147 and 258 VNMC Brigades near Mai Loc on March 29. He stayed overnight at the VNMC Mai Loc Command Center. The next morning, March 30, he could not get out by helicopter to visit the various brigades' outposts due to low cloud ceilings. The VNMC Brigade 147 commander was Lt. Col. Nguyen Nang Bao, and his U.S. adviser was Army Maj. Jim R. Joy. Brigade 147 was responsible for the western segment of the 3d ARVN Division's area of operations. Things were quiet up near the northern defense area. In fact, Lieutenant Colonel Bao told Lieutenant Colonel Turley that Mai Loc had not received any incoming NVA artillery fire for almost two years. It turned out to be a pleasant, quiet night for Gerry Turley. Because he couldn't get to the VNMC outposts, he returned with Major Joy to the 3d ARVN Division headquarters at Ai Tu.

At the 3d ARVN Division command post, Turley and Joy sat in on an MACV Advisory Team 155 readiness presentation where they learned that nearly all U.S. combat support had been withdrawn from Vietnam. During the briefing Turley heard that the 3d ARVN Division was newly constituted and untested. The ARVN division had only been activated on November 1, 1971, and had organized its infantry regiments only one month before. One of its three regiments on the northern front had been operating as a unit for only the last three weeks. It was short of equipment and not fully trained. Basically, the 3d ARVN Division was not ready for combat. U.S. Marine advisers to the division had much respect for the aggressive, professional ARVN commander, Brig. Gen. Vu Van Giai, but were well aware of the need for equipment and training to get truly combat ready along the northern defense lines. General Giai's 3d ARVN Division had the 2d, 56th, and 57th ARVN regiments strung out between Don Ha and Quang Tri City.

While Lieutenant Colonel Turley was at the briefing, the 56th Regiment was in the process of replacing the 2d Regiment at the former U.S. Marine operating areas of Camp Carroll, Khe Gio, and Fire Support Base Fuller. The 2d Regiment was moving to relieve the 56th Regiment at Alpha 4, Charlie 2, and Charlie 3. A composite of twenty-six artillery pieces, ranging from 105mm howitzers to 173mm self-propelled guns, was located at Camp Carroll. The 57th Regiment's area of responsibility covered the rest of the front up to the DMZ from Dong Ha east to Highway QL-1. The area from QL-1 to the coast on the Gulf of Tonkin was the responsibility of the Quang Tri Province chief and his local militia forces.

The Vietnamese Marines consisted of the VNMC Brigade 147 with outposts at Nui Ba Ho and Fire Support Base Sarge defended by the 4th VNMC Battalion and two companies of the 8th VNMC Battalion in the vicinity of Fire Support Base Holcomb, forming the western flank of the defensive arc.

At 1000, while Lieutenant Colonel Turley was attending the 3d ARVN Division headquarters meeting, the 1st VNMC Company had made contact with an enemy platoon northwest of Nui Ba Ho. Reports were slow getting back to the 3d ARVN Division headquarters. In fact, the 8th VNMC Battalion had enemy contact in the vicinity of Fire Support Base Holcomb later in the morning. While those contacts were happening, the NVA began heavy artillery bombardments of Mai Loc and Camp Carroll. Turley, sitting in the 3d ARVN Division's headquarters, had not heard about the NVA actions along the front.

After the briefing, which did not report any new actions along the front, Turley went to lunch. Then, as he left the mess hall after eating, incoming artillery rounds began to impact nearby. Lieutenant Colonel Turley and another U.S. Marine adviser to VNMC Brigade 147, Capt. John D. Murray, ran into the tactical operations center to find out what the situation was.

They soon found out that the entire front was alive with North Vietnamese Army attacks. Supported by Soviet- and Chinese-built tanks and artillery, thirty thousand North Vietnamese infantry soldiers attacked across the demilitarized zone and caught all outposts by surprise. Every outpost and fire support base along the DMZ was taken under accurate and devastating artillery fire.

Due to the intense incoming artillery fire, Lieutenant Colonel Turley could not leave by helicopter for his scheduled trip back to Da Nang and then to his headquarters in Saigon. So Turley stayed at the 3d Division headquarters and tried to assist the MACV Advisory Team 155 as best he could.

The communist heavy artillery fire continued for the next six days. The heavy artillery had begun on March 30. It was immediately followed by infantry attacks by the 304th, 308th, and 324B NVA divisions; five infantry regiments; and several sapper battalions.

The ill-prepared 3d ARVN Division met this onslaught with five infantry regiments, including two VNMC brigades, nine battalions of artillery, armor, and ranger forces. The North Vietnamese attacking divisions had a numerical advantage of more than three to one and quickly began to overwhelm the ill-trained, underequipped 3d ARVN Division, which was responsible for defending the northern area of South Vietnam.

The massed artillery impacted on the division headquarters and forced the defending artillery to seek cover, slowing down any ARVN counterfire.

At this time, Nui Ba Ho—where the U.S. adviser, Marine Capt. Ray Smith, was located—was under heavy attack by the 9th NVA Regiment. Fire Support Base Sarge, two thousand meters to the south, came under a heavy, accurate artillery barrage of more than five hundred rounds. Fifteen VNMC troops were killed. Major Walter E. Boomer was fully exposed to the incoming rounds of NVA fire as he scurried about the defenses while locating the NVA artillery units firing at them from across Highway 9 to the northwest. Despite the heavy incoming upon Camp Carroll and Mai Loc, the defenders were able to fire some counterbattery missions and destroy some NVA gun positions.

The Seventh Fleet's carrier attack aircraft off the coast to the east in the South China Sea and the U.S. Air Force from Thailand and Da Nang could not respond with attack bombers due to the adverse weather over the North Vietnamese invading force.

The command bunker that Major Boomer was in was hit, and equipment in a nearby bunker used for monitoring NVA radio nets was destroyed. Major Boomer rushed out of his bunker to try to help save the VNMC troops in the other bunker, but there were no survivors.

A platoon outpost six hundred meters north of Nui Ba Ho came under intense small-arms fire and rocket-propelled-grenade attacks at 1700. Three human waves of NVA attacked the Marine defenders and were repelled with small arms, hand grenades, and M79 grenade launchers. Then the NVA attacked the squad on the south side of Nui Ba Ho and was also repelled. As darkness fell, the NVA pulled back and regrouped during the night for a morning attack.

At the 3d ARVN Headquarters Combat Base at Ai Tu

The 3d ARVN operations center was jointly manned by ARVN and MACV Advisory Team 155 personnel, and they continued to receive attack reports. U.S. Marine 1st Lt. Joel B. Eisenstein, in charge of Naval Gunfire Team 1-2 of ANGLICO, and the air force tactical air control liaison team were inside the tactical operations center (TOC). Lieutenant Colonel Turley and Captain Murray, adviser to VNMC Brigade 147, were trying to find out how many VNMC units held during the March 30 day attacks along their frontlines. So they remained at the TOC. Turley and Murray were not in the ARVN chain of command but became deeply involved in helping the assistant G-3 adviser, U.S. Army Maj. James Davis. Major Davis, working all day and night under the pressures of the all-out NVA attacks became exhausted. The next morning, March 31, U.S. Army Col. Donald J. Metcalf, the senior adviser, asked the visiting Lieutenant Colonel Turley to assume the duties of senior U.S. adviser within the operations center to relieve the exhausted Major Davis. Colonel Metcalf decided to stay with General Giai and his American assistant senior adviser, U.S. Army Lt. Col. Normand Heon. General Giai had them prepare a more protected command post south of the Thach Han River in Quang Tri City.

Much later, when reporting events to the Marine Corps, Turley said that he had resisted the request to relieve Major Davis as senior adviser because Turley wasn't from that chain of command. Due to the urgency of the situation, Turley accepted Colonel Metcalf's request. Some historians claim there was friction between Colonel Metcalf and Lieutenant Colonel Turley. This subject still appears to be controversial, and only Metcalf and Turley know what was really said.

Turley immediately directed that calls be made to all units that could help defend the northern area, including calls to U.S. naval gunfire support ships of the Seventh Fleet and the 1st Regional Assistance Command in Da Nang. Turley then opened a journal so he could begin recording all the events in the 3d ARVN Division's operational area.

At Nui Ba Ho

At dawn on March 31, the NVA made a mass attack upon the northern section of Nui Ba Ho. A Marine 106mm recoilless rifle on the northern slope with flechette rounds fired into the attacking NVA. The communists withdrew, leaving the bodies of an estimated one hundred dead hanging on the defensive wire. Three more NVA waves attacked and were repelled. At 1000, very accurate NVA 130mm artillery rounds began to chew up the VNMC trench lines and bunkers. At 1500, the NVA unleashed a massive infantry attack upon the northern slope of Nui Ba Ho. The NVA paid a big price, as the outer ring of barbed wire was covered with NVA bodies. At the same time, though, the defensive integrity and mutual supporting firebases were destroyed by the NVA. The NVA then opened up with 75mm recoilless rifles and began to systematically destroy the South Vietnamese defensive positions. Two VNMC 105mm howitzers responded and knocked out two NVA recoilless rifles on the northern slope.

The VNMC had only four squads to defend the positions. At 1730, the weather cleared enough to allow U.S. Air Force F-4 Phantoms to attack and destroy an NVA artillery gun, causing the NVA attackers to disperse to the south.

The NVA resumed the relentless attack at dark. At 2130, a U.S. Air Force Lockheed AC-130 Specter gunship arrived overhead with Gatling guns, but the night haze prevented the gunship crew from finding the NVA even though they dropped flares to illuminate the ground. Finally, one of the flares broke through the haze and the AC-130 crew saw the grim remains of the ground battle below. The NVA had completely inundated the VNMC position.

At 2205, a surviving command post trooper called from the perimeter and reported that the NVA had captured him but he had escaped. He reported that the enemy had control of the hill. He recommended evacuation of the position. U.S. Marine adviser Capt. Ray Smith, from Bravo group of the battalion on Nui Ba Ho, grabbed a PRC-25 radio and M-16 rifle and was the last to clear out of the command bunker. He didn't see anyone he knew outside the bunker but came across three NVA troops just three meters in front of him. He later recounted, "The NVA were as confused as I was by then. I ran right by them." He came across some ARVN survivors huddled against the southwest corner concertina wire. They were afraid to go over the wire because of possible booby traps. Smith ordered twenty-six survivors through the wire as an NVA fired at him; he then turned and shot the NVA trooper who had been firing at him. Smith feared the sound of his shots would bring more NVA to his escape area, so he quickly hurled himself backward onto the wire and became entangled. The survivors quickly climbed over Smith and the wire he covered with his bleeding body; he tore loose from the wire with severe cuts on his arms and legs and crawled down the hill. He rallied the surviving South Vietnamese Marines heading for Mai Loc and evaded the North Vietnamese Army along the eastern slope. In the dark, Smith continued to call in artillery strikes on the top of the hill as he moved away from the now decimated hill. At 2140 on March 31, 1972, combat outpost Nui Ba Ho became the first position lost to the invading NVA. The communist invasion of South Vietnam was two days old.

At Fire Support Base Sarge

On the morning of March 31, 1972, Fire Support Base Sarge came under massive fire and infantry assaults by the 66th NVA Regiment. Major Boomer recognized the situation as grave, since nearby Nui Ba Ho was also under similar massive artillery and infantry attacks. Boomer had radio contact with Captain Smith on Nui Ba Ho and was worried when Smith reported, "If we make it, it'll just be luck." Boomer knew that if Nui Ba Ho fell, Sarge could not stand alone because Nui Ba Ho dominated the approaches to the south toward Sarge.

At 2150, Boomer became concerned when he heard Smith calling in artillery fire on top of the hill position that Bravo group was supposed to be holding. Then he couldn't communicate with Smith who was, at the time, evading the NVA at the overrun position. Boomer thought his personal friend, Smith, had been killed. As Boomer worried about Smith and Nui Ba Ho, his own positions at Sarge were under constant attack throughout the night of March 31. Bad weather continued and precluded air support. By 0200 the next morning of April 1, the NVA overran all the outposts' squad positions north, south, and east and penetrated the defensive perimeter. Despite the bad flying weather, B-52 arc-light strikes hit enemy staging areas west of Highway 9. The NVA continued to attack with wave after wave of infantry against Sarge.

At 0345, during a deluge of rain and under intense NVA fire, what remained of Alpha command group evacuated Sarge. Major Boomer radioed Major Joy at Mai Loc, "We're moving out." Then Major Boomer lost radio contact with the entire 4th VNMC Battalion.

At dawn, the NVA hoisted their victory flag over command post Sarge. Major Boomer and his fatigued survivors, after two full days of fighting and no food, escaped the seemingly ubiquitous encircling enemy by fleeing through the jungle.

During these first battles just south of the DMZ, MACV ordered B-52 strikes against NVA resupply and staging areas at Khe Sanh and Laos, not into the embattled zone. MACV and the RVN joint general staff still believed that the NVA was using these attacks as a feint and that large-scale attacks would not come from across the DMZ. They felt that the main NVA invasion would come farther south into Military Region 2 (MR 2). Therefore, they concentrated their air efforts in the Kontum area to prevent the NVA from seizing Pleiku.

By midday of April 1, 1972, Alpha 2 of the 57th ARVN Regiment at Gio Linh abandoned their exposed positions on the perimeter and sought protection in bunkers in the southern position of the fire support base. ARVN artillerymen refused to leave the safety of their bunkers to fire counterbattery missions that were being screamed for by the ARVN infantry units. Naval gunfire from the USS *Buchanan* and the USS *Joseph Strauss* of the Seventh Fleet was directed by a five-man ANGLICO spot team at Alpha 2. This suppressed the enemy supporting arms fire and impeded the advance of the NVA infantry, allowing the ARVN forces to withdraw from Gio Linh.

Sub Unit One of the 1st Air and Naval Gunfire Liaison Company, commanded by U.S. Marine Lt. Col. D'Wayne Gray, had remained in Vietnam after the removal of U.S. infantry units culminated in 1971. Sub Unit One's ANGLICO headquarters was adjacent to the MACV compound in Saigon. ANGLICO was responsible for coordination of the Seventh Fleet's naval gunfire from destroyers and cruisers and air support for U.S. Army and allied forces. Lieutenant Colonel Gray had assumed command of Sub Unit One in Saigon on July 19, 1971. His spotter units were dispersed all over South Vietnam from the DMZ to the Delta. Marines from ANGLICO were up north at outpost Alpha from Gio Linh just south of the DMZ and as far south as the Ca Mau Peninsula on the Gulf of Siam.

One of Lieutenant Colonel Gray's problems was that the U.S. Air Force refused to allow naval gunfire to shoot while air force aircraft were attacking in the area. At that time, artillery and naval guns were not permitted to fire while air force close air support missions were being flown in the same area. Yet, I was a Marine Corps forward air controller in VMO-2, flying OV-10A Bronco aircraft during the second of my three combat tours in Vietnam, and we were always capable of controlling close air support, naval gunfire, and artillery simultaneously upon the NVA and VC. Therefore, now in 1972, this coordination problem often resulted in ANGLICO not being able to receive naval gunfire support due to ongoing U.S. Air Force air strikes. There was another problem that Lieutenant Colonel Gray's spotters experienced. It had been three years since March 15, 1969, when the battleship USS *New Jersey* (BB-62), with her 16-inch guns, had been ordered back to the United States for decommissioning during the Vietnamization troop draw-down period that commenced in 1968. This left us, at the time of the March 30, 1972, NVA invasion, with only the USS *Newport News* (CA-148) with 8-inch guns. The ship I was on, the USS *Oklahoma City*, had 5- and 6-inch guns, along with the destroyers that had 5-inch guns. The older 5-inch .38-caliber guns, with limited range and required manual loading, were deployed near the coastline. The newer automated, longer-range 5-inch .54-caliber gun was used on targets located farther inland. The 5-inch .54-caliber also fired a rocket-assisted projectile that extended the range but was not very accurate at maximum range. Despite these limitations that ANGLICO encountered, they supported the South Vietnamese with naval gunfire, which was a deterrent to the NVA movements along the coastal areas. ANGLICO had some real American heroes among its ranks. The senior enlisted Marine in Sub Unit One was 1st Sgt. Ernest Benjamin. He had been on his fourth combat tour of Vietnam when he confronted this NVA 1972 spring offensive. Another terrific Marine in ANGLICO was Cpl. James F. "Diamond Jim" Worth, a field radio operator working with 1st Lt. David C. Bruggeman in a spot team working with the 57th ARVN Infantry Regiment at outpost Alpha. The twenty-year-old Worth, from Chicago, Illinois, had been in Vietnam with Sub Unit One since 1971.

When the Alpha 2 outpost was hit with heavy artillery, rocket, and mortar fire and a North Vietnamese ground attack, Worth and his teammates called in naval gunfire suppression, interdiction, and counterbattery fire. This was during critical times when the 3d ARVN Division had lost most of its artillery support and the weather prevented navy and air force air support. When the NVA began to overrun Alpha 2, Lieutenant Bruggeman requested helicopter evacuation for his team through Lieutenant Eisenstein at the division tactical operations center.

From his position on the Alpha 2 observation tower, Corporal Worth watched the ARVN soldiers from the 57th Regiment abandon their fighting holes on the outpost's forward slope. As he looked to his rear, he saw the ARVNs abandon their 105mm howitzers as the NVA infantry closed in on them from three sides of the firebase.

After some delay, Worth and the other Marines spotted a U.S. Army UH-1E. The helicopter, piloted by Warrant Officers Ben Nielsen and Robert Sheridan, flew in and landed. Sheridan and Lieutenant Eisenstein jumped out of the helicopter and began assisting the ANGLICO spotters into the helicopter. At that instant, mortar rounds impacted the landing zone, mortally injuring Lieutenant Bruggeman and dispersing his men. As the Marines scrambled aboard the helicopter, Corporal Worth was not with them. As Warrant Officer Sheridan glanced back, he saw a few shell-shocked ARVN troops, but he couldn't see anyone else in the landing zone.

Warrant Officer Nielson flew the helicopter back to the Ai Tu Combat Base to pick up ANGLICO's Hospital Corpsman 1st Class (HM1) Thomas E. "Doc" Williamson, U.S. Navy corpsman, who attempted lifesaving measures on Lieutenant Bruggeman as they flew toward Da Nang. Lieutenant Bruggeman died of wounds halfway to the Da Nang medical facility. Corporal Worth was never seen again after the fall of outpost Alpha 2; he joined the ranks of the missing Americans who were either dead or captured.

As Alpha 2, Alpha 4, Fuller, Khe Gio, and Holcomb fell to the NVA, General Giai moved his 3d ARVN Division headquarters to the rear. VNMC Brigade 258 was ordered to leave its 3d VNMC Battalion at Dong Ha, move the rest of the brigade to Ai Tu, and assume control of the division forward command post. When Lt. Col. Ngo Van Dinh and his staff arrived at Ai Tu at 1500, together with the 6th VNMC Battalion, which had come from Fire Support Base Barbara, they were greeted with an NVA barrage of more than eight hundred rounds of artillery fire.

On April 1, Lt. Col. Normand Heon, assistant senior adviser to Team 155, directed all remaining U.S. personnel at Ai Tu to withdraw. The U.S. Marine advisers were not subject to that order. They, along with two U.S. Army advisers, voluntarily remained at Ai Tu.

The forward command post at Ai Tu remained the only command and control center north of Da Nang with functional communications. The post, now under the command of Lieutenant Colonel Turley, was manned by thirty personnel from the U.S. Marine Corps, Army, and Air Force.

At 1700 on April 1, outposts Charlie 1 and Charlie 2 fell to the NVA. The withdrawn troops headed south across the Dong Ha Bridge. The outposts were overrun by NVA T-54 main tanks, PT-76 amphibious tanks, and BTR-50 armored personnel carriers.

Two hours later, General Giai and his U.S. adviser, Colonel Metcalf, departed Ai Tu Combat Base and set up a new command post for the 3d ARVN Division at the Citadel in Quang Tri City. According to Lieutenant Colonel Turley's journal, his American group had the only command-and-control radio capabilities for controlling U.S. supporting arms. The nearest operating control center was the headquarters in Da Nang, well to the south, where U.S. Army Gen. Frederick J. Kroesen was located.

This Da Nang command center authorized Lieutenant Colonel Turley's requests for U.S. Air Force B-52 arc-light bombing raids. Turley was then capable of communicating directly with an air force general in Saigon to give his target coordinates for the B-52 raids.

The NVA invasion thrusts were so large and fast that sixty-four B-52 raids called in by Turley did not stop the NVA. They continued to advance upon Cam Lo and Mieu Giang and headed south to the north side of the Cau Viet River.

The Dong Ha Bridge

Lieutenant Colonel Ngo Van Dinh, Vietnamese Brigade 258 commander at Ai Tu, ordered Maj. Le Ba Binh, 3d VNMC Battalion, to defend the bridges at Dong Ha and the city at all costs.

Four jeep-mounted 106mm recoilless rifles for antitank support and newly received U.S. M48 battle tanks were sent up to Dong Ha to assist in defending.

U.S. Marine Maj. Jon T. Easley, senior adviser to VNMC Brigade 258, called U.S. Marine Capt. John W. Ripley at Dong Ha and advised Ripley to expect the worst and not to anticipate any reinforcements.

Refugees streamed south across the Dong Ha Bridge. The NVA had arrived in full view of the north bank of the Cau Viet River. As the 3d VNMC Battalion, joined by the 20th ARVN Tank Battalion, dug in to defend Dong Ha, the NVA began an intense artillery barrage, later described by Captain Ripley as an "absolute firestorm." Many civilians were killed by the NVA heavy artillery fire as they attempted to flee south.

A large group of soldiers from the retreating 57th ARVN Regiment, only some of them armed, mingled with the civilians passing south through Dong Ha. Major Binh, 3d VNMC Battalion commander, shouted to them, "Where are you going?" The shaken ARVN soldiers responded, "No use . . . no use." Major Binh drew his pistol and shot one of the deserters. The retreating mixed civilian and military crowd simply continued southward without being distracted by the shooting of the deserter.

At this time, the 36th NVA Regiment began crossing the partially destroyed railroad bridge near the Dong Ha Bridge. Captain Ripley called for naval gunfire. First Lieutenant Eisenstein, officer in charge of the ANGLICO team, coordinated the naval gunfire support of interdiction fire three hundred meters north of the bridge. Ripley then shifted the NGFS fire upon PT-76 tanks along the north side of the bridge.

As the weather cleared slightly, Vietnamese-piloted A1 McDonnell Douglas Skyraider aircraft bombed and strafed newly arriving NVA tanks to the north of Dong Ha. The Vietnamese airforce aircraft destroyed eleven tanks and lost one A1 Skyraider. ARVN tanks knocked out six NVA tanks.

At noon, the first NVA tank moved onto the north side of the bridge. A lone Vietnamese Marine, Sgt. Huynh Van Luom, placed two ammunition boxes full of dirt and a single strand of concertina wire in front of him. He set up his personal defense on the south side of the bridge. As the first NVA tank came onto the bridge, the tank stopped, quite possibly because the tank commander couldn't believe a lone VNMC trooper stood defending the bridge.

Sergeant Luom fired an M72 light antitank weapon (LAW) at the stationary NVA tank. The LAW flew by the NVA tank, high and to the right. Sergeant Luom fired another LAW rocket. The rocket detonated on the tank's turret ring, jamming the gun turret. The damaged tank backed off the bridge to the north side.

Captain Ripley called Sergeant Luom's decisive action the "bravest single act of heroism I've ever witnessed."

The VNMC defenders on the south side of the river recognized for the first time that an NVA tank could be stopped. But even though the NVA tanks were temporarily halted, we knew they would try again.

ARVN and VNMC tanks dueled with the NVA tanks across the river, while the Dong Ha Bridge was partly wired with explosives by ARVN engineers. Tanks from the 20th Armored Division attempted to shoot supports out from under the bridge, but the bridge remained steady.

Marine Captain Ripley, who had earned a Silver Star during his previous combat tour in 1966, and U.S. Army Maj. James Smock teamed up to prepare to blow up the bridge. Ripley and Smock gathered twenty-five boxes of C-4 and TNT explosive blocks. Ripley jumped over a concertina-topped fence. Smock began lifting the fifty-pound boxes over to Ripley. Ripley placed the explosives under the bridge and began swinging from beam to beam as if he were performing a circus act.

When Ripley completed placing the explosives under the main bridge, Smock and ARVN engineers placed demolitions on the damaged railroad bridge upstream. Ripley placed thirty-minute fuses on the explosives as a backup way to blow up the bridge. After placing blasting caps at the end of communications wire that he had run up to the charges, Ripley jumped back over the fence. He then touched the other end of the communications wire to his electrical detonator and waited. The bridge did not blow up. Ripley and Smock waited some more. Finally, the backup fuses set by Ripley exploded, and suddenly the bridge blew, crashing into the river. The wooden parts of the steel support bridge burned for days. The bridge was destroyed at 1630 on April 2.

That same evening, at 1800, a U.S. Air Force Douglas EB-66 electronic warfare radar jammer aircraft was hit by a communist missile just south of the DMZ. The aircrew's call sign was Bat 21.

The Seventh Air Force headquarters at Tan Son Nhut AFB outside of Saigon, acting for MACV and not comprehending the full-scale NVA invasion that was under way, assumed control of all U.S. supporting arms within the area of the 3d ARVN Division. The search-and-rescue efforts by the U.S. Air Force for a sole survivor of the six-man Bat 21 crew, Bat 21 Bravo, became a major effort — not fully understanding the gravity of the NVA attacks against the ARVN and VNMC units nearby Bat 21 Bravo.

The air force directed a no-fire zone be placed around Bat 21 Bravo to protect him from friendly fire. This preempted any supporting arms control of air, naval gunfire, and artillery into the area around Bat 21 Bravo, and also stopped all firing into a very large area that had a major NVA advancing attack force. ANGLICO's Lieutenant Colonel Gray went into a rage as the NVA poured toward the ARVN and Vietnamese Marine Corps (VNMC) defenses, and his supporting arms coordinators could not fire at them in the no-fire zone created around Bat 21 Bravo. Lieutenant Colonel Gray was quoted as saying, "I was absolutely up the wall. I could not convince the air force colonel at the I Direct Air Support Center at Da Nang to change his position."

Lieutenant Colonel Turley, senior adviser for the ARVN units in direct contact with three major elements of three NVA divisions, was concerned and had something to say about it. He remarked, "The unilateral rear area arrangements of giving the USAF control of all tactical air, naval gunfire, and artillery fire seemed like a rational decision to officers eighty kilometers from the battle line. However, it was a tragic decision for the 3d ARVN Division." Lieutenant Colonel Turley cited that the no-fire zone imposed in that area actually precluded destroying the strategic Cam Lo Bridge prior to its capture by the communist forces.

The 147th VNMC Brigade evacuated Mai Lo and headed to Dong Ha. The 7th VNMC Battalion from the 258th VNMC Brigade was also ordered to withdraw from Mai Loc but had difficulty disengaging from close fighting with the 66th NVA Regiment. As darkness fell, the battalion finally disengaged and withdrew toward Ai Tu.

The 3d ARVN Division had failed to hold the main defensive positions in Quang Tri Province. The NVA was heading for its primary objective, Quang Tri City.

Chapter 3

• • • • • • •

The Fall of Quang Tri City

The destruction of the Dong Ha Bridge slowed the NVA advance. On April 3, Lieutenant General Lam, I Corps commander, requested reinforcements for Quang Tri City area defense. General Lam planned to launch a counteroffensive as soon as the overcast weather would permit close air support.

Lieutenant Colonel Turley, who had not slept for three days, flew down to Saigon to brief Rear Adm. Robert S. Salzer, Commander Naval Forces, Vietnam. Admiral Salzer directed Turley, who was in his chain of command and not in the chain of command of my boss, Seventh Fleet commander, Admiral Mack, to return to MR 1 and rejoin Col. Joshua W. Dorsey at the VNMC division.

During the following week, the VNMC division headquarters and VNMC Brigade 369 moved into the Citadel at Hue City under command of Lt. Gen. Le Nguyen Khang. General Khang was placed in command of the defense of Hue City.

While these events took place, attempts to rescue Bat 21 Bravo continued without success.

The 3d VNMC Battalion and 20th ARVN Tank Battalion repulsed repeated enemy assaults on the severely damaged town of Dong Ha. The NVA began using small boats to cross the river, since the bridge had been destroyed. The battle for Dong Ha raged from April 3 through 8, as rains continued over the contested area.

B-52 arc-light raids hit north of the Cau Viet River. General Khang sent 250 men from the 57th ARVN Regiment to assist the 3d VNMC Battalion and 20th ARVN Tank Battalion to defend Dong

Ha. However, the 57th ARVN unit buckled from the assaults of the NVA on the south side of the river. Major Binh, disgusted with the poor defensive performance of the 57th ARVN, requested that a Vietnamese Marine unit replace the 57th Vietnamese army unit.

On April 6, the NVA increased mortar and rocket attacks upon Dong Ha. The town had been empty of civilians for several days. Captain John Ripley's radio operator was killed, and Maj. Jim Smock was wounded. Ripley convinced the last departing tank from Dong Ha to take Captain Smock and other wounded with them. As the tank departed, Captain Ripley helped more wounded get aboard an M113 armored vehicle as it was withdrawing on orders.

Ripley remained as mortar rounds exploded around him. As he looked around, Ripley realized he was alone on the battlefield. A squad of NVA approached less than fifty meters from him. The NVA stopped and watched Ripley pick up his dead radio operator and walk away carrying the dead soldier toward friendly lines. Ripley expected to be shot in the back, but the NVA didn't shoot. He continued walking away, carrying his dead radio operator. The NVA still didn't shoot. Then they saw Major Binh and two other VNMC personnel return to the area looking for Ripley. The NVA then opened fire upon them and Ripley, but Major Binh, the two Vietnamese Marines, and Ripley got out alive, just as more NVA arrived on the scene.

As Ripley, Major Binh, and two VNMC troops headed south, past the burning buildings in Dong Ha, they saw a large rocket shot from the ground. The rocket blazed skyward at an overhead forward air controller's OV-10A Bronco. Ripley later described the scene to comrades: "It looked like a telephone pole lumbering skyward." The SAM missed the OV-10A. But Ripley and Binh had witnessed, firsthand, the introduction of a new NVA weapon to the battlefield: the Russian-built SA-7 Strella handheld, heat-seeking antiaircraft missile. The SA-7 missile launcher and missile was a copy of the U.S. Redeye shoulder-fired missile system.

The 1st ARVN Armored Brigade, the 4th and 5th Ranger Groups, and the undermanned 57th ARVN Regiment replaced the 3d VNMC Battalion as they withdrew to join the rest of the 3d ARVN Division at Ai Tu, northeast of Quang Tri City. The 3d VNMC Battalion had stopped a full NVA division at the river's edge at Dong Ha. The

South Vietnamese Marines had paid an awful price. Of the seven-hundred-man 3d VNMC Battalion, only two hundred survived the NVA assault on Dong Ha.

Positioned north of Ai Tu, Fire Support Base Pedro came under bombardment from NVA 130mm guns at midnight on April 9. At dawn, sixteen NVA T-54 tanks led NVA infantry on an attack from the west upon Pedro. The NVA lost nine tanks to mines that had been placed around Pedro. Two VNMC companies, with adviser Capt. Lawrence H. Livingston from the 1st VNMC Battalion, and eight M-48 tanks with twelve M-113 armored personnel carriers from the 2d Troop, 20th ARVN Tank Battalion, responded to the NVA tank and infantry attack upon Pedro.

Assisting the reactive defense were VNMC 105mm howitzer fire and two barrages from the Seventh Fleet ships, which drove the NVA infantry back to the Ba Long Valley. A break in the weather allowed four VNAF A-1 Skyraiders to attack the NVA tanks near Pedro; these bombs knocked out five NVA tanks.

On April 10 and 11, Pedro defenders, led by Captain Livingston, beat back more NVA attacks while killing 211 NVA troops.

The battle for Pedro continued as the NVA attacked the Cam Lo area. Marine Lt. Col. Andrew E. "Andy" Anderson—officer in charge of the MACV Studies and Observation Group (SOG) from the Joint Personnel Recovery Center (JPRC)—had flown up to Da Nang from his headquarters in Saigon. He was in the 3d ARVN Division area, just south of where Bat 21 Bravo and another American, Nail 38, had been trapped behind NVA attacking lines for days. After numerous failed helicopter rescue attempts, the two survivors must have been desperately hoping for another rescue attempt.

On April 10, Anderson directed his JPRC team of two Americans and six Vietnamese Special Forces to cross the Cam Lo River dressed as villagers to rescue Bat 21 Bravo and Nail 38 Bravo. U.S. Navy SEAL team member Lt. Tom Norris led the successful mission to rescue Nail 38 Bravo, finding the downed pilot on April 11. Then, on April 13, Norris and his team rescued Bat 21 Bravo.

Within two weeks of the NVA invasion, the two Marine Corps fighter/bomber squadrons that I had directed as Marine air officer on the Seventh Fleet staff had arrived at Da Nang from Iwakuni, Japan. They were flying combat-support missions for the ARVN and VNMC. I also had directed that Marine air observers (AOs) be dispatched to Vietnam from the 3d Marine Amphibious Force on Okinawa. On April 13, the Marine AOs arrived and reported to Sub Unit One at Da Nang AFB. More AOs arrived from Camp Pendleton, California, the next day. The AOs were assigned with FACs to fly in USAF OV-10A Bronco and VNAF O-1 Bird Dog observation aircraft.

The NVA were stopped at Pedro but continued around to push toward Quang Tri City, using the still-standing Cam Lo Bridge to cross the Cam Lo and Mieu Giang rivers. The bridge was still standing partly because of the USAF-imposed no-fire zone in that area due to the rescue attempts to get Bat 21 Bravo out of an area just north of the bridge.

The weather finally broke after two weeks of heavy rain and dense, low cloud cover. The USAF increased B-52 arc-light strikes, and hundreds of U.S. Navy, Marine Corps, and Air Force as well as VNAF tactical air strikes commenced hitting the NVA.

Despite the air strikes and naval gunfire support, on April 14, Fire Support Base Bastogne, southwest of Hue City, fell to units of the 324B NVA Division that had enveloped from the western mountains and the Ho Chi Minh trail, well to the southwest of Quang Tri City.

The 324B NVA Division was in position to attack Hue City. Despite intense defensive fights between General Lam's 1st ARVN Division and the 324B NVA Division, the NVA moved closer, threatening to attack Hue City. General Lam's previous optimistic plan for a full counteroffensive ended.

Fire Support Base Jane came under NVA attack on April 16. The 5th VNMC Battalion held Jane but suffered heavy casualties. USMC advisers Maj. Donald L. Price and Capt. Marshall R. Wells helped to get survivors of the intense battle back to the rear as the 7th VNMC Battalion relieved them in defending Jane.

The NVA shifted their attacks to VNMC Brigade 369. At early dark on April 18, the 304th NVA Division struck toward Quang Tri City as the 308th NVA Division attacked and passed through Camp Carroll and Mai Loc toward Dong Ha.

As the ARVN defenders hung on to Dong Ha, the NVA again shifted their attacks to the western approaches toward Ai Tu and Quang Tri City.

Attack from the West for Quang Tri City

Early on the morning of April 27, the 304th NVA Division launched an attack on Ai Tu from the southwest against the VNMC Brigade 147 and 1st ARVN Armored Brigade. Marine Corps advisers Maj. Robert C. Cockell and Capt. Lawrence H. Livingston were with these defenders as more than five hundred rounds of 82mm mortar fire and artillery impacted their area. Late afternoon, the NVA tanks attacked but lost fifteen tanks as the NVA were driven back. That night, 130mm NVA fire hit the Ai Tu base ammunition bunker and destroyed most of the defenders' ammunition stockpile.

As the situation deteriorated with the continual NVA attacks, U.S. Navy corpsmen were busy at the 3d ARVN Division headquarters at Quang Tri City. Corpsman HM1 Thomas E. Williamson from ANGLICO teamed up with U.S. Navy Lt. John M. Lapoint, HMC Donovan R. Leavitt, HM2 Francis C. Brown, and HM3 James Riddle from the U.S. Naval Advisory Unit to provide medical treatment to the ARVN and Americans who were wounded during the Bat 21 Bravo rescue operations.

On April 27, Corpsman Williamson and U.S. Army Sgt. Roger Shoemaker obtained an ARVN personnel carrier to drive them north to the Thach Han River. Although under fire, they medically evacuated seriously wounded U.S. Army adviser Lt. Col. William C. Camper, saving his life.

Dong Ha collapsed on April 28, and the 57th ARVN Regiment, in disarray, retreated toward Quang Tri City. The 3d ARVN Division directed that the 7th VNMC Battalion withdraw from Fire Support Base Jane and reinforce the VNMC Brigade 147 en route to Quang Tri. Only two companies of Brigade 147 succeeded in breaking through the NVA attacking lines that had begun encircling Quang Tri City. The two companies arrived at Quang Tri just before dark.

At 0200 on April 29, the NVA launched a tank and infantry assault upon the Thach Han River area defended by the 2d ARVN Regiment. The NVA captured the north end of the bridge leading into Quang Tri City and were able to retain control despite the fact that FACs, flying cover overhead, dropped flares and ran air strikes, knocking out three of their tanks.

At dawn, VNMC Brigade 147 assigned two companies of the 7th VNMC Battalion, supported by tanks from the 20th Tank Battalion, to counterattack the NVA holding the north end of the bridge. The Marines recaptured the north end of the bridge and destroyed NVA bunkers.

The 4th and 5th Ranger groups assigned to retain the north end of the bridge at Quang Tri retreated to the Quang Tri City side of the bridge. Colonel Bao assigned the 7th VNMC Battalion to hold the bridge.

The defenses at Ai Tu were crumbling. Despite destructive air attacks upon the NVA, General Giai decided he could no longer defend at Ai Tu and withdrew the Marines. He brought the VNMC 147 Brigade from Ai Tu to Quang Tri City. At this juncture, Colonel Metcalf was quoted as saying, "This was General Giai's last ditch to defend Quang Tri."

As the VNMC Brigade 147 withdrew south from Ai Tu, Major Huff requested fire missions from ANGLICO's Maj. Glen Golden. Golden's naval gunfire support requests were responded to. The Seventh Fleet's cruiser, USS *Newport News*, with the biggest guns, 8-inch shells, fired at the NVA covering the withdrawal from Ai Tu. The VNMC tried to bring their howitzers and vehicles with them, but they couldn't get them across the Thach Han River because the ARVN engineers had already blown up the two bridges. The South Vietnamese Marines had to destroy eighteen of their howitzers and twenty-two vehicles to prevent their capture by the NVA, but sixteen tanks from the 20th ARVN Tank Battalion found a ford to cross. The VNMC infantry swam across to rejoin at their assigned defensive perimeter inside Quang Tri City.

The 1st VNMC Battalion defended the western approach to the city, the 4th VNMC Battalion set up defenses to protect the eastern and southern approaches, and the 8th VNMC Battalion set up to defend north of the city. The headquarters remained inside the Citadel compound.

ARVN units to the north of the city, along the river, seeing the NVA tanks approaching, abandoned their defensive positions. A great exodus of ARVN vehicles began heading south until they ran out of fuel and had to be abandoned.

Major Golden coordinated the Marine advisers' fire support requests for artillery and air force FACs' support flying with Marine ANGLICO aerial observers in OV-10A Broncos. Seventh Fleet naval gunfire could not reach that far inland now that the NVA were primarily concentrated for attacks upon Quang Tri City.

On May 1, General Giai felt that trying to save Quang Tri City was hopeless and would cost too many lives. He decided to direct withdrawal from Quang Tri City and pull his units to a new defensive line at My Chanh. No orderly withdrawal plan was devised—only VNMC Brigade 147 remained in control.

Colonel Metcalf called brigade headquarters and reported, "ARVN forces are pulling out; advisers may stay with their units or join me." Major Joy responded that U.S. Marine advisers to the Vietnamese Marines' Brigade 147 would remain with their units.

Brigade 147 withdrew from Quang Tri. General Giai loaded his staff onto three armored vehicles and departed the Citadel, but he was unable to break through the surrounding NVA. He returned to the Citadel and requested an emergency helicopter evacuation.

U.S. Air Force search-and-rescue helicopters arrived at 1635 to evacuate 118 personnel from inside the Citadel. U.S. Army helicopter gunships escorted the Air Force SAR helicopter evacuation as U.S. Marine and Air Force fighters provided air cover for the withdrawal.

The NVA struck west of Hai Lang district headquarters, stopping all fleeing military and civilians. This stretch of Highway 1 was soon to be called the "highway of horror." An estimated two thousand civilian and military dead filled the three-quarter-mile stretch.

The retreating VNMC Brigade 147 withdrawing from Quang Tri eventually made it back to the lines of the VNMC Brigade 369, south of the My Chanh River, and reassembled at the Hue City Citadel.

On May 1, 1972, Quang Tri City was evacuated by the South Vietnamese and captured by the communists. Throughout the world communists held their usual May Day celebrations; now they could also celebrate their victory over this South Vietnamese city that lay in burned-out ruins.

Chapter 4

• • • • • • •

Bat 21

On Easter Sunday, April 2, 1972, bad weather continued over the northern area of South Vietnam just below the DMZ. The low clouds still masked the hard-charging North Vietnamese Army's divisions that commenced their invasion three days before, on March 30.

A U.S. Air Force cell of three B-52s, call sign Copper, approached over the NVA attacking divisions. The B-52s were dropping bombs, called an arc-light mission, just north of Camp Carroll, near the Cam Lo River and town of Cam Lo.

The area was heavily protected by NVA electronically guided surface-to-air missiles. Two air force EB-66 electronic jammer aircraft from the 42nd Tactical Electronic Warfare Squadron at Korat Air Force Base, Thailand, escorted the B-52s and performed jamming of the NVA SAM radar systems. The EB-66 jammers' call signs were Bat 21 and Bat 22.

The B-52s were also protected by four escort F-105G fighters armed with anti-SAM homing missiles. Also, two F-4C fighters were along to protect against MiGs.

NVA SA-2 Fan Song radar immediately began tracking the B-52 flight, and onboard B-52 jammers reacted. The two EB-66 aircraft began jamming. At least eight SAM missiles plus 100mm antiaircraft fire burst among the attacking aircraft.

One SAM exploded into the Bat 21 EB-66 aircraft. Of the crew of pilot, four electronic warfare officers, and navigator, only the navigator, Lt. Col. Iceal Hambleton, safely ejected and parachuted to the ground. His personal call sign was Bat 21 Bravo.

Hambleton landed right in the middle of a portion of an invading NVA infantry division that had tanks and artillery moving south from the DMZ area.

We, the Seventh Fleet staff on board the USS *Oklahoma City*, heard some of the radio transmissions between the U.S. Air Force and some U.S. Army helicopters about the downing of Bat 21 and that there was a survivor, Bat 21 Bravo.

Little did we realize that this event would trigger the most notorious series of rescue attempts of the war.

Several heroic rescue attempts by U.S. helicopters to get Bat 21 Bravo began to unfold right in the middle of the invasion force of the NVA's push across the border from North Vietnam and the DMZ.

The First Attempt to Rescue Bat 21 Bravo

The first rescue response was by three helicopters from F Troop, U.S. 8th Cavalry from Marble Mountain Airfield near Da Nang. These three U.S. Army helicopters had been up in the area on other support missions. Their flight consisted of:

- AH-1 Cobra, Blueghost 28, piloted by Capt. Mike Rosenberry.
- AH-1 Cobra, Blueghost 24, piloted by Warrant Officer George Ezel.
- UH-1H Huey, Blueghost 39, with crew of: pilot, 1st Lt. Bryon Kulland; pilot, Warrant Officer John Frink; crewchief, Spc5 Ronald Paschall; Gunner-Spc5 Jose Astorga.

The UH-1H, Blueghost 39, was immediately hit by ground fire as it searched for Bat 21 Bravo and made a controlled crash. NVA gunfire poured into the crashed chopper and it blew up. Only Spc5 Jose Astorga, the gunner, survived and was immediately captured by NVA troops.

Second rescue attempt. This was for survivors of the shot-down Blueghost 39.

Two more AH-1 Cobra helicopters launched that same night of April 2 to attempt to look for possible survivors at the Blueghost 39 crash site. The crews of the two Cobras saw the burning wreckage of Blueghost 39 and were driven from the area by heavy NVA ground fire.

Third rescue attempt. On April 3, a third search-and-rescue attempt was executed by the 3d ARRG from Nakhon Phanom, Thailand. They flew two HH-53 rescue helicopters, Jolly Green 65 and Jolly Green 67, and two A-1 Skyraiders, Sandy 07 and Sandy 08.

They were joined overhead of Hambleton's hiding area by two more A-1s, Sandy 05 and Sandy 06.

The weather was solid overcast and unworkable for visually controlling air strikes by the on-scene FAC, Nail 25 flying in a U.S. Air Force OV-10 Bronco. Nail 25, with the crew of Capt. Rocky Smith and Capt. Rick Atchison, ran low on fuel and were replaced by another OV-10 Bronco, Nail 38, with the crew of Capt. Bill Henderson and 1st Lt. Mark Clark. The weather slightly improved as Nail 38 arrived over the survivor.

Jolly Green 65 went under the clouds and Jolly Green 67 followed above the clouds as Nail 38 broke below the overcast clouds. Jolly Green 65 immediately began receiving hits by NVA ground fire. The Jolly Green 65 crewmembers were completely shocked to see, below them, the large mass of enemy infantry forces with many tanks.

Jolly Green 65, piloted by U.S. Coast Guard Lt. Cmdr. Jay Crowe, an exchange pilot on tour assigned to the 37th ARRS squadron at Da Nang, was badly damaged by heavy NVA ground fire. Crowe had to struggle with the HH-53 to make an emergency landing at Phu Bai airfield. Crowe landed his damaged helicopter during a rocket attack by the NVA upon the Phu Bai airfield but safely got his chopper to a parking apron for much-needed repairs.

Jolly Greens 66 and 60 replaced Lieutenant Commander Crowe's flight of two HH-53s over the downed Bat 21 Bravo. This fourth rescue attempt, the third specifically for Hambleton, was controlled by Sandy 03, Lieutenant Burke, Nail 22, who led three other A-1s: Sandy 04, 05, and 06.

Jolly Green 66, piloted by Lt. Col. Bill Harris, commander of the 37th ARRS at Da Nang, dove down below the thick clouds, led by another FAC, Nail 22. Lieutenant Colonel Harris spotted Bat 21 Bravo's position and began an approach descent for pickup of Bat 21 Bravo. Ten NVA tanks in the immediate area began firing at Harris's Jolly Green 66. The intense enemy fire caused the FAC, Nail 22, to direct Harris to abort the pickup and exit south. Harris's HH-53 received numerous hits, and he was forced to land his bullet-riddled helicopter at Phu Bai airfield next to Jolly Green 65.

Sandy A-1 aircraft remained bombing and strafing around Bat 21 Bravo's location.

Later, that same day of April 3, Nail 38, piloted by Capt. Bill Henderson and backseater, 1st Lt. Mark Clark, Nail 38 Bravo, in an OV-10 Bronco, reported to Sandy 01 flying overhead of Bat 21's area. They descended to two thousand feet, below the cloud layer. Almost immediately, Henderson and Clark's OV-10A Bronco was hit by a SAM. Henderson and Clark ejected and landed within two kilometers of the evading Bat 21 Bravo.

Sandy 01 quickly called for a quick snatch of Henderson and Clark by any helicopter in the area. Two Cobras, Blueghost Red and Blueghost 26, piloted respectively by Capt. Tim Sprouse and Capt. Chuck La Celle, responded along with a UH-1E Huey, piloted by Warrant Officer Ben Nielsen, Blueghost 30.

Sandy 01 directed them to the downed OV-10 crew. En route, several SAMs were fired at the three responding helicopters. Then, Nielsen's Huey was badly hit, and he had to abort the SAR mission and return to Quang Tri airfield with all three helicopters.

In the meantime, NVA troops captured the downed Bill Henderson, Nail 38 Alpha. Lieutenant Mark Clark, Nail 38 Bravo, continued to evade the NVA on the ground.

While these SAR attempts were going on, we heard only cryptic, short radio transmissions in our war room on the Seventh Fleet Staff. This same day of April 3, I had sent an execute message to the III Marine Amphibious Force (III MAF) commander on Okinawa to direct a detachment from Marine Composite Reconnaissance Squadron (VMCJ-1) from Japan to fly to Cubi Point in the Philippines and prepare for radar jamming missions. I had also sent a directive message to the CG III MAF to dispatch three Marine Corps fighter squadrons to Cubi Point in the Philippines, and then after refueling to fly to Da Nang and set up flight operations to support the South Vietnamese. These Marine fighter jets arrived in Da Nang on April 5 to give additional support to the Seventh Air Force and provide the 3d ARVN Division and VNMC units close air support.

On April 4, a sixth rescue attempt took place with seven A-1 Sandys and two HH-53s. The nine-aircraft mixture of fixed-wing Skyraiders and Jolly Green helicopters were greeted with heavy volumes of NVA fire. Several of the A-1s and helicopters were badly damaged and limped back to Da Nang. They were without just-captured Bill Henderson and Mark Clark, who was now also a survivor down on the ground, not far from the original survivor, Iceal Hambleton, Bat 21 Bravo.

The next day, April 5, weather was extremely bad, but a few F-4 Phantoms got under the thick cloud layers and dropped CBU-42 antipersonnel bomblets around Bat 21 Bravo's area to discourage NVA troops from getting too close to Hambleton.

This same day, two of the three squadrons of Marine fighter jets that I had directed into Vietnam had arrived in Da Nang: VMFA-115 and VMFA-232 with 26 F-4B McDonnell Phantom aircraft and an airlift of 984 support personnel as well as 2,099,702 pounds of cargo, which arrived under the command of Col. Keith O'Keefe.

The following day, April 6, after the rescue crews had their aircraft repaired and B-52 bombers hit targets in the area of the now two survivors, Hambleton and Clark, another rescue attempt was to be made. Hambleton had been hiding on the ground for four days by this time. He was tired and hungry.

By late afternoon, the weather had improved slightly. Three A-1s (Sandys 02, 05, and 06) and two Jolly Greens (63 and 67) launched from Da Nang. Sandy 03, an A-1, joined the flight for firing a smoke screen to mask the pickup area from the NVA.

The leader, Sandy 01, Capt. Fred Boli, had been briefed that there were five NVA battalions near the downed Hambleton and Clark. They knew they would have to exercise extreme caution to attempt the rescues.

Sandy 03 put down his smoke screen, and Sandys 02, 05, and 06 began strafing attacks to protect Jolly Green 67 as the helicopter approached within one hundred meters of Bat 21 Bravo. The enemy began heavy firing and hit Jolly Green 67 with numerous rounds. Captain Fred Boli, Sandy 01, directed that they all get out of there.

As Jolly Green 67 turned away to abort the SAR mission, more NVA firing hit the helicopter as it attempted to evade to the south. The helicopter caught fire and crashed about one-and-a-half kilometers south of Clark, Nail 38 Bravo. There were no emergency beepers heard by any of the aircrew members above the burning helicopter.

Sandy 01, Boli, determined the area was too dangerous for any more ground rescue with such a large NVA force there, so the rest of the SAR team returned to Da Nang missing one HH-53 helicopter and crew.

Upon return of the damaged search-and-rescue aircraft to Da Nang, meetings and discussions ensued. All realized that both downed airmen, Hambleton and Clark, were trapped in the middle of a full NVA invasion force and that it would be too dangerous to try using helicopters to extract them to safety. They knew they had to figure out another way to get their fellow aviators. On that day, April 6, eighty SAMs were reported launched by the NVA in that area alone.

On April 7, U.S. Air Force 1st Lt. Bruce Walker, 20th TASS (Tactical Air Support Squadron) FAC, Covey 282, in an OV-10A Bronco with backseater, aerial observer U.S. Marine 1st Lt. Larry Potts, from 1st ANGLICO, flew over the area of Dong Ha, not very far from the downed Hambleton.

At about 1115, a SAM hit Covey 282, and Walker and Potts both ejected. Potts had been talking on the radio with First Lieutenant Eisenstein at Ai Tu on the artillery and command-and-control frequency to begin coordinating a naval gunfire support mission when their aircraft was hit by the missile. Not hearing a response from Potts, Eisenstein directed another AO flying in the backseat of another VNAF 0–1 to search the area for a downed OV-10A. The pilot, flying in the O-1 Bird Dog, began to search for Walker and Potts. The Bird Dog aircraft was hit by a Russian-built Strella SA-7 shoulder-fired surface-to-air missile. The O-1 limped back to Quang Tri airfield.

First Lieutenant Bruce Walker, Covey 282 Alpha, evaded the NVA on the ground and reported on his radio that he was unhurt. He also stated that he did not know the status of his backseater, 1st Lt. Larry Potts. Potts, Covey 282 Bravo, was never heard from again. Lieutenant Bruce Walker survived on the ground and was located about six kilometers northeast of Bat 21 Bravo.

Fifteen minutes later, U.S. Navy Lt. David Throop, senior observer to the naval gunfire liaison team, flying in the backseat of another VNAF O-1, commenced a search for the downed OV-10 crew of Walker and Potts; they didn't spot either Walker or Potts. They then directed naval gunfire missions against known SAM sites in the area.

Not too far from that search area, and just north of Dong Ha, a South Vietnamese A-1 and O–1 were shot down by SAMs. No parachutes were seen and no rescue efforts were executed.

Back over in the search-and-rescue area, Capt. Tuck Ernst and backseater, 1st Lt. Dave Talley, Nail 21, flying in an OV-10A, were now searching for Dave Talley's friend, Mark Clark, as well as Hambleton. Ernst and Talley heard Walker's Mayday calls; discussions with Walker indicated he was unhurt on the ground, but they did not see or hear from Potts.

At this point, there were four aviators on the ground: Iceal Hambleton, Bruce Walker, Mark Clark, and Larry Potts.

Nail 21, Ernst and Talley, tried to evade the numerous SAMs by flying at 1,500 feet. Immediately, they spotted Walker's parachute on the ground, six kilometers northeast of Hambleton. Larry Potts never did come up on his radio. A near miss by a SAM caused Ernst to fly his OV-10A out of the area and out to sea, passing right over the *Oklahoma City*. They flew back over land and rendezvoused with Nail 25, Capt. Rocky Smith, and Capt. Rick Atchison, in another OV-10A. Smith and Atchison looked over Ernst's aircraft for possible damage from the SAM near miss but could not find any. Captain Ernst stayed on station another hour looking for Walker but never could find out his exact position. As they were returning to their base at Nakhon Phanom, Laos, another SAM was fired up at them.

As Smith and Atchison flew over the search-and-rescue area, they confirmed Walker's location on the ground. As they did so, numerous SAM warnings from the DMZ area shook them up. As they headed out to sea, they received an audio indicating a SAM had been launched at them. Smith didn't see the SAM approaching the rear of the aircraft, but he took drastic evasive maneuvers just as the missile exploded nearby, without causing any damage to their aircraft. They quickly took a two-minute break over the Gulf of

Tonkin. During that flight, Atchison counted ten missiles launched against them.

The NVA air defense was seriously challenging U.S. air superiority and affecting close air support operations in and below the DMZ.

U.S. Air Force Lt. Col. John O'Gorman, commander of the 421st Tactical Fighter Squadron (TFS), and his counterpart, U.S. Air Force Lt. Col. Walt Bjorneby, commander of the 390th TFS, determined that the NVA air defenses had to be eliminated before any assistance could be developed for the South Vietnamese defenders.

First Lieutenant Bruce Walker evaded on the ground. Lieutenant Colonel Hambleton remained hidden in brush, only about two kilometers northeast of the town of Cam Lo, on the north side of the Cam Lo River. He was smack in the middle of the NVA invasion route from the DMZ. First Lieutenant Mark Clark hid on the south side of the Cam Lo River, about one kilometer east of Hambleton.

On April 7, no search-and-rescue efforts were flown.

On April 8, Lt. Col. Andy Anderson, in charge of the Joint Personnel Recovery Center attached to the J-2 intelligence division in MACV headquarters in Saigon, who had been following the numerous failed SAR attempts up north, felt that a commando team could use the Cau Viet River or the Mieu Giang River to get in and recover the three, possibly four, survivors. Anderson flew up to Da Nang to plan a ground recovery attempt.

On April 9, NVA forces attacked the Cam Lo area east along route QL-9. They encountered the ARVN 20th Armor and 5th Ranger Group just to the west of Dong Ha. The ARVN ground commander declared a tactical emergency, and U.S. Air Force B-52s bombed and stabilized the battlefield. However, an NVA SAM hit one B-52 bomber and damaged it, causing the giant bomber to make an emergency landing at Da Nang.

In the meantime, Lieutenant Colonel Anderson, up at Da Nang, requested the Da Nang–based U.S. Naval Advisory Detachment, which was a cover operating under the Military Assistance Command Observations Group (MACSOG-37), for a small Vietnamese commando team to assist in the rescue attempt. MACSOG-37 was responsible for covert maritime operations, which were being conducted mostly by the South Vietnamese Coastal Security

Service. Anderson was given a commando team under the command of Lieutenant Tho and began coordinating a plan to get Hambleton, Clark, and Walker out from under the noses of the invading North Vietnamese.

Anderson then called Lt. Cmdr. Craig Dorman at STAT 158 in Saigon to request an American to join Lieutenant Tho on the rescue team. Dorman sent an aggressive U.S. Navy SEAL, Lt. Tom Norris, to Da Nang to meet with Anderson.

Anderson coordinated his plan with MACV, Seventh Air Force, Seventh Fleet, First Regional Assistance Command, and the Vietnamese I Corps.

Anderson's plan had Lieutenant Norris and Lieutenant Tho set up along the Mieu Giang River and wait for Hambleton and Clark to float down the river to the rescue team.

Norris felt Anderson's plan was not aggressive enough and was too restrictive. Norris later told Tho, "Don't worry about the plan, we'll execute it as we need to."

As the battles ensued all along the southern area of the DMZ and the NVA-invading forces battled to make their way to their objective of Quang Tri City, Anderson and his commando team flew north in a helicopter from Da Nang. Anderson arrived at the 3d ARVN Division headquarters, where he briefed the commander, General Giai. General Giai was preoccupied with defending his area of responsibility and fully aware of the overwhelming size of the North Vietnamese Army attacking his forces. He was skeptical about Anderson's small commando operation to try to save just three Americans while he was suffering losses in the hundreds.

General Giai gave Anderson a Ranger platoon and three M-48 tanks to allow them to locate along QL-9 within visual observation of the strategic Cam Lo Bridge.

Lieutenant Colonel Louis Wagner, U.S. Army adviser to the ARVN 1st Armor Brigade, briefed Anderson and his team on the awesome NVA invasion situation along the battle lines of defense.

That night, Anderson radio-contacted Bat 21 Bravo. Hambleton was very weak but responded to Anderson on his survival radio. Then Anderson contacted Nail 38 Bravo. Anderson told Clark, who was closer to Anderson than Hambleton, to get into the water and let the current take him down to where Lieutenant Norris and his commandos were along the river.

Anderson repositioned himself and the Rangers downstream to grab Clark if Tom Norris missed him floating down the river.

Numerous NVA patrols wandered along the north side of the river. Anderson coordinated precisely timed air strikes to disrupt the NVA.

SEAL Tom Norris, Vietnamese commando Lieutenant Tho, and a team of three other Vietnamese commandos moved around several NVA patrols and past a column of NVA tanks and trucks moving south across the Cam Lo Bridge.

Norris set up a waiting post on the south side of the Cam Lo River to wait for Clark to float downstream to his team. Occasionally, Norris called in for Seventh Fleet naval gunfire ships to shoot night illumination flares in the general area as he waited for Clark.

A U.S. Air Force FAC, overhead, directed Clark to get to the river and float with the current. Clark saw the night illumination flares fired from the naval gunships and surmised that was where he was to head for the Norris pickup.

Just as First Lieutenant Clark came floating downstream near Norris and his commando team, an NVA patrol of six troops appeared. They passed through the pickup area without seeing Clark in the river or Norris's team along the bank of the river.

Because of the distraction of the NVA patrol, Norris lost sight of Clark in the river. Anderson contacted Clark on the survival radio and directed Clark to get out of the river on the south side.

Norris then got into the river and swam looking for Clark; just before dawn, Norris found him. Norris then contacted Anderson and led Clark back to friendly lines and to an ARVN bunker. An armored personnel carrier drove Clark to Dong Ha, and he was flown to Da Nang.

Anderson then planned the recovery of Bat 21 Bravo and Covey 282 Alpha. Anderson passed locations of enemy tanks to the FAC flying cover overhead. The FAC ran air strikes on another column of NVA tanks approaching the Cam Lo Bridge. The air strikes destroyed the three NVA tanks and several NVA trucks.

The NVA launched an artillery and rocket barrage upon the ARVN forces and Anderson's commandos. FAC Capt. Harold Icke, Bilk 11, flying overhead, ran air strikes that broke up the NVA artillery attack and an NVA ground attack that was commencing. But during the attack, Anderson was wounded and commando Lieutenant Tho was seriously wounded. One of Tho's sea commandos was killed by the NVA artillery barrage.

Lieutenant Tom Norris requested armored personnel carriers to evacuate the wounded while a helicopter picked up Anderson and Tho and flew them to Da Nang. From there, they were flown in a fixed-wing aircraft down to Saigon, where they were placed in a hospital.

The next day, Anderson, worried about the rescue mission, snuck out of a hospital window and met with General Marshall, who loaned him his T-39 jet to fly him back up to Da Nang.

In the meantime, Hambleton was weak from surviving in enemy territory for nine days, and Tom Norris's commando team was down to only three members. Norris, checking with Hambleton on the radio, found Hambleton slowly making his way toward the river.

The next night, Norris led his small commando team back to the river. Hambleton reported on his survival radio to the FAC overhead that he had reached the river. Norris searched the river but couldn't find Hambleton. Just before dawn, Norris returned to the ARVN bunker. Two of his commandos balked on wanting to continue the dangerous search for an American. So, Norris left the two commandos at the bunker and took sea commando Petty Officer Nguyen Van Kiet with him back to the river.

At the river, Norris took a local villager's sampan and searched the river for two hours until it got dangerously light at dawn.

Norris and Kiet returned to the bunker and rested. FAC, Bilk 11, Captain Icke was back overhead the rest of the day. As Captain Icke directed a Sandy 01, Skyraider, to drop a Madden survival pack to Hambleton, Icke was shocked to see Hambleton come out of his hiding and stand out on a sandbar. The two Sandy pilots also saw Hambleton out in the clear waving at them.

All agreed it was too dangerous of an area to again attempt a helicopter pickup of Hambleton, but they knew Hambleton's mental and physical health was now precarious.

Tom Norris knew he had to get in there and get Hambleton out—and soon. Norris waited until dark. He and Petty Officer Kiet dressed as Vietnamese fishermen and got a sampan. They paddled upstream, passing some NVA and a tank assembly area.

Fog rolled in to help cover their sampan paddling upstream. To their shock, though, because of the thick fog, they found themselves directly under the Cam Lo Bridge. NVA troops were passing directly over them, heading south on the bridge. They quietly paddled back downstream. They found Hambleton, partly delirious, in some bushes along the river; they laid him in the sampan and covered him with bamboo.

The FAC, Capt. Harold Icke, Bilk 11, arrived overhead again. Floating in the sampan, back down the river, an NVA patrol began shouting at them, but they finally passed the NVA troops without getting shot at. Farther down the river, they encountered fire from a heavy machine gun. They couldn't get past that, so they paddled to the south bank of the river and hid. Norris then requested air strikes. Overhead, Bilk 11 immediately ran a flight of U.S. Navy A-4 Skyhawks onto Tom Norris's reported NVA positions. Then two U.S. Air Force A-1 Skyraiders, Sandy flight, reported in, and Captain Icke ran the flight onto targets passed to him from Norris. The A-1s not only dropped high-explosive bombs, but also MK47 smoke bombs, creating an ideal smoke screen for Norris, Kiet, and Hambleton.

Immediately after the aerial attack, Norris and Kiet got Hambleton back into the sampan and went farther downstream to safety. Upon reaching the south shore, NVA troops opened fire on them. ARVN forces fired back from the south side at the NVA and helped lift Hambleton out of the sampan, then they carried him to a bunker, administered some first aid, and requested a personnel carrier (PC) for him.

Another mortar and rocket attack upon the bunker position delayed the arrival of the personnel carrier. Finally, it arrived and took Hambleton and Norris back to Brigade headquarters at Dong Ha.

News reporters, well aware of the daring rescue, awaited Hambleton's arrival at Da Nang; he had survived eleven and a half days behind enemy lines.

Hambleton had few words to say to the press. He simply said, "It was a hell of a price to pay for one life . . . I'm very sorry."

The price had been high. During April 1972, eleven Americans who had attempted rescuing Hambleton were killed and two were captured. Lieutenant Colonel Anderson and Lieutenant Tho and others were wounded. Six aircraft were shot down and many were damaged. Seventh Air Force records indicated that more than eight hundred strike sorties, including B-52 strikes, were flown in direct support of the rescue.

SEAL Norris, when asked if it had been a tough rescue, and if he would do that again, answered, "I would do it any time if I could bring back another pilot."

Norris was back at Da Nang, planning the recovery of 1st Lt. Bruce Walker, Covey 282 Alpha. Walker had tried to move south for a river pickup, but too many NVA were in the area. Norris recommended Walker head east, a little each night. This would allow Norris to come over the beach from the east to attempt to find Walker heading toward him.

It was April 16, and Walker was still only about six kilometers from where Hambleton had originally been hiding before he moved to the river for rescue.

FAC, 1st Lt. Mickey Fain, Bilk 35, in his O-2A, continued to fly cover over Walker, taking turns with other FACs.

On April 17, Walker was instructed to make his way east toward the coast.

Walker acknowledged the plan and prepared to move east. No FAC coverage remained over Walker that night because the plan was to have him start moving the next night, April 18.

But Walker decided to move eastward that same night, April 17, without FAC cover. He encountered a South Vietnamese local villager, whose wife quickly notified the local Viet Cong cadre commander in the village of Lam Xuan.

The local Viet Cong began to track Walker eastward during the night. At dawn, First Lieutenant Fain was overhead, in his OV-10A, looking for Walker at his last known hiding site. Fain heard the panicked voice of Walker over his survival radio. Fain finally found Walker about eight kilometers east from the previous night's hiding place. Walker used his survival mirror to assist Fain in locating him, and Fain was shocked to also see the local Viet Cong closing in on Walker.

Fain brought in a flight of U.S. Air Force F-4 Phantoms, call sign Lacy; he had the F-4s drop their MK-82 500-pound bombs as close to Walker as possible to hit the close-in VC, but he had to stop the bombings as the VC got quite close to Walker.

Fain called in another FAC, Capt. J. D. Caven, Bilk 35, flying an OV-10A. Captain Caven, in his Bronco, made repeated low-level attacks upon the VC as they fired back at him. Fain's aircraft was hit and damaged badly enough to force him to leave the area. Fain requested a replacement FAC. Bilk 35 heard Walker call on his radio that the VC were now shooting at him. Those were the last words that Fain or Caven heard from Walker. Fain saw Walker lying in the grass as he flew over him several times; what Fain did not see was a local Viet Cong, Vo Va De, get close to Walker and shoot him six times.

Fain was unaware that Walker was shot and continued to run attacks by the Lacy F-4s upon the VC area until the F-4s expended all their bombs. When the smoke cleared, Fain could no longer see Walker lying in the grass. Fain, low on fuel, was forced to return to Da Nang. FAC, Capt. Harold Icke, Bilk 11, relieved Fain and flew cover over Walker's area. Captain Icke never made visual, or radio, contact with Walker.

After two orbits overhead, Captain Icke heard Vietnamese voices on the emergency survival radio frequency. Icke immediately surmised that Walker had been captured or killed and that the local VC had his radio. Icke ran several more air strikes into the area and had to depart when his O-2A became low on fuel.

FACs covered the Walker area for the next two days but never heard from Walker again. The search-and-rescue efforts for First Lieutenant Walker were terminated on April 20.

Shortly after terminating Walker's rescue attempt, U.S. Navy SEAL lieutenant Tom Norris's commando team was dissolved. Norris reported back to STDAT 158 in Saigon.

The search-and-rescue efforts by Lt. Tom Norris reflected the highest level of heroic actions. Four years later, in April 1976, President Gerald Ford awarded the Medal of Honor to U.S. Navy Lt. Tom Norris. Additionally, South Vietnamese commando Nguyen Van Kiet, received the U.S. Navy Cross, the only Vietnamese so honored during that very long war.

Chapter 5
• • • • • • •

The Seventh Fleet Counterattacks

While President Nixon and special adviser to the president Dr. Henry Kissinger pondered what to direct JCS to do in retaliation, the NVA continued to cross into the South, also attacking from Cambodia. The NVA penetrated twenty miles into South Vietnam. The city of An Loc had to send its last reserves up Highway 13 to relieve the siege at An Loc. This reserve counterattack stopped the NVA at An Loc, but other communist forces attacked the U.S. coastal base at Cam Ranh Bay, killing eleven U.S. support personnel. Down in the Mekong Delta area, the communists doubled their normal number of attacks. The overall thrusts obviously were planned to take as much of South Vietnam as possible. If the North could divide the South into several portions, the North Vietnamese would have more bargaining strength for the ongoing negotiations in Paris. The North Vietnamese wanted to prove that South Vietnam could not shoulder the full defense of their country. The NVA were determined to prove that President Nixon's Vietnamization of the war would not stop the North from taking the South, even with the U.S. air and naval support left in the area, after most of the U.S. ground forces retrograded out of Vietnam the year before.

As assistant amphibious warfare officer on the staff, and the only Marine in the operations section, I hurriedly flew off the *Oklahoma City* in Admiral Mack's personal helicopter, Black Beard One. We flew to Phu Bai airfield, near Hue City. There, we met with the local South Vietnamese Marine Corps commander. I accompanied my boss, Cmdr. Jim Froid, the amphibious warfare officer; Marine Col. Jim Dionisopolous, assistant plans officer; and plans officer, Capt. L. J. Marshall. We explained our support position to the South Vietnamese Marine Corps commander, Brig. Gen. Bui The Lan (pronounced Laan). We stated, "The Seventh Fleet has requested, and received permission, through the chain of command, from JCS to use our Seventh Fleet amphibious landing craft to carry South Vietnamese Marines behind the enemy. This was approved provided we don't land any U.S. ground-fighting Marines on North or South Vietnam soil. Absolutely no reintroduction of U.S. Marines into Vietnam was allowed."

The Vietnamese Marine Corps staff at Phu Bai was elated that we had not abandoned them and that we would render some assistance in fighting the numerically superior NVA forces attacking just to their north. During these two days of initial discussions, I felt uncomfortable at Phu Bai. Looking around, I could not see any Americans, other than the four of us. I was fully aware that our advisers were in harm's way, now under heavy NVA attacks to our immediate north. In the confusion of the land battles under way, I did not know the status of the U.S. Army, Air Force, and Marine advisers. The North Vietnamese Army had begun to envelop Phu Bai from the mountains of the Ho Chi Minh trail in northern Laos, and the NVA division was only twelve miles to our west.

Within two days, a plan was drawn up at Phu Bai for a mini surface counterattack from the sea in our Seventh Fleet's Task Force (TF) 76 amphibious assault boats. Once the plan was solidified, it was up to my boss, Cmdr. Jim Froid, and me, as his assistant, to execute the plan into an operational order with message directives to TF 76 under the watchful eyes of our Seventh Fleet operations officer, U.S. Navy Capt. Bob McKenzie and Admiral Mack.

Following Jim Froid's plan, the amphibious force commander moved his amphibious ships into position. We then had them pick up two thousand VNMC troops and landed them behind the three NVA divisions, south of the banks of the Cau Viet River. This placed the two thousand South Vietnamese Marines to the rear of the NVA forces that were heading for Quang Tri City. This VNMC force was now in position to interdict the NVA supply lines in the eastern area. Because this was a coastal landing, we were able to provide the

VNMC units with naval gunfire support during their amphibious assault to the rear of the enemy. This immediately put pressure on the NVA troops heading for Quang Tri and their supporting artillery units with them. This was the classic Marine Corps amphibious assault from the rear, similar to the U.S. Marines, with army units, at Inchon Harbor, during the early stages of the Korean War that resulted in the recapture of Seoul, Korea.

By now, the South Vietnamese, desperately fighting to prevent the entire fall of South Vietnam, gallantly destroyed 105 NVA tanks using handheld antitank weapons. Their own Vietnamese Air Force and the U.S. military could not help them due to the continual overcast skies. The NVA was still pressing hard toward Quang Tri City and flanking from the west toward Hue–Phu Bai.

Our ship, the *Oklahoma City*, and eight other cruisers and destroyers attacked coastal targets south of the DMZ. Two destroyers, *John R. Craig* (DD-885) and *Rowan* (DD-782), were hit by enemy shore batteries located in North Vietnam while obeying orders from higher authority to stay south of the DMZ. Commander Stu Landersman, our staff surface warfare officer and coordinator with TG 70.8, briefed Admiral Mack, "Admiral, the *Craig* sustained hull and equipment damage and the *Rowan* took light shrapnel hits. Three enemy batteries were destroyed inside the DMZ and eight secondary explosions ignited."

Admiral Mack acknowledged, "Sorry to see casualty reports, but keep our ships hitting them along the coast. Establish a shore bombardment force."

"Aye, aye, Admiral. I'll set up a specific force for that mission," responded Stu Landersman. Stu then hurriedly drafted a message in the war room that directed the Task Group 70.8 commander of surface ships to create a separate task unit dedicated to shore battery attacks. Stu designated this unit as Task Unit 70.8.1 (TU 70.8.1), including our ship, *Oklahoma City*. TU 70.8.1 began day-and-night raids called special naval gunfire operations that began with Freedom Train and continued on into a series called Linebacker.

With the NVA still attempting to penetrate farther into South Vietnam, President Nixon allowed us a little more flexibility. Admiral Bernard A. Clarey, commander in chief, U.S. Pacific Fleet (CINCPACFLT), located in Hawaii, called Admiral Mack on our covered, scrambled-classified voice radio net, located a deck below in the ship's communications center.

Admiral Clarey said to Admiral Mack, "Bill, the commander in chief of the Pacific (CINCPAC), here in Hawaii, reports to me that General Westmoreland, in Saigon, has reported the NVA are coming out of Cambodia. They are slicing through the middle of South Vietnam toward the area of Qui Nhon on the South China Sea. A large NVA force is moving out of the mountains from the Ho Chi Minh trail toward the coastal city of Qui Nhon. It looks like they plan to cut the country in half."

Admiral Mack, hearing that, had Stu Landersman direct our ship and several others to leave the DMZ area and head south toward Qui Nhon. This upset me because it removed us from the close proximity of the South Vietnamese and ARVN forces battling along the NVA northern invasion area.

Our small task group set up a coastal gun position area called Kelly off the coast of Qui Nhon. As the NVA poured out of the hills toward the east and Qui Nhon, our naval gunfire impacted them a distance out. The South Vietnamese artillery, to the west of Qui Nhon, also greeted the invading NVA. For two days, these heavy fires raged to preclude the NVA from actually cutting South Vietnam in half and claiming a victory in doing so. The NVA were finally driven back into the mountains. Our task group, our ship included, quickly sailed back up the coast to reestablish in an area just below the DMZ and close to the Cau Viet River, not too far from Quang Tri City.

The NVA invasion forces near Quang Tri City were continuing their attacks. I felt it was time to bring some of our Marine jet squadrons back into Vietnam, before Hue City and Phu Bai fell. If Quang Tri City fell, followed then by Hue City, the NVA would quickly move south to attack Da Nang. Our Marine jet squadrons had retrograded from Da Nang to Iwakuni, Japan, a year ago in 1971, under Nixon's Vietnamization program. I initially discussed my desire to bring the Marine squadrons back into Vietnam with my immediate boss, Cmdr. Jim Froid. We both then discussed it with our N-3, operations officer, Capt. Bob McKenzie. They agreed that I should direct Marine aircraft assets back into South Vietnam from Japan. I then discussed it with the chief of staff, Capt. Earl F. Godfrey, and finally, with Admiral Mack.

I explained to Admiral Mack: "We must get more attack air into the Quang Tri and Hue areas, or they may fall to the NVA. The enemy still has extensive momentum. I can get our Marine fighter/attack bombers back into Da Nang quickly. If JCS doesn't want them back in-country, they can stop them on their way before they get to Vietnam. By the time the Marine squadrons mount-out from Iwakuni, Japan, after receipt of my execute message, the entire chain of command will have copies of it.

"I will send the Marine jets first to Naval Air Station Cubi Point in the Philippines. I will direct them to refuel there and not refuel in the air en route to Vietnam. By stopping to refuel in the Philippines, we'll give everybody in the chain of command, including JCS, ample time to stop them from going into Vietnam. If politically desired, they can direct the Marine squadrons to return to Japan from the Philippines. Additionally, JCS would have enough time to query Dr. Kissinger at the White House as to whether we should reintroduce Marine jets back into Vietnam.

"If the White House doesn't want them back in Vietnam, there will be time for higher authority to have JCS send us a flash message, via satellite. I can then turn the Marines around and send them back to Japan."

Admiral Mack listened intently, sipped some coffee, and said, "We have the assets. We're still committed to assist South Vietnam. We'd be remiss in our duties in not responding with forces on hand, within the restrictions and rules of engagement dictated to us by Washington. Yes, go ahead ... draft a message. Let me personally see it after Captain McKenzie checks it over.

"I'll call Admiral Clarey at CINCPACFLT on the garbled squawk box to discuss it with him. If he approves, I'll release your execute message."

I drafted a message and took it to our staff N-3, operations officer, Captain McKenzie to carefully check its contents. Basically, my message read:

FMCOMSEVENTHFLT
TOCTF 79

INFO JCS
COMUSMACV
CINCPAC
CINCPACFLT
CDR 7TH AF
CTG 79.1
CTG 79.2
CTG 79.3
AMER AMBAS, TOKYO, JAPAN
NAS CUBI PT, PHI

EXECUTE MESSAGE

THIS IS AN EXECUTE MESSAGE. REPEAT,
EXECUTE MESSAGE. CTG 79 IS DIRECTED
TO DEPLOY THREE (3) FIGHTER ATTACK
SQUADRONS TO DA NANG AFB, RVN, VIA
NAS CUBI PT. ASSURE REFUEL CUBI PT., VICE
AERIAL REFUELING. MINIMUM DEFENSE
FORCE ASSETS TO JOIN AIR GROUP AS SOON AS
FEASIBLE. REPORT FIRST LAUNCH TO ALCON
IMMEDIATELY. REPORT ETA CUBI PT. REPORT
ETA DA NANG. AIR GROUP DESIGNATED CTU
79.3.0 AND CTU 79.3.0 WILL REPORT OPCON
COMSEVENTHFLT. REPEAT. REPORT OPCON
COMSEVENTHFLT.

Admiral Mack, having discussed the situation with Admiral Clarey, read my draft and approved it. The message was released and flashed top priority around the world, via a satellite stationed over the Gulf of Tonkin. My message specifically spelled out that our Marine jets would land at Cubi Point in the Philippines and refuel. In addition to the commander of the Seventh Air Force, I included the U.S. ambassador on the info copies of the message traffic so the ambassador could brief the Japanese legislature, the Diet, in Tokyo before the Marine jets would depart Naval Air Station Cubi Point for Vietnam.

I had definitively directed the Marine mini–air group to report for operational control to my boss, the commander, Seventh Fleet, located on board the *Oklahoma City*. For several reasons, I did not direct, in my message, that the Marine Air Group report OPCON to the commander, Seventh Air Force, located at Tan Son Nhut AFB outside of Saigon.

During my first combat tour in Vietnam, I was well aware that there was an operational control squabble with the Seventh Air Force when Marine jets were first introduced in 1965. I was stationed at Da Nang at that time, and OPCON became a complex issue. The Seventh Air Force wanted control of all Marine air assets, including Marine close air support (CAS) aircraft. The Marines have an extremely close-knit air-ground team. Therefore, the Marines are quite reluctant to break up that team, or give all or portions of it away to any other controlling agencies. The daily close air support training between Marine ground units and the attack air units is unique, the very best in the world. To disrupt this close coordination and very well-trained operational fighting team would endanger the lives of Marine infantry troops. Air force control of these Marine CAS assets weakens the protection of the Marine ground troops because the air force had not fully understood the Marine air-ground team mechanics involved.

When the air force assumes full operational control of assets, including Marine air assets, there obviously is a better overall theater operational control. But, unfortunately, this does severely weaken the protection afforded the Marine infantry and complicates air scheduling, fast-reaction, and fragmentary (frag) orders on what is normally a daily Marine routine. Back in 1965, though, when it became obvious that Marine air assets were going to remain ashore in Vietnam for some time, rather than operate from ship to shore, the air force did get operational control of those Marine Air Groups. Still, the Marines fully controlled day-to-day Marine close air support missions, covering their frontline troops. This control by the Marines of attack aircraft was confined to their Marine tactical area of responsibility in I Corps area of South Vietnam. The fighter aircraft, F-4 Phantoms, when flying long-distance tactical bombing missions and not used for close air support of troops, were a different scheduling situation.

To complicate matters more, all Marine fighter aircraft are always capable of both fighter tactics and close air support bombing missions. It depends on how the missions are scheduled. All Marine air consisting of fighters and attack bombers, particularly the A-6 Intruder when flying tactical missions into North Vietnam, were scheduled and frag-controlled by the Seventh Air Force frag-order system. The CAS missions, particularly the reactive bombing missions in the nearby battlefields of the Marine infantry forces, remained under the control of the Marines, but the Marine CAS missions appeared daily on the Seventh Air Force flight schedule. This schedule was coordinated by the Seventh Air Force Headquarters located at Tan Son Nhut Air Force Base outside of Saigon from 1965 until Marine air assets were pulled out of Vietnam in 1971.

In actuality, out in the combat fields, Marine ground and airborne forward air controllers controlled fighter/attack F-4 Phantoms, A-6 Intruders, and A-4 Skyhawks in their attacks upon the enemy. I happened to have been an airborne forward air controller, flying out of Marble Mountain airfield in an OV-10A Bronco twin-turboprop airplane during my second thirteen-month combat tour in 1969–70.

Now, in 1972, as Marine air officer on the Seventh Fleet staff, I did not want to resurrect that complex problem of the air force controlling the Marine air assets until I was certain that Marine air assets were staying ashore for some time. If we were going to keep them there for only a short counteroffensive period and again retrograde them back out of country, then I wanted my boss, Admiral Mack, to retain OPCON over his own assets.

There were only a handful of Marines in Vietnam at this time serving as advisers to the ARVN and VNMC and within ANGLICO. In terms of the jet squadrons that I was reintroducing into Vietnam, I strongly felt that the operational control, at least initially, belonged to the commander of the Seventh Fleet, who owned these air assets. This set of circumstances would match the doctrine of the amphibious operation, in which the navy operational commander controls all Marine air and ground assets until the Marine amphibious landing force is well established ashore. Then, the theater navy commander formally passes command of both Marine air and ground forces ashore to the Marine ashore commander. Additionally, during this fast-paced set of circumstances that we were in with the rapidly invading North Vietnamese, I felt that if the Seventh Air Force would complain about OPCON of Marine air, I'd hear about it soon enough from the navy chain of command.

Unknown to many, including most air force officials, the Marine Corps invented dive bombing in 1927 when U.S. Marine Maj. Ross E. Roswell led the first dive-bombing attack in history in support of friendly troops against Nicaraguan bandits during the so-called Banana War. This was the first low-level bombing against an organized enemy. This dive-bombing action by Marine Corps pilots was years before Hitler used dive bombing against Poland, at the start of World War II. This long history of close air support for ground troops was refined throughout World War II island-hopping Marine invasions (for example, Iwo Jima and Okinawa) and was also provided during the Korean War. It is obvious why Marines don't want to lose control of these vital air assets in combat because they are normally tactically tied to the support of their Marine ground units.

It should be pointed out that after the National Security Act enactment on September 18, 1947, which unified the army, navy, and newly formed air force into a National Military Establishment, the air force soon diminished their capability to provide realistic close air support to the army. The air force still doesn't practice, nor fully know how to provide, air support to friendly ground troops in close contact with enemy ground units. Use of smart bombs doesn't replace Marine air support.

Therefore, to clarify the situation I was creating, and to ensure that there was good coordination, I discussed the situation with Admiral Mack, the U.S. Air Force liaison staff officer, Lieutenant Colonel Rose, and other staff officers. After the discussions I sent out a second message directive to Task Force 79. The message basically covered the mechanics of control of the Marine air assets being reintroduced into Vietnam. The setup would have a Marine colonel as liaison officer at the Seventh Air Force headquarters in Tan Son Nhut. He would coordinate the daily Marine missions with the Marine Air Group at Da Nang for the next day's schedule. He would then incorporate the daily Marine air schedule into the Seventh Air Force frag orders schedule for the next day. Lieutenant

Colonel Rose discussed the coordination plan with the Seventh Air Force prior to my release of my message. My message read:

```
FM COMSEVENTHFLT
TOCTF 79
INFOJCS
COMUSMACV
CINCPAC
CINCPACFLT
CDR 7TH AF
CTG 79.1
CTG 79.2
CTG 79.3
CTU 79.3.0
```

MARINE AIR ASSETS CONTROL AT DA NANG

REQUEST CTF 79 SEND MARINE AVIATOR, COLONEL, 06, TO SEVENTH AIR FORCE STAFF AT TAN SON NHUT AFB, RVN TO ACT AS FRAG MISSIONS ASSIGNMENTS COORDINATOR AND DAILY SCHEDULING LIAISON OFFICER. ESTABLISH COMMUNICATIONS BETWEEN CTU 79.3.0 DA NANG AND SEVENTH AIR FORCE. KEEP ALCON ADVISED.

This brief message of assigning a Marine colonel to the Seventh Air Force apparently settled all questions at this time. We did not get pressure from above ... from COMUSMACV in Saigon or the Seventh Air Force at Tan Son Nhut.

The Marine F-4 Phantoms were in the air within a few hours of receipt of my execute message and soon landed at Naval Air Station Cubi Point in the Philippines for refueling.

We didn't get any messages from anyone concerning this movement. So I sat there on the ship and waited and watched the message traffic as the Marine jet-fighter jocks took off again. The Marine fighter/bomber jets headed 270 degrees, directly for Da Nang. On April 6, the first two squadrons of McDonnell Douglas F-4B Phantom fighter/bombers to arrive at Da Nang were the Silver Eagles of VMFA-115 and the Red Devils of VMFA-232. On April 14, twelve additional F-4J aircraft from the Lancers of VMFA-212 arrived from Hawaii.

The very next day after the Marine fighter/bomber aircraft arrived at Da Nang, though, we on the Seventh Fleet staff received a message from CINCPACFLT. The commander in chief of the Pacific Fleet asked why the Marines flying from Japan to Vietnam had not notified the U.S. ambassador in Tokyo that they were going back into combat in Vietnam from Japan. CINCPACFLT was concerned politically because the U.S.–Japanese agreements included a required notification by the United States of any military movements from Japan to Vietnam during this period of the war. To answer CINCPACFLT, we conducted a message traffic inquiry to all units involved.

After a short investigation, we found out that my execute message copy had been received at the U.S. embassy in Tokyo on a Friday night. This was after the ambassador had departed Tokyo for a ski resort for the weekend, and his aide at the embassy apparently felt that this particular message was not important enough to cause the aide to call the ambassador at the ski resort hotel. By the time the ambassador returned to the embassy in Tokyo and read his message traffic Monday morning, our Marine jets were already in Vietnam, and maintenance personnel were loading ordnance on their aircraft for missions. The ambassador did not have the time to personally warn the Japanese government, as notifications were required. The ambassador, obviously embarrassed, was probably furious. I had done the right thing in sending the ambassador an info copy of my execute message, though; there was nothing else that could be done. Additionally, because I had directed that the Marine jets refuel in the Philippines, instead of aerial refueling en route, the Japanese could not honestly state that the Marines went directly into Vietnam from Japan. Technically, they flew from the Philippines into the combat area. This fact apparently calmed the large number of complaining Japanese communists who always looked for any excuse to assist their worldwide communist comrades-in-arms.

During the same period, I had another problem. Because our naval gunfire support ships were now allowed to fire on military targets inside the DMZ, we soon realized that we desperately needed day-and-night naval gunfire spotting capabilities. This was required to visually observe the hits, make adjustments, and observe damage inflicted for determining overall assessments of the ships' raids. In the South Vietnam areas, I had an immediate solution to the spotting requirement. I sent a message through the command system to ensure that the ANGLICO unit in Vietnam would disperse among the ARVN and VNMC units along the coast, particularly in the Quang Tri Province. They needed to assist the South Vietnamese with coordination with our Seventh Fleet's naval gunships off the coast.

To my satisfaction, I would learn that U.S. Marine Lt. Col. D'Wayne Gray, ANGLICO Sub Unit One commander in MACV's compound in Saigon, had already done that and his spotters were already contacting our ships for fire-control missions. I had served for fourteen months in 1st ANGLICO in Hawaii, from 1964 until I had received orders to Vietnam for my first combat tour in 1965. So, when I discussed ANGLICO with Admiral Mack and our staff, I knew everything to know about ANGLICO. The staff did not. Therefore, after my briefings of what exactly ANGLICO was and did, our surface operations staff officer, Cmdr. Stu Landersman, sent out a flurry of messages to CTG 70.8. Stu directed that the gunline commander start closely coordinating naval gunfire with the ashore-located ANGLICO units that were supporting the ARVN and VNMC troops in contact with the NVA.

However, for the North Vietnamese occupied DMZ coastal areas requiring naval gunfire interdiction attacks, the fleet had no such existing spotting capability. So, I directed TF 79 Marines to send five TA-4, two-seater versions of the A-4 Skyhawk from Iwakuni, Japan, via Cubi Point to Da Nang. At first, I seriously considered sending a detachment of OV-10A Bronco, twin-turboprop observation aircraft from my old squadron, VMO-2, now located on the island of Okinawa, but we did not have free space on any aircraft carrier. Additionally, at the time, the OV-10A did not have dispensing flare units installed for defensive evasion measures against heat-seeking missiles. Nor did they have SAM alerting and evasion equipment for survival in this more intensive ground-to-air threat by the enemy. Because we had not yet knocked out the tremendous number of SAM sites in the DMZ or North Vietnam, the SAM threat was extremely dangerous to all friendly aircraft near the DMZ or anywhere north of it.

I sent a message to TF 79, the III MAF on Okinawa, requesting that the 1st Marine Aircraft Wing deploy five aerial observers (AOs) from Marine Observation Squadron Two, VMO-2, in Okinawa. The 1st Marine Aircraft Wing not only sent aerial observers from VMO-2, but from other sources as well. These Marine AOs reported to a U.S. Air Force squadron of OV-10A Broncos. This air force squadron in the 20th TASS had the call sign of Covey and was still based at Da Nang. It was one of the few air force squadrons still in Vietnam as a result of Nixon's Vietnamization retrograde of Americans from Vietnam. These Marine AOs would fly in the backseats of the air force Broncos, and they would fly naval gunfire support (NGFS) missions only in South Vietnam.

I coordinated these missions with Cmdr. Stu Landersman and the Marine colonel acting as liaison officer on the Seventh Air Force staff at Tan Son Nhut.

Additional Marine AOs would fly in the backseats of the Marine TA-4 Skyhawks. After some delay for installing handheld laser target designators into the TA-4s, and some very limited crew training using the lasers, our Marine TA-4s arrived at Da Nang on April 16. The two-person teams in the TA-4s were called Fast FACs. These NGFS spot teams gave the Seventh Fleet bombardment ships visual spotting and adjusting capabilities with increased gunfire efficiency. We designated this small Marine spotting team flying their TA-4s CTE 79.3.01 and had them report to the Marine F-4 fighter group settled in Da Nang. For naval gunfire spotting, these air force/Marine flying teams reported directly to our gunline commander of the ships, designated CTU 70.8.0 for their daily fragmentary assigned missions. This was more direct, and therefore much faster for coordination and execution than getting their frag mission assignments from our Marine liaison officer on the Seventh Air Force staff, who normally coordinated the Marine F-4 squadrons' missions with the air force daily flight schedule.

Even using the Marine TA-4s with AOs spotting naval gunfire, we could have used more spotting because of the heavy firing by our fleet against the heavily fortified North Vietnamese coastal defense positions installed just north of the DMZ. Looking the situation over, I felt we could use the fleet's logistics helicopters and the antisubmarine helicopters, some were from navy squadron HSL-3 and located aboard the numerous cruisers and logistics ships in the Gulf of Tonkin.

I strongly believed that these helicopters could fly out to support the cruisers during the raids along the DMZ coast. I brought this concept to Admiral Mack and the staff at the next meeting. Admiral Mack thought it innovative, but I was met with a lot of resistance from my fellow staff officers. Some felt it was too dangerous for a helicopter flying so close to the North Vietnamese coast because of the numerous NVA SAMs.

The next day, I presented a slide briefing that I had obtained from our intelligence section, N-2. The presentation depicted the slant range of the SAMs and maximum-distance efficiency of the SA-7 shoulder-fired Strella heat-seeking missile. This Soviet-supplied copy of our Redeye missile was certainly lethal against helicopters, but it did have performance limits. I briefed the admiral and staff that we could easily keep the navy helicopters midway from the firing ships to shore and no higher than five hundred feet above the water. This would keep the choppers well below the missile envelopes and distant from the ranges of coastal antiaircraft guns. I then coordinated using Marine aerial observers from the Marine TA-4 detachment to get picked up at Da Nang by the navy logistics helicopters. They would then fly out to our ships and train the navy on the rudiments of airborne naval gunfire spotting.

Some of my fellow staffers still resisted supporting my concept, saying that it was too dangerous for the navy logistics helo crews despite the obvious immediate requirement for verifying the Seventh Fleet ships' hits upon targets. To prove the functionality and feasibility of the concept to the entire staff, none of whom had ever controlled gunfire support or air strikes, I asked Admiral Mack, "Could I use your personal helicopter, Black Beard One, because it's right here on the fantail of our ship? I could use it during our ship's next night raid into North Vietnam. I will personally do the naval gunfire spotting for our attacking group of ships, including our *Oklahoma City*."

Without hesitating, the admiral answered, "Sure. We certainly can use the spotting to know what we're hitting. Just don't get too close into shore."

The next night, I went airborne in the copilot's seat of the Kaman-built helicopter from Detachment 32 out of Helicopter Anti-Submarine Squadron 31. The pilot was Lt. Cmdr. E. Sarr. Using night-illumination flare shells, both the pilot and I were amazed by how much better you could see the shore targets, even at night and at a distance, when flying at five hundred feet above the ship. The overcast night sky actually assisted in focusing our eyes on the targets because of the absence of distracting star-studded night conditions.

Our four ships fired on a convoy of trucks that had been picked up on radar in CIC as they came down the coast Highway 1 through the DMZ. I could easily see and report to the *Oklahoma City*, call sign Fire Ball, the specific number of burning trucks and exact number of secondary explosions caused by our 5- and 6-inch gun firings. The radar personnel within all four ships could see the convoy of trucks on their radar screens and directed the gunfire onto the convoy. Without visual observation, though, they could only guess what the actual destruction upon the convoy really was. Reporting to them that they were, indeed, getting direct hits and many secondary explosions out on the trucks on Highway 1 was very satisfying to the gunship crews.

The next morning, our surface operations officer, Stu Landersman, sent out a message to TG 70.8 that the Seventh Fleet staff had utilized the admiral's personal helicopter for naval gunfire spotting and that we would soon implement this spotting within the fleet, using the navy helicopters.

I sent a message directing that a Marine aerial observer (AO) in the TA-4 squadron at Da Nang be prepared to be flown out to ships in a navy helicopter to commence training the navy helicopter crews in naval gunfire spotting for control and damage reporting. This Marine AO immediately began training sessions aboard the ships.

Within two weeks, it was common to hear Stu Landersman briefing the admiral and staff about his incoming messages from TG 70.8 surface gunships that the helicopters' NGFS damage reports were indeed working well. We all had a much better feel for what our ship's interdiction missions were hitting, and what the damage upon the enemy really was, as the NVA continued to move logistics down along the coast. We were able to report the enemy's attrition rate of one of their supply lines more accurately.

As an interim solution to increase this needed information, I directed that four Marine UH-1Es Huey helicopters from one of Jim Froid's LPH helicopter carriers of Task Force 76 be dispatched north, along with four Marine AOs from the afloat 9th Marine Amphibious Brigade (9th MAB), designated CTG 79.1. The staff of CTG 79.1, aboard the TF 76 flagship, USS *Blue Ridge* (LCC-19), responded immediately and said they were prepared to execute the gunfire support mission. Jim Froid immediately sent a message directing that one of our landing platform dock (LPD) ships be located off the North Vietnamese coast. The four Huey helicopters then used this LPD as a base platform to operate in the hostile waters off the coast of the DMZ. This also gave us a useful gunfire support—if we could get permission from higher authority in Washington to strike along the coast north of the DMZ.

During April 1972, the North Vietnamese continued more invasion thrusts deeper into South Vietnam. Finally, the skies began to clear and we were visually able to use our military air power. This was the very first time, during this long war, that U.S. planes flying over South Vietnam had crews actually able to find very worthwhile targets of large-sized NVA units, tanks, artillery, and supplies. Prior to this period, the NVA took great pains to keep their ground units in small cadres to save them from the U.S. air attacks, and they had not fielded tanks, SAMs, and artillery until this big NVA invasion phase of the war.

During the rest of April 1972, the North Vietnamese continued more buildups of ground units, coming from all directions into South Vietnam from Laos and Cambodia out of the Ho Chi Minh trail.

During April, our Seventh Air Force was directed by Washington to rebuild its strength. The buildup in Thailand increased the number of aircraft to a total of 110. They now consisted of five squadrons of F-4 Phantoms, one squadron of F-105 Thuds, and one squadron of EB-66 Douglas twin-engine radar countermeasure aircraft. President Nixon authorized fifty-eight more B-52 bombers to be flown to the western Pacific. During April, Nixon also authorized two more carriers to join the Seventh Fleet. This gave Admiral Mack's Seventh Fleet carrier Task Force 77, under the command of Adm. Damon Cooper, the additional carriers USS *Kitty Hawk* and the USS *Constellation* in the Gulf of Tonkin.

Chapter 6

• • • • • • •

B-52s Return to the North

On April 4, 1972, President Nixon authorized bombings in North Vietnam, as far away as eight miles north of the demilitarized zone. President Nixon then appointed Gen. John Vogt to be the replacement Seventh Air Force commander in Vietnam. The Seventh Air Force operational headquarters, called Blue Chip, remained at Tan Son Nhut Air Force Base near Saigon.

General Vogt arrived as the new Seventh Air Force commander at Tan Son Nhut on April 7, 1972. Lieutenant Colonel Rose, our air force representative on our Seventh Fleet staff, briefed us on some of the plans that General Vogt had promulgated to his command. We all listened closely to the briefing by our fellow staff officer, U.S. Air Force Lieutenant Colonel Rose. He read several messages from his Seventh Air Force command. The briefing reflected that the air force was getting ready to finally do some work that they, and the rest of us, had long been denied authority to execute upon the brash enemy.

On Monday, April 11, a little more than a week after the large-scale NVA invasion, the Joint Chiefs of Staff in Washington directed that B-52 bombers attack North Vietnam, but not as far north as Hanoi or Haiphong. The B-52 bomber crews responded to the directive by rapidly striking military targets around the city of Vinh, 145 miles northwest of the DMZ, along the coast. This was the first time that B-52 crews had bombed North Vietnam in more than four years.

Slowly, Nixon lifted bombing restrictions. On April 16, 1972, he allowed aerial bombings of petroleum storage facilities outside the North Vietnamese capital, Hanoi, and the nearby port city of Haiphong. On April 17, Nixon allowed B-52 raids over Hanoi and Haiphong military targets.

The North Vietnamese, expecting the escalated air raids, began evacuating people from Hanoi; they moved children and old people to rural areas. The North Vietnamese then began dispersing fuel in drums throughout the rural areas to preclude clustered fuel areas as targets for air attacks and destruction.

Nixon's resumed bombings of North Vietnam did not change the minds of the leaders in North Vietnam. The North Vietnamese Army continued their ground attacks in the South. On April 25, 1972, the NVA attacked the city of Kontom. On May 1, 1972, International Communist May Day, the apple of the eye of the North Vietnamese objectives, the South Vietnamese city of Quang Tri fell to the determined North Vietnamese leaders. The NVA immediately began burning the city.

During the massive NVA attack, many civilians were killed as they fled the burning city. Unfortunately, the international press was not there to see, or report, the atrocities committed by the NVA soldiers. But, at the time, I wondered if the press, U.S. press included, would have reported such carnage caused by the NVA, even if they had witnessed it. During my previous two combat tours in Vietnam, I had seen only negative stories published by U.S. reporters about the Americans fighting in Vietnam. During our longest war, I read hundreds of news reports that favorably depicted the enemies, the communist Viet Cong guerrillas and the North Vietnamese Army. Reports of the attrocities of the enemy trickled out with little fanfare. An example was in 1968, during the famous NVA Tet Offensive, when the NVA captured Hue City from the South Vietnamese Army. During their occupation the NVA killed more than one thousand civilians, perhaps as many as six thousand, and buried them in mass graves. Later, when the U.S. Marines recaptured Hue City, the U.S. press was there. Yet, the U.S. press was slow on the uptake and never made a big deal out of those brutal NVA mass murders. The city residents revealed the massacres as they dug up the mass graves to find their relatives and many religious monks. It was months before the media was getting even close to reporting the scope of this purposeful slaughter. But any collateral damage caused by U.S. forces was immediately and endlessly reported.

Now, during this spring 1972 North Vietnamese invasion into the South, there were no longer any press reporters and photographers in the battlefield areas. Only a handful of reporters still remained in South Vietnam, mostly in Saigon, and a few in Da Nang, well below the NVA invasion area. Here, the press occasionally continued to send out misinformation. The U.S. press continued to make the enemy look like they had the right to invade South Vietnam and that the U.S. military assisting in the defense did nothing but commit atrocities. This input consistently fueled the anti–Vietnam War protestors back in the United States.

Up along the DMZ, where our Seventh Fleet ships primarily floated off the coast and gave fire support to the counterattacking South Vietnamese Army and Marine Corps, there were no reporters. The accounts of this period you are now reading, herein, are personal accounts based upon my own observations, as well as reports of pilots flying over the areas contested that I monitored on the radio and others who were there. If you were there, during 1972 and 1973, and saw it differently, report it to the American public and historians.

President Nixon, still concerned about Red China possibly entering the war, maintained a directive that prohibited hitting any targets within ten miles of the Chinese border. The wording of the directive included "no bombing of foreign ships in Vietnamese waters." Obviously, this precluded bombings of ports where these ships were unloading weapons and food.

Within these constraints, JCS reviewed their plans and came up with a large-scale attack plan for targeting North Vietnam. The plan name was called Operation Linebacker. It had the following objectives:

- Stop the flow of troops and supplies into South Vietnam.
- Destroy military supplies and equipment.
- Prevent supplies from being brought into North Vietnam.

Operation Linebacker permitted attacks on military targets and transportation lines anywhere in North Vietnam except close to

China. The plan also allowed for considering mining the approaches to the North Vietnamese ports. Mining, as an option, had been talked about before. Now, it finally was written, as an option, into the contingency plans at JCS, but the plan included very strict directives to avoid civilian casualties. The plan stated that operational commanders were to be held personally accountable for any violations that resulted in civilian casualties.

Commander George Boaz, our TF 77 aircraft carrier staff officer, using an overhead viewgraph depicting maps and areas of responsibilities, briefed Admiral Mack and the rest of us in the war room. Boaz stated:

> In the Operation Linebacker plan, North Vietnam is divided into six route packages that are shared between the air force, navy, and Marine air units for attacks into North Vietnam.
>
> General Vogt's Seventh Air Force will attack targets in the southern area of North Vietnam in Route Package One (RP-1). The air force will coordinate missions for the Marine Corps attack bombers in RP-1. The air force will also attack the RP-5 and RP-6 areas, including Hanoi City area. Admiral Damon Cooper, Commander, Task Force 77, under Admiral Mack's Seventh Fleet Command, is responsible for Route Packages 2, 3, 4, and 6B; sharing attacks upon Hanoi area with the air force.

Commander Boaz continued to brief all of us in greater detail as to the air plan and who had specific responsibility for what route package.

The United States, despite the brash all-out invasion into South Vietnam, still attempted to demonstrate some restraint. Henry Kissinger continued to hold both secret and public meetings with North Vietnamese representative, Le Duc Tho, in Paris.

North Vietnam, using the antiwar demonstrations in the United States to their advantage, continued to use time by cooperating, and then not cooperating, with Kissinger's ceasefire proposals, but on May 2, 1972, Kissinger confronted Tho with what Kissinger later described as "the heaviest artillery barrage of the war by the NVA and large number of NVA tanks."

Tho tried to frustrate Kissinger by referring to the American citizens' unrest at home and telling Kissinger the North Vietnamese had the advantage and victory was ultimately theirs.

Kissinger reported back to President Nixon that, again, the North Vietnamese were not cooperating. Nixon's response was swift. Nixon ordered the mining of Haiphong and other important harbors of North Vietnam to stop the flow of supplies. Later, Kissinger was to state, "That was one of the finest hours of Nixon's presidency."

On May 4, Adm. Thomas H. Moorer, chairman of the Joint Chiefs of Staff in Washington, D.C., personally briefed President Nixon on the specifics of the mine-laying plan for Haiphong Harbor and other North Vietnamese ports. The very next day, JCS sent a message to Adm. John S. McCain II, commander in chief, Pacific, to prepare for the mining operation and to execute it upon receipt of an executive order.

At this time, Admiral McCain's son, Lt. Cmdr. John S. McCain III, was still a prisoner of war in North Vietnam, having been shot down over North Vietnam four and a half years before on October 26, 1967. The same day that Admiral Moorer briefed President Nixon, Henry Kissinger, National Security Adviser, returned from Paris and was very disturbed. There had been another stop in the negotiations with the North Vietnamese in Paris. The North Vietnamese were confident. With their ground successes in South Vietnam, including the recent capture of Quang Tri City, and with their troops well obscured by the extensive cloud coverage over the battlefields, they now would not make any concessions at the talks in Paris.

The North Vietnamese, fully convinced by the tremendous pressure brought to bear upon President Nixon by the American antiwar demonstrators in front of the White House and across the country, believed that Nixon would not return U.S. ground troops to Vietnam to fight them. The North Vietnamese were sure that Nixon would soon buckle under these home-front pressures. They felt strongly that time was on their side, and the "Get out of Vietnam" placard carriers and wavers of the enemy's Viet Cong flag would eventually ensure a communist victory over South Vietnam.

President Nixon was scheduled to meet with Soviet General Secretary Leonid Brezhnev in mid-May in Moscow. This caused some difficult decision making for President Nixon, but Nixon was still determined to go forward with Operation Linebacker. Nixon hoped the added pressure on North Vietnam would get them back to the peace talks and possibly more seriously consider a negotiated peace. Therefore, on May 8, 1972, President Nixon announced his directive to the National Security Council. The NSC executive order was then transmitted down the chain of command, from JCS to CINCPAC to CINCPACFLT, and to us on the COMSEVENTHFLT staff.

When I looked at the JCS message and the time it took to get to our *Oklahoma City* message center, it appeared that the message must have been released from JCS at 0200, Washington, D.C., on May 8, 1972.

Chapter 7

• • • • • • •

MiGs and the Redeye Missile

On board the *Oklahoma City*, our staff officers took turns manning the war room watch center for six-hour periods, day and night. It was called the command duty watch.

One evening in early May 1972, a few weeks before Admiral Mack was relieved of command by Admiral Holloway on May 23, I had the watch. Everyone left for dinner in the wardroom. As they were leaving, Cmdr. Lyle Littlewood, our air antisubmarine warfare officer, teased me as he usually did by saying, "Oh! Oh! Our Marine has the duty watch again. Hell, we won't get any sleep again tonight! Every time he has the watch, all hell breaks loose, and we're all awakened causing us to immediately write emergency messages."

I laughed it off. But it was true—many times, big events did occur when I had that six-hour watch in the war room. I usually wound up busy as hell, waking up various staff action officers to get them up to the war room to respond to some problem in their area of responsibility.

On this particular evening, I knew our ship was going to participate in a raid upon a SAM site in the Dong Hoi area of North Vietnam. The three other destroyers in our group were assigned to fire upon a long truck convoy and the missile site. Our *Oklahoma City* would fire harassment and interdiction (H&I) fire across the city onto the Dong Hoi Airport. Intelligence reported MiGs parked at that airport.

A little later, as I was sitting in the war room culling the evening's incoming heavy fleet message traffic, Navy Chief Epenesa was helping me separate the messages to be given to various action officers. By now, our ship was firing into North Vietnam and our war room was shaking as usual from the outgoing shots. We were the lead ship. Soon, our ship's firing ceased. We were in a sharp, leaning port turn, heading away from the hostile coast. I could hear the destroyers behind us still firing.

My red alert phone on the watch desk rang. I picked it up. "War room, this is Commander Fairchild down in the CIC. I want to alert the command watch."

"Roger, Joe. This is Stoffey. What's happening?"

"Bob, our radar down here has just picked up a MiG taking off from the Dong Hoi airport. Presently, the MiG is very low. He's below two thousand feet and heading southwest, away from us. No major factor at present. I thought I'd give the staff a courtesy heads-up situation report."

"I appreciate it. If there's a change to concern us on the staff, give me the latest sitrep."

It was exactly 1700 hours and dark. I logged Cmdr. Joe Fairchild's sitrep into our command staff log book. It was not only dark out, but the weather was reported to be two thousand feet overcast with light rain showers.

My alert phone rang again. "Bob, Fairchild here. Now, there is a second MiG airborne. He's heading southwest and low like the first jet."

"Thanks for the report," I responded. "Hell, if my MiGs were getting shot at while they were parked at the airport, I'd get them into the air and the hell out of there." I logged Commander Fairchild's report. I culled a few more messages, sipped some coffee, and the red phone rang again. It was Fairchild.

"That second MiG has turned toward the southeast, toward the beach. He now has turned directly toward us! The first MiG has disappeared from the radar screen, heading west. However, the second MiG heading our way is still remaining very low. This may become a problem for us.

"We do have our two Talos missiles out of the missile house and armed, ready to fire. The problem is that this incoming MiG is currently too low for us to get a missile-guidance lock on him. He's still bearing down on us very fast."

"Thanks, Joe. I better notify Captain Godfrey. He can let Admiral Mack know about the incoming MiG. Let me know when the MiG gets feet wet!"

"Roger, Bob. I'll let you know when the MiG crosses the beach for the Gulf of Tonkin."

I quickly called Captain Godfrey. "Sir, this is the command duty watch officer in the war room. CIC has just reported two MiGs airborne from the Dong Hoi airport. One of the MiGs is heading straight for us and is very low. I recommend notifying the admiral. All our ships have their missiles ready, but this MiG coming at us is too low. He's probably this low because of the low overcast ceiling. So, he's boring in on us flying on the deck. Presently, he's below our missile envelope!"

The chief of staff answered, "Thanks, Bob. The admiral and I will be up in the war room in a minute."

The red phone rang again. I snatched it up. "The MiG is now feet wet, still very low and heading straight for our group of ships! Still no missile lock-on!"

"Thanks, Joe. The admiral and chief of staff are on their way up to the war room."

The war room hatch opened behind me and Admiral Mack and Captain Godfrey rushed in. The admiral calmly asked me, "What's the situation?"

I gave a fast verbal sitrep.

The admiral quickly said, "I've got to get out on my bridge to see this. This MiG pilot has guts coming out here that low, in this pitch-black, overcast night."

The admiral knew exactly what was going on. He knew the difficulty that this incoming MiG pilot was experiencing. To find a ship at sea at night, while flying very low and fast, under overcast skies, is not easy, even for a seasoned pilot.

Admiral Mack opened the hatch to the bridge, where only the red combat lights were on. He stepped through the hatchway and onto the bridge. Just as Captain Godfrey followed him through the hatch, we all heard the roar of a jet going by our bow, seeming to turn toward our port side. Almost immediately, there was a loud explosion aft of our starboard.

"Find out what the hell that was," shouted the admiral from out on the bridge.

I picked up the phone and called CIC. I couldn't get Fairchild. Obviously, he was too busy down there. I waited. He then got on the phone and shouted, "Bob, the destroyer *Higbee* has been hit by a bomb. I'll get more information for you soon."

I quickly relayed that information to the admiral. At that moment, another explosion went off. It was not as loud as the previous explosion. It sounded slightly muffled and this time came from the aft port side.

Captain Godfrey stated, "I sure hope that wasn't another hit on a ship."

The phone rang again.

"Bob, the *Sterett* shot down the MiG with a Terrier missile. The *Higbee* is burning badly in the stern area. Captain Kanakanui has *Oklahoma City* slowing down so we can pull beside to render assistance."

I briefed the admiral and chief of staff, and they both quickly ran back out to the admiral's bridge to watch as our ship approached the burning *Higbee*.

By now, many of the other staff officers had piled back into the war room to find out what the explosions were all about. My friend Lyle Littlewood was among them. He quickly jibed me, "See! Every time that Marine has the command watch, something exciting happens around here . . . just like I said!"

As our ship slowed, I momentarily left my watch desk and dashed to the bridge to see the *Higbee* (DDR-806). The fantail of the USS *Higbee* was ablaze. The large flames lit up the entire area. The damaged ship looked eerie in the dark with the low overcast reflecting the light from the fire. I quickly returned to my watch desk just as the phone rang again.

Commander Joe Fairchild reported to me, "*Higbee* took a 500-pound bomb on the fantail. The bomb blast went off below the deck causing a fire in the living quarters. Thank God everybody was at general quarters! There were only four reported injured and nobody killed. The blast severely damaged the aft twin 5-inch gun turret. I'll keep you abreast of things."

I briefed the admiral, who was already reading a rough-drafted message, that the quick-reacting Cmdr. Stu Landersman had prepared to send a fash casrep message to report the ship damage and casualties. Commander Landersman would quickly send the casrep to CINCPACFLT in Hawaii and then follow up with information as he would receive it.

The phone rang . . . it was Fairchild again. "Bob, the crew of the *Higbee* is having a hell of a time fighting the fire. Because the fire is on the fantail [where much of the fire-fighting equipment was located], the crew can't get to the hoses and axes. It's too narrow along the side walkways to properly fight the fire with other minimal equipment. It's quite a problem. Captain Kanakanui is pulling us away from the *Higbee*. There's nothing we can do to fight the fire, and we don't want to be too close in case their ammunition stores explode.

"They only have a corpsman aboard, and he's doing the best he can, but they really need a doctor. Can you have the fleet surgeon available to fly over to the *Higbee*?"

Our *Oklahoma City* doctor, Lieutenant Commander Masstricht, had been high-lined to the underway replenishment ship *Haleakala* (AE-25) that morning to perform an emergency appendectomy. I responded, "I sure can. I'll get Doc Burkhart to the helo right away."

I quickly briefed the admiral. I then called Lt. Ed Sarr, officer in charge of the admiral's helicopter, and told him to crank up Black Beard One and stand by for Capt. Vernon A. "Doc" Burkhart. Our helicopter crew was from Detachment 32 of Helicopter Anti-Submarine Squadron 31, home-ported in Imperial Beach, California. They were assigned to our ship for a six-month tour of duty.

Next I called Captain Burkhart. "Doc, this is the command duty officer, Stoffey, in the war room. The *Higbee* was bombed close to us and has four wounded sailors. The *Higbee* doesn't have a doctor aboard, and our doctor's on the *Haleakala*. We need you to go to the fantail immediately and get into Black Beard One. Two of our ship's corpsmen with emergency medical pack-ups will meet you there and you'll be flown to the *Higbee*."

"Okay, Bob. I'm on my way," responded Burkhart.

"Thanks, Doc. Be careful over there. The *Higbee* is still burning from the bomb blast," I told him.

What I didn't tell Doc Burkhart was that the damage to the *Higbee* was on the fantail—where the helicopter platform was. Our chopper would not be able to land. They'd probably have to drop Captain Burkhart and the corpsmen onto the bow by winch and horse collar from the helicopter's rescue hoist. I didn't want to worry the doc, so I didn't elaborate on the situation. He was a personal friend, who had had quite a few rounds of drinks with me when our ship visited liberty ports.

It bothered me to be sending an older navy captain like this, one who had risen to become the seventh fleet surgeon but hadn't performed basic medicine for some time due to his high-level administrative duties. I sat there with the horrible image of Doc Burkhart hanging onto the sling suspended from the helicopter and onto a bobbing bow of a burning ship while the ship was moving and rolling in the fire-created glowing night.

At 0615 the next morning, after finishing my war room watch assignment, I was eating breakfast in the officers' wardroom. The hatch to the wardroom opened and a very tired-looking Captain Burkhart stepped through the hatchway. Looking angry, Doc Burkhart headed directly for me. He glared at me and said, "You bastard! You didn't tell me last night that I'd be hoisted down in the helicopter's rescue sling onto the moving, rolling, pitching bow of the *Higbee* in the middle of the night."

I forked a piece of scrambled egg, chewed it a little and responded, "If I had told you, would you have gone?"

The beat-looking doctor grimaced and parted, shaking his head. I had a flash thought of what the doc probably had experienced. He had been hanging in the swinging sling with the noise of the helicopter directly overhead. The bow of the *Higbee* had been bobbing up at him, and then instantly dropping far below his dangling feet. The eerie night was aglow from the burning ship probably casting shadows upon the badly damaged ship, adding to the disorientation of a night hoist drop.

Just prior to my departing the war room command watch position, I passed the follow-up information of the MiG-17 attack upon the *Higbee* to the chief of staff. It consisted of the following:

Shortly after the MiG–17 attack upon the *Higbee*, a navy F-4 fighter aircraft arrived overhead of our small task group of ships. Disc, a navy EC-121 radar-tracking aircraft, was directing eight additional A-7 Corsair II aircraft toward our task group. The A-7s would be under the direct radar control of the USS *Sterett* [DLG-31] for defensive intercept protection as our group of ships retired from the coastal area. The *Sterett* reported still having bogey contact in the area, and the USS *Lloyd Thomas* [DDE-764] got a radar-lock on one MiG, now closing on us at fifty-six miles. The *Thomas* then reported firing as the MiG approached closer. The MiG turned and departed the area for the beach without further incidents.

The burning *Higbee* is heading directly in the direction of Subic Bay in the Philippines for damage repairs.

Many of us gathered on the admiral's bridge to watch flames finally being beaten down by the exhausted crew of the *Higbee*.

At the next morning briefing, Admiral Mack said, "Well, we've just proven one of my major concerns for years. We are all aware that we no longer have antiaircraft guns on our ships, like we did during World War II. The missiles are great, but not for close-in, low altitude air attacks. If ever I get into a position to change that, I certainly will." (Much later, Admiral Mack's relief, Vice Adm. James L. Holloway III, after his tour of duty as Seventh Fleet commander, went to Washington and eventually became Chief of Naval Operations [CNO] and ensured that vulcan machine guns for air defense were installed on all combat ships.)

Admiral Mack continued talking to us in the war room about the MiG problem.

He said, "Do any of you staff members have any quick fixes for close-in protection of our ships in the event more MiGs start coming out to challenge our ships in a possibly new phase of their defense?" Nobody was offering any temporary or long-term solution. Then I said, "Admiral, I have an idea that would certainly help. It wouldn't be the perfect solution, but it would immediately assist in filling the gap in the ships' defenses for now.

"I could get handheld Redeye heat-seeking, shoulder-fired, surface-to-air missile systems from our Marines located on Okinawa. We could phase them into our combat ships for close-in protection. Additionally, the ships that have Marines on board, like ours, should have M-60 machine guns manned up on the decks, when any ship is making a raid into North Vietnam."

Admiral Mack thought about it for a few minutes, then he said, "It sounds good. Work out the details and brief me. If I like the plan, you can implement it."

I worked out a training plan and logistics phase-in plan for implementing the Redeye missiles into the Seventh Fleet. I briefed Admiral Mack. He approved and authorized my activities. I immediately began writing a series of message instructions to the Marine commander, Task Force 79 (CTF 79), on Okinawa. I sent copies to the navy commander, Task Group 70.8 (CTG 70.8), afloat in the Gulf of Tonkin. Commander Stu Landersman coordinated the surface gunships of cruisers and destroyers for setting up the training and installation of the Redeye missiles aboard the ships.

It so happened that our *Oklahoma City* had been scheduled to return to Subic Bay in the Philippines for the rebarreling of a 5-inch gun that had burned out during heavy firing in North Vietnam. The sailing time from the Gulf of Tonkin gave me an opportunity to coordinate setting up a school at Subic Bay for our Marine Redeye instructors. At Subic, they would teach sailors how to shoot the handheld missile launcher on each gunship as the ships cycled in and out of Subic Bay.

The plan called for each ship that cycled through Subic Bay from off the gunline, or en route to the gunline, to have stanchions built for four Redeye gunners per ship. Two stanchions were installed forward on the ships and two stanchions aft on the ship. These stanchions, or stands, gave physical support for the gunner, who also was strapped into the stanchion. Subic Bay's ships repair facility's personnel also installed two steel vertical rods on either side of the gunners' firing position to limit the gunners from moving their Redeye launcher too widely to the sides of their standing positions. This would minimize the possibility of a fired Redeye heat-seeking missile erroneously tracking onto the ship's large heat-emitting exhaust stacks of the engine rooms. In other words, we didn't want our own defending Redeye shooters hitting our own ships' exhaust stacks.

General Jones, Fleet Marine Forces Pacific (CG FMFPAC) in Hawaii, authorized the Marines to deploy missile teams from California on May 7, 1972, for employing shoulder-fired missiles on board Seventh Fleet ships. Using the California-based teams and missiles precluded a draw-down of the missiles then currently stored in Okinawa so they could be readily available for the 9th Marine Amphibious Brigade (MAB) or other elements of the 3d Marine Division.

On May 8, 1972, 1st Lt. James B. Dowling, in charge of the 3d Redeye Platoon, 3d Marine Aircraft Wing, departed Marine Corps Air Station, El Toro, California. The platoon of forty-two men took with them forty-four missile systems, six night-viewing devices, and associated support equipment. They were assigned under the operational control of Brig. Gen. Edward J. Miller, CG 9th Marine Amphibious Brigade afloat in the Gulf of Tonkin, and they would set up their training school at Subic Bay.

When our *Oklahoma City* tied up pierside at Subic Bay, I was able to personally coordinate things instead of doing so by message traffic. I went ashore to meet the Marine Redeye platoon and personally describe our situation and need for their assets.

A few days later, I had arranged for two members of the Redeye platoon to come aboard *Oklahoma City* and personally brief Admiral Mack and our staff on the functionality of the Redeye system. When that young Marine captain and sergeant strode into our war room, dressed in full field gear, carrying a Redeye launcher and missile, they were impressive. I was an extremely proud Marine seeing them and their military bearing. They impressed the admiral and the whole staff.

The admiral obviously enjoyed his firsthand exposure to this lethal weapon and better understood the specifics of the weapon system that twenty-two of his destroyers and cruisers, including our *Oklahoma City*, would soon have on board. This would result in the ships having improved protection against possible attacking North Vietnamese aircraft when making strikes against North Vietnam's coastal areas. The Seventh Fleet would not have to divert carrier aircraft to cover ships unless something extreme happened.

As soon as the Redeye platoon was training navy personnel and the stanchions were being installed on ships as they cycled in and out of Subic Bay, our Seventh Fleet staff logistics officer, Cmdr. C. W. "Woody" Long, ordered the navy logistics system to commence supplying navy Redeye missiles. These navy missiles would then replace the Marine Corps missiles, so we could return the borrowed missiles to the Marines.

Chapter 8
• • • • • • •

Mining Haiphong Harbor

In 1966, Premier Ky of South Vietnam had requested that President Lyndon B. Johnson authorize the U.S. Navy to mine the harbor at Haiphong, North Vietnam. General Maxwell Taylor had publicly backed the idea, but President Johnson had denied Ky's request. At this point, though, after so many years, we on the Seventh Fleet staff had been receiving warning messages from JCS for several months to prepare plans for mining the harbor in North Vietnam's busiest port.

Lieutenant Commander Larry Emarine, the Seventh Fleet mine warfare officer on staff, had the responsibility to coordinate the plan for execution of the mining of the North Vietnamese harbors and selected inland waterways. It was also his responsibility to coordinate the mine sweeping operations that may ultimately have to be accomplished, if and when directed by higher authority at a later date.

Larry Emarine shared a small office in back operations with Cmdr. Jack Beaver, our submarine warfare officer; Cmdr. Lyle Littlewood, the air antisubmarine warfare officer; my boss, Cmdr. Jim Froid; and Larry Emarine sat right next to me. It was a cramped and busy office. There was another operations office forward and on the same deck, next to the war room. That office was called front operations. It had in it: Cmdr. George Boaz, air warfare officer; Cmdr. Ole Carlson, conventional air warfare officer; Cmdr. Frank Presenti, nuclear warfare officer; Comdr. R. A. Hall, electronic warfare officer; Cmdr. Stu Landersman, surface warfare officer; Cmdr. Dave

Grosshuesch, readiness officer; and Cmdr. Ron Stoddart, carrier air warfare officer. The Plans Division was located one deck above us, and the Communications Division was two decks below.

As Larry Emarine began to plot the areas that were to be mined, Cmdr. Jim Froid and I had to closely watch Larry's activities. Eventually, we would have to utilize assets of our amphibious ships of TF 76 and Marine helicopters from the Marine amphibious ready groups, Alpha and Bravo, within TF 79. These Marine helicopters would be combined with navy mine sweeping helicopters to execute neutralizing the mines in the sea-lanes.

On May 8, 1972, President Nixon went on nationwide radio and television to announce to the American people that he was authorizing the mining of North Vietnam's major ports. The president stated, "The United States respects the Soviet Union as a great power and recognizes the Soviet's right to defend its interests when they are threatened. But no Soviet soldiers are threatened in Vietnam, while the lives of sixty thousand Americans who are still in there are endangered."

The president outlined four actions to curb aggression across the demilitarized zone separating the two Vietnams. They included:

- Mining of all entrances to North Vietnamese ports to prevent access and to prevent North Vietnamese naval operations from there;
- U.S. forces to interdict the delivery of supplies within the internal and claimed territorial waters of North Vietnam;
- Cutting off rail and other communications to the maximum possible extent; and
- Continuing air and naval strikes against military targets in North Vietnam.

The president then added, "The countries with ships presently in North Vietnamese ports were notified that they would have three daylight periods to leave the harbors in safety. After that, the mines would become active and any ships attempting to leave or enter these ports would do so at their own risk. There is only one way to stop the killing in Vietnam, and that is to keep the weapons of war out of the hands of the international outlaws of North Vietnam."

This announcement by President Nixon resulted in the directive to execute both an American aerial offensive and the mining against the North Vietnamese ports. The code name given for the operational execution of that directive was Linebacker.

On that same day, May 8, 1972, Commander Boaz briefed us in the war room, saying, "Navy squadron VF-96 from the carrier *Constellation*, responding to Linebacker directives, flew an air strike against the Hai Duong rail yards, near Haiphong." Boaz then added, "Navy pilot, Lt. Randy Cunningham and his radar intercept officer, Lt. j.g. Willie Driscoll, shot down a MiG-17 for the second MiG kill to their credit." This announcement by Boaz had the staff in the war room sounding out a round of applause with great elation.

Also on May 8, 1972, we received an execute message from CINCPACFLT that read:

FMCINCPACFLT
TOCOMSEVENTHFLT

INFO JCS
CINCPAC
COMUSMACV
CTF 77
CDR 7TH AF

EXECUTE MINING HAIPHONG HARBOR
CHANNEL

THIS IS AN EXECUTE MESSAGE. REPEAT.
EXECUTE MINING
MESSAGE. EXECUTE MINING PLAN FOR THE
HAIPHONG HARBOR
CHANNEL IMMEDIATELY. PREPARE PLANS FOR
SUBSEQUENT MININGS OF OTHER MAJOR PORT
OFFLOADING SITES IN NORTH
VIETNAM. REPORT FIRST MINING OPS TO
ALCON.

Larry Emarine, our mine warfare officer, quickly got together with George Boaz, carrier air officer, and jointly laid out their detailed plans to our staff plans officer, Capt. Leo Marshall. They then jointly briefed Admiral Mack.

Commander Boaz drafted a message for release to the Carrier Air Group, under the command of Task Force 77, to execute the mining of the Haiphong Channel.

At 0800 that same day of May 8, despite intense antiaircraft fire and volleys of SAMs, Navy Cmdr. Roger Sheets led six navy A-7 Corsairs and three Marine A-6A Intruders from the USS *Coral Sea*. They dropped the first mines into the Haiphong Channel, which runs to the port of Haiphong. These attack aircraft laid strings of thirty-six 1,000-pound, Mark 52 mines. This started what would be days, and then months, of laying thousands of these Mark 52 mines, plus thousands of 500-pound Mark 36 Destructors, into the seaway and secondary ports of North Vietnam. Mines eventually were dropped into parts of the Gulf of Tonkin, off the cities of Cam Phan, Thanh, Vinh, and Hon Gai.

The mines were modern, unlike the old floating mines of World War I, World War II, and the Korean War. They were special aerial-type bombs dropped by very-low-flying attack aircraft. Each drop was specifically plotted exactly where they were dropped in the channel and off the coast. They were geographically noted on the Task Force 77 war room charts, and a copy was sent to Lt. Cmdr. Larry Emarine so he could work the charts in our back operations office on the *Oklahoma City*. Larry then briefed Admiral Mack on the exact layout of the mining patterns sown in North Vietnam. Larry had pertinent, detailed data for his planning, which enabled him to coordinate sweeping of the mines at a later date when he would be directed to do so.

The mines all had time fuses on them. They were all set to be active, or alive, no sooner than three days after their drops. This delay would comply with President Nixon's statement that the neutral ships, such as the Canadian trading ships and North Vietnamese ally ships of Russia, Cuba, and China, had time to get out of the mined channel.

We received messages from the carriers *Constellation* and *Enterprise* (CVA-65) that aircraft dropping the mines, or slick bombs, came under intense gunfire. Luckily, though, none of the attack bombers were shot down while seeding the mines. We assumed that the dropping of hundreds of bombs into the waterways must have initially confused the North Vietnamese gunners, who probably wondered why the hell the aircraft were bombing the waters rather than them or other targets.

The mines dropped were slick-bomb-styled containers, and therefore when impacting the water they penetrated to the very bottom of the channel, some burying themselves into the silt. Some mines would become automatically activated within three days. Other mines would activate in five days from drop time. Still others would simply lie on the bottom of the channel and not become active mines until thirty days past drop day.

Once activated, the mines became lethal, lying in wait for any ship passing above on the surface of the water. The mines could be detonated by any ship's hull that passed over them and were powerful enough explosive devices that they could sink most ships, if exploded directly under them. How anyone could sweep such new and revolutionary mines was indeed puzzling to the North Vietnamese and possibly the Soviet Union. The United States had never seeded these types of mines before. Everyone still used the old World War II–type floating mines that the United States had last used during the Korean War.

During the same day of the initial mine seeding operation, Cmdr. Lyle Littlewood, from our back operations office, had briefed to Admiral Mack and our staff on his P-3 Orion patrol aircraft activities. Littlewood stated, "The P-3 aircrews, operating from the Philippines and Japan, have been tracking three Soviet freighters that are heading for North Vietnam."

Commander Jack Beaver then briefed Admiral Mack and said, "Our submarines have also been tracking the same three Soviet freighters since their departures from Vladivostok." Commander Frank A. Hantz, intelligence officer in N-2, also briefed the admiral and staff, saying, "The freighters are carrying tanks, trucks, SAMs, and food."

It was interesting to watch Littlewood and Beaver brief us from their patrol aircraft and submarine monitoring information regarding these three Soviet ships as they continued toward North Vietnam. Would these Soviet ships try to enter the mined Haiphong Channel to unload their war-making supplies destined for Haiphong Harbor? Within a few days, Littlewood and Beaver briefed us that their sources reported the Soviet ships had turned around and were headed back toward the Soviet Union.

President Nixon ordered U.S. strength in Vietnam to continue personnel reductions from the remaining sixty thousand down to a targeted forty-nine thousand by June 30, 1972. President Nixon's mining executive order sent from Washington, D.C., had allowed time for all foreign ships to leave North Vietnamese ports before the first set of mines that had been dropped would become active and deadly. Ships and crews desiring to leave had to be out of the mined areas by 1800, Hanoi-time, on May 11, otherwise they risked being sunk by the activated mines.

We, on the staff, carefully watched the reporting of several ships leaving the Haiphong Harbor, the port serving Hanoi and Haiphong. As the ships proceeded down the Haiphong Channel, we hoped we had been accurate on the time-delays of the mines already seeded in the channel. We hoped that no mines would explode and sink, or damage, a departing ship. Thirty-two large merchant ships, including sixteen Soviet, five communist Chinese, three Polish ships, two Cuban, one East German, five Somalian, and four Hong Kong–registry British ships decided to remain in port. After the deadline, they were trapped in the Haiphong Harbor.

The JCS execute order message to mine had also included the statement: "The time may come when we must sweep the mines that have been placed in the waters adjacent to North Vietnam. Consequently, we must take and maintain an accurate inventory of all mine sweeping assets and be prepared to assemble these assets."

This awesome responsibility fell directly upon Lt. Cmdr. Larry Emarine. Larry, as the mine warfare officer on our staff, shifted into longer days and nights of detailed work, pulling in all the mine-warfare assets to start the planning for the inevitable sweep operations.

Our immediate boss, Admiral Mack, had Capt. Burr M. Wilcox, Commander Mine Flotilla 1, report to our staff on board the *Oklahoma City* to discuss mining and sweep plans on May 9.

In late May 1972, Rear Adm. J. A. Dare, former Commander of the Mine Warfare Force, who had retired a month before the mining of North Vietnam, was recalled for mining consultation.

Numerous meetings took place back in the United States between Vice Adm. Robert L. Long, Commander Naval Ships Systems

Command; civilian, William White of the Naval Ship Engineering Center; civilian, William Emshwiller, Naval Air Systems Command; and Capt. J. J. Strom, manager, Airborne Mine Countermeasures with the Commander Mine Warfare Force based in Charleston, South Carolina.

The spring 1972 mine countermeasures that planned to use, for the first time, helicopters for airborne mine countermeasures was under way, with much message traffic transmitted to and from our staff, primarily involving Lt. Cmdr. Larry Emarine.

The mine sweep planning stage had begun.

Chapter 9
• • • • • • •

Operation Linebacker

From watching communications traffic in our war room and listening to staff briefings to Admiral Mack, including briefings from our air force representative on our staff, Lt. Col. R. F. Rose, I saw the events unfolding.

At 2145 on May 8, 1972, Washington, D.C., time, or about forty-five minutes after President Nixon's TV announcement revealing Operation Linebacker, the Joint Chiefs of Staff issued the executive order to execute the follow-on phase of Linebacker, now that the mines had been seeded.

Lieutenant Colonel Rose reported to Admiral Mack, "The Seventh Air Force has prepared their target lists and air attack schedules."

Commander George Boaz reported to Admiral Mack, "The Seventh Fleet carrier air wings have prepared their target lists and schedules to attack and support aircraft squadrons, and the surface ships are also ready to go."

All units were readied for the most massive air strikes thus far allowed against North Vietnam. The selected date for the full-scale, intensive air attacks was May 10, 1972.

At two minutes past midnight, early morning on May 10, Gulf of Tonkin time, the *Oklahoma City*, with Admiral Mack and our staff aboard, sailed northward from off the DMZ. We formed a special surface attack task group that Stu Landersman pulled together via his message writing. It consisted of two other cruisers, the large *Newport News* with her 8-inch guns and the *Providence* (CLG-6). The *New Jersey*'s 16-inch guns sure would have been nice to have for this attack run, but the battlship had already been placed back into the mothball fleet. Along with our cruisers, we had the destroyers *Buchanan*, *Myles C. Fox* (DDR-829), and *Hanson* (DD-832) join us. We quickly departed the DMZ coastal area and silently glided on the calm, moonless Gulf of Tonkin toward North Vietnam. Within a few hours, the *Newport News* began firing its 5- and 8-inch guns at targeted military installations near the Haiphong Harbor coastal area. As NVA coastal defense (CD) sites fired back, the rest of our task group began attacking, primarily at North Vietnamese CD sites. It was 0230 when the Seventh Fleet surface gunships initiated Nixon's Operation Linebacker strikes against North Vietnam.

As our ships retired from the coastal attacks against North Vietnam, air war preparations were vigorously under way. The tempo of activities dramatically increased throughout Southeast Asia.

Lieutenant Colonel Rose briefed us in the war room on the air force activities under way. He said, "At 0400, Hanoi time, the Air Force at Kadena Air Force Base on Okinawa launched a Boeing RC-135 reconnaissance aircraft from the 82nd Strategic Reconnaissance Squadron." At about 0700 hours, that recee aircraft would be over North Vietnam. That recee aircraft was followed by a U-2 Reconnaissance aircraft that lifted off the U-Tapo Air Force Base in Thailand. The U-2 would be the intelligence link in relaying communications from an altitude of about sixty-eight thousand feet over North Vietnam.

Soon after the departure of the high-flying U-2 aircraft, an air force weather reconnaissance RF-4C aircraft took off from Udorn Air Force Base in Thailand. This RF-4C crew would report the weather conditions over the target areas.

When Lieutenant Colonel Rose was finished, Commander Boaz briefed us on the following naval aviation scenario: "At Yankee Station, in the Gulf of Tonkin, at 0730, an E-2B Hawkeye propeller-driven, radar-warning aircraft will be catapulted from the attack carrier, *Constellation*. The carrier and its escort task group of ships will then continue north. The E-2B, being slow, will be given an early, headstart launch to the target areas. The jets will soon launch to follow the slower prop-driven radar-warning aircraft to the targets."

Our staff members were anxious, apprehensive, and alert as we gathered in the war room to watch events unfold. Most of us had not slept during our ship's night raid. We simply stayed up, if not working in the war room, when something hot was going on. Normally, if nothing eventful was happening, we slept in our staterooms. We would be awakened individually when a message came in that directly concerned that particular staff officer. I would frequently be awakened by a communications officer's thrusting an action message into my face to read. But this particular night, most of us were gathered in the war room because our ship was involved in a night raid. And we all knew this day was going to be very exciting, particularly in the air war in the north. This day was the kick-off of Linebacker. We were curious to see how much damage our illustrious leaders back in Washington, D.C., were going to allow our military to inflict upon a terribly aggressive enemy after all these worthless years of meaningless sacrifices.

Soon the air war would commence, and soon more formal briefings to the admiral would start. The daily briefing to Admiral Mack normally took place at 0900; we knew this particular briefing would be interesting. We all sat around the war room reading each message brought in from the message center. We knew things were going to begin happening, very soon, in a big way, this morning of May 10, 1972. We also knew that Nixon's halt to the bombings of North Vietnam, as a goodwill gesture, had given the enemy time to greatly improve their air defenses during that respite. This worried everyone.

There certainly was good reason to worry. With the respite during Nixon's bombing halt in North Vietnam initiated in 1968 until now in May 1972, the build-up of antiaircraft weapons in North Vietnam was sure to be awesome.

May 1972 intelligence reports indicated that North Vietnam now had 3,300 antiaircraft guns, most of them located north of the 20th parallel, or DMZ. The antiaircraft weapons consisted of 23mm optical-controlled guns, 37mm optical-controlled guns, 57mm optical-controlled guns, 85mm radar-controlled guns, and 100mm radar-controlled guns. The effective firepower altitude ranges of these weapons varied from six thousand feet up to thirty-nine thousand feet. The radar-controlled guns operated with the Soviet-built SON-9, NATO code name Firecan systems.

The antiaircraft guns were backed up with Soviet-built Dvina, NATO code name Guideline, SA-2 surface-to-air missiles. There were reported to be ten SAM concentrations of four to six launchers with fire-controlled radar, NATO code name Fan Song, systems around Haiphong and thirteen such launch concentrations around Hanoi.

(Later, reports indicated that during the raids of May 10, 1972, ninety-three SAMs were fired at U.S. Navy, Marine, and Air Force attacking aircraft.)

At 0835, a navy EP-3 Orion Signet plane from VQ-1 at Da Nang was joined up in the northern skies by an E-2B Hawkeye from the USS *Constellation* and another E-2B from the carrier *Kitty Hawk*.

The USS *Chicago* (CG-11), call sign Red Crown, a heavy guided-missile cruiser with large Talos surface-to-surface and surface-to-air missiles, was the designated control ship in the northern Gulf of Tonkin. Down inside the radar intercept control room of the *Chicago* was Chief Radarman Larry Nowell. Chief Nowell was in charge of a group of radar technicians responsible for tracking both friendly and enemy aircraft; North Vietnamese MiG intercept aircraft were tracked by the *Chicago*. Hanoi City was designated as the center of the radar-tracking grid and was designated as the bull's-eye on the grid system.

At this point, EKA-2B navy tankers went airborne to be available to refuel our attack aircraft off the north coast. This would enable the attacking aircraft from the carriers to fly their missions and then refuel in the air en route back to their carriers in the Gulf of Tonkin.

While we were attending our 0900 briefing, air force prestrike aircraft from Korat, Thailand, arrived over North Vietnam. They consisted of EB-66 radar-jamming, defense-suppression F-105 Wild Weasel aircraft along with F-4 Phantom chaff-layers from Udorn, Thailand.

The air force chaff-dropping flights of F-4s consisted of Dingus flight from the 433rd Tactical Fighter Squadron. This flight was led by Maj. Bob Blake and his wingman, Capt. Sam O'Donnell. Their sections consisted of Lieutenants Jim Dunn and Richard Howser with the third section of two F-4s flown by Capt. Larry Honeycutt and Lt. Charlie Crisp. The fourth section of the two F-4s were flown by Capt. Mike White and Lt. Barry Morgan.

Another four F-4 chaff-dropping division was called Hi Test flight from the 435th Tactical Fighter Squadron. Hi Test was led by

Maj. Phil Mentesana and his wingman, Capt. Gregory Krosnoff. Number two section of two F-4s had Capt. Bill Byrns and Lt. Charlie Hostenke. They were followed by the third section of two birds, flown by Lt. Ron Moore and Capt. Ryan Cobb. Tail-end Charlie, or the last section of two chaff-droppers, consisted of Capt. Mike Suhy and Lt. Lanny Toups.

The stage was set for the strikes. Lieutenant Colonel Rose continued filling us in on the air force activities as he received messages from the Seventh Air Force. His information kept the navy up on the air force activities and even included the names of the players in this big game of life and death. Having the names of some of the pilots would be helpful in the event they were shot down and our navy search-and-rescue choppers had to go into North Vietnam to rescue them.

The air strikes started to shower years of pent-up anger upon the North. After all, North Vietnam had wrought holy hell upon South Vietnam for all these years. Minutes after 1000, the attacks commenced. Initially, sixteen air force F-4Ds, carrying 2,000-pound bombs, including laser-guided bombs (or smart bombs), struck the famous Paul Doumer Bridge—the most important bridge in North Vietnam. It is both a rail and highway bridge over the Red River and is located just east of Hanoi City. It is the vital main supply route between the port of Haiphong and the capital, Hanoi. The bridge had been named after a governor from the French rule of Indochina; it had been attacked in 1967 and again in 1968. During those attacks, it had sustained some damage. Each time it had been struck, it was rapidly repaired. As of May 10, 1972, though, it had not been attacked for four years.

Records reflect the attack group upon the Paul Doumer Bridge, by the air force F-4s, was led by Col. Carl Miller from the Goatee flight out of the 435th Tactical Fighter Squadron. His flight of four F-4Ds carried electro-optical-guided 2,000-pound bombs. Four more F-4Ds, carrying laser-guided 2000-pound bombs, were led by Col. Dick Horne. His flight was called Napkin flight. Captain Lynn High, leader of Biloxi flight from the 25th Tactical Fighter Squadron, carried laser-guided bombs. The final division of four F-4Ds was called Jingle flight, with Lt. Col. Dick Hilton as leader. They were from the 433rd Tactical Fighter Squadron, and they carried laser-guided 2,000-pound bombs.

As the chaff-laying flights of Dingus and Hi Test came into the Hanoi SAM area at twenty-three thousand feet about sixteen miles south of Hanoi; they flew in a horizontal separation of two thousand feet abreast of each other. Immediately, they began dropping their chaff to jam the SAM and radar-controlled antiaircraft guns. Major Bob Blake, flight leader, commanded, "Drop chaff . . . pickle chaff now!"

The descending chaff bombs opened. This released loads of metal chaff strips that tumbled earthward, causing much confusion on the North Vietnamese radar screens. SA-2 SAMs were immediately launched at the chaff-dispensing F-4s as they flew level and in abreast formations, but all F-4s successfully evaded the missiles, as the falling chaff confused the radar and some aircrew executed evasive flight tactics.

The Paul Doumer Bridge attack force, which consisted of sixteen F-4 bombers, four F-4 fighter escorts, and four F-105 Wild Weasel aircraft, entered the SAM-protected area. The chaff fell and then the Dingey and Hi Test flights departed the target areas. Behind the Paul Doumer Bridge attack force was the Yen Vien attack force. This force consisted of sixteen F-4 bombers, eight F-4 fighter escorts, and four F-105 Wild Weasels. Each Wild Weasel carried three antiradar missiles, a mix of two Shrikes and one long-range Standard ARM missile, to home-in on enemy radar signals. The Wild Weasels descended well below the strike forces, and as the enemy radars scanned the skies, the Wild Weasels homed-in on the radar and fired at the Fan Song missile control radar sites with Standard missiles. While the F-105s attacked the radar sites, the EB-66 aircraft continued jamming radar systems of the SAMs and antiaircraft guns.

Twenty miles southwest of Hanoi, Col. Carl Miller led his division of Goatee flight of four in level abreast flight with two thousand feet of separation between aircraft. This is the radar-jamming formation. Their jamming pods were all turned on, as the rest of the twelve F-4s followed, all at fourteen thousand feet. Closing fast on Hanoi at 550 knots indicated airspeed, Colonel Miller called his section of four, but in actuality he was heard by his full attack force as he spoke into his microphone inside his oxygen mask: "I can't believe this CAVU (clear and visibility unlimited) weather. We can see for miles." Just then, the first wave of SAMs rose up to attempt to destroy them.

Colonel Miller stated, "Keep the jamming formation. Don't sweat the SAMs, unless you get a three-ringer." At this point, several pilots began reporting seeing the SAMs rising toward them. Close to Hanoi, some three-ringer SAM lock-on indicators in cockpits were observed as the close tracking of the SAMs met the flight. Several of the four-plane divisions' aircraft had to descend several thousand feet and maneuver as SAMs arced rapidly over them, missing them.

Colonel Miller then called, "Goatee flight, I'm rolling in, both 2,000-pounders armed!"

With the sun to his back as he attacked, the shadows of the bridge would not hamper the electro-optical TV-guided systems of the falling bombs. All four planes descended and Colonel Miller broadcast, "Goatee flight, pickle your bombs!"

The next four aircraft, Napkin flight, followed in the diving attacks upon the Paul Doumer Bridge. Then came Biloxi flight, and finally, the wave of Jingle flight dropped their ordnance loads.

As the bombs hurled earthward toward the Paul Doumer Bridge, the sky was laced with lethal 37mm and 57mm tracer lines. The bridge was indeed heavily defended. The bombs burst on and about the massive bridge.

MiG fighters jumped Colonel Miller's flight the minute they cleared the target area. There were several passes by MiGs and an exchange of missiles fired by opposing aircraft. There were no hits sustained upon any air-to-air battling aircraft. It was a swift encounter, as Colonel Miller then said, "I want those sonic booms over Hanoi. The Hanoi Hilton is down there somewhere. Let our POWs hear us!"

Within minutes, eight F-4s, a division called Bow-leg flight, attacked the Yen Vien rail yards. As they commenced their attack runs, the residents of Hanoi were hearing Colonel Miller's sonic booms from his division, departing the Paul Doumer Bridge attack area, but with all the bombs exploding around and upon the bridge, the sonic booms were probably not as effective noise makers as were desired by Colonel Miller. Possibly some day a former American POW who was at the Hanoi Hilton during this raid can tell us if he heard any sonic booms above the noise of the battle.

General John W. Vogt Jr., in his Blue Chip Seventh Air Force command center at Tan Son Nhut Air Force Base outside of Saigon, listened to the radio relays of the dynamic raid. He said to his staff, "Sounds like we're getting some good hits on the bridge, but that bridge can take a hell of a pounding. It was struck hard years ago, so here's hoping it goes down today. We'll soon see—after the post-strike photos are in here."

A little earlier, back over North Vietnam, the Yen Vien rail yard attack force Bow-leg was led by Maj. Al Munsch of Gopher flight of the 25th Tactical Fighter Squadron. As his flight was about to roll in for their attack upon the rail yards, his entire flight witnessed the ongoing attack upon the Paul Doumer Bridge. They saw the enormous quantity of bomb explosions. It looked to them as if most bombs hit on, or very close to, the bridge.

Major Munsch came up on his tactical common UHF frequency and stated to his flight, "Wow! Look at those hits! They must have severed that big bridge, but look at all that crap coming up at them. I hope we don't meet the same kind of resistance on our run. Hang in there, guys. Here we go!"

Luckily, Major Munsch's flight did not encounter the stiff antiaircraft resistance of SAMs and AAA over the rail yards like that encountered by the attackers over the bridge, but as his flight departed the rail yard target area, MiGs came up to attack them. No major aerial combat fight developed as Munsch's flight swiftly departed west from what appeared to them as a now badly damaged, smoking rail marshalling yard.

Now came the navy contribution to the day's strikes. The first formations from the USS *Constellation*'s air wing arrived in the area. Following them roared the assembled air wings from the USS *Coral Sea* and the USS *Kitty Hawk*, all en route to Haiphong.

First into the attack area were the navy A-7E Corsair II aircraft. They were Iron Hand aircraft that would strike the enemy's SAM radars. Along with them charged the EKA-3B electronic warfare aircraft to perform radar jamming for the navy attack aircraft, which were inbound, headed for the Haiphong petroleum storage areas of the Route Package VIB area assigned to the navy. Then came the navy A-6 Intruders, carrying CBU cluster bombs.

The A-7E Busy Bee flight of Iron Hand aircraft began firing Shrike homing missiles at the North Vietnamese Fan Song radars. These attacks forced the enemy to shut down their Fan Song fire-control radar systems that operated their SA-2 SAM systems. Those systems that were not shut down were immediately homed-in and struck by the Shrike homing missiles of the A-7E aircraft.

By the time the A-6 Intruders, call sign Boomer flight, arrived to bomb, many of the SAM missiles were up to greet them, but without their ground radar-guidance systems operating, the enemy missiles flew harmlessly past the navy attacking Intruders.

Throughout the air strikes, the Red Crown MiG warning radar system on the USS *Chicago* was up and operating proficiently. Aircraft Intercept Controller and Chief Radarman Larry Nowell was extremely busy in charge of radar technicians running radar intercepts for the navy F-4J Phantom fighter escorts called Showtime flight.

Larry Nowell's radar technicians were very successful this strike day. Later, at our Seventh Fleet staff briefing on the *Oklahoma City*, it was announced that Chief Nowell was credited with supervising radar technicians in directing and thereby assisting navy fighters responsible for three MiG kills on this big strike day, May 10, 1972. Nowell, during his busy days, actually directed more air force than navy MiG engagements.

The USS *Biddle* (DLG-34), with exceptionally fine radar control and keen operators, also significantly contributed to protecting the navy attack aircrews.

Later, back in our Seventh Fleet war room, as we all anxiously awaited air force results of the strike, Lieutenant Colonel Rose briefed us: "After the 10 May morning bombings, which were very intense and fairly accurate, the Paul Doumer Bridge still stands intact." The bridge was still standing! "It sustained extensive damage, including two eastern spans that were completely destroyed. However, the main spans are still standing supporting the overall structure. The bridge has not been totally severed, or knocked down. Fortunately, due to the extensive damage, the bridge is not usable for vehicles or trains. Only foot-traffic can use the damaged bridge. In many areas, the bridge is a mass of twisted steel."

When the air force jets departed from their strikes upon the Paul Doumer Bridge, they purposely flew directly over Hanoi City at low altitude and broke the sound barrier. This sonic booming of the city was a spontaneous decision, not in their original formal briefing. It was led by enthusiastic flight leaders who wanted their sonic booms to be heard not only by the North Vietnamese residents of Hanoi, but primarily by the American prisoners of war, who were being held nearby in the Hanoi Hilton POW camp. The departing attack pilots hoped these sonic booms would raise the morale level of the POWs and show them they were not forgotten. . . . There was hope.

While the air force F-4s departed over Hanoi, air force F-4s with F-105G suppression Iron Clad aircraft, with sixteen F-4s carrying 500-pound bombs, attacked the Yen Vien rail yards.

Photo coverage and visual reports at Seventh Air Force headquarters indicate that nine of the thirteen rail tracks were severed and cratered in numerous areas. "It will take the North Vietnamese some hard work and some time to repair this vital rail center."

With Lieutenant Colonel Rose's briefing completed, Cmdr. George Boaz began to brief us by saying, "In the meantime, the navy carrier *Constellation* launched the fuel tanker planes KA-6s and EK-3Bs. They began refueling navy aircraft that were en route to attack Haiphong. The three navy air wings from three carriers were a mix of A-6 Intruders, A-7 Corsair II, and F-4 Phantom aircraft.

"The *Constellation*'s wing attacked the petroleum storage area west of Haiphong City. The *Coral Sea*'s air wing struck the Haiphong main rail yard. The *Kitty Hawk*'s aircraft attacked the main rail center and bridge at Haiphong Port."

My boss, Cmdr. Jim Froid, then briefed with the following statement: "I had relocated Task Force Seventy-Six with the Marine amphibious helicopter carrier USS *Okinawa* (LPH-3) well north of the DMZ, placing it to just sixty miles southwest of Haiphong. At 0800, three navy Sea Knight Sikorsky HH-3A helicopters from squadron HC-7 launched from the LPH and flew thirty miles off the coast of North Vietnam to serve as search-and-rescue helicopters for the attack strikes."

These navy search-and-rescue birds did not have any armament aboard. This contrasted with the air force Sikorsky H-53B Jolly Greens, which had two 7.62mm electrically operated mini Gatling guns. If the navy choppers had to go ashore to pick up downed aircrews inside of North Vietnam, they would have a helluva time without self-protective guns.

After all these years of conducting limited warfare upon the North Vietnamese, the United States had given the enemy the time it needed to build up their defenses into one of the most well-defended cities of the world. And when we were finally directed to attack these lethal, well-protected areas, we were authorized to hit only Washington-selected military targets. Our intelligence reported, at this time, that the enemy was ready and waiting.

Commander Frank Hantz, our intelligence officer, N-2, briefed us, saying, "North Vietnam had about 3,500 antiaircraft guns, all of Soviet caliber of 23mm, 37mm, 57mm, 85mm, and 100mm. These large-caliber antiaircraft weapons were also reinforced by all kinds of smaller-type weapons, ranging from .50-caliber machine guns to the standard Russian-Chinese AK-47 automatic rifles for use against low-flying attacking aircraft." To make things more critical for our attacking pilots, the North Vietnamese moved their antiaircraft guns every day. They moved them about as if playing a chess game. There were thirteen Soviet Dvina SA-2 surface-to-air missile sites around Hanoi and ten SAM sites around Haiphong. The North Vietnamese also moved these SAM weapons systems almost daily.

Commander Hantz continued, "The People's Army of Vietnam Air Force had forty MiG-15s, fifty MiG-17s, thirty-five MiG-19s, and eighty MiG-21s. All were excellent fighter interceptors, with the MiG-21 Fishbed a very high-performance, supersonic, high-rate-of-turn aircraft."

From Cmdr. George Boaz's briefings of Task Force 77 activity, we got a good idea of the air war. He also stated, "As the navy air wings attacked, they encountered the same intense, lethal flak from 37mm and 57mm antiaircraft guns that the air force encountered. SAMs also flew up to meet them. Then, as expected, the silver MiG-21 fighters encountered our navy flyers. Over Kep airfield, a navy F-4 Phantom shot down a MiG-21 as it came up to engage it.

"Shortly after that shoot-down, a navy F-4 shot down a MiG-17 off the coast. By early afternoon, six MiG-17s had been shot down over Hai Duong. Two navy F-4s were shot down by MiG-19s, and one navy F-4 was downed by antiaircraft fire over Hai Duong."

Commander Boaz's briefing, based upon Task Force 77 message reports, continued, "After the Navy raid on Hai Duong, and while near the coast, Lt. Randy Cunningham and his backseater (RIO), Willie Driscoll from VF-96 off the *Constellation*, shot down three MiG-17s." This two-man F-4J fighter team aircrew, having shot down five MiGs, had just become the first aces of the Vietnam War!

"As Cunningham and Driscoll, low on fuel, departed the North Vietnamese coast for feet wet, a SAM exploded near their F-4 and severely damaged their aircraft. They immediately punched-out over the Gulf of Tonkin. Aircrews in navy HC-7 helicopters lifted them from the water and flew them back to the helicopter landing platform on the *Okinawa*, where Commander Froid had placed the ship off the north coast, specifically for the search-and-rescue missions. On board the *Okinawa*, Cunningham and Driscoll were welcomed as the war's first aces. Later, a Marine CH-46 helicopter returned them to their carrier *Constellation*."

Naturally, during and upon completion of Commander Boaz's briefing, there was much excitement in our war room, now that the navy had their first aces of this long war. The navy beat the air force in this deadly business of aerial combat achievement! Returned safely to their carrier, they gave some details of their action that opening day, May 10, 1972, of the Linebacker campaign:

Cunningham and Driscoll were catapulted off the *Connie's* angled deck at 200 knots in their F-4J Phantom. Using the call sign Showtime 100, they first refueled from an aerial tanker as they flew toward North Vietnam. Their assigned mission was to provide destruction of antiaircraft guns and protection against MiGs for their attack bomber companions, the navy Intruders and Corsair IIs bombing the Hai Duong railroad complex.

Over the target area, Cunningham's wingman shouted a warning to him and Driscoll that MiG-17s were on their tail firing at them.

Cunningham pulled a hard port (left) turn and one MiG-17 overshot their F-4J.

Cunningham fired a Sidewinder heat-seeking missile and it flew up the exhaust of the MiG-17 engine. The MiG-17 immediately exploded.

A wild dogfight ensued with F-4Js against MiG-17s, MiG-19s, and MiG-21s directly over Hai Duong.

As another U.S. Navy F-4J was attacked by three bogies, Cunningham closed on the MiGs and fired another heat-seeking missile. A MiG-17 blew up for a second Cunningham and Driscoll kill of this day.

Cunningham and Driscoll then headed for the coast as a MiG-17 headed directly at them while firing the MiG-17's 37mm guns. Cunningham pulled back on the stick and his Phantom went into a vertical climb. The enemy MiG-17 pulled nose-up and stayed in a vertical climb with Cunningham and Driscoll. The enemy aircraft was only about three hundred feet from the U.S. Phantom, and both were in vertical flight and parallel to each other. Both pilots personally had a good look at each other. Many years later it was thought the enemy pilot might have been North Vietnam's top ace, Maj. Dinh Ton, who had ten U.S. aircraft kills to his credit.

Cunningham immediately pushed his throttles into afterburner and rolled inverted over the top, and dove toward the ground. Major Ton fired as he rolled inverted behind Cunningham.

Cunningham and Ton again went into matching vertical climbs. In their climbs Cunningham abruptly yanked his two throttles back and popped open his speed brakes. His F-4J rapidly slowed down to 150 knots of airspeed, as Major Ton's MiG-17 zipped past him. Cunningham quickly pulled behind Ton and accelerated after him in a dive. Cunningham fired his third Sidewinder missile. The heat-seeker missile quickly exploded into Ton's MiG and the plane spun earthward, billowing black smoke. Since Cunningham and Driscoll already had two MiG kills in previous days' aerial battles, this third kill on May 10, 1972, promptly made Cunningham and Driscoll America's first aces of the Vietnam War.

More MiGs closed in on Cunningham and Driscoll, so they again headed for the coast. Task Force 77 message traffic reported that a North Vietnamese SA-2 Guideline SAM had exploded out in front of Cunningham and Driscoll's F-4J, damaging it. They continued flying the stricken jet, crossing the coastline. At this point, they could not keep the plane safely flying. All systems shut down on their F-4J, and they had to eject over the water.

Promptly, three navy HC-7 search-and-rescue Sea Knight helicopters arrived over them. U.S. Navy Lieutenant Frank Pinegar from HC-7 led the Sea Knight helicopters. Pinegar's call sign was Big Mother 62, and his wingman, Big Mother 65, picked up Cunningham from the water. Pinegar flew his helicopter over to the bobbing Driscoll. Pinegar's navy swimmer, Elvin Milledge, jumped from the helicopter into the water to help Driscoll untangle from his rubber raft. Milledge then helped Driscoll hook up to the helicopter rescue hoist system, and it plucked him from the sea. The HC-7 helicopters then flew both pilot Cunningham and radar intercept officer Driscoll to the LPH *Okinawa*. A Marine CH-46 Sea Knight helicopter then flew the first aces of the war to their carrier, USS *Constellation*.

Historian John Sherwood, PhD, Naval Historical Center, in 2003 reported to me that he interviewed Randy Cunningham, then a congressman representing the San Diego area. Congressman Cunningham stated that shortly after being reunited with his shipmates on the *Constellation*, the navy flew him to Saigon to meet with air force intelligence officers at the Seventh Air Force Command Center, code name Blue Chip.

The air force intelligence officers confirmed the third kill of the day for Cunningham and Driscoll and identified the North Vietnamese pilot as a Colonel Tomb or Toon. In recent years, however, historians doubt it may have been a Colonel Tomb or Toon because Cunningham and Driscoll had shot down a MiG-17, and a MiG-21 had been reported flown by the mysterious Tomb or Toon. Therefore, it could have been some other Vietnamese People's Air Force pilot. (As discussed in the Preface, the third MiG shot down by Cunningham and Driscoll could possibly have been piloted by a Maj. Dinh Ton.)

Much of the air-to-air combat success for the navy on May 10th was due to Task Force 77 radar controllers on cruisers and destroyers. The USS *Chicago* and USS *Biddle* had advanced powerful radar systems. Instrumental in warning and directing the navy pilots over the skies of North Vietnam was Chief Radarman Larry H. Nowell, who was in charge of the group of radar technicians responsible for tracking the enemy aircraft.

Later in this war, Chief Nowell would be recognized for having been responsible for his technicians directing navy fighters while in their radar rooms for a total of twelve MiG kills.

Marine A-6 Intruders from VMA-AW-224, flying off the *Coral Sea*, participated in attacks at Hai Duong, along with the navy attack bombers. Although the Marine A-6 Intruders received some damage to several of their aircraft, to my personal relief as the Seventh Fleet Marine air officer, they luckily had none of their A-6s shot down; all safely returned to the *Coral Sea*. The most damaged Marine A-6 was serial number 155649. It had suffered a two-foot hole in the starboard horizontal stabilizer.

That dynamic day of May 10th saw navy ex–Blue Angel pilot Lt. Steve Shoemaker and his radar intercept officer, Lt. Keith Crenshaw, shoot down a MiG-17 near Hai Duong. Lieutenant Tom Blonski and his backseater, Lt. Matt Connelly, shot down two MiG-17s. Lieutenant Curt Dose and, RIO, Lt. Jim McDevitt shot down a MiG-21, while Lt. Ken Cannon downed a MiG-17.

Air force pilots Capt. Steve Richie and backseater Capt. Chuck DeBellevue vaporized a MiG-21. Also, Maj. Bob Lodge and backseater, Captain Locher, in their F-4, shot down a MiG-21. As soon as they downed the MiG, however, they were immediately shot down by another MiG-19 in the aerial battle.

By the end of the day, eleven MiGs were shot down and two F-4 Phantoms were shot down by MiGs. With about ninety-five SAM missiles recorded being fired at the Americans, only one U.S. aircraft was downed by a SA-2 SAM that day. Another U.S. aircraft was shot down by antiaircraft artillery fire.

May 10th had been a helluva long, action-packed day. Although many more air raids were to follow, including massive B-52 raids during the fall and winter of 1972, none would be of this magnitude.

Lieutenant Colonel Rose, reporting the air force results, stated, "The air force, during this twenty-four hour period, flew 120 combat sorties in support of all attack roles. This included sixty-six B-52 bomber sorties."

Commander George Boaz received his afteraction reports and briefed us: "During that same period of high intensity, the U.S. Navy and Marine Corps flew a total of 294 sorties from navy carriers."

As heavy message traffic poured into our Seventh Fleet staff war room through our *Oklahoma City* communications center, supervised by Lt. B. Humphrey and Chief V. Syrovatka, all us staff members read each word carefully.

Attack carrier Task Force 77 (TF 77), led by Adm. Damon Cooper, kept us well informed of their three air wings' aerial activities. Additionally, private, scrambled, covered voice communications between Admiral Mack and Admiral Cooper rounded out the exchange of timely information.

Operation Linebacker had started with a big bang. It was to continue, at a slightly lower pace, for many months. It was in the wee hours of the next morning before I left the busy war room to hit my rack for a few hours of sleep. I would soon be back up there in the war room preparing my amphibious warfare and Marine air briefings for Admiral Mack for our daily 0900 war room briefings.

As I lay in my bunk trying to get some much-needed sleep, I couldn't get all of the day's air action out of my mind. I was sure that Adm. Thomas H. Moorer, chairman of JCS at the Pentagon, and Adm. Elmo R. Zumwalt, CNO, had followed this day's events very closely, watching and digesting the same reports that we had read.

Needless to say, Adm. Bernard A. Clarey, commander in chief, U.S. Pacific Fleet in Hawaii, both closer to the action and more directly responsible, watched the events unfold. Clarey not only directed all U.S. naval/Marine forces, but he was located on Oahu Island in Hawaii near Adm. John S. McCain II.

Admiral John S. McCain II, commander in chief, Pacific, who directed all U.S. military operations of all armed forces in the Pacific theater, had a special interest in this war at this time. His son, Lt. Cmdr. John S. McCain III, had been shot down back on October 26, 1967. Young McCain had been flying a mission over North Vietnam from the carrier *Hancock*. Here it was, four and a half years later, and McCain was still a prisoner of war somewhere in North Vietnam.

I thought what most of my fellow staffers must have thought, and I'm sure that Admiral McCain must have thought of the same thing this day ... our navy, Marine, and air force bombers might have accidentally killed his son in his POW camp.

The McCains were a navy family. Our commander in chief, Pacific, Adm. John S. McCain II, was the son of Adm. John S. McCain, who had been commander of Task Force 38 aboard the carrier *Hancock* in 1945. He personally had directed air strikes against the Japanese occupiers in Indochina. All these years later, his grandson, John S. McCain III, after flying off the newer *Hancock*, was a POW in North Vietnam, an area once part of Indochina.

The next day came and the war room remained a beehive of activity. The daily actions continued at a rapid pace as President Nixon tried desperately to force the invading North Vietnamese back to the negotiating table in Paris.

Chapter 10
• • • • • • • •

The Defense of
Hue City

By the time MACV in Saigon fully recognized the full extent of
the NVA invasion, the Marine Amphibious Force, for which I
was the staff cognizant officer of the Seventh Fleet, had been directed
to build to four amphibious ready groups (ARGs). These ARGs
were afloat on Task Force 76 amphibious ships off Vietnam. TF 76
was under the command of Rear Adm. Walter D. Gaddes, who was
aboard the task force flagship, USS *Blue Ridge*.

Meanwhile, Lt. Col. D'Wayne Gray, in command of
ANGLICO, received 210 more Marines and strategically dispersed
them in South Vietnam. Lieutenant Colonel Gray, a supporting
arms professional, briefed Brig. Gen. William H. Langan, J-3,
MACV, that to defend Hue City, in view of the loss of Quang Tri
City nearby, much improvement was needed between the existing
disconnect of U.S. air support and the South Vietnamese ground
units. Lieutenant Colonel Gray expressed that coordination centers
for effective targeting had to be established because the South
Vietnamese had not yet learned how to do this. Gray said that the
supporting arms control had to be better coordinated to use the
U.S. supporting arms of air and naval gunfire.

On May 4, the South Vietnamese Joint General Staff in Saigon
replaced I Corps commander General Lam in Da Nang with Lt.
Gen. Ngo Quang Truong. General Truong immediately moved his
headquarters north to Hue City from Da Nang.

General Truong had command of ARVN airborne divisions and Vietnamese Marines responsible for the northern and northwestern areas of Thua Thien Province. He had control of the 1st ARVN Division south and southwest of Hue and the 2d ARVN Division in MR 1's southern provinces. He began establishing the defense of Hue City.

U.S. Marine Brig. Gen. Edward J. Miller, commander of the 9th Marine Amphibious Brigade, who had his Marines dispersed on the amphibious ships that my immediate boss, Cmdr. Jim Froid, and I were responsible for on Admiral Holloway's staff, came ashore at Hue City. Brigadier General Miller met with U.S. Marine Col. Joshua Dorsey, senior Marine adviser to the VNMC division, and Vietnamese Marine Brig. Gen. Bui The Lan, commander of the South Vietnamese Marine Corps.

To establish the defense of Hue, they set up a combat operations center in a schoolhouse in the coastal village of Huong Dien. They drew fire-support coordination personnel from ANGLICO, 1st Radio Battalion, the U.S. Air Force's 20th Tactical Air Support Squadron, and the U.S. Army's 14th Signal Company.

Because the NVA halted their attacks north of the My Chanh River, the 1st Regional Assistance Command declared everything north of the river a free-fire zone. They now faced the NVA 304th, 308th, and 324B divisions, the NVA 202d and 203d Armored regiments, and their supporting arms of tanks, artillery, and antiaircraft missiles.

The NVA 130mm guns dueled with the ARVN 175mm guns near the Marine defenders up along the My Chanh River. The now reorganized Marine division fire support coordination center at Hue provided good targets that resulted in inflicting substantial damage upon the NVA.

Because the NVA brought handheld SA-7 Strella heat-seeking antiaircraft missiles with them, dispersed within their artillery units, U.S. and South Vietnamese forward air controllers had to fly above the 9,500 feet range of the SA-7s. This made it difficult for the FACs to locate precisely the muzzle flashes of the NVA guns. Additionally, the NVA wisely spread out their artillery units. The NVA generally had no more than two platoons, or two to four guns, in any single location.

General Truong initiated a series of limited objective attacks and raids against the NVA. He began using combined air, artillery, and naval gunfire support, with Brigadier General Lan planning the operations. Colonel Dorsey recommended a heliborne assault into the Hai Lang District. General Truong concurred and asked General Abrams in Saigon for permission to request our Seventh Fleet assistance. We, on the Seventh Fleet staff, responded by planning a helicopter raid, using our Marine helicopters under my staff cognizance.

The raid was called Song Than 5-72, and it commenced on the night of May 12. South Vietnamese Marine Corps 1st Lt. Thu Xuan, communications officer of the 9th VNMC Battalion, and a small group swam across the My Chanh River and established a communication site to coordinate the next morning's raid.

I had directed, via messages, that the 9th Marine Amphibious Brigade furnish Marine helicopters. Early on May 13, Marine Corps Lt. Col. Ed Hertberg's HMM-164 squadron of helicopters lifted twenty VNMC troops in each CH-46 helicopter and sixty VNMC troops in each CH-53 helicopter for maximum capacity lifts. Major Don Brodie, who had flown in HMM-161 with me in Hawaii in 1962–64, was the HMM-164 operations officer. He directed that the Marine helicopters fly nap-of-the-earth height, at forty feet above the ground, to attempt to avoid SAMs. The Marine Corps helicopters launched from the USS *Okinawa* and loaded the VNMC troops from Lieutenant Colonel Luong's 369th Brigade at Fire Support Base Sally. The U.S. Army's F Troop, 4th Air Cavalry, flying from Hue–Phu Bai, provided attack helicopter escort for the Marine Corps assault helicopter transports.

Our staff officer, Cmdr. Stu Landersman, ensured that there was naval gunfire support available as U.S. Air Force and Navy aircraft pounded the assault landing zone.

At 0930 on May 13, the Marine Corps helicopters landed in the landing zone, discharging the VNMC troops, and returned to LZ Sally for another load of troops.

The NVA hit three Marine Corps CH-46s and damaged one CH-53 that had to remain in the landing zone. The downed CH-53 had to be destroyed to prevent capture by the NVA.

The 9th Marine Amphibious Brigade (MAB)'s helicopter detachment, HML-367, flying off the USS *Denver* (LPD-9), provided naval gunfire support spotting in the landing zone area.

Receiving reports of Marine air assets that I was responsible for, I knew we had lost a CH-53 in the landing zone and that a CH-46 had crashed in the Gulf of Tonkin—and that one U.S. Marine was wounded.

The two VNMC battalions swept out from the LZ and headed south, to the rear of the NVA along the north side of the My Chanh River, as the 9th VNMC Battalion attacked north across the My Chanh River to link up with the two helo-lifted battalions. They trapped the 66th NVA Regiment.

Captain Richard H. Hodory, assistant battalion adviser to the 3d VNMC Battalion, had also landed with the VNMC battalions in the USMC helicopter assault in the landing zone. He immediately began calling in supporting VNMC artillery and U.S. air strikes and naval gunfire, which caused the NVA 66th Regiment to break their defense and receive severe casualties.

As the VNMC battalions linked up, they freed 150 civilians who had been held captive by the 66th NVA Regiment. Three NVA tanks and two 130mm guns were destroyed, and 240 NVA soldiers were killed by the VNMC Song Than 5-72 raid.

The VNMC helo raid caught the NVA by surprise. On May 21, however, the NVA mounted a full-scale armor and infantry attack along the My Chanh Line and penetrated the VNMC Brigade 369 area. The overwhelming NVA armor forced the two VNMC battalions to withdraw initially. After a full day of fighting, supported by U.S. air strikes and the ARVN armored cavalry, the VNMC pushed the NVA north back toward the My Chanh River.

On May 22, at 0100, the NVA launched a twenty-five-tank-supported infantry attack against the 3d VNMC Battalion. With tanks and superior numbers, the NVA overran the forward battalion. But the NVA lost eight tanks in the fight, including tank losses inflicted by a U.S. Army adviser firing a newly arrived U.S. tube-launched, optically tracked, wire-guided (TOW) missile. Brigade adviser, U.S. Army Maj. Robert F. Sheridan and adviser Maj. Donald L. Price directed use of the new weapons. These new weapons destroyed five NVA armored vehicles. By 0930 a total of ten NVA tanks had been destroyed.

The 8th VNMC Battalion then counterattacked. The NVA retreated, leaving their dead and wounded. The South Vietnamese defense of the My Chanh Line held.

On the morning of May 23, we, on the Seventh Fleet staff, began coordinating—with the Marine Corps 9th MAB commander, Brigadier General Miller, Vietnamese Colonel Lan, and Lt. Col. Do Ky of the VNMC—a plan for an attack called Song Than 6-72. We were working out the details in both our operations office and our plans office aboard the *Oklahoma City*, while at the same time our ship was firing her 6-inch guns at several 133mm Russian-built coastal defense guns that the North Vietnamese had mounted on railroad tracks. These guns were well concealed inside caves and came out only to fire at our navy ships. In this instance, we were firing at guns located well to the north of the Cau Viet River and slightly north of the DMZ. In the middle of all of this, though, we had something else that needed attending to: there was to be a change of command of the Seventh Fleet, at sea, in combat.

The *Oklahoma City* ceased firing at 0900 and glided out a safe distance from the large coastal defense guns. Admiral Mack's personal helicopter, Black Beard One, had just returned from a trip to Da Nang and back. Now aboard Black Beard One was Adm. Bernard A. Clarey, commander in chief, U.S. Pacific Fleet, and Vice Adm. James L. Holloway III. In the late morning heat of the Gulf of Tonkin, and while our ship's 6-inch gun barrels were still smoking and hot from firing, the ship was decorated with flags and took on the atmosphere of a military parade.

Just seconds before the ceremony, as sailors, Marines, and officers formed ranks on the fantail, we were bracketed by incoming NVA shore bombardment. General alarm was sounded, and we went to battlestations as *Oklahoma City* moved farther out from shore to a spot well beyond the maximum range of fire of the coastal defense guns. Then we got back to the ceremony on the fantail, below the rear of the missile house. With two large Talos missiles standing out from the missile house in the firing position for background, our entire staff, me included, stood at attention. Farther in the background, our other cruisers continued exchanging gunfire with the North Vietnamese coastal defense sites.

Our departing Seventh Fleet commander, Vice Adm. William Paden Mack, spoke briefly. Then our new commander, Vice Adm. James L. Holloway III, gave a brief acceptance-of-command speech.

This was followed by a speech from the guest speaker, Admiral Clarey, CINCPACFLT. Admiral Clarey then presented Admiral Mack with the Distinguished Service Medal. Admiral Holloway assumed command of the Seventh Fleet, which consisted of 91,000 men, including 27,000 Marines and 130 ships.

Vice Admiral James L. Holloway III, a stocky, young-looking man, was very impressive. He wore his full array of colorful military decorations on his short-sleeved, white uniform shirt. His military ribbons represented his personal service to his country from World War II, the Korean War, and to this date in the waters off Vietnam.

Holloway was shorter of stature than the gaunt, gray-haired, and seasoned departing leader, Admiral Mack. Holloway looked aggressively eager to assume command and get on with running his assigned duties of this Washington-restrained war. The outgoing and incoming admirals shook hands. Admiral Mack bade farewell and the ceremony ended. With the brief, formal ceremony completed, the nearby cruisers' shelling of the North Vietnamese coast seemed louder. The colorful change-of-command ceremony, in the middle of the war, became a memory of U.S. naval history.

We had a little informal gathering on the fantail with Admiral Clarey. He spoke to each of us staff officers. Later, after a formal briefing in the war room, Black Beard One arrived back upon our ship's fantail. In minutes, Black Beard One was airborne with Admiral Clarey and departing former Seventh Fleet commander Admiral Mack aboard. The helicopter departed for Da Nang. From there, Admiral Clarey would head back to his CINPACFLT command headquarters in Hawaii, and Admiral Mack was heading back to the continental United States to assume command of the U.S. Naval Academy.

After the brief reprieve of the ceremony, it was back to finalizing the plans for Song Than 6-72. Jim Froid and I coordinated with our Marine amphibious ready groups (ARGs) Bravo and Charlie, while our air force liaison officer, Lieutenant Colonel Rose, coordinated B-52 arc-light strikes for another raid. Stu Landersman assembled his naval gunfire ships off Wunder Beach, the famous Street Without Joy area, located a few miles southeast of Quang Tri City. This would be the attack area.

Jim Froid directed the TF 76 amphibious ships, *Cayuga* (LST-1186) and *Duluth* (LPD-6), as well as the *Schenectady* (LST-1185) and the *Manitowoc* (LST-1180), to load the VNMC 4th, 6th, and 7th battalions of the 147th VNMC Brigade at Tan My Naval Base.

On the morning of May 24, Stu Landersman's surface ships from TG 70.8 bombarded Red Beach and the VNMC coordinated artillery and air strikes upon Red Beach to soften it up.

Helicopters from Marine squadrons from HMM-164 lifted off the USS *Okinawa* and flew to Tan My to pick up 550 VNMC assault troops. Meanwhile, our LSTs launched twenty amphibious tractors (amtracs) full of VNMC assault troops. As the amtracs closed on the beach, a final B-52 arc-light raid dropped strings of bombs along the beach. When the amtracs hit the beach, the dust was settling from the supporting arms. The VNMC troops were met by only scattered NVA infantry and artillery incoming.

The destroyer USS *Hanson* joined other gunfire support ships and silenced the NVA artillery batteries.

Major Walter E. Boomer, adviser to the 7th VNMC Battalion, made the landing with his VNMC troops. Initially, reports indicated that Operation Song Than 6-72 caught the NVA by surprise again behind their lines. The 7th VNMC Battalion quickly secured their objective, killing fifty NVA and capturing large amounts of NVA weapons and food caches.

As the VNMC units that landed across Red Beach consolidated their objective, Marine Corps helicopters from squadron HMM-164 launched with elements of the 4th and 6th VNMC battalions from Tan My to an LZ Columbus objective at the road junction of Routes 555 and 602, near NVA-held Quang Tri City. Soon after the helos landed, the VNMC troops encountered elements of the 18th NVA Regiment and 325th NVA Division. During the battle, it was reported that two captured NVA troops stated that they had just arrived in the area and that their 18th NVA Regiment was preparing to attack along the My Chanh Line.

After effectively countering the NVA for the second time in eleven days, the Vietnamese Marines, supported by the Seventh Fleet's 9th MAB and Task Force 76, countered the NVA invasion threat to Hue City.

After we each briefed Admiral Holloway on May 24, changes began. Every new commander incorporates his, or her, own style and personality into the command. Admiral Holloway, a naval aviator, several years before had been the commanding officer of the nuclear-powered attack aircraft carrier USS *Enterprise*. What he wanted for briefings differed from his predecessor, Admiral Mack. We staff officers quickly adjusted our briefing presentations to the style desired by our new commander. We also quickly adapted to the style of message writing that Admiral Holloway expected. One thing I was to learn from Admiral Holloway, regarding message drafting, was that a message should be clearly understandable and specific. Military messages normally are very cryptic, and due to shortness, sometime important information can be misunderstood. Admiral Holloway emphasized detailed message drafting that would not let the recipient be confused or in any doubt as to the directive or information conveyed. As a result, our messages sent out as directives or reports were longer and more detailed. We were soon to realize that Admiral Holloway was not only an excellent commander, but also a very good teacher.

The day after the successful Operation Song Than 6-72, on May 25 at 0530, the NVA tried another ferocious attack along the My Chanh Line. Despite employing unprecedented quantities of NVA armor, the NVA prematurely exposed their attacking infantry to U.S.–Vietnamese supporting arms. The countryside was littered with burned-out NVA armored vehicles, and the My Chanh River became polluted from hundreds of NVA bodies. After the battle, Maj. Robert F. Sheridan, adviser to the VNMC Brigade 369, stated, "The air observers and forward air controllers, flying low over the battlefield, day and night, were our link to the outside world."

Again, in the early morning of May 26, a reinforced NVA battalion savagely attacked against VNMC Brigade 258's western flank. At the same time, the 1st VNMC Battalion was attacked by the 88th NVA Regiment supported by tanks, mortars, recoilless rifles, and heavy artillery fire.

Marine Corps Cap. Robert K. Redlin directed heavy Seventh Fleet naval gunfire and U.S. Navy and Air Force strikes upon the aggressive NVA attacking the 9th VNMC Battalion. Marine Corps

Capt. Lawrence H. Livingston, with the 1st VNMC Battalion, quickly called in air strikes as the NVA attacked his assigned battalion. The South Vietnamese halted the third hard drive by the NVA to attack the Hue City area. The NVA left 220 dead as they withdrew from this failed attack.

During May, the NVA lost 2,900 dead, 1,080 weapons captured, and 64 armored vehicles destroyed along the My Chanh River defense line. The North Vietnamese communists failed to capture Hue City.

May ended with the South Vietnamese Marines not only defending Hue City, but building up their strength to fifteen thousand Vietnamese Marines.

During June 1972, limited South Vietnamese thrusts were launched to the north across the My Chanh River. U.S. Army Maj. Gen. Howard H. Cooksey replaced General Kroesen as the senior U.S. adviser to MR 1. Down in Saigon, U.S. Army Gen. Frederick C. Weyand replaced Gen. Creighton W. Abrams as U.S. Military Assistance Command Vietnam (MACV) commander.

On June 8, three VNMC brigades launched a spoiling attack named Song Than 8-72 across the My Chanh River, under close supporting arms cover of tactical air strikes, artillery, naval gunfire, and B-52 strikes. The NVA were well entrenched.

The NVA took a beating and lost 320 dead, 7 tanks and 102 weapons destroyed, including SA-7 handheld Strella heat-seeking antiaircraft missile launchers. The VNMC units held the recaptured ground in Quang Tri Province.

After building pontoon bridges across the My Chanh River, the VNMC launched another spoiling attack, Song Than 8A-72. They attacked along Route 555 into the notorious Street Without Joy coastal area.

The NVA then counterattacked the VNMC battalion on June 20. VNMC artillery quickly mass-fired upon the NVA attacking tanks, but about fifty NVA infantry troops broke through the 6th VNMC Battalion and got into the battalion command post.

Marine Corps Maj. James M. Tulley, ANGLICO naval gunfire spot team, called in supporting arms as the eight-hour battle raged around him. Tulley called in U.S. Navy, Marine, and Air Force tactical air support and naval gunfire. The air force B-52 bombers arrived to help as the 6th VNMC Battalion pushed the NVA from their penetrated position. The NVA's 130mm artillery guns in the rolling hills to the west responded and fired throughout the battle. Those NVA guns were miles beyond the reach of the Seventh Fleet's naval gunfire ships.

By June 27, the VNMC established a solid defense line four kilometers north of the My Chanh River, killing 761 NVA, destroying 8 tanks, and freeing hundreds of captive villagers. The liberated Vietnamese from the hamlet in Hai Lang District described their life under the invading communists as "full of terror and forced labor." They were forced by the NVA to carry supplies, dig weapons caches, build field fortifications, and harvest their own rice to supply food to the North Vietnamese invaders.

Thus ended the defense of Hue and the initial counterattacks by the South Vietnamese.

U.S. Marine Col. James G. Dionisopoulos, fleet Marine officer working in our Seventh Fleet staff plans section, and I, representing Marines in our operations section, continuously discussed the dismal situation. We reviewed our usual plans that we had for amphibious landing attacks directly into North Vietnam to take the pressure off of South Vietnam. We worked straight through many nights, working up specific plans for attacks behind the enemy north of the DMZ. Despite these plans to attack into North Vietnam, we all felt that President Nixon and Henry Kissinger would never authorize these invasion plans.

The navy staff officers in plans, working with Col. Jim Dionisopoulos, Cmdr. Jim Froid, and me, refined several attack plans to utilize two amphibious ready groups that we had afloat off the Vietnamese coast in amphibious Task Force 76 ships. We decided on one option that we felt would impact the North Vietnamese. We submitted the plan to Admiral Holloway. Admiral Holloway studied the plan intently. Being the tiger that he was, Admiral Holloway did not hesitate to submit the plan up through the chain of command to Admiral Clarey at CINCPACFLT in Hawaii. It should be noted that Admiral Holloway certainly had within his Seventh Fleet resources the physical assets to destroy the North Vietnamese will to wage war. If allowed by Washington, he would have proven he was, without doubt, the Halsey and Nimitz of this or any other war. Unfortunately, our political leaders in Washington, history will record, did not allow the combat commanders to run this war. Therefore, history will record that great U.S. military leaders during the Vietnam War were not authorized to fully exhibit the true U.S. military skills they had . . . skills that once made our country so great.

Our message requesting permission to invade North Vietnam went from Admiral Clarey, CINCPACFLT, to CINCPAC, also located on Oahu, Hawaii, and then to JCS in Washington, D.C. Because we did not receive a response for several days, we, on the Seventh Fleet staff, assumed that JCS must have sent our request message over to the White House. We felt that Dr. Kissinger was probably evaluating and discussing our plan with President Nixon. Because of the unusual time delay for a flash message response request, I thought they might actually approve our invasion plan, however, one week later, we received a rejection of our request to thrust our amphibious Marine forces into North Vietnam.

After the JCS rejection of our invasion plan, and after many discussions in our section, primarily with Colonel Dionisopoulos and his boss, Captain Marshall, we decided on an alternative response plan to the North Vietnamese massive invasion into South Vietnam. We felt we might obtain permission from Washington to use our TF 76 landing craft to simply carry the South Vietnamese Marines on assault landing craft onto a beachhead behind the NVA, just south of the DMZ, inside of South Vietnam. And, if Washington authorized us, we could also utilize our 9th Marine Amphibious Brigade (MAB) helicopters from off the LPH helicopter carriers. With the surface assault boats and the helicopters, we could simultaneously envelop behind the NVA lines northeast and north of Quang Tri City. This would greatly reduce the pressure upon the South Vietnamese from the NVA, as the NVA fought their way toward Hue City. We worked out a classic Marine Corps surface landing assault from the sea and helicopter envelopment plan. Captain Marshall submitted the plan to Admiral Holloway for evaluation. The admiral allowed the chief of staff to release a message of our plan to CINCPACFLT with a request for approval.

A few days later, CINCPAC, apparently with higher approval, sent a message to CINCPACFLT approving our plan and giving execute authority. Within hours, CINCPACFLT sent us an approval message to execute. I was happy with that approval. Finally, we could somehow support the beleaguered South Vietnamese Army and Marine Corps in Quang Tri Province, although I really had hoped to do it the correct military tactical way and invade North Vietnam.

If we had invaded North Vietnam years before, the war would have ended a long time ago, and South Vietnamese troops would have occupied the North. The other option always had been to have the United States give heavy naval bombardment and air support to the South Vietnamese against targets in North Vietnam as the South Vietnamese invaded directly into North Vietnam. This was always the logical option, which would have carried the ravaging war to the enemy homeland, instead of continually defending against the North Vietnamese invasions in the South, where the NVA killed so many South Vietnamese and destroyed so many homes and buildings. There was a constant fear, particularly expressed by Secretary of Defense Robert McNamara, years earlier in the war, that the Red Chinese would rush into the war to prevent North Vietnam from falling to the South Vietnamese. This concern precluded the civilian Washington leadership from brashly running a war the way it should have been directed. Common sense dictated that, at the time, our government should have at least sent someone into communist China to discuss the situation and find out what their reactions might have been if we had invaded North Vietnam or supported a South Vietnamese invasion into North Vietnam to end the war. Red China might not have defended North Vietnam. They actually might have been more satisfied to have South Vietnamese–controlled Vietnam as a neighbor. A few years later, soon after this war ended, Red China carried on its own invasion skirmishes into North Vietnam over territorial rights along their mutual border. The Red Chinese were never very good neighbors to North Vietnam, despite both countries being communist controlled.

This, however, was only speculation of various options at this time in history. Because we, on the Seventh Fleet staff, received approval to use our assets to support the South Vietnamese in an attack behind the North Vietnamese Army, albeit only inside South Vietnam, we would improve the effectiveness of the South Vietnamese to counterattack the invading North Vietnamese Army. I felt that we should conduct a classic amphibious feint, as taught to me in Amphibious Warfare School at Quantico, Virginia. It was even possible that we might actually get permission to execute an amphibious feint, or simulated raid, into North Vietnam. I thought about it for a day. I then left my operations section and went up the ladder to N-6, plans section, to discuss my desires. After lengthy discussions in N-6, we felt that a large-scale amphibious feint might cause the North Vietnamese Army to pull back some of their invasion elements from South Vietnam and send them back north to defend their homeland. This would take the pressure off the South Vietnamese defenders. Immediately after a feint in the north, an actual surface landing of South Vietnamese Marines in the south, behind the NVA lines would take place. Simultaneously, a vertical envelopment by South Vietnamese Marines flown into a landing zone by the U.S. Marine helicopters, behind the NVA lines, would help significantly toward the eventual recapture of Quang Tri City. The South Vietnamese Army and Marine Corps could attack from the south as our helicopters landed behind the NVA northeast of Quang Tri City. The plans section worked up the proposed plan, with both Cmdr. Jim Froid and me deeply involved. Captain Marshall, from plans, submitted the plan to the chief of staff and to Admiral Holloway. The admiral approved the plan and had the plan sent in a message up the chain of command, requesting approval.

To our surprise, within two days, our plan for an amphibious feint off the coast of North Vietnam was approved. Commander Froid directed that TF 76 amphibious forces prepare voice tapes to be played over the radios of their command ship, USS *Blue Ridge*. The tapes would simulate a large attack fleet preparing for an amphibious invasion into North Vietnam. The tapes would create a lot of radio communications between simulated ships and landing forces. All taped conversations would discuss numerous kinds of ships and Marine troop preparations for an invasion into North Vietnam. Jim Froid then directed that all thirty-two TF 76 ships sail to a rendezvous location off the coast of North Vietnam, about fifty miles north of the DMZ.

In our original plan to invade North Vietnam, the plan that JCS denied execution, we had intended a beach assault outside Vinh City in North Vietnam. In our original plan, our Marine helicopters from two LPH carriers would have flown a vertical assault battalion around Vinh and landed directly upon Vinh City Airport, located southwest of the city. Other Marines, simultaneously, would have landed on the beach by surface assault boats. The objective was to capture Vinh and stop all supply lines on Highway 1. The plan called for our U.S. Marines holding Vinh City for three days. After three days, all units would retrograde back to the ships.

We felt strongly that holding these North Vietnamese areas for three days would have resulted in the North Vietnamese seriously assuming that the Americans were going to stay in North Vietnam, cut it in half, and that more Americans would invade into North Vietnam. This quick seize-and-hold operation might have been enough for the North Vietnamese to react, and possibly pull two divisions from South Vietnam and head back north to defend their own homeland. We felt that a reduction of NVA in the Quang Tri area could result in a more evenly matched numbers contest for the South Vietnamese troops in their attempt to fight off the invading NVA. This would then help the South Vietnamese regain the initiative for a counterattack and assist in the recapture of Quang Tri City and possibly the northern areas of Quang Tri Province.

Because the real invasion plan had been denied by Washington, and we had the approval for a feint operation, we set about duplicating some parts of the original invasion plan. We simulated units' call signs, using them on radio tapes broadcast from the amphibious flagship *Blue Ridge*. In the actual movement of equipment and people, we would execute only the initial assault waves of surface boats, without any troops inside the boats. Additionally, we would execute this new feint plan only slightly north of the DMZ in North Vietnam's territory. We could not send TF 76 elements too far north of the DMZ because we would have to quickly sail them back south and reorganize them for the actual coordinated South Vietnamese Marine Corps attack behind the NVA lines. This actual attack would place South Vietnamese Marines behind the NVA located at Quang Tri City, using the very same ships, assault boats, and U.S. Marine helicopters used up north for the feint operation.

On our feint plan for the North, the empty, except for drivers, landing craft assault waves would go only into the high-water mark of the beach gradients in North Vietnam and then immediately turn around and head back to their mother-ships. There would not be any U.S. Marine combat troops on these U.S. Navy amphibious assault boats. Likewise, our U.S. Marine helicopters would also be empty of assault troops, except for the U.S. flight crews. The helicopters would be flown from the carriers to just off the beach of North Vietnam. They then would turn around and fly back to their respective carrier ships. To ensure realism for the amphibious feint plan, and to improve an anticipated NVA reaction, we requested and received three consecutive days of air force B-52 bombing raids in the Vinh City area. This was well coordinated with heavy Seventh Fleet ship bombardments. We knew that the NVA had been monitoring our increased shipboard radio communications chatter by now. Intelligence began intercepting communications between NVA field commanders in South Vietnam and higher commands up in the Hanoi area. This indicated that the NVA were concerned about a possible U.S. invasion thrust into North Vietnam. Possibly, the communists even remembered the historical U.S. Marine amphibious landing, with U.S. Army participation, at Inchon Harbor in Korea, behind the North Korean Army lines during the Korean War. The stage was now set.

The execute message was sent by Commander Froid to Task Force 76. The feint operation commenced. The B-52 bomber raids began hitting the busy Highway 1 bridges in the Vinh area and struck massive truck convoys in parking areas outside of Vinh. Then the amphibious feint raid commenced. The massed TF 76 amphibious ships were a beehive of activity. TG 70.8 surface ships began pounding the North Vietnamese coastal defense guns. Our cruisers dueled heavily with the enemy's Soviet-supplied coastal guns. Again I thought it certainly would have been nice to have the mothballed *New Jersey*'s 16-inch guns, which would have been a much better match against the large coastal defense guns that were sure to be hiding inside caves, rolling out on railroad tracks, and firing at our cruisers, which had much shorter firing ranges. During my previous combat tour as a forward air controller flying an OV-10A Bronco in South Vietnam, I had personally controlled naval gunfire missions of the *New Jersey*. She was an accurate, lethal fire support platform, which is essential, particularly during an amphibious attack upon the beaches.

As this amphibious feint operation continued, the empty navy landing craft and empty Marine helicopters, with crewmembers only, swiftly headed for the shore inside the territorial waters of North Vietnam. The NVA shore batteries that had been exchanging fire with our cruisers shifted their firing to the approaching assault boats. Antiaircraft fire rose up to greet the faster incoming Marine transport helicopters and their UH-1E Huey gunship escort helicopters.

As the Marine helicopters approached the beach, they quickly turned around and headed back to their LPH carriers *New Orleans* (LPH-11) and *Okinawa*. Below them, the assault boats approached the beach under enemy fire. The assault boats then turned away through the breakers and headed back to their mother-ships.

During this feint, or simulated attack into the north, Colonel Dionisopoulos, representing plans, and Commander Froid and I, representing Operations, were helo-lifted from the *Oklahoma City* to Hue City. There we met with the South Vietnamese Marines to help finalize our actual amphibious assault and helicopter envelopment plan for the *real* attack behind the NVA lines near Quang Tri City.

The South Vietnamese Marines were eager and ready to participate in a counterattack at Quang Tri City. They wanted Quang Tri City back. They also wanted to prove they could recapture the city because their army airborne division had been unable to do so, after trying repeatedly during the last several weeks. This planning session turned into an operation plan that the South Vietnamese named Operation Lam Son 72. If it failed, the remainder of South Vietnam's northern area could fall completely within a few weeks.

Upon our return to the *Oklahoma City*, and as I prepared my briefing for Admiral Holloway, I remembered a previous Lam Son Operation. U.S. Marines had participated in Lam Son 719 with AH-1G Cobra helicopters escorting CH-46 and CH-53 transport helicopters during a large-scale raid into Laos by the South Vietnamese Army on February 8, 1971. This was executed near the city of Tchepone, Laos. The U.S. Marine helicopter support given the ARVN troops was provided just before the receipt of the directive for the retrograde withdrawal of all U.S. Marines out of Vietnam in 1971, one year before we were now planning to support another Lam Son. The name *Lam Son* was based upon an ancient fifteenth-century Vietnamese victory over Chinese invaders. The Lam Son 719 raid into Laos executed in 1971 was not very successful. The extremely heavy concentration of North Vietnamese troops near Tchepone, Laos, was simply too large for the ARVN troops to handle. The NVA rapidly counterattacked the ARVN infantry and artillery. The ARVN commanders had to request assistance to withdraw, or they would have lost too many troops to the pitched battle inside Laos. The U.S. Marine chopper crews heroically flew into intense enemy fire and pulled out the ARVN troops from Laos. The whole operation only temporarily disrupted the NVA supply routes along the Ho Chi Minh trail and the massing of the NVA forces in that part of Laos.

Now, more than a year later, I was personally involved in another Lam Son operation. This one was designated Lam Son 72. Naturally, I thought . . . this one had better be more successful.

Chapter 11

• • • • • • • •

Lam Son 72

South Vietnamese I Corps commander Lt. Gen. Ngo Quang Truong not only wanted to defend Hue City, his goal was to mount a major counteroffensive and recapture Quang Tri City. His limited offensive operations north across the My Chanh River, and then holding positions solidly along the river, gave him time to rebuild his assets.

General Truong's primary objectives were first to strike the NVA forces and supply lines to weaken them, and then go for Quang Tri City.

Lieutenant Colonel D'Wayne Gray had dispersed his ANGLICO teams throughout four military regions.

The defense of Hue City leadership included the South Vietnamese Marine Corps commander, Brig. Gen. Bui The Lan, with the assistance of Col. Joshua Dorsey, senior Marine Corps adviser. Brigadier General Edward J. Miller, 9th Marine Amphibious Brigade Commander, made trips into Hue City from his flagship, USS *Blue Ridge*, to confer with the Hue City defenders.

As the May 1972 defense of Hue City improved, the South Vietnamese Army units, located west of the Vietnamese Marine Corps units, began counterattacks south of Quang Tri City. These attacks met with strong resistance by the NVA. For weeks, the ARVN tried, without regaining the NVA captured ground. The South Vietnamese Airborne Division was brought up along the mountains to the southwest of Quang Tri City. They joined the ARVN counterattacks but could not penetrate the NVA lines. Now, with our plan, which included an amphibious feint, or demonstration, north of the DMZ, which we had discussed at Hue City with the Vietnamese Marines, the VNMC forces were ready to join with the South Vietnamese Airborne Division and the army to counterattack the NVA with increased numbers. Lam Son 72 was ready to begin.

On June 27, 1972, the morning before the selected D-Day, I briefed Admiral Holloway and our staff in the war room. The briefing went something like this:

> The Republic of Vietnam Armed Forces has launched a counteroffensive campaign named Lam Son 72. The objective of Lam Son 72 is to regain major portions of Quang Tri Province.
>
> The operation involves Vietnamese Marine battalions helo-lifted by Seventh Fleet Marine Corps helicopters. CINCPAC has authorized CINCPACFLT to allow us to utilize CTF 76 Amphibious Ready Group CTG 76.1, Marine Amphibious Unit sealift and airlift assets, to support this operation. We have not been authorized to use any of our Amphibious Ready Group infantry forces.
>
> The Seventh Air Force will support the operation by providing:
>
> * Arc-light B-52 air strikes;
> * Pre–H-Hour LZ prep aerial bombardment, close air support, and combat air patrol (CAP; and
> * Two forward air controllers on-station in OV-10A Bronco aircraft.
>
> Surface ships of Task Unit 70.8.9 will provide pre–H-Hour neutralization and destruction fires in the area of operations, LZ prep, helo approach lane suppression fire, and on-call naval gunfire support.
>
> The U.S. Fourth Army Cavalry will provide AH-1G Cobra helicopter gunship escorts from Da Nang for the LZ prep and escort protection for our Marine CH-46 and CH-53 helicopters. This is due to the fact that I am using the Marine Cobras up in North Vietnam's coastal waters in my MarHuk Program and don't have any backup Marine Cobras for this

operation. If the situation eventually dictates, as the battle unravels, I can relocate our Marine Cobras into this Lam Son 72 Operation, however, I would have to close down the MarHuk Operation currently under way.

The counteroffensive will include an amphibious feint, or demonstration, north of the DMZ. This demonstration is now under way, as I speak. It consists of pre–D-Day fires, pre–H-Hour prep fires, and launching Marine helicopters, led by Lt. Col. Charles "Doc" Egges, commanding officer of HMM-165, flying off the USS *Tripoli* (LPH-10).

A preplanned turnaway by the helicopters from a simulated assault landing will be executed when the helicopters get five thousand yards from the beach. The surface assault boats will also simultaneously execute a swift turnaround upon getting close to the beach. For deception purposes, communications will provide simulated surface landings at Red Beach and simulated helicopter landings in LZ Robin. This demonstration initially commenced with a command post exercise by CTF 76 and GTG 76.1 and GTG 79.1 while naval gunfire units from CTG 72 conducted actual fire attacks upon targets in the simulated invasion area of North Vietnam.

The Seventh Air Force has conducted photo recee flights and target attacks on coastal gun sites, AAA and SAM sites, and main route choke points. Rehearsal was conducted yesterday by units of TG 76.1 and TG 79.1. Today, two B-52 arc-light bombing strikes will be conducted prior to the 0800 turnaround time of the simulated assault boat surface attacks and the simulated helicopter assault landings. After the turnaround of the simulated invasion and after the surface assault boats and helicopters are back aboard TG 76.1 ships, the assigned amphibious task group ships will immediately sail south of the DMZ to the actual counterattack staging area off the Cau Viet River to prepare for D-Day.

D-Day for the actual attacks from the sea for Lam Son 72 is scheduled for tomorrow, June 28. However, at 0800 today, the feint, or demonstration, commenced as D-Minus One. The plan of Lt. Gen. Ngo Quang Truong, Commander,

Vietnamese I Corps is that the counteroffensive of Lam Son 72 will be conducted in the following three phases:

Phase I. Actual supporting arms fire for Lam Son 72 will commence today, D-Minus One. Today, starting at 0800, tactical air, artillery, and naval gunfire prep fires will continue until H-Hour, 0800, D-Day tomorrow. This will include 206 B-52 Stratofortresses from Guam and Thailand. They will conduct arc-light raids with each bomber dropping 84 750-pound high-explosive bombs near Quang Tri City.

Phase II. Tomorrow, June 28, D-Day, at H-Hour, the ARVN airborne and VNMC divisions will attack the NVA from the rear, carried by U.S. Navy surface assault boats and U.S. Marine Corps helicopters. They will attack to seize the eastern highway that runs up to Wunder Beach, which is Objective A. They then will seize Hai Lang, Firebase Lavang, and finally, Quang Tri City.

Phase III. On order, ARVN airborne and VNMC divisions will continue attacks across the ground and by way of Marine Corps helicopters to seize Quang Tri airfield and Fire Support Base Pedro. They then will block the northern approaches to Quang Tri City and destroy the enemy therein.

Support during Phase III will utilize fourteen U.S. and three VNN naval gunfire support ships with priority for naval gunfire going to the VNMC division. Thirty B-52 arc-light strikes and 260 tactical air missions are scheduled for each day by the U.S. Air Force.

At L-Hour, 0900, on D-Plus One, sixteen Marine Corps CH-46 and CH-53 assault helicopters from the 31st Marine Amphibious Unit (MAU) will lift off from the LPH USS *Tripoli*. They will be joined by six CH-46 and two CH-53 choppers from the LPH *Okinawa* of the 33rd MAU. The helicopters will lift seven hundred Vietnamese Marines of the 258th VNMC Brigade from a rear area, at Tam My, and head for LZ Flaming. When the helicopters land, the

Vietnamese Marines will push directly for Objective Charlie. Two hours later, a second helicopter lift from Tam Ky consisting of another battalion of seven hundred Vietnamese Marines will be landed in LZ Dove. After capture of Objective Charlie, they will drive toward seizure of Objective Delta. U.S. Marine light helicopter squadron 367 (HML 367) will provide two UH-1E Huey helicopters for command-and-control communications during the helo assaults. Following the helo landings, the transport helicopters will be on-call to land a seven-hundred-man reserve battalion of Vietnamese Marines in a single helo lift to Objective Echo, located just to the north of Quang Tri City. The helicopters will also be available to provide medevac and emergency resupply. The officer-in-charge of the Beachmaster Unit One Team will assume OPCON of the causeway pier and warping tugs set up by the Seabees at Wunder Beach.

On D-Plus Two, the Second Vietnamese Marine Brigade will be landed by VNAF and U.S. Army helicopters in the vicinity of Objective Two. Artillery will be displaced forward by the U.S. Army CH-47 heavy-lift helicopters. Upon link-up of the Second and Third Vietnamese Marine brigades, the Second Brigade will continue the attack to seize Objective Three, followed by attacks against the Quang Tri City area.

Following seizure of Quang Tri City, and on order, one battalion of the First Brigade will continue the attack to seize Quang Tri Airfield, Objective Four, and proceed to attack Firebase Pedro, Objective Five.

The Seventh Fleet support will be primarily for the Vietnamese Marine Corps Division concept of operations. To support this concept, ARG/MAU assets will stage in Area Alpha. LPH *Okinawa* holding area is in Area Bravo and the LPH *Tripoli* will hold back in Area Charlie. Our ship, *Oklahoma City*, will be the turn-back rendezvous point for the helicopters coming out to sea from Tam My Beach, north of Hue City. This will make the NVA think the helicopters are flying out to our ships. As they pass over us, they will turn back inland to the beach, heading directly for the LZ near Quang Tri City. A causeway, or docking pier, will be installed on Wunder Beach for adequate supply logistics. This pier installation has been coordinated by our staff officer, Cmdr. Jim Froid.

The 1st ARVN Division will defend Hue City with four regiments. One regiment will defend the Phu Bai airfield complex.

Admiral Holloway and our staff listened to my briefing. We all waited for the execution of the plan.

As the operation got under way, the North Vietnamese reacted rapidly, just as we had hoped. Although they did not pull back two full divisions as a result of our feint operation, they did pull back one full division from the Quang Tri City area. The one NVA division moved back north across the Cau Viet River and passed north, continuing through the DMZ back into North Vietnam. Our feint operation had taken place where the NVA had moved their one division of troops back into North Vietnam. As the NVA division headed back toward North Vietnam, our ships fired heavily upon them.

The feint operation executed up north on June 27, 1972, was a complete success. It created the opportunity to commence the Lam Son 72 counteroffensive.

On D-Day, June 28, 1972, the 3d ARVN Division in I Corps had the 3d, 5th, 7th, and 8th VNMC battalions jump off and attack north. The NVA, well-dug-in, strongly resisted.

As the NVA refused to withdraw, General Lan directed execution of Lam Son 72. His helicopter-borne assault behind the NVA commenced. General Lan's 1st and 4th VNMC battalions, supported by the U.S. Marines 9th MAB, commenced the helicopter assault by securing key objectives along Route 555.

On D-Plus One, June 29, Marine Corps helicopters lifted off the carriers *Okinawa* and *Tripoli*. They flew to the beach at Tam My, as planned, and loaded aboard the VNMC troops. They then flew out from Tam My and headed for our ships, which sat just off the entrance to the Cau Viet River. As the helicopters flew over our *Oklahoma City* ship, they immediately turned 270 degrees toward the beach and headed directly for the LZs Flamingo and Hawk, northeast of Quang Tri City. It was assumed in the plan that the NVA observing the helo-lift departing from the Tam My beach would think the helicopters were going out to the ships. Instead, they turned back inbound for a rapid flanking attack into the prebriefed landing zone, which was located just to the northeast of Quang Tri City.

Some of my fellow staffers and I had been out on the admiral's bridge when the wave of our Marine helicopters, loaded with Vietnamese Marines, crossed over us and then headed inland for the assault. I took personal movies of the Marine choppers flying overhead. They were right on schedule and escorted by U.S. Army Cobra helicopters that had tiger teeth painted on their noses. I continued taking movies of them as they turned inland over our ship and headed for the beach, eventually flying past the dense smoke that rose about one thousand feet high from the B-52 arc-light bombings. They flew into their LZ. When they were out of sight, I stopped taking movies and ran from the bridge of the ship into the war room to sit, wait, and listen at the radios. The Marine helicopter crews were on their own; there was nothing more that we could do for them. The actual operation was being directed down at the operational level of Task Force 76 amphibious command by the 9th Marine Amphibious Brigade commander, Brig. Gen. Edward J. Miller, and fully coordinated by the Vietnamese Marine Corps Division headquarters at Hue City.

The ANGLICO naval gunfire coordination and control organization was established ashore with the now-trained VNMC naval gunfire spotters, calling U.S. naval gunfire strikes upon the NVA positions. I carefully listened to radios and logged pertinent activities into the war room watch log book.

As the Marine helos, escorted by the army Cobras, headed from our ship toward the enemy positions ashore, I experienced personal thoughts and concerns. Having flown 440 combat missions in Vietnam during my previous two combat tours and having been shot down twice, I felt emotional during this Lam Son 72 helicopter assault. I knew the apprehension the aircrews must have been experiencing, flying into the unknown. How ready was the enemy for a helicopter landing attack to their rear? I had flashbacks, as I heard the wop . . . wop . . . wop of their rotor blades overhead, then fading toward the shore. I well remembered Monday, March 8, 1966, when flying an H-34, lovingly called the Dog, a Sikorsky-built troop transport helicopter, along with twenty-five other choppers. We were moving 465 ARVN troops of the Fifth Airborne Battalion from Tam Ky, in the southern area of Quang Tri Province, to an LZ twenty-five miles south of Da Nang. The antiaircraft fire was intense, and one H-34 was shot down; the copilot was killed, and the pilot was severely wounded. Five other choppers were badly shot up, a total of two crewmembers killed and nineteen wounded. I found, upon my return to base, that my own helicopter had twenty-two bullet holes in it.

My mind swept back in time to several other similar hairy events. One particular day, dubbed Black Sunday, came to mind as I was sitting in the war room on the *Oklahoma City*. That Sunday we suffered five helicopters shot down right in the landing zone. KIAs and WIAs in the LZ, along with damaged helicopters, precluded other choppers from getting into the LZ for immediate rescues. It was a mess.

That thought process lingered with me as the Lam Son 72 helicopters had already passed overhead and landed inside their landing zone, near Quang Tri. Privately, I wished them luck. Yet I knew that on every attack of every war it was a gamble, due to unknown factors that could arise abruptly. I even thought of other situations. I thought about my older brother, John Stoffey, when he was in the famous Eighth Air Force during World War II. On one mission, referred to as Black Thursday, Col. Budd Peaselee, commander of the 384th Bomb Group flying out of England on October 14, 1943, led an enormous air strike against the ball-bearing factory located in Schweinfurt, Germany. In excess of one thousand B-17 Flying Fortresses flew over that target. Sixty B-17 bombers were shot down, with ten-man crews in each bomber. Those staggering losses of six hundred aircrew members on one daylight mission were the greatest aircrew losses ever on one day during that big but relatively short war.

When thinking of that unbelievable fact of war, while sitting at my desk in the war room, my mind continued to wander. I even asked myself, in light of those phenomenal statistics, were we right to be in Europe? Was Hitler more of a threat to the United States in those terrible days in Europe than the North Vietnamese were now, backed by communist nations worldwide? Presently, during this Vietnam War, the North Vietnamese pacts with worldwide communist armies and their supplies by the Soviet Union and Red China were indeed a realistic threat and still growing. Now, more of the world had been dominated by communist armies . . . much more than Hitler had ever imagined he might achieve. The Soviet Union, with its immense nuclear arsenal aimed at the United States, the eastern European captive countries, massive China, aggressive North Korea, Cuba, and many parts of Africa were all under the full control of communism . . . and on the march daily, with a common theme and bond, "Destroy Capitalism." Now, I was hoping and praying that this Lam Son 72 vertical envelopment helicopter assault behind the enemy, near Quang Tri, would result in only minimal casualties. I was acutely aware that most of these Marine chopper aircrews had not been in any previous combat. U.S. Marines, except for a few advisers, had been out of Vietnam a year, since retrograding in 1971. Most of those who last served in-country had already rotated back to the States. Only a handful of these aircrews might have been veterans of real combat. I knew that this would be traumatic for the first-time assault crews.

As I listened in the war room to the radios chattering, I could hear the chopper crews talking to each other. I heard their radio chatter as they were transmitting locations of enemy fire directed at them as they headed for the landing zone. The first wave of CH-46 helicopters landed in the landing zone one minute late. I did not hear anyone reporting taking any hits in the zone. Apparently, they landed close to a North Vietnamese artillery unit, which the South Vietnamese Marines quickly overran, but the subsequent waves of choppers came under intense NVA fire, some getting hits. All choppers returned for a second wave of seven hundred troops and got back into and out of the hot zone safely, despite increasing enemy fire.

U.S. Air Force Capt. Steven L. Bennett, a forward air controller, and his backseater, Marine Corps Capt. Michael B. Brown, ANGLICO aerial observer (AO), in an air force 20th TASS OV-10A Bronco flying out of Da Nang, supported the operation on June 29. Captain Bennett rolled in on a strafe run. On pull-out of his fifth strafe run, an NVA SA-7 Strella heat-seeking missile hit his OV-10A. Bennett, his Bronco on fire, attempted to eject, but his ejection system was damaged. He headed to the Gulf of Tonkin and ditched. The Bronco cartwheeled on impact with the water. Captain Bennett could not get out of the aircraft and sank with it. Captain Brown swam to safety.

That same day of June 29, 1972, Gen. Creighton W. Abrams, who had been the Commander, U.S. Forces, Vietnam, for the last four years, left the war zone to return to the continental United States. He was assigned as the army's chief of staff in Washington, D.C. General Frederick C. Weyand took his position as Commander, MACV in Saigon.

The beginning of Lam Son 72 was successful during June. The ARVN-VNMC, with U.S. Air Force and VNAF air support and U.S. naval gunfire support, killed 1,515 NVA troops; they also captured 15 NVA tanks and took 15 NVA prisoners.

The battle raged around Quang Tri City for two weeks as U.S. Marine and U.S. Army helicopter crews gallantly resupplied the South Vietnamese Marines.

By July 10, the VNMC 1st, 3d, 7th, and 8th battalions formed a line from Route 555 west toward Quang Tri City.

The ARVN Airborne Division was meeting heavy resistance from the NVA on the outskirts of Quang Tri City. Brigadier General Bui The Lan with Col. Joshua Dorsey directed a helicopter assault of one VNMC battalion across the Vinh Dinh River to the northeast of the city as they had two battalions attack the NVA from the east. General Lan requested use of our U.S. Marine helicopters for troop transportation, and we complied. His battalions' missions were to cut off the NVA supply route from the northeast.

On July 11, 1972, at 0600, supporting arms prepped the landing zone area. An arc-light B-52 raid hit fifteen minutes prior to our Marine helicopters landing at noon, L-Hour. HMM-164 and HMM-165 launched thirty-four helicopters from the *Okinawa* and *Tripoli*, lifting 840 1st VNMC Battalion troops, ammunition, and rations for the attack. They were escorted by U.S. Army Cobra helicopters. They flew the eight-mile distance as low to the ground as possible in an attempt to avoid the SA-7 Strella missile threat.

One U.S. Army Cobra attack helicopter knocked out an NVA tank in the landing zone with a TOW antitank missile as the transport helicopters were landing. Twenty-eight of the Marine helicopters received hits by NVA small-arms fire, and five escort Cobra helicopters sustained hits.

During this helo-lift, I was in the war room of the *Oklahoma City* when we received several reports that a CH-53 Sea Stallion, a heavy hauler helicopter, had been shot down. One departing pilot in that area reported that the CH-53 had been shot down as it approached the landing zone. The report indicated that the large helicopter was hit, crashed, and burned.

One of the early reports received from TF 76 indicated that all crewmembers and VNMC troops perished in the flaming wreckage. Later, reports indicated that two Marine Corps crewmembers were reported missing in action and three were wounded. Fifty VNMC troops perished in the burning CH-53. Twenty-nine of the thirty-one Marine helicopters received hits from NVA ground fire.

Some reports stated that some of the other helicopter pilots in the landing zone area had seen a missile home-in on the right exhaust stack of the two-engine CH-53 helicopter. Within minutes, a CH-46 pilot reported that his helicopter had been hit badly by gunfire. He reported that he would have to abandon the helicopter in the landing zone. Another chopper crew flew into the hot zone and picked up the downed helicopter crew. A few minutes later, a second CH-46 troop transport helicopter was reported shot down. The crew was lucky. They got out of their damaged chopper and were picked up by another CH-46 crew. The remaining Marine helicopters returned safely to their LPH carrier. Their army escort Cobras flew south to Marble Mountain airfield, near Da Nang.

Soon after things calmed down, I sent a message to the Marines in the Amphibious Ready Group of CTG 79.1. I asked them if they knew what had shot down the CH-53.

After receiving several messages with descriptions of the shoot-down, I was fairly convinced that the missile downing the CH-53 had to have been a Soviet-built SA-7 Strella missile. At this time on the staff, we had not yet received any messages confirming any shoot-downs of helicopters or fixed-wing aircraft by Strella missiles.

We had not yet received confirmation reports that a Strella had shot down Captains Bennett and Brown, forcing them to ditch in the Gulf of Tonkin. We had assumed their 20th TASS Bronco had been hit by antiaircraft artillery fire.

Our intelligence had told us the NVA artillery units had the SA-7 Strella with them. But until now, we had not sighted any SA-7s south of the DMZ. This first downing of a CH-53 helicopter by a Strella missile opened a Pandora's box. This was a new combat situation. The introduction of this lethal weapon, fired from close proximity of the NVA artillery and infantry, posed a formidable threat, not only to our helicopters but also to our fast-moving jet attack bombers.

I quickly briefed Admiral Holloway on the loss of the CH-53 due to what we thought might have been a Strella missile. The admiral became concerned. Immediately, I sent a message to CTG 79.1 commanding general, First Marine Aircraft Wing (1st MAW), in Iwakuni, Japan. My message directed they ensure that the word got out to all operational Marine jet and helicopter squadrons about the newly introduced threat of the SA-7 Strella, handheld, shoulder-fired heat-seeking missile. My message directed the 1st MAW to ensure that they install ALE-20 flare dispensers and chaff dispensers on all combat fixed-wing, if they hadn't done so yet. Therefore, on their fixed-wing attack aircraft runs they would dispense chaff to jam the antiaircraft radar gun systems, and when dispensing the decoy flares, the SA-7 missiles would, hopefully, home-in on the flares instead of the heat from the exhaust plumes of the engines.

I followed that message with a message I sent to CTF 79, CTG 79.3, and CTF 76 to have them plan to install ALE-29 flare dispensers on all Marine helicopters and OV-10A Broncos as soon as their logistics could supply them with the ALE-29 systems. This would take time and a lot of work by the fixed-wing and helicopter maintenance crews.

The SA-7 Strella missile system is a handheld, shoulder-fired weapon that is an almost exact copy of our hand-fired Redeye missile. The Redeye was the predecessor to the current Stinger shoulder-fired, infrared, heat-seeking missile designed to shoot down low-flying aircraft that pose a danger to frontline troops. The U.S. Marines did not take the Redeye into Vietnam during their years there from 1965 through Nixon's mandated retrograde departure of

1971. They never felt there was an enemy air threat to their ground units in South Vietnam. Therefore, they went into South Vietnam without the Redeyes to preclude their possible capture by the Viet Cong or North Vietnamese Army units. They stockpiled the weapons on Okinawa Island. There were some rare exceptions to that policy, dictated by special circumstances.

Admiral Holloway, always thinking of the big picture, mentioned to me, "I am concerned that the NVA now has introduced this lethal Strella weapon into the south. Now, it could be showing up in the hands of not only the regular NVA units, but in the hands of what is left of the VC. It could possibly be used around major airports such as Tan Son Nhut and Da Nang. It now may become easy to knock down a military transport approaching or departing any airfield. Possibly, they could shoot down a transport carrying a high-ranking official. This type of act could easily, and very cost effectively, influence major events."

Several hours later, we received confirmed field reports that found that of the sixty-eight Vietnamese Marines and U.S. crewmembers in the shot-down CH-53, only five U.S. crewmembers, with several wounded, survived. Two U.S. crewmembers died; eleven South Vietnamese Marines survived, and fifty South Vietnamese Marines were killed. This certainly was bad news, but luckily, there were some survivors from the North Vietnamese Army's newly introduced battlefield weapon. It did not, however, diminish the impact of losing that number of troops nor the losses of the CH-53 and CH-46 helicopters.

As Admiral Holloway pondered the introduction of the SA-7 missile system by the NVA into the battlefield, the Lam Son 72 counterattack continued. Now that the weather had finally cleared, the North Vietnamese were trapped by U.S. Air Force, Navy, and Marine Corps aircraft bombings, including B-52 arc-light massive bombings. This aerial bombing campaign was coupled with daily naval surface ship gunfire from our Seventh Fleet cruisers and destroyers of Task Group 70.8 along the coast, just south of the Cau Viet River.

As limited U.S. support continued, it greatly assisted the South Vietnamese in wearing down the North Vietnamese invaders. The South Vietnamese were slowly regaining their homeland. Our brave chopper crews continued to be exposed to the risks of the full-scale battle. The now-trapped NVA fought hard and maneuvered desperately about the battlefield. The NVA tried to survive the heavy B-52 bombings and stave off South Vietnamese ground counterattacks all along the lines while also subjected to attacking VNMC units to their rear, airlifted by Marine Corps helicopters.

One participant in Lam Son 72, a nineteen-year-old, hard-charging Marine lance corporal and helicopter ground support member by the name of Thomas J. Murphy from Philadelphia, Pennsylvania, volunteered to fly a helicopter combat mission. Young Tom Murphy was not an assigned helicopter crewmember. Tom had joined the Marine Corps and wanted to go to Vietnam. On July 11, 1972, while flying in a CH-46 helicopter assault wave upon the North Vietnamese, just to the northeast of Quang Tri City, Tom Murphy flew into the raging battle, shuttling South Vietnamese Marines for another entrapment attack upon the NVA invaders.

Tom Murphy had been assigned to Marine Medium Helicopter Squadron 165, one of several squadrons in Marine Air Group 36 aboard the LPH carrier USS *Tripoli*. Taking off in a CH-46 assault transport helicopter, Tom was at his assigned position as a waist-gunner. The division of four helicopters made an uneventful, routine flight ashore to a pickup landing zone. They picked up VNMC troops and headed directly to their planned drop-off landing zone, but this leg of the flight was to be far from routine. They were going into the heart of a many-days-old battle area, flying into a heavily defended landing zone. The NVA were everywhere and fighting for their own lives against a strong South Vietnamese counterattack.

Lance Corporal Murphy was excited and ready with his .50-caliber machine gun. He was all pumped up to see the war zone firsthand; this was his first combat mission. The Marine choppers rapidly swept in and soon neared Quang Tri City area.

As they approached the landing zone, which was about three thousand meters northeast of Quang Tri City, they made a landing almost on top of some NVA troops. Tom's CH-46 immediately began taking intense enemy fire. All helicopter waist-gunners returned fire with their .50-caliber machine guns. Tom Murphy was shooting intently when an enemy bullet struck him in the head, passing through his skull and brain and exiting the other side of his head. Despite his severe head injury, Tom continued at his post, firing. Only after the CH-46 helicopter climbed out of the hot zone did young Tom Murphy collapse from extensive bleeding, pain, and trauma. His aircrew members came to his assistance, rendering what little help they could offer to a brain-injured fellow Marine.

That brief battle and moment in U.S. history was to affect this brave Marine's entire life, and that of his close family. Tom Murphy's severe brain damage was to remain with him. A Marine hero to the completion of the mission, serving his country in time of war, Tom was to pay an extremely high personal price. His gallant contributions in the fight would be historically significant toward the eventual fall of this once radically growing, aggressive world menace of communism. Lance Corporal Thomas J. Murphy laid it all on the line, with unwavering devotion to duty.

Back on board the *Oklahoma City*, we finally received more information about the CH-53 that had apparently been shot down by a Strella missile. Reports indicated that Cpl. Stephen Lively, a Marine combat photographer assigned to Battalion Landing Team 1/9, had been aboard that ill-fated CH-53 as it crashed and burst into flames from the missile hit. Corporal Lively assisted the copilot and a crewmember in getting out of the downed burning inferno. Later, Corporal Lively was to receive the Purple Heart and the Vietnamese Cross of Gallantry from Lt. Gen. Louis Metzger, commanding general, III Marine Amphibious Force. Major General Joseph C. Fegan Jr., commanding general, 3d Marine Division, then meritoriously promoted Stephen Lively to sergeant.

Another hero in this same incident of that shot-down CH-53 was Cpl. L. E. Cox, a crewchief of a CH-46 helicopter from squadron HMM-165. He received serious burns when he left his own CH-46 in the hot landing zone, ran over to the blazing CH-53, and helped two U.S. crewmembers and two Vietnamese Marines get out of the burning helicopter. Later, Corporal Cox also received the Purple Heart and Vietnamese Cross of Gallantry.

Within weeks, Lam Son 72, the South Vietnamese counteroffensive campaign to regain major areas of Quang Tri Province, would prove to be a major military success. Without U.S. ground forces, and aided only by U.S. air and sea power, the South Vietnamese Army 3d Division with the South Vietnamese Marines recaptured control of the area from the communists. They were ready to attempt to recapture the North Vietnamese prize of Quang Tri City.

Chapter 12

• • • • • • • •

Retaking Quang Tri City

The 325th NVA Division, reinforced by elements of the 308th and 320th NVA divisions, defended their hold on Quang Tri City.

Each day of July and August 1972, the VNMC Brigade 258 slowly fought forward as they increased their attacks against the now-defending NVA at the Quang Tri Citadel.

As the Lam Son 72 attacks by the Vietnamese Marines began with the objective of retaking Quang Tri City, the 1st VNMC Battalion, commanded by Maj. Nguyen Dang Hoa, landed in a landing zone beside the city. They immediately encountered heavy NVA fire and began taking casualties as they fought elements of the 320B NVA Division.

Major Hoa led his troops in a charge into two trench lines of NVA defenders, killing 126 communists, capturing 6 NVA, and strategically flanking the NVA position.

Marine Corps 1st Lt. Stephen G. Biddulph, ANGLICO naval gunfire spot team officer, was wounded in the leg, shortly after disembarking from one of the assault helicopters. Marine Corps Capt. Lawrence H. Livingston, adviser to the 1st VNMC Battalion, carried the wounded Lieutenant Biddulph to safety. ANGLICO Cpl. Jose F. Hernandez came under heavy NVA fire as he helped wounded VNMC troops. At the same time, he called in naval gunfire to halt attacking NVA reinforcements.

Hand-to-hand fighting followed as the 1st VNMC Battalion fought to expand their perimeter and forced the NVA to withdraw to the west toward Quang Tri City.

During this same three-day period, the 7th VNMC Battalion attacked an armored regiment command post destroying numerous NVA tracked vehicles and trucks.

Because of the extended attacking locations of the VNMC Battalions that were helicopter-lifted behind the NVA, resupply would become a problem. Therefore, a request came in for the Seventh Fleet commander, Admiral Holloway, to provide a five-section causeway pier at Wunder Beach, now fully under control of the South Vietnamese.

My boss, Jim Froid, rapidly coordinated providing the USS *Alamo* (LSD-33) and a tugboat for support of the causeway pier. He also dispatched an underwater demolition team to clear the area of obstacles.

On July 13, naval construction personnel, Seabees, began installing the pier. The Seabees completed installation by 1300 the same day. A U.S. Marine shore party and naval beachmaster went ashore from TF 76 to supervise the Vietnamese for operation of the pier.

By July, the Vietnamese Marines had cut the NVA line to Quang Tri City along Route 560. By July 20, the VNMC Division positions were consolidated to prepare to attack the NVA holding Quang Tri City. The NVA, defending Quang Tri City, intent on keeping it as a symbol, dug in to fight and retain it.

General Lan, fully aware the NVA were concentrating on defending Quang Tri, executed raids against other NVA units on the NVA left, or eastern flank, along the coast.

Using our Marine helicopters and the VNMC Brigade 147, with three battalions, the VNMC enveloped the NVA. This forced the NVA to retreat north back across the Thach Han River.

This helicopter assault took place on July 22 when Lieutenant Colonel Hertberg's HMM-164 helicopters launched with the VNMC 5th Battalion in two waves of 688 troops in each wave. U.S. Army F Troop Cobra helicopter gunships escorted the U.S. Marine assault helicopters carrying the VNMC troops into LZ Lima. The VNMC 5th Battalion, after meeting some resistance, linked up with two ground-assaulting VNMC battalions. The battle ended on July 24 with 133 communist troops killed. Three NVA tanks and two armored command vehicles were captured. Numerous NVA weapons were captured along with an NVA one-hundred-bed hospital.

During the night of July 27, the VNMC Brigade 258 moved forward and relieved the ARNV Airborne units that had been attempting to defeat the NVA at the Quang Tri Citadel. For the next four days, the NVA fired more than one thousand artillery and mortar rounds against the Marines, who responded with their own heavy firings.

Marine Corps 1st Lt. Edward G. Hayden II, ANGLICO, was killed. Marine Corps Capt. David D. Harris, adviser to the VNMC, who was next to Hayden, was wounded with severe leg and back injuries.

The communists continued to defend the city strongly with their 325th NVA Division, reinforced by elements of the 308th and 320th NVA divisions and supporting units in southeastern Quang Tri and Thua Thien provinces. During July, these communist forces paid a heavy price in their defense of invaded territories in the Quang Tri City area. The NVA suffered 1,880 killed, and the VNMC captured 51 armored vehicles, 7 antiaircraft guns, 4 artillery pieces, a 20-ton ammunition dump, and 1,200 individual weapons. Yet, during the start of August 1972, the NVA still held control of most of Quang Tri City. The NVA still had many artillery units in the Ai Tu combat base area and the area west of the Thach Han River. Sub Unit One, 1st ANGLICO, under command of Lt. Col. George E. Jones, was extremely busy coordinating counter fire of naval gunfire and air strikes against the NVA artillery. ANGLICO aerial observers flew dawn to dusk forward air control spotting for U.S. and Vietnamese Air Force attack bombers.

On August 22, a large NVA force occupying Quang Tri City attempted to break out from the Citadel. The attacking 8th VNMC Battalion forced the NVA back into the Citadel. This certainly was an indication that the NVA realized the South Vietnamese counteroffensive had the North Vietnamese divisions trapped inside of Quang Tri City, the prize the North Vietnamese intended to hold. The Lam Son 72 counteroffensive was well under way. At this juncture, the VNMC had suffered 1,358 killed and 5,522 wounded during this five-month battle period, while killing 10,285 communists.

After a month of shelling and attacks upon the NVA inside the Quang Tri Citadel, the VNMC 1st, 3d, 5th, 6th, and 8th battalions attacked through the rubble to reach the Citadel. On September 5, the NVA attempted a counterattack but failed.

At 1015, on September 15, the VNMC 3d, 6th, and 7th battalions reached the Citadel walls as massive NVA artillery fire rained upon them.

At 1700 on September 15, the Vietnamese Marines had gotten into the Citadel and had complete control of it as the NVA retreated. The VNMC 6th Battalion raised the red and yellow flag of the Republic of South Vietnam over Quang Tri City's west gate at 1245. The city was liberated.

During the seven-week battle to recapture Quang Tri City, the VNMC suffered 3,658 casualties, 25 percent of the entire South Vietnamese Marine Corps, which had proven its fighting capabilities with its recapture of Quang Tri City.

With this victory, the VNMC began movements back toward the north on September 25, 1972, to reoccupy territory lost during the NVA Easter invasion.

Six NVA divisions still remained in Quang Tri Province as the heavy monsoon rains began to fall in October. The heavy rains would continue until the end of the year.

The U.S. Air Force began dropping propaganda leaflets onto North Vietnam. The reason for this was to stir up the populace by telling them that unless they got their leaders to leave South Vietnam alone, the B-52 raids would increase. Simultaneously, our Seventh Fleet started a navy radio broadcast program, using Vietnamese language tapes, directed into North Vietnam. The information disseminated by the leaflet drops and the Seventh Fleet radio broadcasts said about the same thing. The only problem with the navy radio transmission program was that the large number of rural peasants in North Vietnam did not have radios like the city folk in the Haiphong–Hanoi areas. To move along with the propaganda program, the navy rapidly purchased thousands of inexpensive mini-radios from a commercial source in Japan. These simple radios had only one station or frequency band. The Seventh Fleet began parachuting these mini-radios with special-ordered small parachutes, which were normally used for night illumination flare-drops. Along with this operation, my boss, Jim Froid, placed the USS *Ogden* (LPD-5) off the North Vietnamese coast.

Commander Froid, with minimal assistance from me, set up a program using weather balloons tied to the mini-radios. After establishing everything by message traffic, Froid flew over to the *Ogden* in the admiral's Black Beard One helicopter. While on the *Ogden*, the ship's crew began launching hundreds of mini-radios into North Vietnam. Using the prevailing winds from the sea, the airborne balloons carried the radios into North Vietnam. There was no scientific way to determine exactly where all the balloons were falling into North Vietnam, and therefore it was not known how effective this was. The navy continued the Vietnamese radio broadcasts, and soon we found out that the balloon-carried radios must have been received by many of the rural peasants in North Vietnam. Within three weeks of commencing the balloon-carried radios program from the *Ogden*, it stirred unrest in the communist propaganda world when they found out the radios had been manufactured in Japan. Because Japan was not involved in this war, and we were holding the defensive shield up for Japan against the continual ravenous expansion of communism in this area of the world, the communists immediately began to exploit this navy program. Magically, communists worldwide began screaming in the liberal news media that Japan was supporting the U.S. war effort in Vietnam. The Japanese Communist Party, particularly, began exerting political pressure upon the Japanese government, claiming Japan was getting involved in the Vietnam War.

During one period of launching mini-radios from the *Ogden*, the crew ran out of weather balloons. Typical innovative sailors, the crew promptly came up with an immediate, temporary solution, which—when I read the message to us from the *Ogden*—left me wondering exactly how to brief the admiral the next morning. Commander Froid and I discussed it and decided to tell the admiral exactly what was happening.

Because Jim Froid and I daily briefed the admiral, Jim covering his responsibilities of the amphibious ships and I jointly responsible for the amphibious Marines aboard those ships, we often briefed simultaneously. During the briefing, covering numerous ships and associated Marine activities, I nervously said to the admiral, "Admiral, the *Ogden* ran out of weather balloons late yesterday afternoon. The crew quickly improvised and continued launching the radio operation using available prophylactics . . . condoms . . . rubbers, filled with helium."

The admiral looked amazed. The rest of the staff began to laugh. Froid continued, "According to a message from the *Ogden*, the condoms worked perfectly and carried the mini-radios directly over the enemy's homeland."

Naturally, there were mixed expressions on the admiral's face, and the staff quickly teased Jim and me about the impact this would have when the *Ogden* hit ports for liberty. "The VD rate in the fleet is certain to go up, with the loss of so many condoms used for the war effort. However, on the brighter side, the VD rate in North Vietnam should drop significantly."

As the Paris peace talks continually experienced ups and downs, during the fall of 1972, rumors swept around the world that the end of the war was near.

On October 27, 1972, the North Vietnamese said they were willing to meet again in Paris with Henry A. Kissinger, but they demanded a Vietnam Peace Treaty be signed by October 31, 1972. North Vietnamese chief negotiators Le Duc Tho and Xuan Thuy invited Kissinger to have champagne and tea with them in Paris because they felt there was nothing more to negotiate. They quoted, "President Nixon, himself, approved the text of the lengthy treaty. The North Vietnamese feel that the text had been heavily discussed and was completed since October 20. The text had been sent by message from the United States to the North Vietnamese Prime Minister, Pham Van Dong." We then read the message traffic that laid out Hanoi's peace terms in Paris, which had been forwarded to our staff, via the chain of command:

Both parties agree that the following will take place:

- Stop the bombing and mining in North Vietnam
- Sign the peace agreement
- Ceasefire takes effect in South Vietnam
- Preparations for elections in South Vietnam will commence
- All U.S. and allied troops withdraw from South Vietnam within sixty days
- Prisoners of war to be returned

- Gradual unification of North and South Vietnam
- United States to contribute to North Vietnam for reconstruction

We all read the various documents the lawyers at the Paris negotiation teams drafted. As the talks continued, some of the language within the text changed. Because we on the Seventh Fleet staff would be responsible for executing the U.S. side of much of those agreements, we carefully studied each new Paris text change to ensure we understood our forthcoming obligations. Naturally, though, the most important item to all of us continued to be the return of the prisoners of war.

More weeks passed and nothing new came out of Paris, or the Joint Chiefs of Staff.

On November 1, 1972, Saigon headquarters directed the VNMC to send Marines north, across the Thach Han River. The NVA counterattacked with massive firepower. The 6th VNMC Battalion could not advance farther. This was to be the last major effort by the South Vietnamese Marines to cross the Thach Han River before the ceasefire agreement in January 1973.

On November 11, 1972, the 4th VNMC Battalion made another attempt to cross to the north side of the Cau Viet River. The NVA strongly resisted and held the northern side of the Cau Viet River.

During December 1972, as Kissinger continued negotiations at the Paris peace talks, the frontlines remained about the same. The North Vietnamese units of the 27th NVA Regiment, 48th NVA Regiment, and 101st NVA Regiment dug in and continued to hold their captured territory north of the Cau Viet River, south of the DMZ inside of South Vietnam.

ANGLICO transitioned the South Vietnamese to give their artillery forward observers the naval gunfire support capability. By the end of December 1972, the South Vietnamese began calling upon our Seventh Fleet's Task Group 70.8 naval gunships for fire support.

Captain Leo Marshall became our new chief of staff, relieving Captain Godfrey. The new plans officer was Capt. Edward Briggs, young and sharp and very enthusiastic. His full crop of blonde hair made him look much younger than his years of experienced naval service reflected. He rapidly applied that experience and became deeply involved in all Seventh Fleet activities and our daily staff actions in support of Admiral Holloway's objectives, eventually becoming chief of staff.

Considering the massive numbers of North Vietnamese, reinforced with large numbers of tanks and heavy artillery, they were up against, the U.S. supporting units and the South Vietnamese casualties were minimal. Despite the heavy losses suffered by the South Vietnamese Marines during the recapture of Quang Tri City, when compared with the numbers of NVA troops and supporting artillery and tanks, the losses were less than they could have been. This was primarily due to air and naval gunfire support. Historically, from a military viewpoint, Lam Son 72 was this long war's most successful strategic military victory. It totally prevented devastating defeat at the hands of the large North Vietnamese invasion force. The North Vietnamese plan to divide the south and conquer it had failed.

The Marine Corps helicopters' vertical envelopment behind the NVA, carrying South Vietnamese Marines and landing close in to the units, was totally successful. It was a classic maneuver for future military historians and tactical commanders to keep in mind.

This helicopter vertical envelopment concept was invented by the Marine Corps in the 1950s, and then followed by heavy usage in U.S. Army tactics. It was, and continues to be, practiced by the Marine Corps amphibious forces.

The all-out invasion launched by North Vietnam on March 30, 1972, had failed to accomplish its objectives. General Vo Nguyen Giap of North Vietnam had set as his announced goals to destroy the South Vietnamese Army, demonstrate the failure of the Nixon administration program, overthrow the regime of South Vietnamese President Thieu, and capture Saigon for a total victory.

When the dust settled in late 1972, General Giap had lost more than 60,000 killed of the 200,000 regular NVA troops committed in the invasion through and around the DMZ, the central highlands of Kontum and Pleiku, and from Cambodia into the Mekong, attacking toward Saigon. Giap had lost 400 tanks of the 600 tanks that he had committed into South Vietnam. Most important of all, Giap had not witnessed any so-called liberated South Vietnamese civilians joining his North Vietnamese liberators as supporters.

What General Giap did learn, the hard way, was that conventional warfare requires air superiority, and in or near coastal areas, naval gunfire support is paramount.

Our Seventh Fleet support of the South Vietnamese Lam Son 72 counterattack cost us, and the U.S. Air Force, the loss of a fair amount of jet attack aircraft and aircrews, until we knocked out the SAM sites in the DMZ. The Seventh Fleet also lost a CH-53 helicopter to the SA-7 Strella missile, costing the lives of two Americans and many South Vietnamese Marines. The Seventh Fleet also lost two CH-46 helicopters plus several severely wounded Marines, which impacted us all. The U.S. Army and Air Force lost more helicopter aircrews during this time frame due not only to supporting Lam Son 72 but also search-and-rescue efforts.

The reports of these brave Americans killed and wounded made me think back in time again . . . seven years ago . . . during the summer of 1965, when I was stationed at Da Nang. Many others, at that time, had the same thoughts that I had. Put simply, we had the common sense question: Why didn't the Americans fighting in Vietnam get permission and congressional approval and support to declare war and bomb the hell out of the enemy in Hanoi? We could have started the systematic destruction of their communications system and then their troops in North Vietnam, followed by our supporting an invasion of North Vietnam by the South Vietnamese, across the DMZ, and a U.S.-supported amphibious assault at the heart of the enemy, Haiphong Harbor. This would have immediately brought the war to the enemy's homeland. North Vietnam's cities and villages would have been ravished as the battlefield, not the cities and villages of unfortunate South Vietnam. Non-supporting congressional members created pressure on several of our serving presidents in a row. As a result, limits were placed upon military commanders at all levels under directives dictating Rules of Engagement, which quite often were rules favorable to an aggressive communist army. The U.S. military, during the Vietnam War, was directed to fight as if, during World War II, we had tried to free France from Hitler's army by purposely fighting only in France and not bombing, and then not invading, the heartland of Germany. The old saying remains true: "If you're going to talk, then talk. If you're going to fight, then fight. But if you're going to fight, fight to win with all that you have at your disposal." While the South Vietnamese were recapturing much of the

NVA-invaded land using Lam Son 72 and other counterattacks, our Seventh Fleet staff was heavily engaged in numerous other activities. We were deeply involved in squeezing North Vietnam by mining Haiphong Harbor and North Vietnam's waterways. During this period of vicious land war of 1972, the Seventh Fleet and the Seventh Air Force were finally authorized to bomb North Vietnam and sever main supply routes from communist China and the Soviet Union.

As this took place, our staff members' orientation also turned to the activities of our bumbling politicians in Washington and Paris. What would our political leaders returning to the Paris peace talks demand and obtain from the North Vietnamese communists who had just suffered a major defeat on the battlefields? What would they give to the North Vietnamese? Would our civilian leaders leverage the North Vietnamese failure of their major invasion into South Vietnam . . . while the United States did not recommit ground-fighting units back into Vietnam to help the south?

Chapter 13
• • • • • • • •

Stranglehold on North Vietnam

The U.S. Air Force continued dropping propaganda leaflets into North Vietnam. The USS *Ogden* also continued sending helium-filled balloons carrying suspended mini-radios so that North Vietnamese peasants could hear, in their own language, a plea to them to demand that their communist government stop their invasion into South Vietnam and that the bombings would continue until they did so.

Our *Oklahoma City* returned to the gunline from Subic Bay and continued day-and-night gunfire raids into North Vietnam and on-call naval gunfire support to the South Vietnamese south of the DMZ.

Our Marine detachment was elated and the morale was high. First Lieutenant M. E. Shivers, working for the detachment commander, Capt. J. D. Chase, stated, "We finally got a piece of the action. The troops are happy at being able to take turns topside with their M-60 machine guns set up for antiair defense, teaming with the navy Redeye missile gunners up there, during the day-and-night raids into North Vietnam. The troops are getting a chance to see our ship's 5- and 6-inch guns hit the enemy shore batteries and other targets. They also enjoy watching other ships pounding the coastal defense sites, including watching the magnificent, classic cruiser *Newport News*, the largest gunship on the line since the departure and re-mothballing of the battleship USS *New Jersey*." Colonel Jim Dionisopoulos, in the plans division, made arrangements so some of the Marines assigned to the Marine barracks, Yokosuka, Japan, could cycle down from Japan and join our *Oklahoma City* Marine detachment for temporary duty. This gave these young, eager Marines actual participation in raids, while assigned topside on the ship's teak-wood deck, manning M-60 machine guns during the day-and-night shore bombardments. These young Marines just loved it.

By now, the stranglehold noose was around North Vietnam and tightening daily. This was something that could have easily been executed seven years prior, back in 1965, if Secretary of Defense Robert S. McNamara had used some common sense to carry the defense of South Vietnam to the enemy in North Vietnam as was tactically done during World War II.

Laser-guided bombs had been developed. The air force had a video-guided, laser bomb system and had used several such bombs to see how accurate they were. They worked fairly well but needed improvements. Their accuracy did help minimize civilian collateral damage in North Vietnam, and it certainly added to the air force inventory. The term *collateral damage* became commonplace, coming from the Department of Defense due to communist sympathizers exerting pressures within the United States claiming Americans were killing and injuring civilians during our strikes against military targets. This certainly was not a term bantered about during our World War II struggles in Europe or Asia; in fact, the reverse was true. The collateral damage to civilians was immense during WWII and helped turn the enemies' peoples against the adventures of their dictatorial governments in Germany and Japan. But communists worldwide, and their supporters in the United States, pushed this concept and the term, resulting in not only endangering our aviators and aircrews but causing many of their deaths.

Admiral Holloway, now in command of the Seventh Fleet, strongly felt his fleet should also be using laser-guided bombs from Task Force 77 aircraft carriers' attack groups, but the fleet did not yet have inventory of laser-guided equipment or bombs. The admiral was disappointed because he always was on the leading-edge of warfare, and he wanted to utilize these new bomb technologies but didn't have them.

Admiral Holloway was an exemplary leader. I had tremendous admiration for his style of leadership. I strongly felt that if this Vietnam War had been World War II, Admiral Holloway would have been known worldwide as another "Bull" Halsey or Chester Nimitz. Holloway was daring, in depth in his decision making, and followed through on his decisions. In this particular case, the navy was still only in the testing stage of laser-guided bombs at their China Lake Naval Test Center in California.

I knew, though, that the reliable Marine Corps had already tested handheld laser-guidance systems and had them in their inventory for use by our ground units' forward air controllers. The ground FAC, holding the laser designator, could illuminate the target for the smart bomb dropped by an aircraft. The smart bomb would pick up the illumination, or designation, and the bomb would adjust and home-in on the illuminated, designated target. Because I had already recently sent five two-seater TA-4F jets into Da Nang for naval gunfire spotting and had assigned aerial observers to fly in the backseats for naval gunfire support, all I had to do was tie in the handheld laser-guidance system personnel and equipment with the detachment of TA-4Fs. First, though, the flight crews would have to conduct some training of flying with, and using, the handheld laser designators.

I then coordinated sending some of the TA-4Fs with aircrews from Da Nang to the Naval Air Station Cubi Point in the Philippines. There, they practiced with aerial observers in the backseat of the TA-4Fs, using the handheld laser-designator guidance system. The designating AO could control the direction of the falling bombs by illuminating, or laser spotting, the target from the backseat of the TA-4F. The bombs dropped by Marine TA-4Fs would then track onto the laser-illuminated target until impact. This system worked well for visual control of the bomb, from drop to hit. The only shortcoming was that the TA-4F aircrew would have to stay near the target area until impact of the laser-illuminated target destruction. This would expose the aircrews to much antiaircraft weapons danger.

While the Marine Corps TA-4F laser-guided bomb training was continuing in the Philippines, the U.S. Air Force continued dropping their laser-guided bombs upon targets in North Vietnam. The North Vietnamese soon found out the U.S. Air Force was using sophisticated, laser-guided bombs and that the video-tracking devices they used were Japanese Sony TV monitors.

The communist-influenced news media and other liberal news media quickly picked up on this and again focused on accusations that Japanese TV monitors were helping American bombs score hits onto North Vietnamese military targets. The communists, in cities around the world, rallied again. Communists and associated anti–Vietnam War protestors went to the streets shouting that the Japanese were participating in this war against communist North Vietnam. And yet, in reality, Japan should have been involved in defending South Vietnam against communist invasions to protect their own capitalistic nation. Because Vietnam was a helluva lot closer to Japan for communism to militarily move after Vietnam, Japan certainly should have been in some sort of supporting role for South Vietnam's defense because their constitution prevented them from participating in military activities. We Americans were again holding up the free enterprise shield of defense at a cost of tremendous financial and human sacrifice as capitalism (free enterprise) flourished in Japan, and they concentrated on non-military technology for their commercial markets of the world while reaping enormous financial rewards.

In the meantime, Admiral Holloway expedited the navy laser-guidance system. He began incorporating them into his Seventh Fleet carrier task groups.

Another sensitive problem arose for our staff to determine what to do. The North Vietnamese had three full divisions in Cambodia. The NVA had been temporarily pushed back into Cambodia from South Vietnam. These NVA units presented a grave danger to Saigon because they could counterattack anytime from Cambodia toward Saigon.

JCS directed us to do limited, surgical bombing inside Cambodia upon known locations of these NVA divisions. Because we did not have any armed forces inside of Cambodia at this time, nor were there airborne forward air controllers, we had to devise some method to pinpoint the NVA troops in Cambodia and control the precise bombing upon the enemy.

It so happened, as usual, that the Marine Corps had in its inventory something tangible that I could use for that Cambodian problem — the Marine Corps had navigational backpack radio beacons called RABFACs. A ground operator would simply turn on the beacon transmitter and it would emit a radio signal. Our Marine Corps all-weather A-6A Intruder attack bomber aircrews would then home-in on the beacon. The clandestine Cambodian ground FAC would then give the Marine A-6A aircrew a distance in kilometers and a heading from the beacon to the target, the NVA troops. The A-6A aircrews would then drop their bombs on that verbally directed location from the RABFAC homer.

We Marines had these devices in our amphibious forces so that when Marines would be directed to hit the beaches during an amphibious assault, their company-level units' ground FACs could get bombing support immediately if the weather turned bad and precluded visually controlled close air support.

I could not pull the RABFAC equipment from our Marines in TG 79.1 in Commander Froid's Task Force 76 amphibious ready groups afloat off Vietnam. One never knew when Washington might have approved a major amphibious invasion of North Vietnam. These ARGs had to be ready to attack ashore anytime. Their parent organization, the 3d Marine Amphibious Force, back in Okinawa, did have a limited number of backup RABFAC beacon units spread throughout the 3d Marine Division.

I sent messages to CG III MAF to coordinate pulling twenty-eight RABFAC beacon units from the Marines on Okinawa. We then coordinated having the RABFAC equipment delivered to clandestine operators spread throughout eastern Cambodia, where we knew the North Vietnamese troops were poised to invade South Vietnam again.

Suffice it to say that command and control over these RABFAC beacon devices, once inside Cambodia, was extremely difficult. Additionally, I did not receive daily reports from the Cambodian operatives. Usually, I received a once-a-week summary report from the Cambodian operatives. I did get a daily report from the Marines that they had flown the missions, but they would not know if they hit any worthwhile target on the ground. I used this sketchy bomb damage assessment information for briefing the admiral and staff. The real results of these bombings were questionable. We really had no way of confirming if the bomb damage assessments given to us from the Cambodian clandestine operatives were accurate, but it was all we had at the time to attempt to strike those NVA troops poised in sanctuaries of Cambodia. I continued monitoring this RABFAC operation in Cambodia, even after the Vietnam War ceasefire, until JCS directed that all bombings in Cambodia should cease.

During this period, the South Vietnamese had captured a document from a high-level Viet Cong in Quang Tri Province. It was translated and turned out to be the Viet Cong ceasefire plan.

This plan was to be implemented immediately upon a Paris ceasefire agreement. The plan first incorporated a new name for the Viet Cong forces. They would change their name from People's Liberation Armed Forces to that of Army of Unity. The plan included some of the following:

- Families in South Vietnam have been ordered to enlarge their bunkers and dig additional tunnels to conceal North Vietnamese and Viet Cong troops and store weapons and supplies until the puppet army is in a nonfighting posture.
- Each family has been ordered to prepare a pot of mud to blot out all painted South Vietnamese flags and slogans from buildings.
- Each family has been ordered to prepare at least seven of the red and blue, gold-starred Viet Cong flags, which will be used in civilian victory parades preceding the Army of Unity troops in villages and hamlets, which the communists may take under control in any truce agreement.
- All South Vietnamese government documents, including individual identity cards and land titles, must be destroyed.
- In addition to the Viet Cong flags, each family will prepare a peace flag with the outline of a dove on a white background.
- A twenty-three-category death list for individuals marked for execution including students who attended schools abroad, regardless of duration or purpose of study; key personnel of religious sects; clerks who once worked for the French or Japanese or are currently employed on foreign-owned (French) plantations; persons who retain economic relationships with French business or carry on correspondence with Frenchmen, and organizations such as malaria prevention or land survey; government

administrative personnel above the district level; members of reactionary South Vietnamese political parties, including the governmental opposition Dai Viet Party; members of ethnic minorities who are discontents, sorcerers, scoundrels, robbers, blackmailers, prostitutes, speculators, smugglers, and squad leaders of the home guard.

To those of us reading that and other documents, the inclusion of sorcerers on the death list was rather interesting because Xuan Thuy, who headed the Hanoi delegation in the Paris peace talks, had made his living in 1945 as a traveling sorcerer. He was then known as Thay Phap, the evangelist. He had traveled through north and central Vietnam, selling curses, spells, and cures.

The South Vietnamese were still concerned about those NVA divisions in Cambodia, near Saigon, and asked for more U.S. attack-aircraft support. JCS authorized the Seventh Fleet to send more aircraft into South Vietnam, close to Saigon.

I drafted a message to the Marine command on Okinawa to dispatch, from the 1st Marine Aircraft Wing in Iwakuni, Japan, two Marine attack jet squadrons of A-4E Skyhawks to Bien Hoa airfield, near Saigon. Marines had not previously been stationed at Bien Hoa. Then I had to get approval from our new operations officer, Capt. Bill Russell. Russell, like McKenzie before him, was a naval aviator and equally astute—a fine man to work with. He had adapted rapidly to our hectic combat circumstances and fast-decision-making activities. After Russell gave me his okay, I sent the message to the 3d Marine Amphibious Force Commander (CG III MAF), Lt. Gen. Louis Metzger, and an information copy to the commanding general, 1st Marine Aircraft Wing, Maj. Gen. Leslie Brown. The message read as follows:

FMCOMSEVENTHFLT
TOCTF 79
INFOJCS
US AMB TOKYO, JAPAN
CINCPAC
COMUSMACV
CINCPACFLT

7TH AF
CTG 79.3
EXECUTE DIRECT ATTACK AIRCRAFT TO RVN
THIS IS AN EXECUTE MESSAGE. REPEAT.
EXECUTE MESSAGE. DIRECT TWO FULL
SQUADRONS OF A-4E AIRCRAFT TO BIEN HOA
AIRFIELD, RVN. NO GROUND SECURITY UNITS
REQUIRED. ROUTE FLIGHT VIA CUBI POINT,
PHILIPPINES FOR GROUND REFUELING. DO
NOT UTILIZE AERIAL REFUELING. DESGINATE
DETACHMENT CTU 79.3.7 OPCON REMAINS
COMSEVENTHFLT. MISSION FRAGS FROM CDR
7TH AIR FORCE VIA MARINE LIAISON OFFICER.
REPORT ALCON WHEN AIRCRAFT LAND CUBI
POINT.

Within two hours, Admiral Holloway personally called me and said, "Meet me down in the communications center. Admiral Clarey, CINCPACFLT, wants to talk about your recent execute message regarding OPCON of your two Marine A-4E squadrons going into Bien Hoa."

Soon, the admiral and I were inside the ship's communication center. From there, Admiral Holloway had a long discussion with Admiral Clarey over the garbled classified communications net. Clarey expressed concern about OPCON remaining with the Seventh Fleet commander, instead of relinquishing it to the Seventh Air Force commander at Tan Son Nhut Air Force Base, near Saigon. Because Bien Hoa Air Base was close to Saigon, Admiral Clarey was concerned about what the air force might think and say regarding OPCON of the Marine attack bombers. Admiral Holloway put me on the classified, covered radio network, and I explained my position to Admiral Clarey. He seemed satisfied and replied, "If those Marine jets stay there for some length of time, you may have to change that operational control to the Seventh Air Force."

Within two days, on May 17, 1972, two Marine A-4E jet squadrons from Marine Air Group 12 in Iwakuni, Japan, VMA-211 and VMA-311, arrived at Bien Hoa. They were led by Lt. Col. Willis E. Wilson, commanding officer of VMA-211, the Avengers, and Lt. Col. Kevin M. Johnston, commanding officer of VMA-311, the Tomcats. Two days later, the Marine Air Group 12 A-4E pilots began flying combat missions, building to thirty-six sortie flights a day by the end of May. The Marine A-4E squadrons flew a variety of missions against the NVA divisions that were advancing upon the provincial capital of An Loc. The NVA forces consisted of the 5th, 7th, and 9th NVA divisions, 33d NVA Infantry Regiment, 274th VC Regiment, and the 74B NVA Regiment. The NVA had tanks, artillery, and the ubiquitous SA-7 shoulder-fired, heat-seeking antiaircraft weapon. Never before had such NVA firepower been seen in this part of South Vietnam.

Marine Air Group (MAG) 12's A-4E squadrons supported the 5th ARVN Division, 21st ARVN Division, 3d ARVN Ranger Group, and the 3d ARVN Armored Brigade. The air control was coordinated by the Direct Air Control at Bien Hoa, the Tactical Air Control Center at Tan Son Nhut, and by the 21st Air Support Squadron and VNAF flying airborne FACs out of Tan Son Nhut.

On May 21, 1972, General Metzger ordered a rifle company to form the 3d Battalion, 9th Marines, to be sent to Bien Hoa for ninety days to protect MAG-12 aircraft and personnel. Captain Nathaniel R. Hoskot Jr. brought his 161 Marines to Bien Hoa and set up defensive positions. On May 23, the NVA launched a rocket attack against the VMA-211 and VMA-311 flightline.

On September 26, Marine Capt. James P. "Waldo" Walsh from VMA-211 was flying a mission to attack NVA troops that had captured the Quan Loi airfield, near An Loc. On pulling off a bombing run, Walsh's A-4E was hit by NVA 37mm antiaircraft fire. He ejected. The airborne FAC controller lost sight of Walsh's parachute as Walsh disappeared into dense jungle. A search-and-rescue helicopter was immediately launched, and the aircrews homed-in on Walsh's intermittent radio beeper signals. The lead helicopter was hit by NVA ground fire, and darkness and thunderstorms quickly cancelled the search-and-rescue effort. NVA troops quickly captured Walsh. Captain Walsh made an attempt at escape by diving under water during a stream crossing, but the communists quickly recaptured him. Captain James P. Walsh was listed missing in action by his squadron VMA-211, but he was alive and was the last Marine to be captured by the North Vietnamese communists. He survived POW camp, making it home in 1973.

In October 1972, the NVA fired sixty-one rockets upon Bien Hoa. Unpredictable fall weather added an additional challenge to the bombing efforts of the A-4E aircrews. Maintenance crews activated avionics equipment that assisted the A-4E aircrews during periods of reduced visibility by allowing the aircraft to pull out of high-angle attack dives at six thousand feet.

By December 9, 1972, Marine Air Group 12 had flown its ten-thousandth combat sortie, averaging forty-nine sorties per day over a seven-month period. At the end of 1972, MAG-12's two A4-E squadrons had completed 12,574 combat sorties, flying 15,214 hours, and had dropped 18,903 tons of ordnance. During that period, MAG-12 had three Marines killed, one missing in action, and eleven wounded, and lost three A-4E aircraft.

Secretary of the Navy John W. Warner cited MAG-12 for its efforts in providing close air support within fifty meters of friendly positions in defense of Hue, Kontum, and An Loc during the successful allied effort in these campaigns.

One day, when our ship had moved away from the hostile shore of North Vietnam, I went for a jog on the deck of the *Oklahoma City*. While on deck, I met a young Marine corporal, Andy Parker, who was temporarily assigned to our ship from the Marine barracks in Yokosuka, Japan. The Marines were serving a few weeks on the M-60 machine guns, providing cover against low-flying MiG attacks during the ship's day-and-night raids.

Parker said, "Sir, I'm sure glad to be aboard as a gunner."

"You can thank Colonel Dionisopoulos for getting you Marines down here for a rotation on the M-60s, Corporal."

"Sir, I only recently joined the Yokosuka Barracks from Camp Pendleton, and you wouldn't believe the turmoil back in the States. At Camp Pendleton protestors picket the main gate every day. Jane Fonda rents a house nearby in Oceanside and uses it as anti-war headquarters. The protestors carry the enemy's flags, both Viet Cong and North Vietnamese. They're all screwed up."

"Yes, they're completely wrong in supporting the communists. Their actions fuel the hope of the enemy in Hanoi. The North

Vietnamese actually think that these activists will start a communist revolution back in the States."

"They've got the good guys completely mixed up with the bad guys. They don't understand what this battle is all about."

"It's not just about communism versus free enterprise. We're fighting for many freedoms that some countries don't have. That includes freedom of speech, of course, but the activities of some of these protestors is not free speech—not while our young men are being killed by the communists—it's supporting the enemy. Fonda's as much a traitor as Benedict Arnold. Some day she'll look in the mirror and realize what she's done."

Just as we both finished our laps around the deck, the ship's alarm sounded for general quarters. In minutes, our ship thundered with the fire of her 5- and 6-inch guns to help keep the communists from completing their long-range conquests.

President Nixon maintained his Vietnamization program as the retrograde of U.S. troops from South Vietnam continued. On May 11, 1972, Adm. Thomas H. Moorer and the JCS had approved a plan to move MAG-15 from Da Nang to Nam Phong, Thailand, specifying that the Marines' opening operations at Nam Phong would be on an austere basis. Major General Leslie E. Brown, commanding general of the 1st Marine Aircraft Wing, said, "Austere basis was an understatement."

General Brown and his assistant wing commander literally got down on their hands and knees to look over maps to determine just where the hell Nam Phong was located in Thailand. Soon, intelligence reports indicated to General Brown that there wasn't anything there. There was no electrical power, little water, and no fuel. All fuel would have to be driven up from ports at Utapao and Sattahip by trucks.

Nam Phong had a ten-thousand-foot concrete runway and an eight-thousand-square-foot hangar that had been built by the U.S. Air Force in 1967, as directed by Secretary of Defense Robert S. McNamara. The runways, with absolutely nothing else, were located fifteen miles northeast of the town of Khon Kaen. The runways were centrally located 340 miles west of Da Nang and 300 miles southwest of Hanoi, Democratic Republic of Vietnam (North Vietnam).

General Les Brown, one of the sharpest Marine aviation generals in the history of the Corps, immediately realized that Nam Phong was just on the edge of the flying range of the F-4s and A-6As to be able to support ground actions in the Military Region 1 area of South Vietnam.

On May 14, General Metzger, III MAF commander, had General Brown, 1st MAW commander, fly down from Iwakuni, Japan, to a meeting on Okinawa. The meeting included the 3d Marine Division and 3d Force Service Support Regiment to figure out how to handle this tasking and move MAG-15 from Da Nang to Nam Phong and support it in the middle of nowhere.

Brigadier General Andrew W. O'Donnell, the assistant wing commander, was dispatched to Thailand with a survey team to determine existing facilities and to coordinate with the U.S. Embassy, the Military Advisory Command, Thailand (MACThai), Seventh Air Force, and other supporting agencies.

As a result, during July 1972, in the middle of our supporting the South Vietnamese against the North Vietnamese massive invasion, we received a directive from CINCPACFLT. We were directed to withdraw MAG-15's three F-4 Phantom squadrons, VMFA-115, VMFA-211, VMFA-232 and the A-6 Intruder squadron, and VMA (AW)-553 from Da Nang and order them to move to Nam Phong, Thailand. We were specifically directed to leave the MAG-12 two squadrons of VMA-211 and VMA-311 at Bien Hoa because the South Vietnamese made a special request to Washington to keep MAG-12 near Saigon.

The objectives of military defense assistance to the Republic of Vietnam remained the same. We were not to draw down on the air strike capabilities. Yet, we were directed to be prepared to eventually withdraw all combat aircraft from South Vietnam.

Upon receipt of the CINCPACFLT directive as originated by JCS, I quickly drafted a message, and Capt. Bill Russell, our operations officer, released the message to all Marine commands.

Task Force Delta was organized at Iwakuni, Japan, on May 24, 1972, and included the headquarters of Task Force Delta, 7th Counter Intelligence Team, Detachment 152, Detachment 36, Logistics Support Group, and the MAG-15 at Da Nang. MAG-15 promptly packed up and began relocating from Da Nang to Nam Phong, Thailand, on June 16, 1972, when eleven F4B aircraft of VMFA-115 launched from Da Nang, flew combat missions en route, and landed at Nam Phong. The next day, June 17, combat air strike sorties began from Nam Phong. Task Force Delta was to remain as an organization in Nam Phong until well after U.S. involvement in Vietnam ended. It is hard to believe, but MAG-15 executed this directive to relocate without missing a single combat mission. Task Force Delta (MAG-15) began flying combat sorties out of Nam Phong, Thailand, on June 24, 1972, under the command of Brig. Gen. Andy O'Donnell. General O'Donnell, personally, eventually flew twenty-five combat missions out of Nam Phong with VMFA-115.

As soon as the Marines from Task Force Delta got somewhat settled in at Nam Phong, Colonel Dionisopoulos, our Seventh Fleet Marine officer in our plans office, and I flew off the fantail of the *Oklahoma City* in the admiral's Black Beard One helicopter to Da Nang. En route to Da Nang, we flew low over China Beach and what was once our Marble Mountain airfield. Now, only a U.S. Army aviation unit occupied the western side of the airfield. As we flew over the half-abandoned airfield, I looked at the eastern side where MAG-16 had operated and I had flown helicopters and OV-10A Broncos out of during my two thirteen-month combat tours in Vietnam. The U.S. Marines had retrograded from Marble Mountain airfield in 1971 under the Vietnamization program.

As we crossed over Marble Mountain airfield at five hundred feet, heading for Da Nang, three miles west, I looked down and actually saw the old Quonset hut where I spent thirteen months and the area where I spent another thirteen-month tour living in a tent. But the nostalgic thing was when I saw the still-standing, weather-beaten, white-painted chapel we had built there for our Catholic chaplain, Father Paul Toland, in 1965. My tent-mate, Father Toland, and I personally had looked all over Da Nang City until we found a small foundry to cast a bell for that small base chapel.

Black Beard One quickly landed at Da Nang. There, Colonel Dionisopoulos and I were scheduled to meet an incoming navy Lear jet from Naval Air Station Cubi Point, Philippines. The jet would fly us to Nam Phong, Thailand, so we could see how the Marines were settling in. We then could brief Admiral Holloway on the Nam Phong situation.

The admiral's chopper dropped us off at Da Nang and departed. We looked around for the jet, but we didn't see one. We checked with a small navy detachment that operated P-3 patrol aircraft from Da Nang and had them query NAS Cubi Point, Philippines as to the location of the jet. The navy at Cubi Point reported that the scheduled jet had mechanical problems and wouldn't pick us up until the next morning. We were stuck there for the night.

As we wandered along the flight line, more rumors circulated that everybody in Da Nang expected the war to end that night. The local Vietnamese seemed to really believe the war was about to end, but Jim Dionisopoulos and I had not seen any message traffic on the Seventh Fleet staff that might indicate there could be truth to the rumor. Naturally, we didn't believe all the talk going around.

Because we were stuck, and we were the only U.S. Marines there, we settled in for a peaceful evening. We wandered over to the famous Red Dog Saloon on what had been the Marine Corps side of the runway up until the retrograde of 1971 and the recent departure of MAG-15 to Nam Phong, Thailand. The bar was located about two hundred feet west of the runway, in the middle of the sprawling base. As we walked into the once-lively bar, we saw a few navy P-3 aircrew members and heard nothing but dead quiet.

After I had a few rum and Cokes and cooled down, I left the Red Dog to find a place to sleep. Colonel Dionisopoulos had gotten into a serious card game, and I knew he'd be playing until the wee hours of the morning. I told him I'd look for a place to sleep in the abandoned Marine barracks behind the saloon. In minutes, I had found a place to sleep. It was stinking hot, just as I remembered Da Nang from my previous two tours of duty, but despite the heat I soon fell asleep.

I must have been sleeping only about twenty minutes when the NVA fired five rockets into the Da Nang airfield, which all exploded right in the area where I had been sacked out. One rocket exploded right outside the wall next to where I had been sleeping. Luckily, the rocket exploded on the other side of a concrete telephone pole. The explosion blew the pole down against the wall of the barracks. Fortunately for me, the exploding steel shrapnel was divided by impacting the concrete pole before it ripped through the wall of the barracks. I was sitting up, startled from the terrific bang of the rocket, as the hot steel pieces flew by on both sides of me. Several more rockets exploded nearby. I was too shaken to get up and run to a bunker. I just sat there and thought . . . *Yep, this is the night they expect the war to end.*

After about five minutes, Colonel Dionisopoulos rushed into the barracks to see if I might have been hit by one of the rockets. He stopped halfway down the barracks and just stared in amazement. First he looked at me sitting in the cot. Then he looked at the two large holes sliced through the barracks wall, and then he saw the steel shrapnel lying on both sides of my cot. Some of the shrapnel had landed on both cots either side of me, and although the steel pieces on the floor seemed to have cooled, both cots were still smoking from the hot steel impacts.

Dionisopoulos shook his head and said, "Goddamn it, Bob! What the hell did you do the last time you were in town to piss off the NVA so badly? How the hell did they know you were back in town?" Then he broke out in laughter. I didn't think it was very funny.

I responded, "Hell, Colonel, here I am . . . I've been out of this damn country for two years now. I'm out there on the water sitting safely on a ship, where I can't be rocketed. I come to town bearing good tidings of peace and joy, for just one night. I didn't even bring a gun, and these bastards fire rockets at me. They just don't appreciate my goodwill gestures and fine cooperative personality."

The next morning, the navy jet arrived from Cubi Point to pick us up. The young navy pilot let me fly as copilot. We climbed out from runway three-six and turned west, heading toward Thailand. We quickly crossed the Ho Chi Minh superhighway trail, without any antiaircraft fire coming up at us. We continued uneventfully across Laos, passing over Ban Tang Vai and Kong Kok until we crossed over the Thai border. We finally landed at the isolated Nam Phong Task Force Delta airfield in Thailand.

It had just rained, and the entire Nam Phong airbase, except for the concrete runway and taxiways, was knee-deep in mud. We were met by a young Marine captain in a jeep who drove us to the Task Force Delta headquarters tent. Only then did we find out that General O'Donnell was back in Japan. MAG-15 commander Col. Aubrey W.

Talbert greeted us and proceeded to brief us on all activities. We then took a jeep tour of the airbase so we could get a general sense of the facility and see all the construction work that was under way. Totally isolated and muddy from the heavy rains, it was a godforsaken, forlorn area to have to live in. It didn't take long for the Marines at Nam Phong to nickname the base the "Rose Garden," after the Marine Corps recruiting slogan "We don't promise you a rose garden," which was popular at the time. I took a photograph of a small one-man structure built to keep sentries dry during the heavy rains. This structure was on the only road leading to the entrance to the base.

The Task Force Delta Marines, with the hardworking, skilled Navy Mobile Construction Battalion 5 (Seabees), Marine Air Base Squadron–15, and Headquarters and Maintenance Squadron–15 had been doing wonders at this isolated airfield. A 200,000-gallon tactical aviation fuel dispensing system and storage for 360,000 gallons of bulk fuel was constructed. A bomb dump and 310 strong-back huts for living quarters as well as 128 administrative and maintenance structures were erected.

Colonel Dionisopoulos and I thanked Colonel Talbert for his informative tour of the isolated airfield and departed for Da Nang in the navy jet. A Marine CH-46 picked us up at Da Nang and flew us out to the *Oklahoma City* as it steamed off from Hue City.

The next morning I briefed Admiral Holloway and the staff in the war room, offering them a vivid description and photographic tour of the wonders of the Rose Garden. The slides accurately depicted the bleak, muddy nothingness of the new Marine air base at Nam Phong, Thailand.

After the briefing, Admiral Holloway jokingly said, "That's just the way you Marines like to live . . . in the mud and tents. You just love austerity."

On August 23, General O'Donnell passed command of Task Force Delta to Brig. Gen. Robert W. Taylor.

Admiral Holloway had a great sense of humor and would jibe me frequently about the Marine Corps. Sometimes he was joking, sometimes he wasn't. An example was when the attack aircraft carrier USS *America* (CVA-66) joined our Seventh Fleet from the Atlantic Sixth Fleet. The *America* had aboard a Marine F-4J Phantom squadron, Marine Fighter/Attack Squadron (VMFA)-333, the Shamrocks, from Marine Corps Air Station (MCAS) Cherry Point, North Carolina. The commanding officer of VMFA-333 was Lt. Col. John K. Cochran, the executive officer Maj. Lee Lasseter.

Admiral Holloway, a naval aviator and former commanding officer of the carrier USS *Enterprise*, upon having the *America* "chop" to control of his Seventh Fleet, was fast to chide me about the incoming Marines on one of his carriers by saying, "Oh! Oh! Here come the Marines on our carrier. We're sure to have problems."

Over the next few weeks, though, the Marine pilots proved their outstanding flight operations off the carrier *America*. On July 14, VMFA-333 began combat flight operations off the *America*, flying missions of fighter patrol and ground attacks in Route Packages 3 and 4. In August, they began flying night armed reconnaissance missions. In September, they began flying missions in Route Package 6b.

In late August, the *Oklahoma City* was scheduled for an R&R visit to Singapore so the crew could have some time away from the gunline. En route, Captain Kanakanui directed the ship to head a little south so we'd cross the equator. (By navy tradition, men who have never crossed the equator are called "polliwogs"; men who have crossed the equator are called "shellbacks"—a somewhat more desirable moniker.) As the ship crossed the equator, we humble servants of King Neptune had to crawl the length of the deck on our hands and knees while the superior shellbacks beat our backs and asses with wooden broomsticks and taunted us with insults. The sailors knew me and took particular pleasure in having the opportunity to beat a Marine officer.

Then we were forced to crawl through putrid, rotting food as it baked in the August heat. The stench was sickening. As if that weren't enough, we had to kiss the fat, garbage-smeared belly of King Neptune (played by one of the ship's navy chiefs). The shellbacks reveled in the entire scene, while 750 polliwogs endured to become proud shellbacks themselves, initiated into the solemn mysteries of the deep.

Crossing-the-line ceremonies are among the most ancient naval traditions. Since antiquity, seafaring men have used the crossing sea frontier of the equator as a test of the worthiness of inexperienced seamen.

Once we docked just north of Singapore, still sore from the beatings, I was ready to leave the ship. My boss, Commander Froid, would cover my job as I went ashore for a few hours of liberty. My wife, Eleanor, and several other staff wives had flown to Singapore from Tokyo to join us during our ship's exotic port visit. The U.S. ambassador to Singapore had invited Admiral Holloway and his wife, Dabney, and our staff and their wives to an embassy "Welcome to Singapore" party.

It just happened that the USS *America* had arrived in Singapore and anchored in the bay the day before. Its crew and pilots needed R&R from the gunline as well, so the ambassador invited the commanding officer and his staff and the commanding officers of the fighter/attack squadrons to the party as well.

At the party, I introduced Lt. Col. John Cochran, CO, VMFA-333, to Admiral Holloway. Despite some teasing of Cochran by Holloway about Marine flying versus navy flying, John Cochran enjoyed the party. Among the hearty, aggressive Marine pilots from VMFA-333 was Capt. Andrew S. "Scotty" Dudley Jr., who had been an enlisted Marine in 1967, when the Vietnam War had been going on for two years for the Americans. Dudley was sharp and had been selected for the enlisted commission program. After officer candidate and basic school, Dudley was selected for pilot training at Pensacola, Florida. He would eventually make a career out of being a Marine Corps pilot.

Two weeks or so after the embassy party, while both the *America* and *Oklahoma City* were back in the Gulf of Tonkin, VMFA-333 were again flying missions, now in the Route Package 6B area.

On September 11, two VMFA-333 F-4J Phantoms launched for combat air patrol. Major Lee T. "Bear" Lasseter and his radar intercept officer, Capt. John D. "Little John" Cummings, flew aircraft call sign Red One. Captains Andrew S. "Scotty" Dudley Jr. and James W. "Diamond Jim" Brady manned Red Two.

Red One and wingman Red Two were flying in a heavily defended airspace in North Vietnam. This was their second flight of the day, covering air attacks of targets north of Haiphong. Both F-4Js were armed with Sparrow AIM-7E2 and four Sidewinder AIM-9D missiles. The USS *England* (DLG-22) was the tactical air commander and ground control intercept operator controlling the flights.

The Red flight met an airborne KA-6 fuel tanker to top off for the mission. Red One, piloted by Lasseter, had finished fueling, and Red Two, piloted by Dudley, was still refueling when the strike force aircraft they were assigned to cover arrived and began their attacks. Dudley had not completed refueling, but Lasseter felt his wingman had enough fuel to complete the mission and ordered Dudley to disconnect from the tanker and join him to their assigned combat air patrol station.

Prior to arriving at their combat air patrol (CAP) location, Chief Radarman Dutch Schultz on the *England* reported locations of two bogey MiGs at twenty thousand feet over Phuc Yen airfield, ten miles northwest of Hanoi.

Lasseter's flight closed on the MiGs, and at seven miles they recognized two MiG-21 Fishbeds. The MiGs were low at one thousand feet. Dudley called, "Tally ho! Tally ho! Twelve o'clock. Keep going straight."

Lasseter fired two Sparrow missiles, and the silver-colored MiG turned inside the missile and climbed. The second MiG reversed course and flew out of the area to the north.

Lasseter and the remaining MiG engaged at subsonic maneuvers below one thousand feet directly over the Phuc Yen runway. Cummings, in the backseat of Lasseter's Red One, reported SAM and antiaircraft warnings were going off. Lasseter fired two more Sparrows and two Sidewinders during the chase, but the MiG stayed close to the ground and evaded the missiles. Dudley, now dangerously low on fuel, was ready to disengage from the chase. Suddenly, the MiG reversed his turn and Lasseter had a clear shot at it and fired a Sidewinder. The MiG-21 exploded in a fireball. Cummings shouted, "Okay, splash one MiG-21!"

Red One and Red Two rejoined and headed back toward the *America*, but a third MiG made a pass on Red Two, Dudley and Brady. Pilots Lasseter and Dudley each fired their remaining Sidewinder. The MiG quickly left the area.

Dudley was critically low on fuel, and both aircraft slowed and climbed to fourteen thousand feet in an effort to reach the safety of the sea. They flew directly over Hanoi City to cut short their departure route. Massive ground fire attempted to hit them, and SAM and antiaircraft artillery warnings continued inside their cockpits.

Lasseter's Red One was hit by a SAM and was burning. Dudley and Brady in Red Two were unable to link up with a tanker aircraft. Dudley and Brady stayed with Lasseter and Cummings as their Red One fighter's engine flamed out. Lasseter and Cummings ejected feet wet into the Gulf of Tonkin. Dudley and Brady were out of fuel and ejected over the sea. The *England* launched a helicopter combat search squadron (HC-7) chopper to pick up Lasseter and Cummings. The USS *Biddle* recovered Dudley and Brady.

This was the only MiG kill of the war by a Marine Corps unit, but two other Marines did shoot down enemy aircraft during the war as exchange officers with the U.S. Air Force: Capt. Doyle D. Baker on December 17, 1967, with the 13th Fighter Squadron, and Capt. Lawrence G. Richard on August 11, 1972, with the 585th Tactical Fighter Squadron.

VMFA-333 continued combat flight operations and flew reconnaissance missions during the bombing halt above the 20th parallel directed by President Nixon in October 1972. On President Nixon's resumption of bombings north of the 20th parallel on December 18, VMFA-333 resumed attack missions.

On December 23, 1972, I had to brief Admiral Holloway that Cochran, commanding officer of VMFA-333, had been shot down while on a mission over North Vietnam from the *America*. Cochran and his backseat radar intercept officer ejected just east of the Haiphong Channel inlet. A navy search-and-rescue helicopter crew promptly plucked them from the sea and returned them to the *America*. Cochran had suffered a cracked tailbone from the ejection shot. He had to be relieved by Lasseter, who assumed command of VMFA-333.

Admiral Holloway again worked me over the coals about this Marine pilot that he met briefly at the embassy party in Singapore some months back. Personally, I felt terrible that Cochran had to give up his squadron because of a simple injured tailbone.

As I thought about John Cochran, I remembered the embassy party and our ship's visit to Singapore. I had to chuckle about an episode my wife and I had during that visit when we traveled to the Malayasian city of Johor Bahru. After we arrived, we found a taxi and asked the driver to take us to the sultan of Johor Bahru's castle where, thirty-one years earlier, famous Marine Corps pilot Col. Gregory H. "Pappy" Boyington, of Black Sheep Squadron fame, had visited the sultan's castle.

It was 1941, and the sultan and Boyington were drinking and partying in Singapore. Because they got along so well, the sultan invited Boyington back to his castle in Johor Bahru. After they arrived, Boyington discovered that the walls in one of the sultan's bathrooms were plastered with nude photos of American movie starlets. Pappy later said that he was "surprised" by the decorative wall hangings he found there (this was years before *Playboy* magazine).

Now, because my wife and I were right outside the entrance to the castle, we wondered if the photos of nude movie stars still lined the bathroom walls. Eager to find out, I walked right up to the gate and asked the guard on duty straight out. He had a good laugh and said that he'd heard that story years ago.

In 1965, I had been stationed at Da Nang, when Pappy Boyington was also there, representing an electronics firm, so I specifically asked him if the story about the nude pictures in the sultan's bathroom were true. Pappy swore it was.

Leaving the sultan's castle, Eleanor and I returned to Singapore to meet our staff fleet surgeon, Doc Burkhart, and his wife, Nancy, at a bar in the nostalgic Raffles Hotel. I told Doc Burkhart that my wife and I had failed to conclusively verify Pappy Boyington's story about the nudie pictures in the sultan's bathroom.

The next morning, we sailed back to the Gulf of Tonkin on the *Oklahoma City*. Eleanor flew back to Japan. I was to meet Eleanor again in a few months when our ship was due to visit Bangkok, Thailand, and much later in Hong Kong. Those financially costly rendezvous made up for the long months at sea when Eleanor and I could not be together. They also gave Eleanor the opportunity to visit the major cities in Asia.

In October 1972, while off North Vietnam on the *Oklahoma City*, I was reviewing some of the message traffic sent from CINCPACFLT, and I read an unclassified message sent to all the Seventh Fleet, stating:

FM CINCPACFLT MAKALAPA HI
TOALPACFLT

UNCLAS//N0300//

POSSIBLE SEDITIOUS BROADCASTS OVER RADIO
HANOI
CINCPAC 0622457 OCT 72 (PASEP)
REF (A) SETS FORTH REQUIREMENT TO
DETERMINE IF CERTAIN JULY 1972 BROADCASTS
OF SPEECHES ALLEGEDLY MADE BY JANE
FONDA DURING A TRIP TO NORTH VIETNAM
WERE HEARD BY ANY MEMBERS OF U.S. ARMED
FORCES IN SOUTHEAST ASIA, AND IF SO, THE
NAMES OF SUCH SERVICEMEN, CIRCUMSTANCES
UNDER WHICH THE BROADCASTS WERE HEARD
WERE ALSO REQUESTED.
ADDRESSEES ARE TO MAKE SUCH
DETERMINATIONS
WITHIN THEIR COMMANDS AND ADVISE
ORIGINATOR NLT 11 OCTOBER, FOR
CONSOLIDATION INPUT TO CINCPAC.
NEGATIVE REPLIES NOT REQUIRED.

We never heard anything more officially about Jane Fonda and her broadcasts and other activities while she visited the enemy in North Vietnam—and we were supporting South Vietnam against the massive 1972 invasion from the North Vietnamese. But I have heard many combat personnel—both then and during the years since—express tremendous anger with Fonda for her visit to the enemy's capital as the United States waged war against that enemy and as that enemy killed and captured U.S. troops by the hour. Many felt Fonda was a traitor and called for legal action against her for her alleged treasonable activities in and around Hanoi in July 1972.

Later, millions of people, including me, did see several French photos and North Vietnamese–released photographs of Jane Fonda in magazines and newspapers. She was pictured wearing an NVA helmet as she sat beside an antiaircraft gun, ostensibly scanning the skies for U.S. bombers as if she were preparing to gun them down. There were also photographs of the communist supporter capitalist shaking hands with North Vietnamese soldiers outside Hanoi.

Despite the ultimate free-world victory over the Soviet communists, this is a part of American history that cannot be erased, nor can the memories of those who fought in Vietnam against the North Vietnamese and Viet Cong. These propaganda photos were released worldwide, and they forever placed Jane Fonda in the documented history of the Cold War between U.S. democracy and Soviet-backed communism.

The North Vietnamese—both privately at the Paris peace talks and publicly in the news media—frequently claimed that Jane Fonda and other U.S. antiwar protestors would soon force the United States to withdraw its support for South Vietnam's defense against the North Vietnamese invasions. So the war was actually *prolonged* by the protestors who waved North Vietnamese and Viet Cong flags by giving Hanoi the incentive to hold on until U.S. withdrawal instead of negotiating an immediate end to the war. And as the war dragged on, we continued our work on the Seventh Fleet staff to help the South Vietnamese defend their homeland.

On November 26, 1972, I presented a personal opinion paper to Admiral Holloway in which I claimed that the U.S. Navy did not have the capability in the western Pacific to move an entire Marine amphibious force anywhere due to the lack of adequate numbers of amphibious ships. Additionally, I claimed that if we did have that movement capability, we would still have a significant challenge if we were to attempt to conduct a full-scale invasion anywhere. Because the battleship USS *New Jersey* had been returned to the United States in 1971, we simply didn't have the big guns like those that covered the Marine Corps invasions and island-hopping quests during World War II.

The heavy cruiser USS *Newport News* was the only ship in the active fleet with major 8-inch guns. Our *Oklahoma City* had the next-largest guns, at 5 and 6 inches. Without the 16-inch guns of the WWII battleships, it was questionable just how effective a full-scale invasion would be against the Soviet-supplied North Vietnamese 130mm coastal defense guns.

USS *Oklahoma City* (CLG-5), light missile cruiser and Seventh Fleet flagship, under way from Japan to Vietnam, January 1972. *USN Photo*

Six-inch guns firing from the *Oklahoma City* off the coast of North Vietnam, April 1972. *USN Photo*

Vice Admiral W. P. Mack (seated, fifth from left) and the Seventh Fleet staff aboard the *Oklahoma City*, May 22, 1972. *USN Photo*

Lieutenant Colonel Robert E. Stoffey, Assistant Amphibious Warfare Officer and Marine Air Officer, in his Seventh Fleet operations office aboard the *Oklahoma City*. *USN Photo*

Vice Admiral James L. Holloway III, Commander, Seventh Fleet, from 1972 to 1973. *USN Photo*

Eight-inch guns firing from heavy cruiser USS *Newport News* (CA-148) during the North Vietnamese Army (NVA) 1972 Easter Offensive. *Department of Defense Photo (USN) 1151898*

The Dong Ha Bridge shortly after USMC Capt. John W. Ripley set off demolition charges he had placed, slowing the NVA advance into Dong Ha (at left). *Courtesy of USMC Col. John W. Ripley*

NVA Soviet-built tank passing through destroyed city of Dong Ha, April 1972. *Courtesy of USMC Maj. Charles D. Melson*

NVA Soviet-built AT-3 Sagger wire-guided antitank missile. Just visible behind it is a Soviet-built SA-7 Strella handheld surface-to-air missile (SAM). Both proved deadly during the Easter Offensive. *Courtesy of USMC Capt. Edwin W. Besch, Ret.*

Vice Admiral James L. Holloway III, Commander, Seventh Fleet, wears a flight suit while visiting one of his attack carriers to discuss combat flight operations. *USN Photo*

Admiral John S. McCain II, Commander-in-Chief, Pacific Command (at left), and Gen. Creighton M. Abrams, Commander, U.S. Military Assistance Command Vietnam, at Tan Son Nhut airbase, Republic of Vietnam. *USN Photo*

Marine F-4B Phantom from squadron VMFA-312, which was reintroduced into Da Nang to assist the South Vietnamese in counterattacking the North Vietnamese invasion of 1972. *USMC Photo*

Oil storage facility in Hanoi after a U.S. Navy airstrike destroyed twelve buildings and damaged thirteen more. Eighteen storage tanks were destroyed and thirteen damaged, cutting Hanoi's oil storage capacity by 80 percent. *Department of Defense Photo*

Navy F-4B Phantom, from squadron VF-154 off the carrier USS *Ranger* (CVA-61), drops 1,000-pound bombs on North Vietnamese military target. *USN Photo*

After parked MiGs and antiaircraft weapons have been taken out, Navy A-4 Skyhawk attack aircraft go after the runway itself with 1,000-pound bombs. *USN Photo*

North Vietnam's principal oil-storage complex, estimated to have had a storage capacity of 76,000 metric tons, on the Cam Cau River, two miles outside of Haiphong City. Navy pilots from the carriers USS *Hancock* (CVA-19) and *Ranger* destroyed storage tanks, buildings, and docking facilities. *USN Photo*

The Haiphong railway and highway bridges, destroyed by U.S. Navy A-6 Intruders from the USS *Enterprise* (CVAN-65). *USN Photo*

Landing craft transporting South Vietnamese Marines (VNMC) head for the well deck of the USS *Juneau* (LPD-10) during preparations for Operation Lam Son 72, July 11, 1972. *Department of Defense Photo A800676 by USMC Gunnery Sgt. R. E. Priseler*

Marine CH-46 transport helicopters from the USS *Tripoli* (LPH-10) land VNMC near Hue City for Lam Son 72. *Department of Defense Photo A800670 by USMC Cpl. Stephen Lively*

South Vietnamese Army Lt. Gen. Truong, Commanding General, I Corps (left), and USMC Brig. Gen. Edward J. Miller, Commanding General, 9th Marine Amphibious Brigade, inspect captured NVA weapons in Hue City. *Department of Defense Photo A800649 by USMC Gunnery Sgt. R. E. Priseler*

Marine AH-1J Cobra helicopter lifting off from the fantail of LPD ship similar to that used in Marine Hunter Killer (MARHUK) operations in 1972. *Bell-Textron Photo*

The USS *Cleveland* (LPD-7) provided the operational platform for Cobras conducting MARHUK operations against waterborne logistic craft offloading from Chinese merchant ships. *Courtesy of Carol McCaleb*

A Chinese merchant ship leaves a trail of bags of rice to float ashore. By 1972 U.S. forces had destroyed all main supply routes and mined major harbors and waterways, effectively cutting off supplies to North Vietnam. *Author Collection*

U.S. Air Force B-52D dropping 750-pound bombs over Haiphong area during Operation Linebacker II, December 1972. *National Archives*

Vice Admiral James L. Holloway III (left) with Lt. Col. Robert E. Stoffey and his wife, Eleanor, after the admiral presented Stoffey with the Vietnamese Air Cross of Gallantry, November 10, 1972. *USN Photo*

Stoffey inspects a Redeye SAM gunner's stanchion aboard *Oklahoma City*. Stoffey introduced the position on twenty-two Navy ships after a low-flying MiG bombed the destroyer USS *Higbee* (DD-806). *Author Collection*

Stoffey served two thirteen-month combat tours, flying 440 combat missions before joining the staff of the Seventh Fleet commander for a third combat tour of two years. *USMC Photo*

The USS *New Orleans* (LPH-11), with a mix of Navy and Marine CH-53 helicopters aboard, prepares to neutralize mines in Haiphong Harbor during Operation End Sweep. *USN Photo*

Three Navy CH-53D helicopters aboard the USS *Dubuque* (LPD-8). The MK-105 hydrofoil sled in the open well deck will be attached to a towline for mine clearance sweeps in Haiphong Channel, February 29, 1973. *National Archives*

A Navy CH-53D Sea Stallion from squadron HM-12 pulls an MK-105 mine-sweeping sled in the main shipping lane of Haiphong Channel during End Sweep. *National Archives*

A U.S. Navy mine explodes in Haiphong Channel during End Sweep, 1973. The photo was released to the media to prove that the U.S. was clearing the mines as agreed in the Paris Peace Accords. *USN Photo*

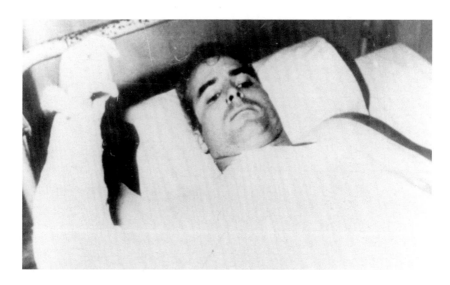

Lieutenant Commander John S. McCain III after being shot down and captured in North Vietnam on October 26, 1967. He remained a POW until the end of the war in 1973. After retiring from the Navy in 1981, he continued serving his country by starting a long career in politics. *National Archives*

American POW returnees depart the bus that brought them to Hanoi's Gia Lam Airport on March 27, 1973. Twenty-seven POWs were released that day. The war was finally over for them. *USAF Photo by Staff Sgt. Larry Wright*

Admiral Holloway acknowledged my point paper with a written return note on it stating, "Well expressed and of much interest. If I am in a position some day to change that situation, I will."

I had hoped that the ideas I presented would go with this dynamic admiral wherever he would go. Admiral James L. Holloway III would go on to become Vice Chief of Naval Operations (VCNO) and then CNO and member of the Joint Chiefs of Staff at the Pentagon in Washington, D.C. While he was CNO, he was instrumental in laying the groundwork for President Reagan's approval to bring the battleship *New Jersey* back into the fleet. Admiral Holloway was also influential in having the rapid-fire Vulcan antiaircraft guns installed on numerous ships to back up the existing installed missile defenses.

Chapter 14

• • • • • • • •

Marine Hunter Killers

As the ground battles continued to rage just south of the DMZ, we were finally allowed to go after the real enemy, North Vietnam. With the mining of North Vietnam's Haiphong Harbor, the air raids by B-52s, and other attack jets bombing North Vietnam, strangulation of all major supply routes from the Soviet Union and communist China into North Vietnam systematically took place. The continual supply of SAMs, trucks, ammunition, and food had to be fully stopped.

Our staff received an information copy of a message sent from the Joint Chiefs of Staff to CINCPAC headquarters in Hawaii. It read something to the effect of:

FROM: JCS, WASH DC
TO: CINCPAC, HI
INFO: CINCPACFLT, MAKALAPA, HI

SUBJ: PREVENTION OF SUPPLIES TO DRV

INTEL REPORTS INDICATE THAT LARGE
PERCENTAGE OF SUPPLIES ARE REPORTED
INTERDICTED BY BOMBING RAIDS ALONG
NORTHERN BORDER OF DRV AND BY
BLOCKADE OF SHIPPING DUE TO MINING.
HOWEVER, REPORTS INDICATE THAT SMALL
PERCENTAGE IS COMING IN VIA CHICOM
MERSHIPS AT HON NIEU AND HON LA
ANCHORAGES OFF COAST OF DRV. REQUEST

CURTAILMENT AS SOON AS FEASIBLE. REPORT ACTIONS TO ALCON.

Admiral Holloway read the message at our 0900 war room briefing. He said, "You staffers have a new, sensitive requirement. We have to take this message for action. We now have Chinese civilian merchant ships sailing right by our Seventh Fleet ships out here in the Gulf of Tonkin. You've all seen them. In fact, you've seen their Chinese crews waving to us as they pass en route to North Vietnam. According to intelligence, the merchant ships steam to two anchorages located three miles off the coast of North Vietnam. There, they anchor and unload their cargo of ammunition, equipment, and food into North Vietnamese waterborne logistic craft (WBLC). These long, motorized junks then motor into the beaches to offload the supplies. The problem we have is, how do we stop these supplies? We can't stop the Chinese merchant ships at sea. We can't bomb their ships, or they might use it as an excuse to enter the war. We can't bomb the WBLC close to a Chinese ship, or we might accidentally hit a Chinese ship with bomb fragments. We don't want to hit a Chinese ship! Our Department of State has already received Chinese communist warning number 402. Another warning issued by communist China about any incidents could be critical at this time and cause our State Department and administration some real headaches.

"I want this staff to seek a solution. We must come up with a plan for stopping this last trickle of supplies into North Vietnam. Obviously, we will get an execute message from CINCPACFLT, very soon, to take that JCS message for action.

"Give me some options and recommendations at tomorrow's briefing."

When the full briefing period was completed and Admiral Holloway left for his stateroom, the rest of us sat around talking about the few options we had to take against this WBLC activity in North Vietnam. Some of the options were:

- Position naval attack aircraft over the Chinese merchant ships, day and night, then attack the small wooden WBLC when they were loaded and well clear of the Chinese merchant ship (mership).

- Run Seventh Air Force jets or Marine Corps jets out of Da Nang onto the beaches where the waterborne logistic craft were offloading ashore and bomb them.
- Have the land-based Seventh Air Force or Marine Corps attack jet bombers drop napalm on those offloading beach areas to discourage their offloading of the WBLC ashore. The navy does not carry napalm mixtures and associated drop-tanks aboard aircraft carriers. It's simply too dangerous for storage of such a volatile mix for shipboard handling.

The Seventh Air Force liaison officer on our staff, Lieutenant Colonel Rose, stated that all of the air force attack assets were committed to bombing main supply routes and strategic targets in North Vietnam. There simply were not any leftover air force assets to do this merchant ship interdiction mission at this time.

Commander George Boaz then added a similar statement: "Task Force 77 aircraft carriers are completely committed, around-the-clock, along with the Marine jets out of Da Nang, bombing the railroads and bridges coming from China, on the North Vietnamese side, as well as the main supply routes and antiaircraft artillery and SAM sites. We do not have extra aircraft to assign to this problem of the merships and WBLC."

After listening to the problem that appeared not to have an immediate solution, I thought of all possible Marine Corps assets in the inventory I was responsible for representing on this staff. I came up with an idea to utilize the fantastic flexibility of the Marine amphibious forces afloat and operating from Task Force 76 ships. I decided that I would propose my idea as a plan presentation to Admiral Holloway. I would recommend we use our AH-1J Cobra attack helicopters. These would be improved versions of the Cobras that I personally flew in squadron VMO-2 out of Marble Mountain airfield in 1969. That is when we Marines first introduced the AH-1G Cobra into combat. These newer Cobras were assigned to Marine Attack Helicopter Squadron 369 (HMA-369).

I would ask my boss, Commander Froid, to make available one of his amphibious ships to use as a helicopter platform for my concept of the operation to handle the WBLC problem. We could locate the ship just fifteen miles over the horizon in North Vietnamese waters. Originally, our Cobra inventory consisted of eight AH-1Gs in Vietnam in 1969. However, my tent-mate, Maj. "Benny" Reinhart lost one. Benny had been refueling his Cobra at An Hoi airstrip when incoming NVA rockets blew it up. Benny was wounded, and we never received a replacement for the lost Cobra in VMO-2. Despite three years and the fact the Marine Cobras had been retrograded back to the island of Okinawa since 1971, there remained only seven Marine Cobras in the inventory. Ironically, when planning my scenario, seven Cobras worked out very well because that is all we could pack on the aft end of an LPD for the mission. With seven AH-1J Cobras, it would be extremely cramped and dangerous cycling them off and onto the fantail of the LPD for the WBLC attack missions. The working conditions would be hazardous for the maintenance crews.

I discussed the idea/plan with Commander Froid. Jim said, "I can place the LPD USS *Denver* up there. As you know, it's sitting off the Cau Viet River with troops, so we'll have to send the *Denver* back to Okinawa Island and offload the combat Marines and their equipment at White Beach. You can then direct your Marines to reconfigure for this special operation. That would leave me short one LPD for our amphibious forces of the 9th Marine Amphibious Brigade (MAB), and they would obviously be short some assault troops. That is a risk factor that the admiral might not go for. However, each passing day, it seems to be more unlikely that Washington will ever approve us invading into North Vietnam or even South Vietnam with our 9th MAB. It appears to me that the risk factor is minimal, considering the Washington politics as they have been all these years of this war."

I responded, "I think we can pull this off. I'll send some advance planning information that this might become a reality to the 3d Marine Amphibious Force on Okinawa Island. My counterpart on the III MAF staff, Lt. Col. K. D. Waters, will be able to alert the III MAF in Okinawa and the 1st Marine Aircraft Wing in Iwakuni, Japan. Lieutenant Colonel Waters can have the Wing assign the personnel and have them prepare a sixty-day maintenance support mount-out package. They can have all the aircrews selected and the mount-out package ready for when the *Denver* sails into White Beach, Okinawa, provided Admiral Holloway approves this operation."

The next morning, all staff options were presented and discussed by Lieutenant Colonel Rose and Commander Boaz, without Admiral Holloway getting any useful recommendations to hang his hat on. The air force and navy air assets were simply fully committed elsewhere and could not be available for the WBLC problem.

I briefed Admiral Holloway on my proposal to use the *Denver* and the Marine AH-1J Cobra helicopters to attack the WBLC. I strongly emphasized that the Cobras would attack only after the WBLC were a safe distance from the Chinese merchant ships.

Admiral Holloway, after thinking in depth about all aspects, liked my proposal. He immediately warned me that there were no navy search-and-rescue units operating in those areas off the coast of North Vietnam. All search-and-rescue assets were committed farther north to cover the aircraft carrier operations. The absence of search-and-rescue assets would be a major risk factor for the Cobra pilots, but you have to take risks in war. There wouldn't necessarily be search-and-rescue assistance in the area in the event a helicopter got shot down. There are no friendly fighters anywhere near those two North Vietnamese anchorages to cover your Cobras. All jets are farther up north bombing on very tight schedules. Additionally, if helicopters get too close to the shore, the many NVA antiaircraft batteries and missiles will shoot them down. Our surface ship assets can afford, occasionally, to cruise by the operating area of the LPD, but we cannot assign any dedicated protective gunships to watch over the *Denver* continuously.

I responded, "The Cobra crews will be carefully briefed. They will have to use their own helicopter assets for search and rescue because there are no other SAR units nearby. Additionally, I will personally brief and warn them not to get too close to the shore."

Admiral Holloway said, "Let's go ahead. Implement it. We'll see how it goes."

I did implement it by sending the appropriate messages. Lieutenant Colonel K. D. Waters, at the III MAF staff on Okinawa, had all the skids greased. Waters had the 3d Division and 1st Marine Aircraft Wing all prebriefed before my execute message reached him on Okinawa.

However, before I sent my MARHUK execute message, the advance information messages I had conveyed to Lieutenant Colonel Waters caused much concern at III MAF.

The III MAF commander, Lt. Gen. Louis Metzger, believed the value to stopping a WBLC sampan and its cargo was not worth the possible loss of any Cobra gunship helicopter. General Metzger, understandably, also objected to depriving Brig. Gen. Edward J. Miller, commander of the 9th MAB, with his two amphibious ready groups aboard TF 76 ships off of Vietnam, of troops during a critical period.

Despite these high-level Marine Corps concerns, Maj. Gen. Leslie E. Brown, commander, First Marine Aircraft Wing, directed the acting squadron commander of HMA-369, Capt. Ronald G. Osborne, to be ready to deploy if ordered by higher authority. During this get-ready stage, Maj. Dawson P. "Rusty" Hansen assumed command of Marine Helicopter Squadron 369 (HMA-369), located on Okinawa.

Lieutenant Colonel Waters, via back channel communications that only he and I could read, notified me about the III MAF's objections and concerns of taking the TF 79 troops off the *Denver* and loading Cobra helicopters on board. I told Waters I was going to direct it anyway, and they had better be ready because it's the only operation we know of that can actually stop the WBLC from taking the communist Chinese weapons, ammunitions, and other supplies into North Vietnam. Waters responded that they were ready to execute Marine Corps–style, if directed by the Commander, Seventh Fleet.

I then sent the execute message to the commanding general of III MAF to implement what we called Marine Hunter Killer Operation, or MARHUK Operation.

On June 17, 1972, the Marines began loading eighteen officers, ninety-nine enlisted men, seven AH-1J Cobra attack helicopters, and a maintenance mount-out package of spare parts and tools on board the USS *Denver* at White Beach, Okinawa.

My boss, Admiral Holloway, had preferred that we use the larger-type helicopter carrier, an LPH, but the 9th MAB required the LPH for combat readiness in the event we were permitted to invade North Vietnam. So, we settled on using the *Denver*.

HMA-369 had to overcome some problems to adjust for the MARHUK Operation. Major Hansen, working with his maintenance officer, Capt. David L. Caldon, solved the problems related to supply, missile countermeasure modifications, avionics support, ordnance handling, and the acquisition of 5-inch Zuni rockets, not normally fired from helicopters.

There was no existing doctrine, or experiences, for this MARHUK Operation to draw readiness from. My message simply directed the Marines to do it. I knew Marines would do it, and do it well.

Major Hansen, HMA-369 commander, and his operations officer, Capt. David C. Corbett, had to use innovative imaginations to develop a concept of employment to accomplish the Seventh Fleet assigned mission.

They came up with a two-part execution for handling the situation with:

1. The Chinese merchant ships at Hon La anchorage
2. The destruction of motorized sampans or WBLC
    running cargo ashore from the People's Republic of
    China merchant ships

Based upon my messages and personal briefings and those of my immediate boss, Cmdr. Jim Froid, the MARHUK Rules of Engagement required the Marine Cobras to stay at least five hundred yards from the Chinese merchant ships that were offloading supplies into North Vietnamese waterborne logistics craft. Additionally, my message directive explicitly required that the AH-1J Cobras remain over water at all times.

Coordinating with Commanders Froid and Boaz, Task Force 77 was directed to control the daily flight sorties of the Cobras and coordinate air, naval gunfire, and rescue support if it became available.

Because the AH-1J Cobra helicopters lacked radio cryptologic equipment, radio silence was mandatory to prevent and deceive the North Vietnamese radio monitoring. Obviously, later, when the MARHUK pilots began flying night operations over water without using radio communications, it was dangerous and demonstrated the flying skills of the pilots in HMA-369.

The *Denver* arrived from the Gulf of Tonkin to offload the combat troops of the 9th MAB. Within a few days, the seven AH-1J Cobra gunship helicopters were loaded aboard the *Denver*. Within two weeks, the *Denver* was floating off the coast of North Vietnam.

As soon as they arrived at their assigned location, just over the horizon from North Vietnam's coast near Hon La and Hon Nieu anchorages, Jim Froid and I flew over in Admiral Holloway's Black Beard One helicopter to personally brief the aircrews. Jim also talked to the skipper of the USS *Denver* as I continued discussions with the Cobra aircrews. I emphasized the dangers involved and the fact that they would have to provide their own search and rescue because there were no navy SAR choppers in their vicinity. All SAR birds were farther north, near Haiphong, due to the heavy bombing raids under way up there. I previously told them not to get anywhere near the beach, feet dry, or they'd get shot down. I told them that if shot down on, or near, the beach, they'd probably get captured. I didn't tell them my own ass was hanging out with this wild MARHUK Operation and that it had better work without the loss of Cobras, or worse, the loss of the *Denver*. The operation was gutsy and risky. The admiral knew it. I knew it. Our staff knew it. Even with the great radar control and coverage offered by the USS *Chicago* in the Gulf of Tonkin, it was doubtful that navy fighters could have scrambled from carriers, in the far north, fast enough to prevent MiGs from rapidly coming out and bombing the *Denver*. The MiG bases were located only minutes away from the *Denver*'s operating location off the North Vietnamese coast.

As the *Denver* set up operations, a large communist Chinese merchant ship (Chicom mership) was unloading supplies at the Hon La anchorage. It was June 22, 1972, when the first Marine Cobra attack helicopter took off from the fantail of the USS *Denver*. The Cobra headed for the Chicom mership area just over the horizon to the west. The Cobra pilot and front gunner (another pilot) flew close by the Chicom mership and watched the Chinese deck handlers unloading cargo with a crane. The cargo was dropped down into a long North Vietnamese motorized junk. As the Cobra swept by at five hundred feet and indicated airspeed of 160 knots, the gunner up front said in the cockpit, "Shit! Look toward the beach. There must be at least twenty of these WBLCs!"

The pilot, in the elevated rear seat, answered, "Roger that. I can see them. Let's start this MARHUK Operation the right way. I'll fire the outboard 2.75-inch rocket pods. You work the junks over with your 20mm gun turret."

Roaring in for their first attack, they began firing. The pilot's gunsight homed-in on the long, narrow WBLC closest to them. It was the farthest WBLC from the shore. This WBLC was a good mile away from the offloading Chinese merchant ship. The North Vietnamese WBLC crew never knew where the hell the Cobra came from. They didn't even know what the Cobra was. In seconds, their WBLC deck was exploding from rockets and 20mm cannon fire. Within a minute, the Cobra pulled off the attack run as the center of the WBLC blew sky-high. Both the stern and bow flew out of the water, and the middle of the boat was aflame with orange-red explosions. Secondary explosions continued, even as the center portion of the long structure of the motorized junk sank underwater.

"Goddamn! Look at those secondaries! That sonuvabitch was really loaded with ammo!" shouted the pilot in the backseat of the AH-1J Cobra. The single Cobra immediately began attacking one junk after another. Within a half hour, they had sunk fourteen large logistic motorized craft. Each of the WBLC had exploded with tremendous secondary explosions, obviously proving that they had been heavily loaded with ammunition shipped from communist China.

Thus started a daily operation right in the backyard of the enemy in North Vietnam waters. Jim Froid had set up a daily reporting system that had the Cobra Detachment officer in charge report the daily flying actions to the skipper of the *Denver*. The captain of the *Denver* then reported to his commander, the commander of Task Force 76, who then sent an afteraction report to our commander on the *Oklahoma City*.

I started to receive the daily messages from CTF 76, reported from the *Denver*. The reports reflected strikes of sorties flown by the Marine Cobra aircrews and estimated damages, with exact number of WBLC sinkings. It was immediately apparent to all on our staff that, at least initially, this operation was going to be successful.

After the second day of my briefing on MARHUK Operation, Admiral Holloway thrilled me. He stated, "You Marines always have a rabbit to pull from your magical hat!" I was quite proud of all the flexibility our Marines exhibited and offered to the Seventh Fleet due to the Marine's capability to task organize and rapidly deploy for a peculiar problem at hand.

It became common during crises that I had a solution to an unusual problem that the navy didn't have assets for solving. Being the only Marine on the operations section of the staff was not easy at first. After proving that our Marine flexibility was always available, I was well accepted by the navy staff officers. Eventually, lifelong friendships developed. I think that my fellow staff members soon found out by watching my activities that the Marine Corps has unique capabilities that make it a formidable force, despite its small size.

Soon this small, aggressive detachment of HMA-369 Cobra pilots and hardworking maintenance personnel was known throughout the Seventh Fleet as the Marine Hunter Killer Detachment, devastatingly executing the MARHUK Operation.

On July 1, 1972, we had the MARHUK Cobras begin night operations. They began night attacks using their landing lights for searching for the WBLC and then firing upon these logistics craft. We now had day-and-night interdiction of the last supplies coming into North Vietnam. It wasn't long before we received a beautiful "Well done!" message sent through the chain of command from JCS in Washington. I immediately sent a copy of the message to the MARHUK Detachment aboard the *Denver* and TF 79. Froid sent a copy to the captain of the *Denver* and TF 76 congratulating them for their continued support in the war effort.

Soon we decided to give the Cobra aircrews an extra punch. I sent a message to CINCPACFLT, with an info copy to CG, FMFPAC, asking if they would investigate how the testing of the firing of the 5-inch Zuni rockets from Cobras at the Naval Test Center, China Lake, California, was progressing.

I received a swift answer that stated the tests were coming along nicely. Marine Maj. D. E. P. Miller, a test pilot at China Lake, had been firing the 5-inch Zuni high-explosive rockets from the AH-1J Cobra. There was no better-qualified pilot to do the testing. Major Miller had flown the very first AH-1G Cobra combat mission for the Marines, along with Maj. Benny Reinhardt in Vietnam in early 1969. I was also lucky enough to fly with each of them, in squadron VMO-2, when we first introduced the Cobras to combat that year.

Back at China Lake, Major Miller had a slight surprise during one of his firing runs. A blast from one of the Zuni rockets blew off the ammunition loading and storage compartment door. Quick modifications were made to the Cobra to incorporate firing the Zuni rockets. After a few more test flights, Major Miller's tests resulted in the navy approving firing the Zuni rockets from the Cobras as soon as the necessary modifications on all Cobras were accomplished. As soon as U.S. Navy and Marine Corps aviation authorities approved use of the Zuni on the Cobra, we were ready to use them for MARHUK Operations.

In one incident, a Cobra was fired at by a North Vietnamese 12.7mm machine gun. Chief Warrant Officer James F. Doner Jr., the aerial observer in the front seat, was surprised when his pilot whipped the Cobra around at the enemy machine-gun position and fired a 5-inch Zuni rocket. This was Doner's first exposure to firing a Zuni rocket from an AH-1J Cobra helicopter. Doner instinctively shouted, "We've been hit!" Later, he said, "The pilot didn't tell me he was about to fire a Zuni rocket." The Zuni rocket, much larger than what the Cobra normally fired, 2.75-inch rockets, enveloped the Cobra in smoke and sparks from the rocket motor and shook the helicopter as it was fired from the rocket pod. Just three years later, I was to fly many times with Doner, the aerial observer in my backseat, while piloting OV-10A Broncos as the commanding officer of VMO-2 at Camp Pendleton, California. Doner relayed to me other experiences he had during his MARHUK Cobra flights that were equally interesting.

Very soon, the waterborne logistics craft carrying supplies from Red Chinese merchant ships were being exploded by a larger warhead, the 5-inch Zuni rocket, now fired from the Marine Cobras.

As the MARHUK Operation continued, the North Vietnamese began firing at the Marine helicopters. The North Vietnamese had positioned 23mm, 37mm, and 57mm antiaircraft guns around the three-sided Hon La anchorage. Nine HMA-369 Cobras were hit by a variety of small arms during 140 reported enemy firing incidents. Early in the operation, though, the Hon La anchorage crews of the coastal defense sites recognized that when they fired at the Cobras, they could expect the Cobras to fire back; in addition, naval gunfire and navy fixed-wing aircraft would engage them.

Major Hansen was then relieved by Maj. David L. Ross as the MARHUK commander on the *Denver* off of North Vietnam. Later, Major Ross was quoted as saying, "I believe the Sea Cobra's small profile, maneuverability, and firepower prevented Cobra losses."

The AH-1Js fired 20mm guns, 2.75-inch rockets, and 5-inch Zuni rockets. Additionally, two Marine aerial observers, Chief Warrant Officers Doner and James R. Owens, often flew in the front seat of the Cobra's gunner's cockpit position. Soon, these seasoned AOs taught the Cobra pilots airborne spotting and naval gunfire control.

We then phased in another capability to utilize the Marine Cobras of the MARHUK Operation. We began using the AH-1J pilots, trained by the two assigned AOs, as forward air controllers. While the Cobras were often flying in between the Chinese merships and the North Vietnamese shore, and when not attacking WBLC, they could be used for controlling navy attack bombers. They began adjusting the air strikes and visually controlling the jet bombers onto defense sites along the North Vietnamese coast, near the offshore anchorages. This perplexed the North Vietnamese gunners along the coast. They could not fire back at the Cobras for fear they may accidentally hit their supply source, the Chinese merchant ships at anchor behind the low-flying Cobra helicopters.

Operational Control (OPCON) for the MARHUK Operation was then passed to CTG 77.0, a navy carrier task group, because the Cobras began forward air controlling their attack bombers when the jets would report in for air strikes on coastal defense sites.

Because of the MARHUK Operation's continual effectiveness, the operation went on for the next eight months. At times, during the bad weather of the monsoon season, and when the Marine A-6A all-weather Intruder attack bombers weren't flying, the only Marine air attacks that I was briefing Admiral Holloway about were the damage assessments and sorties flown by our AH-1J Cobra MARHUK pilots. During these heavy seasonal rains, the Cobra crews flew about four hundred feet above the Gulf of Tonkin and just below the solid overcast skies, near the merchant ship offloading anchorages, while blowing up WBLC. Sometimes during these severe weather conditions, nothing else was flying in the war zone except for the Marine Cobras.

From June 1972 through July 1972, the Chicom merships were unsuccessful in attempts to get their supplies ashore near Hon Nieu and Hon La anchorages. The Cobra crews often sank as many as forty to sixty WBLC a day. Each WBLC that was blown up resulted in many secondary explosions due to the concentrated loads of ammunition being ferried ashore from the communist Chinese merchant ships.

The *Denver* was relieved for crew rest to go to Subic Bay in the Philippines. The USS *Cleveland* (LPD-7) arrived on July 13, 1972, to ensure continuation of the MARHUK Operation. Because we had only seven AH-1J Cobra helicopters in all of the 1st Marine Aircraft Wing in Asia, this HMA-369 detachment of aircrews and maintenance personnel had to remain at sea and were transferred from the *Denver* to the *Cleveland*. It was very unfortunate not to be able to have the HMA-369 detachment get some well-needed rest and relaxation in Olongapo City in the Philippines like the *Denver* crew. Both the mechanics and pilots had been busting their asses with day-and-night flying activities. It really was time to get them off the ship for a few days. I personally felt badly about them not getting some shore liberty, particularly because they were continuing day-and-night operations at this time. Eventually, the Marine Corps personnel system would catch up with these hardworking crews and get them some personnel replacements.

Several more weeks went by, and the Marine Helicopter Attack Squadron (HMA-369) detachment, flying from the LPD *Cleveland*, continued destroying WBLC.

All of a sudden, the daily reports of damage assessment and sorties flown by the Cobra detachment were reflecting no sightings of WBLC. The Cobra aircrews reported that they were flying fairly close in to the Chinese merchant ship, and still they saw no activity on board, and no WBLC coming and going from ship to shore. It was very strange because the Cobras continued flying in the vicinity of the merchant ship, day and night. Could North Vietnam have given up on this waterborne logistics craft supply line because our Marine Cobra crews were blowing them sky-high? Or was it simply that the merchant ship, still at anchor, had been emptied of all supplies but was not yet ready to sail from the anchorage for China?

This particular Chinese mership had only recently arrived. Additionally, our intelligence division reported that when the ship arrived, it was riding low in the water. Later intelligence reported that the ship was riding much higher in the water. Photos were taken to prove that the ship obviously had been unloading supplies and was, indeed, riding considerably higher in the water.

Somehow, supplies had been offloaded in such a manner that the alert MARHUK aircrews had not seen any unloading or transporting of supplies to shore. This really was a mystery for everyone, including us on the Seventh Fleet staff.

A few more days went by, and I still had nothing to report to Admiral Holloway and the staff on this, one of my many operations. Then, one morning, we received a rather strange message from the intelligence-gathering community. Marine Capt. Bill Tehan, from our staff intelligence section, came down the ladder to our office to show me the message. We both read and reread the message trying to figure out exactly what it meant. The message had been sent from the aircraft carrier USS *Enterprise* to Task Force 77. We, at COMSEVENTHFLT, had received an informational message. The message simply read:

FMUSS ENTERPRISE
TOCTF 77
INFOCOMSEVENTHFLT
CTF 76
CTF 79
CTG 77.00

CTG 79.1
USS CLEVELAND
UNUSUAL SIGHTINGS BY TACAIR

A-7 ATTK SQDN PILOT REPORTED SIGHTING SHINY OBJECT UNDERWATER, MIDWAY BETWEEN CHICOM MERSHIP AND BEACH AT HON LA. PILOT WAS ON PULL-OUT OF ATTK RUN ON COASTAL DEFENSE POSITION.

Captain Tehan and I again read this strange report. I then said, "Captain, what the hell do you think this pilot saw underwater?"

Tehan responded, "I don't know what he saw, sir. He obviously saw something, or he wouldn't have reported it to intelligence."

At the next morning's briefing, we all discussed what that pilot might have seen underwater in the Hon La anchorage area. Nobody, including Admiral Holloway, could guess what that attack pilot might have seen underwater, in an area where the WBLC no longer were actively transporting supplies from the Chinese merchant ship.

I sent a brief message to CTF 77 requesting that the MARHUK pilots get back out there and investigate to see what was under the water near the merchant ship and the general anchorage area.

A day later, I received a message from Task Force 77 stating that nothing was found by the Cobra aircrews that day, but the very next morning, a flash message report came in from CTF 77 reporting that Cobras flying the previous night, using their night landing lights for illumination of the area, still saw nothing. They then flew much closer to the Chinese ship than they had ever flown before. To their surprise and amazement, they caught the Chicom mership deck crewmembers very busy hand-cranking a large wheel and pulley mounted on the fantail of the ship. The large pulley had a steel cable running off of it and into the water. On the steel cable were attached boxes, obviously supplies being hand-cranked underwater all the way to shore. Apparently, the Cobras had been flying around, day and night, for sometime without seeing anything, while the Chicoms had been slipping supplies to the North Vietnamese, unseen, underwater.

I briefed Admiral Holloway on the weird situation on our hands. He questioned the entire staff, saying, "How do we bomb a thin steel cable that is underwater, without accidentally having frags hit the Chinese mership?" He thought about it for a while, and then said, "Let's give it a try. Let's see if we can hit something that long and thin."

Commander Boaz, after discussing the problem at length with the admiral, sent a message to CTF 77 requesting that they run a division of four A-7 attack bombers on the beach-end of where the cable might possibly be coming ashore on the beach. That same afternoon, we received a report back from CTF 77 that the first division of A-7 aircraft unloaded some 500-pound bombs in the general area. They hit nothing, and they received a helluva lot of flak from antiaircraft guns on the coast. A second division of A-7 attack aircraft bombed in the same area. They struck paydirt.

Another message followed with details that read:

```
FMCTF 77
TO COMSEVENTHFLT
INFOCTG 79.1
USS CLEVELAND
CABLE DESTROYED


ATTK AIR BOMBED SHORE END OF CHICOM
MERSHIP CABLE AND HIT IT. CABLE SNAPPED
LIKE GUITAR STRING AND LASHED
WILDLY IN AND OUT OF THE WATER TOWARD
MERSHIP, CAUSING MERSHIP FANTAIL TO RISE
HIGH IN THE WATER AND THEN CRASH BACK
INTO THE SEA. THE CHICOM CREW RAN ABOUT
THE DECK WILDLY, AS THE SHIP OSCILLATED
SEVERAL TIMES.
```

Admiral Holloway didn't think the message was comical. He was concerned that the Chinese communists (Chicom) might lodge a complaint of some ship damage to our State Department. The admiral immediately told George Boaz, "Commander, if they place another cable out there in the water from their fantail, don't bomb it. We'll have to figure out another way to skin this cat."

I thought that if the Chicom did place another steel cable into the water from the hand-crank on the fantail, I would request the Commander Task Force 79 to have some of his Marine reconnaissance forces get out there in rubber boats, at night, and cut the cable, but the Chicoms did not install a replacement cable. Instead, nothing happened for two full weeks. The ship just sat there with no apparent activity, as the Cobras continued flying around the area, day and night. There simply were no unusual activities reported. We all waited to see if the offloading to the WBLC would resume . . . or, if the ship would depart the area. Nothing happened.

On the third week, we received another unusual message. This message came from our cruiser-destroyer commander, CTG 70.8. Commander Stu Landersman read the message to Admiral Holloway and the staff. It read something like this:

FMCTG 70.8
TOCOMSEVENTHFLT
UNKOWN FLOATING OBJECTS SIGHTED

USS STERETT REPORTED SIGHTING FIVE
FLOATING OBJECTS APPROX THREE FEET
BY TWO FEET IN SIZE. CONCERNED ABOUT
POSSIBLE FLOATING MINES. STERETT DID NOT
APPROACH TOO CLOSE. OBJECTS AFLOAT TWO-
MILES NORTH OF END OF CAU VIET RIVER.

No staff member could think of what was floating way down south, below the DMZ area. Admiral Holloway was rightfully concerned. He stated, "What if they are North Vietnamese mines? After all, we mined Haiphong Harbor and other areas. Possibly, they are mining off their coast to keep us back off the beachheads."

The admiral then turned to Commander Landersman and said, "Send a message to CTG 70.8. Tell them to investigate and carefully get closer to the floating objects. Tell them to have a crewmember shoot a rifle at the floating objects to determine if they will explode. If the objects don't explode, have the crew pick up the objects to determine just what the hell they are."

Landersman's message directive went out. Several hours later we received a response stating that a cruiser came up to the objects and a crewmember fired a rifle at several floating objects. Nothing exploded.

Another message soon arrived and reported that the crew of the cruiser fished out several of the floating objects. The objects turned out to be black plastic bags of rice inside of potato-type sacks. The message ended stating that the crew in the mess hall of the ship had cooked the rice in their galley and were eating it with their dinner.

The reports about the floating bags of rice, off the DMZ, had only just settled in our minds when we received a message report of the latest results of the MARHUK Cobra flights. The report stated that the Cobra aircrews had sighted hundreds of floating objects in the anchorage area and toward the beach.

I sent the MARHUK detachment a message directive, via their chain of command, stating they should fly closer in toward the shore, but not too close to be shot down. I wanted to determine if they could see if any of those floating objects, possibly also bags of rice, were actually being washed up on the shore of North Vietnam.

We quickly received a response indicating that the Cobra crews saw hundreds of bags piled up on the beach, directly inland from the Chicom mership. It was obvious that the Chicom mership crew, determined to unload rice bags and unable to unload heavy ammunition and weapons boxes, decided to simply throw hundreds of bags of rice off the ship and hope the tide would wash them ashore. Apparently, many floated ashore and many did not. Many bags got caught in offshore currents and floated hundreds of miles south of the DMZ. It was hard to believe they could have floated so far south, but they apparently were the same types of rice-filled bags that the cruiser had picked up, and the cruiser crew had eaten the rice for dinner.

It seemed like an awful waste of ammunition, but the Marine Cobras began shooting at the floating bags of rice and sinking them. This actually served two purposes. It stopped rice from reaching the enemy, who finally was bottled up under an ever-tightening strangulation of all supplies. It also provided the Cobra aircrews with daily target practice. It was better than expending the same amount of ammunition in training back home in the States, at some make-believe targets on a range.

Additionally, it discouraged the Chicoms and the North Vietnamese from continuing the futile offloading of the game the merchant ships had been playing. This small but important MARHUK Operation continued to add another dimension to the already tight noose squeezing North Vietnam, and it severed the enemy's lifelines, which were needed to continue their invasion war in South Vietnam.

The LPDs continued to cycle, relieving each other, in the MARHUK Operation area off the North Vietnamese coast. During December 1972, the USS *Dubuque* (LPD-8) also joined in the relieving cycle of LPDs for the seven AH-1J Cobra helicopters support. When this unusual interdiction operation finally ended, HMA-369 had conducted the operation from June 22, 1972, until January 26, 1973. Despite heavy monsoon rains and hostile fire directed at the Cobras, their flight crews flew 982 combat sorties for 1,216 flight hours utilizing their rockets and 20mm cannon fire to destroy enemy supplies. Cobras destroyed 123 sampans carrying approximately 5,600 containers and 5,444 one-hundred-pound bags of rice, an estimated total of 241 tons of communist Chinese supplies destroyed by this aggressive seven-helicopter detachment operating from the fantail of the three cycling LPDs.

A 1973 Center for Naval Analysis Study concluded that the employment of HMA-369 had released two navy destroyers and numerous carrier aircraft sorties otherwise required for this supply interdiction mission.

Marine Maj. David L. Ross was certainly qualified when he stated, "The squadron did more than shoot up sampans . . . most of all the last six months of the operation had given the AH-1J Cobra the opportunity to prove it deserves the designation of an attack helicopter."

A little later, Adm. Elmo R. Zumwalt, CNO, came out from Washington to visit us on the *Oklahoma City*. When he came aboard our flagship, I personally briefed Admiral Zumwalt on the remarkable success the MARHUK Operation was.

Admiral Zumwalt responded, "I followed the message traffic reports of this unusual military operation very carefully. I am impressed with the historically unique military effort exhibited by this MARHUK Operation. It really added to fully slamming the doors shut on the enemy."

Months later, when the war was officially ended, I was still on the Commander, Seventh Fleet's staff. I personally wrote up the HMA-369 detachment for a navy unit citation. It was sent up through the chain of command to the CNO. Much later, the unit received the citation. The Secretary of the Navy recognized that the squadron maintained a sustained pace of heavy combat operations during all types of weather, "responding gallantly to the almost overwhelming tasks of providing a three-fold role of attack, supply movement interdiction, and constant surveillance of the enemy." As the war continued, though, we continued our daily staff activities and our ship, *Oklahoma City*, continued its shore bombardments as part of a task unit. I would read the *Oklahoma City*'s *Plan of the Day* daily newspaper, which the ship's executive officer, Joe Fairchild, published. A typical statement listing the ship's daily routine and schedule would include something like:

Oklahoma City, together with the destroyers of the task unit, conducted naval gunfire strikes against military targets in the vicinity of the city of Vinh during the night.

Early this morning, we conducted strikes against North Vietnamese troop positions and an oil storage area around Cap Lay, just a few miles south of the DMZ.

Some other of our *Oklahoma City* morning papers read roughly as follows:

Last night the *Oklahoma City* continued to strike at enemy targets in the city of Vinh. The targets were heavy coastal defense batteries on the island of Hon Mat and a petroleum storage area on Hon Me Island. Early this morning, we struck a coastal defense battery near Than Hoa, 180 miles north of the DMZ.

Last night the *Oklahoma City* struck targets twenty miles south of Haiphong, about thirty miles north of the 20th parallel. We also attacked a missile site and bridge at Than Hoa.

Tuesday night, the *Oklahoma City* fired more than 500 rounds of main 5-inch and secondary 3-inch armament against North Vietnamese troops south of the Cau Viet River.

Yesterday, *Oklahoma City* took two tanks under fire with the 5/38 gun battery and observed secondary explosions as the vehicles were destroyed.

Yesterday afternoon, *Oklahoma City*, in the company of several destroyers, fired on a radar installation near the DMZ at Cap Lay. Last night strikes were made on the Don Hoi airfield, thirty miles north of the DMZ. Following that, a strike was made on a large coastal defense site at Cap Lay and left the CD site burning after a large secondary explosion was observed. The spotting helicopter from the USS *Sterett* confirmed the hit.

Those daily news stories of our own ship's activities helped let the ship's crewmembers know what their efforts contributed toward the war effort.

My two-officer living quarters' stateroom was located forward on the ship and directly behind the 6-inch gun turret mount. There was no way I could be in my room when those 6-inch guns fired. The entire room shook and the noise was intolerable, so I had to stay two decks up in my office when the ship made day-and-night raids. Occasionally, I would stuff cotton in my ears and wear my helmet and go into the gun mount control room. There, I was always amazed at how hard these young sailors worked. They would be working like hell and sweating in that smoky, confined area while moving heavy shell casings around for firing. The ship's Marine detachment would also assist the sailors by being in there, humping those large shells around. They formed a smooth, coordinated group. I was and still am proud to have met them all and to have talked to them individually during my two years on their beloved ship, the *Oklahoma City*.

As I watched these dedicated, hardworking young men during the day-and-night raids, I had to think of an old saying by an unknown author: "There are no great men. There are only ordinary men who meet great challenges." I believe that has always applied to fighting men, worldwide, in the service of their countries.

Chapter 15

• • • • • • • •

Preparing for End Sweep

The Seventh Fleet staff received constant updates of the progress, or lack of progress, of the on-again-off-again Paris peace negotiations between Kissinger and Le Duc Tho.

We on the staff were therefore well aware that if and when a ceasefire agreement were to be signed, a related protocol of that agreement would require the United States to neutralize the mines we had laid in North Vietnam's waters.

The peace negotiations that began in 1968 and had progressed sporadically were suspended indefinitely on May 4, 1972, as a direct result of the Easter invasion by communist North Vietnamese into South Vietnam. Of course, we had to be prepared for resumption of the peace talks and a possible ceasefire, which would result in our executing the neutralization of those mines.

At this point in time, though, our staff was deeply involved in planning for the top secret mine sweeping operation code named End Sweep.

Lieutenant Commander Larry L. Emarine, sitting at his desk to my left, in back operations, had plotted where all the 500-pound Mark 36 Destructor bombs and 1,000-pound MK 52 mine bombs were dropped in the Haiphong Channel. Larry Emarine had carefully tracked and charted each batch of bombs that were now sitting at the bottom of the Haiphong Channel with their deadly acoustic, magnetic, time-delayed fuses. Emarine then had George Boaz request that Task Force 77 carrier aircraft reseed certain areas in the channel from time to time because some of the time periods of the set fuses had passed, and those mines were no longer active, or alive.

Because End Sweep would use Jim Froid's Task Force 76 amphibious ships and my assigned Marine helicopters aboard those ships, Jim and I began working closely with Larry Emarine on a daily basis to be fully prepared for execution of the operation.

During November and December 1972, our planning changed to establishing actual training and rehearsals for the mine sweeping operation. The training and rehearsals would take place in Subic Bay in the Philippines. We would duplicate the Haiphong Channel and train realistically to be ready for the anticipated execute message.

On November 3, 1972, Rear Adm. Brian McCauley, Commander, Mine Warfare Force from Charleston, South Carolina, arrived with his staff at Naval Base Subic Bay. He was joined by Cap. Felix Vecchione, Commander, Mobile Mine Countermeasures Command. Vecchione was to become the operations officer for the neutralization of the mines, code name End Sweep. Admiral McCauley would soon be designated Commander of Task Force 78 in charge of the mine clearance in North Vietnam. Key members of End Sweep gathered in Subic Bay. Some of the attendees included Admiral McCauley, Captain Vecchione, Seventh Fleet Plans Officer Capt. Edward Briggs, Colonel Dionisopoulos, Commander Froid, Lieutenant Commander Emarine, myself, and other mine warfare personnel. Admiral McCauley briefed Vice Adm. James L. Holloway III, Commander, Seventh Fleet.

Admiral McCauley would eventually, after Seventh Fleet meetings on board the *Oklahoma City*, move to the amphibious flagship of Task Force 78, the USS *Worden*. There he worked closely with the chief of staff, Cmdr. Paul L. Gruendl, also a mine warfare expert; Rear Adm. Wycliffe D. Toole Jr., Commander of Task Force 76 (CTF 76); and Brig. Gen. Edward J. Miller, Commander of Task Group 79.1.

This first meeting primarily dealt with command and control, organizational functions, and planning to assemble the assets required for execution of End Sweep.

The giant air force C-5As and C-141 s began flying in the mine warfare CH-53D helicopters from navy squadron HM-12 from Charleston, South Carolina, to Naval Air Station Cubi Point, Philippines.

I began writing messages to assemble three Marine helicopter squadrons (HMM-164 [CH-46s], HMM-165 [CH-46s], and HMM-462 [CH-53]) from TG 79.1 Marine units aboard TF 76 ships, including the *New Orleans*.

The *Okinawa* had already returned to San Diego for normal scheduled repair work, so we were lacking one LPH helicopter transport carrier to execute our mine sweeping plans. I sent a message to CTG 79.1 to move the Marine helicopters from the *New Orleans* to NAS Cubi Point for installation of mine sweeping equipment and to prepare for mine sweeping training in Subic Bay, Philippines.

Admiral Holloway directed that Admiral McCauley form Task Force 78, which included Amphibious Squadron 1, Mobile Mine Countermeasures, Mine Flotilla 1, Base Support, Mine Countermeasures, Inland Waterways, and Diving and Salvage.

Commander Froid coordinated with TF 76 the movements and involvement of the amphibious ships with TF 78. I coordinated, with Captain Vecchione, the types and numbers of helicopters assigned to each ship as TF 78 was formed. Captain Vecchione and I had some minor conflicts in deciding the helicopter mix aboard the ships, particularly the LPHs. Captain Vecchione wanted to place an army CH-47 Crane helicopter aboard the LPH *New Orleans*. Basically, I thought the Crane helicopter was too large and would have consumed too much deck space and would have impacted upon flight operations of TF 78. Captain Vecchione wanted the flying Crane aboard the LPH to salvage any helicopters that might crash in the water during End Sweep. It would have been a good idea if we had the deck space. Additionally, the army Crane rotor blades were not built to fold for deck parking like the Marine Corps helicopters. I insisted that the Crane would not go aboard the LPH, and we debated the issue in our war room on the *Oklahoma City*. While Admiral McCauley and Captain Vecchione discussed their viewpoints with me, Admiral Holloway settled the issue. The army flying Crane did not go aboard the *New Orleans*.

As preparations got under way at Cubi Point, each Marine Corps CH-53A helicopter required a towing cable rig to accommodate towing a Mark 105 (MK 105) hydrofoil turbine-powered magnetic sweep sled, with a Mark 104 (MK 104) acoustic device attached in tandem to it. A long magnetic pipe was attached trailing behind the MK 104. The pipe was painted orange and was therefore called magnetic orange pipe, MOP. The HM-12 navy squadron CH-53Ds already had all necessary mine sweeping equipment installed back in Charleston, South Carolina.

The MK 105 mine sweeping sled would simulate the magnetic characteristics of a ship, and the MK 104 acoustic mine sweeping device would generate noise to detonate acoustic mines.

Additionally, each CH-53 helicopter had installed auxiliary fuel tanks providing the choppers with four hours of flight time capability, and inside each helicopter cockpit, behind the pilots, was a Raydist tracking panel that would take fixes from antennas installed ashore to track the patterns of the MK 105 sled towed by the helicopter. This allowed the pilots to fly precise flight paths using electronic-generated grid-heading lines for navigational flying. A Raydist crewmember would observe the flight track and give directional changes to the pilots forward in the cockpit. This tracking would ensure that the helicopters flew the tow track patterns without missing an area in the mine sweep efforts.

The situation that concerned us was that the ongoing Paris peace talks had created documents being sent to us which indicated that an agreement would require the United States to guarantee a 95 percent sweep coverage. To ensure such a high coverage, the areas could not be swept by flying only visually. The pilots would require electronic tracking, and therefore, the Raydists were of utmost importance.

Initially, these Hastings "T" Raydist Navigational System transmitter towers would have to be installed along the Subic Bay shore. This tracking system would be used for rehearsal training at Subic Bay by duplicating a grid that would be created in the Haiphong Channel. Obviously, this would require ultimate installation of Raydist towers inside of North Vietnam to create the electronic grids for the pilots to fly along precisely.

Another control panel was also installed in the CH-53 helicopters to allow the pilots to control, on board, the towed MK 105 hydrofoil with its simulated electrical signature of various types for various kinds of ships. When the electrical circuit between two buoyant magnetic conductor cables is completed, these electrical pulses activate the magnetic mine firing devices of the actuated live mines.

The MK 105 turbine-powered, magnetic, hydrofoil sweep sleds were built by the Edo Corporation. The MK 105 weighs six thousand pounds and is launched from the rear of an LPD after being attached to a tow cable affixed to the aft end of a hovering CH-53 helicopter. The MK 105 has hydrofoils that are like the inverted wings of a gull bird. The inverted wings, or hydrofoils, can be extended or retracted by the helicopter pilot. Two hollow floats contain fuel tanks for nine hundred pounds of JP-5 fuel for the turbine engine mounted upon it. It is towed from the helicopter after hook-up from the stern of the LPD. The CH-53 helicopter flies at fifty-five feet of altitude above the water, at a speed of only fifteen knots. To explode an acoustical mine during sweeping, the MK 104 acoustic device is added, in tandem tow, to the MK 105 magnetic generating sled.

Some of our staff officers were skeptical about of a helicopter being capable of towing a six-thousand-pound sled through the water, but I produced a document that depicted a Marine CH-53A helicopter, during military acceptance testing and qualifications of that helicopter, pulling a fourteen-thousand-ton LPD, USS *Austin* (LPD-4). The negative comments ceased as I passed the document with the photos around the war room.

In the meantime, Lieutenant Commander Emarine had requested standard mine sweeping operation ships (MSOs) from Guam. They were wooden-hulled ships specifically designed for clearing the old WWII–type floating mines, or moored, tethered mines.

An MK 103 system was also available for snagging and cutting loose moored mines so they would float to the surface for exploding by crewmembers of the MSO ships. The United States did not seed such floating mines in and around North Vietnam, but we were not sure if the North Vietnamese had set some of those old-fashioned moored-type mines off their coasts to keep our gunships away from their coastal waterways.

Because this would be the U.S. Navy's first major mine sweeping campaign since extensive mine sweeping at Wonsan, Korea, in 1950–51, the Seventh Fleet had to be prepared for sweeping possible North Vietnamese floating mines. The first task was to have the *Engage*

(MSO-433), *Fortify* (MSO-446), *Force* (MSO-445), and *Impervious* (MSO-449) sweep an area thirty-five nautical miles southeast of the entrance to the Haiphong Channel to ensure a safe anchorage area for assembling the newly formed TF 78 ships. The destroyers, USS *Epperson* (DD-719) and USS *Worden* (DLG-18), escorted the MSOs to their sweep area off the coast of North Vietnam.

Because we were short one helicopter transport LPH ship, due to the return of the *Okinawa* to San Diego, Commander Froid knew we needed two LPHs and three LPDs to be able to carry a total of sixty mine sweep helicopters to fully support Operation End Sweep.

Froid and I reviewed all previous mine sweeping message traffic, and Jim found a simple line statement in one of the JCS messages that read, in part:

TO ACCOMPLISH THE MINE SWEEP OPERATION, WORLDWIDE ASSETS ARE AVAILABLE.

Using that JCS quote, Froid immediately drafted a message to CINCPACFLT, referring to JCS's quote, requesting that an available Atlantic Sixth Fleet LPH be dispatched to join TF 78 for Operation End Sweep. To Jim's surprise, numerous messages flashed around the world through various chains of command.

The USS *Inchon* (LPH-12) was in a liberty port in Norway when she received a directive to leave the Sixth Fleet and join the Seventh Fleet in the western Pacific. The *Inchon* crossed the Atlantic Ocean, passed through the Panama Canal, and briefly stopped in Hawaii.

In the meantime, the Marine and navy helicopter squadrons had begun training of mine sweeping in Subic Bay, where TF 78 had laid out a simulated Haiphong Channel using the Raydist equipment.

While I was briefing Admiral Holloway on the status of the sweep training, he asked me a question I didn't expect, "Where do they have the Raydist beacons located ashore for training in Subic?"

I responded, "Admiral, they are located on four of my favorite drinking bars in downtown Olongapo City, and some are along the Subic Bay Base."

"On top of bars downtown?" asked the admiral.

"Yes sir, Admiral, they have to be located somewhere in the city to transmit out to Subic Bay. The bars that I selected all are two-story buildings. This allows the Raydist electronic transponders to transmit unrestricted by any taller obstacles. No matter where we would place them downtown, someone might come across them. It is unlikely someone will be walking around on top of those bars. Besides, if someone found one, they wouldn't know what it was, suspended up a tall pole as they are."

The admiral murmured, "On the tops of bars . . . you Marines started in Tun Tavern in Philadelphia in 1775, and now, almost two hundred years later, you're still involved in bars!" He gave a sly smile and shook his head in near disbelief.

During one of our returns from Subic Bay in the Philippines, after repairs to our guns, the *Oklahoma City* cruised south from Subic Bay past Mindoro Island and the many other Philippine islands. Sailing southward from the main Philippine island of Luzon, past the Siuyan Sea and island of Palawan, was the most beautiful cruise of my life. The natural beauty of the southern Philippines with its many islands and dense, green vegetation is absolutely remarkable. We then sailed through the Sulu Sea, north of Borneo, and then northwest to the South China Sea.

Once back into the South China Sea, our ship held a missile firing exercise to test-fire our large Talos guided-missile system. We fired one of these automobile-sized missiles, and it shot off the ship's missile house perfectly.

Admiral Holloway had the *Oklahoma City* fire that practice missile for a reason.

Upon reaching the gunline off North Vietnam, the admiral requested, via the chain of command to JCS, and received a one-time-only permission to fire a single Talos missile into North Vietnam.

Prior to this, the heavy missile cruiser USS *Chicago*, up at Yankee Station, had routinely fired Talos missiles in surface-to-air mode to shoot down North Vietnamese MiGs. Higher authority had never allowed us to fire any missile surface-to-surface into North Vietnam. Admiral Holloway felt that we should try such firing in this limited war effort.

With Admiral Holloway finally getting approval for his request to fire a single Talos missile, surface-to-surface at the enemy inside of North Vietnam, our fleet set up a coordinated stage. The *Chicago* moved farther north. Our *Oklahoma City* moved north to an area below Haiphong Harbor. The navy aircraft carrier launched an attack upon North Vietnam to stir up MiGs around Haiphong. The navy attack aircraft purposely departed the North Vietnamese area slowly with the objective of drawing up the MiGs. The trap was set. As the MiGs closed on the slow-departing navy attack bombers, the navy jets accelerated, drawing the MiGs farther out to sea. The trap began to close on the enemy. As the MiGs got a distance out from the North Vietnam coast, our *Oklahoma City* missile house fired one Talos missile. I just happened to have had the war room watch as Seventh Fleet duty officer assignment at that time. I listened to the countdown of the missile as reported to me from the missile house firing area and CIC. The missile fired perfectly, and then I heard the countdown to impact to target. The target was a North Vietnamese ground control intercept radar site (GCI). The site had been radar-guiding the MiGs for their attack upon the navy jets retiring to the Gulf of Tonkin. On the fired countdown of twenty-three, I heard the word *Splash!* This was the verbal report of the missile impact, announced by the missile crew and CIC. The Talos apparently impacted upon the GCI site. The enemy never knew what hit them.

The next morning, we sent a drone (pilotless) plane over the impacted target area to take photos. The drone returned to our ship area, and the photos were quickly developed. The photos showed the admiral and staff that the enemy's GCI site had been totally destroyed.

That was the only time that I know of during the entire war we were allowed, by JCS, to fire a surface-to-surface missile into North Vietnam. This reflected the mentality of our civilian politicians that created the term *limited war* as they used it in Korea and again in Vietnam.

Soon after the *Oklahoma City* returned south along the gunline, we received a message from the commanding general, III Marine Amphibious Force, Lt. Gen. Louis Metzger. General Metzger was coming out to the Gulf of Tonkin from Okinawa to see his troops along the gunline. Commander Froid sent a message out to TF 76 to string out their ships so that helicopter flying distances between the ships leading up to our *Oklahoma City* would be minimized. This would enable the general to visit his troops on board the amphibious ships and visit Admiral Holloway on the *Oklahoma City*.

One mid-morning, General Metzger arrived overhead the *Oklahoma City* by Marine CH-46 helicopter. Prior to the general's arrival overhead, the *Oklahoma City* had been firing at North Vietnamese coastal gun batteries. The ship ceased firing, and then our ship's public address system announced that the ship was going to flight quarters. The ship moved farther from shore. The crew readied for taking the general's helicopter aboard the fantail. I heard the flight quarters announcement and knew the general would soon be landing. I went aft to the fantail helo-deck to greet the general and to lead him alongside the ship to Admiral Holloway's flag dining room.

The helicopter landed as his wingman continued circling above. General Metzger got out of the landed helicopter. I saluted and greeted him. I motioned for him to follow me forward, along the narrow teak passageway. Just as we briskly walked the deck along the side of the ship, a North Vietnamese coastal defense battery began firing at our ship. A shell impacted the water off our starboard side. Water showered General Metzger and me. Automatically, we both began running. We heard the ship's engines increasing speed as the ship moved farther from shore, away from the North Vietnamese 130mm guns. As I opened a side hatch and jumped through the hatchway, another shell impacted and hit the antennae mast of the ship. Flak and antennae parts flew down upon the deck with loud metallic impacting noises. General Metzger jumped inside the hatchway. The admiral stood down the red carpeted passageway leading to his dining cabin. Admiral Holloway stood there laughing like hell at General Metzger and me, as water was dripping down our now-soaked clothing. We walked up to meet the admiral, and Admiral Holloway and General Metzger shook hands. The general quickly said, "Admiral, I didn't know the navy got shot at in this war!"

Admiral Holloway continued laughing and responded, "On occasion, General, on occasion."

A few days after General Metzger's departure, while reading the daily message traffic, I came across a statement within the message covering the USS *Inchon*'s movement report of their departure from Hawaii, en route to join us for End Sweep. The short statement that caught my eye read:

CH-53 HELICOPTERS FROM HMH-463 AT
KANEOHE, HAWAII, ARE LOADED ABOARD
INCHON.

I read and reread the message again. I had not sent any message to anyone requesting additional Marine Corps helicopters. To my knowledge, General Metzger didn't request any additional Marine choppers to be moved to the western Pacific. I didn't see any message traffic from the 1st Marine Aircraft Wing, Gen. Les Brown, at Iwakuni, Japan, asking for more helicopters for Operation End Sweep.

My immediate boss, Commander Froid, had asked for an additional LPH and knew he was getting the *Inchon*, but he never asked for nor expected to hear that Marine helicopters from Hawaii were inbound to the Seventh Fleet. Jim asked me, "What are you going to do with them?"

I responded, "I don't know! I have no idea why they're coming."

I knew Admiral Holloway would soon be asking what that message meant . . . and I didn't know. I quickly sent a message to CINCPACFLT, asking why they were sending a full squadron of CH-53A helicopters in HMH-463, to us?

I noticed that in related message traffic, HMH-463 was commanded by Lt. Col. John Van Nortwick III. I flew old Korean War vintage HRS-3 helicopters with John back in 1958 in Japan. He was a sharp officer and pilot in those days, and I knew he would also have a fine squadron of well-prepared Marine helicopter pilots who could handle any assignment. The problem confronting General Metzger, General Brown, and me was where do we place these twelve large CH-53A Sea Stallions? We simply did not have any deck space for an additional twelve helicopters. I had just recently completed my debate with Captain Vecchione over my resistance to placing an army CH-47 flying Crane on the LPH *New Orleans*. There was no place to put this additional squadron, and I was the Marine helicopter-mix decision maker . . . or so I thought. My question, of course, was who ordered HMH-463 aboard the incoming *Inchon* from Hawaii?

I quickly briefed Admiral Holloway that the Marine CH-53A squadron had been loaded aboard the *Inchon* at Pearl Harbor, Hawaii, and I didn't know who ordered it. The admiral was also confused.

Soon, a CINCPACFLT message response came in. It simply directed that COMSEVENTHFLT was to integrate HMH-463 squadron into Operation End Sweep.

In the meantime, General Brown of the 1st Marine Aircraft Wing sent a message to his immediate boss, Lieutenant General Metzger at III MAF, asking the same question. CG III MAF sent us a message to determine if we had requested that additional squadron. We responded that we had not.

I drafted a message to have the *Inchon* stop at Okinawa, en route to join us in the Gulf of Tonkin, and drop off HMH-463 for backup readiness because I could not fit them onto our amphibious helicopter-borne ships. The admiral stopped me from sending the message and said, "Let them go to NAS Cubi Point in the Philippines, and we can use them as reserves from there. They'll be closer to us in North Vietnam."

I responded to the admiral's desire, and Commander Froid and I jointly sent a message to the USS *Inchon* and TF 79, directing the offloading of HMH-463 at NAS Cubi Point.

Shortly, a blockbuster message came in from CINCPACFLT. It directed COMSEVENTHFLT to use HMH-463 as the main Marine helicopter squadron, joining the navy HM-12 squadron of CH-53D helicopters for Operation End Sweep.

We were shocked. For the last month and a half, Marine squadron HMH-462, a composite squadron of CH-53A choppers and HMM-165 with CH-46 helos, had been training for End Sweep at Subic Bay. Additionally, all of their helicopters were already fully modified with the mine sweeping equipment enabling them to tow the devices and to use the Raydist electronic tracking monitors. They also had installed ALE-29 flare dispensers for evading heat-seeking missiles, particularly for the SA-7 Strella handheld SAM.

However, we found out that General Victor Krulak, commanding general, Fleet Marine Forces Pacific (CG FMFPAC) in Hawaii, had assigned HMH-463 to Gen. Les Brown's 1st Marine Aircraft Wing. Additionally, we heard that the FMFPAC commander had coordinated with our CINCPACFLT commander, also located in Hawaii, and had offered HMH-463 to board the *Inchon* as it stopped in Hawaii, en route to join us in the western Pacific. But, because it was coming from higher authority outside the war zone, I thought that we might be directed to include HMH-463 into the sweep operation if we had time to train them before an actual Paris ceasefire agreement was signed. Therefore, I began making plans to place HMH-463 back onto the *Inchon* after their mine sweeping training and equipment installations at NAS Cubi Point. That would result in HMM-165 being a composite squadron of CH-46s and CH-53s going on the LPH *New Orleans*.

The *Oklahoma City* had to leave the gunline for a two-day repair of guns in Subic Bay, Philippines. This would save an airplane flight for Larry Emarine and me from Vietnam to Subic Bay because we had to get to Subic Bay to discuss End Sweep training, and now the HMH-463 situation, with the Task Force 78 staff on the LPH *New Orleans*.

The *Oklahoma City* stopped in Manila Bay, Philippines, en route to Subic Bay. Admiral Holloway stated to me, "When we tie-up dockside in Manila, I will call Admiral Clarey at CINCPACFLT on a classified covered line and discuss the HMH-463 situation with him to determine what really is going on."

Larry Emarine and I arranged with TF 78 to have a Marine helicopter pick us up at the U.S. embassy helicopter pad in Manila and fly us to the *New Orleans* in Subic Bay as soon as our ship docked in Manila. Larry and I had to have a face-to-face meeting with the staff of TF 78 to figure out what to do with the incoming HMH-463 on board the *Inchon*. We had to discuss what impacts this might have with Admiral McCauley, Captain Vecchione, and their staff regarding the ongoing training being done by composite Marine squadron HMM-165, the assigned Marine helicopter squadron that was to work with navy HM-12 in the actual mine sweeping operation.

We sent a message to the *New Orleans* to dispatch a helicopter to the helo-pad at the U.S. embassy in Manila to pick up Larry Emarine and myself. By the time our ship docked in Manila, we had received a message from General Metzger, CG III MAF. The message stated that Gen. Les Brown, CTG 79.3, the commander of the 1st Marine Aircraft Wing in Japan, was sending Col. Bill Maloney to Cubi Point to meet with me. It further stated that Colonel Maloney would request me to coordinate a meeting between Colonel Maloney and Admiral Holloway when our *Oklahoma City* arrived in Subic Bay from Manila. Colonel Maloney was dispatched by General Brown to discuss the incoming HMH-463 situation.

I was an old friend of Col. Bill Maloney, having flown HOK-1 helicopters and OE-1 Bird Dog airplanes with him in VMO-2 on Okinawa in 1959.

After the *Oklahoma City* had tied up at the pier in Manila, Larry and I got off the ship and rushed by cab to the U.S. embassy. The scheduled Marine helicopter pickup of Larry and me at the embassy was only minutes later. We entered past the Marine sentry at the embassy gate and walked over to the helicopter landing pad. An American-looking man in civilian clothing was standing at the helo-pad. I introduced Larry and myself to the man, who was holding a two-way radio. I told him that we were waiting for an incoming Marine helicopter to land and whisk us away to the *New Orleans*. He promptly responded by telling us he was a White House secret service agent and that there would be no Marine helicopter landing at that pad today, except for the one for Vice President Agnew. He continued to explain that Vice President Agnew was visiting Manila today and that the embassy helicopter pad was reserved all day only for his helicopter and that the pad was closed to all other helo traffic. He said that the vice president's Marine Corps helicopter was parked at the Manila International Airport and would be coming over to the embassy when Vice President Agnew had completed his visit to Manila.

I quickly asked the secret service agent where his boss was. He quipped, "He's inside the embassy."

Larry and I quickly ran into the embassy seeking the senior secret service member and found him. We jointly explained that we had an urgent requirement to fly out of the helo-pad and gave him some non-classified background of what we were in the middle of.

He was not too impressed. I then opened my briefcase that I had handcuffed to my left arm and showed him the tops of several papers marked in red titled TOP SECRET SENSITIVE. That got his attention. I explained to him that we were directly engaged in an operation that was tied to the Paris peace talks and the safe return of the POWs from North Vietnam. I couldn't tell him what it was we were involved with, but he became convinced we were bonafide military men on an important trip to Subic Bay. He spoke on his radio and talked to the other agent at Manila Airport. He then said,

"The agent at the Manila Airport confirmed that there was a Marine CH-46 parked not far from the vice president's helicopter and that the crew acknowledged they were sent to pick up two Seventh Fleet staff personnel at the embassy." The agent then said, "I'll have to clear this with a few other people, so hang in here."

Larry and I looked at each other, and it seemed this waiting session could turn into an all-day waiting game for permission to use the pad. We decided to tell the agent we were going to grab a cab and head for the Manila Airport, or we might never connect with the Marine helicopter waiting for us there. We rushed out the gate, called a cab, and it drove us about one hundred yards. The cab ran smack into Manila's rush-hour traffic. The cab stopped. As we sat there for ten minutes, we saw a Marine CH-46 helicopter flying low about three miles, coming from the direction of the Manila Airport. We quickly exited the cab and ran back the one hundred yards to the embassy. The agent at the helo-pad said, "I'm glad you came back. I now have authority to allow your helicopter to land here. The agent at the airport has told your helicopter crew they could come over and pick you up."

Larry and I stood there soaking wet from the run in the Manila heat of the day as we watched our CH-46 helicopter approaching across Manila Bay.

Within minutes we were aboard the CH-46, heading for Subic Bay and the *New Orleans*.

When Larry and I arrived aboard the *New Orleans*, anxious Task Force 78 staff members met us. We got out of the helicopter and were barraged by a series of angry questions concerning the confusion regarding what was going on with bringing HMH-463 to Subic Bay on the *Inchon*. By the time we made our way down to the operations room on the ship, the TF 78 staff was aware that neither we on the Seventh Fleet nor the III Marine Amphibious Force commander or his 1st Marine Air Wing commander had requested the additional CH-53 squadron.

During the tense meeting with TF 78 staff, Captain Vecchione conveyed an in-depth presentation of where the Marine HMM-165 composite squadron had progressed to in flight training with the mine sweep equipment over the past weeks. Lieutenant Commander Emarine then gave a presentation of the layout of where the mines were seeded and the areas that would need to be neutralized, and in what order.

I needed all specific statistical facts of the flight training already accomplished by HMM-165 at Subic Bay so that I could convey that to Admiral Holloway, who was en route to Subic Bay aboard the *Oklahoma City* from the visit in Manila. Captain Vecchione kept expressing that he did not understand why HMH-463 was joining the sweep operation. I could not answer that other than to say we are trying to find that out, too. We did know that higher authority had directed HMH-463 to board the *Inchon* at Pearl Harbor and that we, on the Seventh Fleet staff, had no plans for just how we would utilize HMH-463 other than as a possible backup squadron, remaining at NAS Cubi Point. Or, the other possibility might develop into having HMH-463 go ashore into North Vietnam to assist the North Vietnamese in sweeping the inland waterways of mines we laid.

Captain Vecchione, after presenting Lieutenant Commander Emarine and me with all kinds of facts and statistical sheets to take to Admiral Holloway, strongly stated, "It is not feasible at this juncture of the training of Marine composite squadron HMM-165 to switch sweep rolls with HMH-463. HMM-165 is already 65 percent completed with the required training syllabus, and all their aircraft have had the sweep equipment installed for weeks." The question arose . . . what if the Paris peace talks result in an agreement and the protocol of agreement requires immediate execution of End Sweep? If the agreement were signed, just as we switched Marine helicopter squadrons and in the middle of installing the equipment into HMH-463 helicopters, chaos would result with only having the navy squadron HM-12 sweep squadron ready to sail for Haiphong from the Philippines.

Any delay in commencing the mine sweep operations in Haiphong Harbor would no doubt cause a delay in getting our POWs back. It would take at least another month to train the newly arriving squadron.

At the end of the second day of our meetings aboard the *New Orleans*, the *Oklahoma City* steamed into Subic Bay from Manila. Larry Emarine and I quickly departed the *New Orleans* by helicopter and returned to *Oklahoma City*.

Lieutenant Commander Emarine and I jointly briefed Admiral Holloway on the situation and questioned why higher authority insisted that TF 78 use HMH-463 as the main Marine helicopter mine sweep squadron. We briefed the admiral on the exact training syllabus HMH-463 would have to complete to get ready and explained that HMM-165 was already 65 percent completed with the required training, and we explained that all of the HMM-165 helicopters had sweep equipment installed weeks ago.

Admiral Holloway, armed with the training statistics we brought from the meeting with TF 78 staff on the *New Orleans*, got on the secure-voice telephone in the communications department of the *Oklahoma City*. The admiral called Adm. Bernard A. Clarey, CINCPACFLT in Hawaii. Admiral Holloway explained the situation. He recommended that the Seventh Fleet utilize HMH-463 as the backup helicopter squadron, keeping it at Subic Bay during the sweep operations. He also expressed the other option of eventually moving HMH-463 ashore into North Vietnam to assist the North Vietnamese in sweeping the inland waterways, if the Paris ceasefire agreement and sweep protocol were to dictate U.S. assets ashore in North Vietnam.

After a long discussion, Admiral Holloway hung up the phone and shook his head at me. He said something to the effect of, "Somehow the commanding general, Fleet Marine Forces, Pacific, in Hawaii, must have convinced Admiral Clarey that the Hawaiian-based HMH-463 coming out here on the *Inchon* should be the primary Marine helicopter sweep squadron working jointly with the navy HM-12 squadron for executing End Sweep, and that is why CINCPACFLT directed HMH-463 to sail aboard the *Inchon* to the western Pacific." Admiral Holloway and I walked up the ladder from the communications center. The admiral added, "Admiral Clarey will be sending a specific message directing that HMH-463 be the assigned primary Marine helicopter squadron for working with the navy HM-12 squadron and that the training of HMH-463 must commence as quickly as feasible upon their arrival at Subic Bay.

Very shortly a top secret message arrived in our war room from CINPACFLT reiterating that directive.

Our staff couldn't believe it. I flew back over to the *New Orleans* to brief Captain Vecchione so he knew that we'd be sending that message for his TF 78 staff to take action. Captain Vecchione was in shock. He couldn't believe it either. By the time I flew back to the *Oklahoma*

City, the ready and trained squadron HMM-165 had gotten the word from Captain Vecchione and were, no doubt, beyond belief; they had trained hard and were ready and now had no idea what their role in End Sweep would be. The morale must have plummeted.

A totally new, from scratch, training regimen would have to be executed here at Subic Bay while we all sweated out the exact date when the Paris peace talks would result in an execute message for End Sweep.

The general consensus was . . . if the balloon goes up, we got us a real bag of worms . . . caught in the middle of removing tow and electronic equipment from one Marine squadron and installing it into helicopters from another squadron. Obviously, we'd be caught between an almost trained squadron and one just commencing training for towing the sweep equipment.

As I pondered over the problem thrust upon us, I again read a message that came in from CG III MAF alerting us that the commanding general, 1st Marine Air Wing, Maj. Gen. Les Brown, was sending Col. Bill Maloney down from Iwakuni, Japan. Colonel Maloney would request a visit with Admiral Holloway and expressed the desire that the wing commander did not want HMH-463 to replace the almost-trained HMM-165 squadron at this critical juncture in time. I briefed Admiral Holloway that Colonel Maloney was en route to NAS Cubi Point in a C-130 transport and that I would meet him at the airfield and bring him aboard the *Oklahoma City* to meet with Admiral Holloway.

I met Colonel Maloney at the airport and drove him dockside of the *Oklahoma City*. We exchanged briefings. I briefed him on the exact circumstances we confronted as briefed to me by TF 78's Captain Vecchione. Colonel Maloney strongly expressed General Brown's desire to retain HMM-165 as the primary Marine sweep squadron. Colonel Maloney, like me, felt it was great that we were receiving extra aircrews and helicopters we could use as reserve backup support, if needed. But he also expressed his support for General Brown in that this was a critical training time for HMM-165, and this was no time to risk placing an unfamiliar squadron into that preparation cycle to replace HMM-165. I took Colonel Maloney to my operations office, and we further discussed the situation. I showed him the top secret message sent from Admiral Clarey to Admiral

Holloway, directing that HMH-463 be the prime Marine squadron for the sweep. He read the message dictating also that training should commence as soon as the squadron could possibly do so, after arrival and offloading from the LPH *Inchon* in Subic Bay.

Colonel Bill Maloney read and then reread the short, explicit message directive. He sipped his coffee, shook his head, looked me in the eye, and said, "With this in hand there is nothing we can do about it. There is no sense in my seeing Admiral Holloway about our resistance to this directive. Would you please send a copy of this directive to General Brown so he can understand just how it all went?"

I responded, "I already sent a copy to General Metzger and General Brown."

"Well, not much I can do here. No reason to see the admiral. Take me back to Cubi Point and I'll fly back up to Japan and brief General Brown that it all slid downhill and there's nothing we can do about it."

As soon as Colonel Maloney left in the C-130 for Japan, I flew over to the *New Orleans*, which was anchored in Subic Bay. I first met with Captain Vecchione and then I met with U.S. Marines Lt. Col. Charles B. Redman and Lt. Col. James C. Robinson on TF 78's staff.

There, I spent considerable time with them as they tried to figure out just how they would convey the bad news to the hardworking aircrews of HMM-165 composite squadron consisting of HMM-164 and HMH-462. It wasn't going to be easy to pass this information to these dedicated aircrews.

Later, I heard just how badly some of the aircrews took this upsetting swap-of-squadrons directive. It didn't go over very well. Hard feelings would remain a lifetime for those aircrews of HMM-165. It didn't matter to them that CTF 78 or COMSEVNTHFLT didn't dream up this upheaval. They finally got the word that the directive had come from outside the western Pacific and they were relegated to a lesser role after such a major training effort.

Within days, the *Inchon* arrived in Subic Bay. HMH-463 was offloaded and relocated to nearby NAS Cubi Point. Major General Leslie E. Brown, commanding general, 1st Marine Aircraft Wing, and Col. Bill Maloney flew down from Japan and warmly greeted HMH-463 upon their arrival from Hawaii.

The big task of training this squadron would begin once again for TF 78. HMM-165, the original Marine squadron assigned to End Sweep, was to be out of the initial End Sweep phase of the operation. They were assigned to remain at NAS Cubi Point as a backup unit for possible inland waterways sweeping if directed by higher authority. Their morale was devastated. After months of planning, training, and the excitement of expecting to perform the history-making first helicopter-borne sweep of mines, they were, all of a sudden, relegated to be the backup unit. I personally was disturbed by the turmoil created and the risk of the critical timing involved by switching squadrons at this juncture. Each day, we sweated out the Paris peace talks. What if they reached an agreement in the middle of this initial training stage of HMH-463 helicopter towing of the sweep equipment? How could we respond immediately to a JCS execute directive of End Sweep?

Soon, the world press was trying to find out exactly what the mine sweep training was all about in Subic Bay. They knew the mines seeded in the Haiphong Channel were different from previous mines used in World War II and the Korean War. The press wanted to know exactly how the sweeping of these different types of mines would be accomplished. Finally, when Washington wanted the world to know, higher authority passed the word down to our staff to let a little information out to the press.

Admiral Holloway set up a press conference on board the *New Orleans* in Subic Bay. He told the press roughly how the neutralization of the mines in Haiphong Harbor would eventually be conducted when dictated by a Paris peace accord. Admiral Holloway also provided the news media with a photographic session of an actual airborne sweep training demonstration.

As we stood, with press personnel on the *New Orleans* in Subic Bay, the admiral told the news reporters that shortly a navy CH-53D helicopter would be flying by, low, towing a MK 105 sweep sled. The press held their cameras ready. Then, finally, the anticipation of the press was greeted with a large green helicopter coming across the bay, towing a MK 105 sweep sled. We all waited a little more as the chopper approached closer. Then, to all our surprise, out in front of us now was not the anticipated navy blue CH-53D helicopter. Instead, there was a Marine CH-53A. It was painted green and had on the side of the fuselage a large white word, MARINES. The

Marine helicopter flew slowly past us towing the MK 105 sweep device. The cameras clicked away at history in the making ... the first time in warfare that sweeping of mines would be performed by airborne methods.

The admiral turned to me and said, "Where is the navy helicopter that was scheduled to pull the MK105 for this demonstration?"

"Admiral, I don't know. I'll go belowdeck and find out from the Task Force 78 operations officer. I'll report back, sir."

I ran down the nearest ladder, through several passageways and hatchways, and into the operations office. The operations officer briefed me and I ran back topside to brief the admiral.

When I returned to the admiral, I said, "Admiral, Task Force 78 schedules' officer told me the navy helicopter that was scheduled for the MK 105 tow demonstration had mechanical problems after the pilot started his engines. It just so happened that the assigned backup helicopter on the schedule for today was a Marine helicopter."

The admiral looked suspiciously at me and said, "You Marines are something." He continued looking at me while shaking his head in disbelief.

It was to have been a full navy show. And now, the Marine helicopter stole the act. Worldwide news articles depicted photos of the Marine helicopter demonstrating and revealing the sweep activities to the world for the first time.

For days, many of my fellow staff officers kidded me about that incident and accused me of swapping the Marine helicopter for the navy chopper during that important press coverage demonstration.

Leaving Subic Bay on the *Oklahoma City*, our staff sailed for the Gulf of Tonkin. We all had strong mixed emotions on the turmoil forced upon us at, what we thought, was the last minute to integrate this newly arrived squadron into Operation End Sweep.

The installation of the mine sweep equipment, including the electronic tracking equipment, was now under way in HMH-463. Detailed briefings of the aircrews leading up to actual flight training towing the sweep equipment would soon follow.

Being a Marine pilot myself, though, I knew these newly assigned low-flying leathernecks from HMH-463 would do an outstanding professional job. I felt comforted becuase I knew HMH-463's commanding officer, Lt. Col. John Van Nortwick. I knew that if all the other pilots in his squadron were as professional as John, this squadron, if given the time to prepare and complete the training, would do the job in the highest Marine Corps traditional way. But it would take a lot of people a helluva lot of hard work at Subic Bay to get ready for execution of End Sweep.

Chapter 16

• • • • • • • • •

Linebacker II

President Nixon had authorized the resumption of B-52 raids, which they commenced over Hanoi and Haiphong on April 17, 1972. The resumed raids, due to the massive North Vietnamese invasion into South Vietnam beginning on March 30, 1972, caused a storm of controversy among U.S. war protestors and communist supporters worldwide, claiming a major escalation of the war by the Americans. But President Nixon continued the B-52 raids as the Seventh Fleet rebuilt its forces in the area by placing six carriers in the Gulf of Tonkin by July 1972: *America, Hancock, Kitty Hawk, Midway* (CVA-41), *Oriskany* (CVA-34), and *Saratoga* (CVA-60).

Despite the peace terms dictated to Dr. Henry Kissinger by the communists at the October 1972 peace talks in Paris, and the communists' demand for an October 31, 1972, signing of a ceasefire agreement, the war rumbled on. President Nixon personally approved the wording in the sought-after treaty. As a goodwill gesture, Nixon directed a stop to all bombing north of the 20th parallel. The North Vietnamese dropped serious arguments and appeared ready to work forward to an agreement. Then they slowed the progress again with some minor bickering, including accusations against the South Vietnamese. The South Vietnamese added their discontent with the talks because they were now making progress in their counterattack against the massive North Vietnamese invasion. On December 13, 1972, the North Vietnamese abruptly walked out of the Paris peace talks.

The North Vietnamese walk-out from the Paris negotiations forced President Nixon to respond. Nixon ordered a full-strength resumption of bombings in upper North Vietnam. On December 18, 1972, "Linebacker II" was unleashed against military targets in the Hanoi and Haiphong areas. Waves of U.S. Air Force F-111 bombers and B-52s, from Thailand and Guam, struck swiftly. The communists sent up a hail of antiaircraft artillery fire. Numerous SAMs and MiG fighters rose into the air to greet the raids. The MiGs climbed out from northern sanctuary airfields that we previously were not allowed by our leaders in Washington to destroy. We finally had authority to strike these airfields if our level of command felt it necessary. Of course, now they were more highly defended with SAMs.

Lieutenant Colonel Rose, the air force representative on our staff, reported to us from his reading the air force message traffic: "Three B-52 bombers were shot down on this kick-off date of Linebacker II. Also, one MiG was shot down by a tail gunner in a B-52. This was the very first MiG kill by a tail gunner in a B-52 bomber during this very long war."

The on-again, off-again bombing attacks against North Vietnam caused by the on-again and off-again negotiations at Paris proved deadly and costly for the American aircrews of all our flying services. Again, we had foolishly given Hanoi time to rebuild formidable air defenses. Our aircrews were paying the supreme price during their Linebacker II air attacks upon the most defended complex of these two cities, Hanoi and Haiphong. This gradual escalation of attacks had given the enemy time to build air defenses, which were now the best defended targets in the world. The North Vietnamese air defenses were better than the defenses ringing Moscow.

One major problem confronting us, after these many years of conflict, was that the Russians and Chinese were still supplying North Vietnam with the older Russian model of surface-to-air missiles, the SA-2. Our sophisticated jamming aircraft of the air force and navy had already been converted primarily to electronically countering the Soviet Union's technology of their new SA-3 missiles. Our new radar-jamming aircraft were now capable of countering that ring of SA-3s around Moscow and other parts of that vast Soviet country.

Now that President Nixon approved the go ahead to bomb military targets in those highly populated areas in North Vietnam, we had another problem. Our concern now was what losses we would incur due to the enemy having the old SA-2 missiles in North

Vietnam, while our air force and navy had upgraded to electronic equipment designed to counter the SA-3 SAM systems. To further complicate the problem, the North Vietnamese had switched their SA-2 guidance radar to new radar with high-frequency I-Band range. Initially, this was a great concern for the staff of the Seventh Air Force and our own staff at Seventh Fleet command.

After listening to some heavy debates in the war room, and hearing that the air force did not have radar jamming of the I-Band, I was again in a position to offer a unique Marine Corps solution to a problem.

And there was a Marine Corps solution readily available. It was fate and luck that our Marine EA-6A electronic warfare aircraft had the jamming capabilities against the just-introduced North Vietnamese I-Band radar guidance system for the North Vietnamese SA-2 missiles. The newer navy EA-6B aircraft were used to jamming the Fan Song target-acquisition radars of the SA-2 SAMs. This radar acquisition system had a broader band beam that enabled the navy EA-6B equipment to sweep and more easily acquire and suppress it.

When we discussed the entire set of circumstances, only the Marines had, in their inventory, an answer for deterring the enemy's I-Band system.

I briefed Admiral Holloway and sent a message to CG III MAF, info copy to CG 3d MAW, to move Marine EA-6A squadron VMCJ-1 from Iwakuni, Japan, to NAS Cubi Point, Philippines. I then coordinated a message with Cmdr. George Boaz, of our staff, to the commander of carriers, CTF 77. We directed the Marine EA-6A Detachment from VMCJ-2 aboard the USS *Saratoga* to relocate from the carrier in the Gulf of Tonkin to join with VMCJ-1 at NAS Cubi Point. This combined force of Marine Corps EA-6A electronic-jamming aircraft would become a formidable defensive force located at NAS Cubi Point in the Philippines.

We then coordinated a system with the air force to enable the Marine Corps EA-6A electronic aircraft to jam North Vietnamese SAM sites. When the air force scheduled their large-scale B-52 bombing raids in December 1972 against the extremely defended Haiphong and Hanoi areas, we had two, and sometimes four, Marine EA-6A jamming aircraft launch from NAS Cubi Point. Each flight of EA-6As, preceded by a single Marine KC-130 refueler aircraft from VMGR-152, would head for Da Nang. The KC-130 cargo/tanker aircraft carried a limited number of aircraft maintenance crews that flew from Cubi Point to Da Nang. They usually took off at Cubi Point at 0300 each morning. These maintenance crews then refueled the Marine EA-6A aircraft from composite squadron VMCJ-1/VMCJ-2 at Da Nang. The EA-6As then flew from Da Nang to North Vietnam. The EA-6As set up a racetrack pattern just off the Haiphong Channel inlet area in the Gulf of Tonkin. From that traffic pattern, the EA-6As could jam the SAM systems in the Haiphong and Hanoi areas.

They would commence jamming prior to the arrival of the air force B-52 bombers over the target areas. Despite the daily, heavy jamming of the missile sites, the SA-2 surface-to-air missiles, referred to as flying telephone poles by the aircrews, flew skyward at the B-52 bombers and the navy attack bombers in unbelievably large numbers. SA-2 missiles did shoot down B-52s and navy attack bombers simply by the large quantity of missiles launched by the North Vietnamese. Of course, many more bombers would have been shot down if it had not been for the electronic jamming by the Marine Corps EA-6A aircraft. Due to the large number of enemy SAMs fired skyward at the bombers, there was much collateral damage upon the North Vietnamese on the ground from their own exploding surface-to-air missiles. The missiles that missed U.S. aircraft exploded, and the debris naturally fell back upon North Vietnam.

After jamming the SA-2 radar sites, the Marine EA-6A aircraft returned to Da Nang and refueled. They again would get airborne and fly 090 degrees back to their base at Cubi Point, ending a tough eight-hour flying day for the aircrews. Later, after the EA-6As were airborne en route to their base at Cubi Point, the maintenance crews would get back into their KC-130 tanker and also fly back to the Philippines.

This extremely tiring work cycle had to be accomplished daily due to our own self-imposed political situation. President Nixon's withdrawal timetable of military units retrograding out of Vietnam precluded me from having directed the Marine VMCJ-1 and VMCJ-2 units to relocate into and operate out of Da Nang in South Vietnam. This long-day flying cycle was the only feasible way I could utilize these Marine EA-6A jammers in an authorized manner. If I had kept the VMCJ-2 Detachment aboard the *Saratoga*, we would have lost their jamming availability when that ship cycled off the gunline for port visits, leaving only VMCJ-1 to protect the air force B-52 bombers and our own navy attack bombers over North Vietnam. This physically tiring routine for the dedicated Marine aircrews and maintenance crews continued daily until the end of the war. The tempo actually increased during late December 1972 when more intensive B-52 bombing raids struck the Hanoi and Haiphong military complexes.

The combining of the VMCJ-1 and VMCJ-2 Detachments was a merging of two slightly different groups of Marine Corps pilots and electronic warfare officers. It required some personality adjustments. The VMCJ-2 pilots were from MCAS Cherry Point, North Carolina, originally assigned to the carrier *Saratoga* out of Norfolk, Virginia. They had volunteered to form a special Marine detachment of EA-6As to deploy aboard the carrier *Saratoga*. On the other hand, the VMCJ-1 aircrews were out of Iwakuni, Japan, and were mostly non-combat-experienced newcomers to the war. This melting pot of prima donnas and inexperienced aircrews initially caused some aircrew ready-room strain. After several combat missions, though, the combined units settled down into a cohesive, professional team.

The sharp *Saratoga* VMCJ-2 Detachment was led by the officer in charge, Maj. Fred Ogline. Their training officer was Captain Johnson. Another entity was added when Capt. Dick Vogel and Capt. Ed Ashman from VMCJ-3 at El Toro, California, joined the other combined VMCJ units at Cubi Point, Philippines, to beef up the unit.

Later, I talked with Capt. Ed Ashman. He related some of the following incidents he experienced. This was one situation he described:

> Flying above a solid overcast, just south of Haiphong, I happened to be the only EA-6A available to cover three cycles of B-52 alpha strikes, so I had to refuel from a navy A-3 tanker. The A-3 tanker had refueling hose problems. Because it was getting close to the B-52 target time and time for me to begin jamming, I had the A-3 tanker drag me north so I could refuel while returning en route to the target area. What

I didn't know was that the tanker's radar was malfunctioning, and I was hooked up to the tanker gulping fuel. I had turned off my radar to stand by, figuring that the tanker crew knew where they were, heading north. The A-3 tanker pilot really didn't know exactly where he was and didn't say a thing about it to me, as we jointly droned northward.

As we neared the Haiphong area, my electronic countermeasures officer (ECMO) sitting next to me began receiving a Fan Song missile-guidance system signal. I broke off the refueling connection from the A-3 tanker, and my ECMO began his electronic-jamming system. Luckily, we jammed just in time, as two SA-2 SAMs came out of the solid clouds below us and the SAMs were not guiding. With some quick turns, we evaded the fast-climbing surface-to-air missiles that exploded beyond us.

Captain Ashman then related another personal incident:

While jamming in orbit during a B-52 strike off the city of Vinh, we were actively working some SAM sites when one of our monitoring radar units broadcast a warning locating Bandits coming at us from Hanoi, called Bullseye. The MiGs were heading straight for us. It was a clear day. The calls continued to report that the MiGs were continuing toward us, but we could not leave our jamming track without endangering the incoming air force B-52 bomber strike force that we were protecting.

Our EA-6A was a heavy and slow aircraft. We were too slow to outrun MiGs. We couldn't do much about our circumstances. I quickly called our MiG combat air patrol (MiG CAP). MiG CAP responded rapidly, just as I visually observed two MiGs coming in on us fast. Just then, the MiG CAP aircraft pilot called that he was rolling in on a MiG. I glanced at seven o'clock high, and sure enough, a navy F-8 fighter was rolling in on me. I screamed loudly into the UHF radio to the navy F-8 pilot that the MiG he thought he was rolling in on was I, in my EA-6A aircraft, and that he was attacking the wrong target.

The F-8 pilot either heard my shouting or at the last second recognized my big, ugly EA-6A and zoomed closely by me. For some unknown reason, the two actual MiGs that had been picked up on radar and were heading for me did a fast 180-degree turn and departed. Maybe our aerial act simply confused the MiG pilots and they decided to get out of there.

The squeeze was on the North Vietnamese. The United States wanted our prisoners of war returned. The North Vietnamese wanted the United States to stop bombing them, clear the mines from the Haiphong Channel and other ports and waterways, and have the Yankees go home.

The previous Linebacker bombing flights had all been flown from Thailand's bases and aircraft carriers, and with a limited number from airfields in South Vietnam. Now, Linebacker II B-52 bombers were also flying from Guam. This intense activity continued, except for Christmas Eve and Christmas Day. On December 26, 1972, a massive raid of more than one hundred B-52 bombers from Guam and Thailand struck Hanoi and Haiphong military complexes. All aircraft released their heavy bomb loads over these two city areas within fifteen minutes. The extensive waves of B-52 aircraft coming in from various directions impacted upon the North Vietnamese air defense command. They shot down only two B-52 bombers. Marine EA-6A jamming, combined with air force and navy jamming and navy attack bombing raids upon MiG bases, especially Kep Airfield near Hanoi, suppressed the SAMs and MiGs, prior to the arrival of the B-52s.

The following days, the air force continued the B-52 raids. The navy, Marine Corps, and air force fighter/attack bombers attacked the main supply routes (MSRs) connecting Red China with North Vietnam as well as the other MSRs in North Vietnam. The tight squeeze was now being drawn tighter. The noose was closing. Virtually no quantitative supplies were coming into North Vietnam. All ports were blocked due to our mining. The overland routes were continually attacked, including bridges. Key bridges were destroyed or badly damaged. The strangulation hold was in place. This, of course, could have been accomplished many, many years before if the U.S. Congress had cooperated with committed presidents and if the antiwar groups supporting North Vietnam had not prevented our full pursuit of winning this war.

The North Vietnamese finally realized they would run out of military supplies and even food in a rather short period of time. The tremendous quantities of SAMs they had fired would not be replaced due to the stranglehold we had upon North Vietnam. North Vietnam communicated to President Nixon that they would like to resume the broken-off negotiations of the Paris peace talks.

On December 29, 1972, President Nixon directed that all bombings of North Vietnam again be stopped north of the 20th parallel. Linebacker II ended. The skies over Hanoi and Haiphong were quiet once again. Our Seventh Fleet ships ceased coastal bombardments north of the 20th parallel. U.S. Air Force, Navy, and Marine Corps fighter attack bombers and occasional B-52 raids continued in South Vietnam, assisting the South Vietnamese to fend off the continuing assaults from the NVA invasion divisions.

During Linebacker II, the air force had flown 3,500 B-52 bomber sorties along with thousands of fighter/attack bomber missions. During that same phase, from December 18 through December 29, 1972, fifteen B-52 bombers were shot down. An estimated 900 surface-to-air missiles had been fired by the North Vietnamese. The air force shot down only three MiG fighters during this whole month of December with their F-4 Phantoms. Two MiG fighters were also shot down by B-52 tail gunners. The navy, with an F-4 Phantom from off the USS *Enterprise*, shot down only one MiG during December 1972. Obviously, the dramatic dogfights of the major raids of May 10, 1972, never were repeated during Linebacker II. The navy attacks upon enemy airfields prior to the arrival of air force B-52s and the suppression of radar-tracking systems, kept the MiGs from defending their homeland.

During December 1972, B-52 bombers conducted eleven consecutive days of intensive bombing, which, combined with the navy mining of all harbors and key inland waterways, finally forced the North Vietnamese to conclude the Paris peace talks with agreements. The last B-52 missions ended when they concluded the raid on the Tai Ca surface-to-air missile storage area at midnight on December 29, 1972. The air force lost fifteen B-52s during the Hanoi and Haiphong air raids with ninety-two aircrew members killed or captured during December 1972. B-52 bombers accounted for the destruction of 80 percent of the electrical generating capacity, one-fourth of the petroleum reserves of North Vietnam, and most of the SAM storage areas.

With all rail lines severed from the People's Republic of China and the effective mining of Haiphong Channel, other harbors, and key inland waterways, which stopped all shipping, technically, we actually won the military war at that stage of the long conflict. We in the military knew it, and the North Vietnamese leaders knew it, too. Unfortunately, our poor examples of what we called statesmen didn't know it, or understand it. Or they were simply too incapable in their positions and lacked the negotiating skills required to end the war honorably. These statesmen, representing our interests at the Paris peace talks, did not demand any guarantees to protect the Republic of Vietnam. Therefore, all of the long, sweat-filled, bloody years of American GIs' sacrifices were lost at the negotiating table. There is no doubt the intense home-front pressures upon the Nixon administration by communist supporters were instrumental in adding to the rush-job of our negotiators to hurry up, get our POWs home, and get the hell out of Vietnam. This left a lot of unresolved issues at the Paris peace talks as the negotiators moved swiftly to end the fighting, now that we had strangled the enemy.

The war in South Vietnam continued, but not the bombings of the Hanoi and Haiphong areas of North Vietnam. Still, aerial bombings were authorized below the 20th parallel in North Vietnam and south of the DMZ.

As the war ensued, so did the life-threatening combat action encounters by all combatant participants. Each personal encounter with the enemy, by an individual, is a story unto its own.

Chapter 17

• • • • • • • •

The End Nears

On January 5, 1973, just seven days after President Nixon directed the end to American bombings north of the 20th parallel and Linebacker II ended, the USS *Leonard F. Mason* (DD-852), a Gearing-class destroyer, cut swiftly through the night in the Gulf of Tonkin. The crew aboard the *Mason* included Lt. j.g. Fred H. Cherrick. Lieutenant Cherrick awoke in his bunk to the shrill call of the bosun's pipe over the loudspeaker. It was the call to general quarters (GQ). Fred Cherrick had been briefed a few hours earlier by the ship's captain. His ship had participated in the previous Linebacker II attacks on North Vietnam. Now that Linebacker II had ceased, air and naval strikes continued only below the 20th parallel in North Vietnam, in support of the South Vietnamese in South Vietnam.

The call to GQ battle stations created much activity throughout the ship. It was 0030, or just past midnight. Cherrick jumped into his trousers and quickly buttoned his shirt. Within minutes, Fred was on his way to the bridge of the *Mason.*

As the officer of the deck during battle stations, it was Cherrick's duty to provide the conning instructions to the helmsman. Under the captain of the ship, Cherrick had the responsibility to make sure the ship responded to any circumstances that might arise, including hostile action and the navigational situation.

The captain of the *Mason* was Cmdr. Robert L. Warren. At age thirty-five, he had a few years' head start compared to previous captains of the *Mason,* who had been in their late thirties and early forties.

Commander Warren, some years before, had been to the U.S. Naval Academy, while he was serving as an enlisted man on an aircraft carrier. Although firm and clearly in control, he smiled frequently in a boyish manner. Commander Warren expected the crew to do their jobs, and once done, he was as lenient as possible in providing a pleasant environment on the ship.

Commander Warren was pleased with the performance of the crew since he arrived aboard the *Mason*. Lieutenant Cherrick viewed Commander Warren as a trim, five-foot-nine-inch-tall outstanding tennis player who could pass for a young man in his late twenties.

As an active youngster, Commander Warren had been raised in Ferguson, Missouri. Lieutenant Cherrick sensed that Commander Warren had some trying times in his youth, and Cherrick observed that Warren was always calm and capable in precluding disruptions or upheavals on his ship, rather than creating them, like some skippers. Fred Cherrick thought highly of his captain and felt Warren was the ideal skipper.

Two months earlier, Warren had given Cherrick the job of officer of the deck. Cherrick was surprised that Warren would assign such a responsible position as this while in the middle of general quarters during an actual raid. Cherrick was still a fairly junior officer. Now, Cherrick was involved in more action than he had figured he would see. Not only did the action face him, but Cherrick was a very responsible part of it.

Fred Cherrick was only twenty-three and had been in the navy since graduating from Purdue University as an electrical engineer. Fred had volunteered for the navy and the Pacific Fleet, influenced by his desire to travel. Much to his surprise, the Vietnam War had continued well beyond all of his projections and expectations. He was no longer on the Purdue campus; he was part of this long, frustrating war.

After adjusting from the life of college student, Cherrick found he liked most aspects of the navy. He felt attached and loyal to his ship, *Mason*. It was almost a love for the twenty-five-year-old naval vessel. The ship was two years older than Cherrick. It was hard not to empathize with a ship that listed two degrees to the starboard when it was fully loaded, though no one could figure out why. The ship had been planned during the end of World War II. Her age somehow gave the ship a unique personality and created a cohesively efficient working unit. Yet, despite the ship's shortcomings due to its age, she was called upon for an important role. The *Mason* had seen combat action during the Korean War and had participated in six cruises to the Gulf of Tonkin war zone.

The crew of the *Mason*, 250 men, came from all parts of the country and were as varied as possible. Nevertheless, the crew got along well together. The crew's personnel faced their jobs with a spirit of mutual expectation for teamwork, and the navy was successful in creating this type of environment. Within the capabilities of the equipment, the ship performed just what the crew directed her to do.

Cherrick was making his second combat cruise to the Gulf of Tonkin. Unlike his first cruise here in 1971 and early 1972, the war had grown much more active from the standpoint of his destroyer's activities. As Cherrick hurried to the bridge during the general quarters just past midnight, he was well aware of where he was as his mind swept past the years back to his youth.

Few people expected this war would have continued so long. While Cherrick was in high school in Clayton, Missouri, the war began, and it had seemed so remote. Like most other high school students, Cherrick did not believe this war would impact upon him. Later, while he was attending Purdue University, the war got closer for him. There were a few students who were either coming back from the Far East or leaving for military service, but Cherrick still had four years of college to attend. Anti–Vietnam War demonstrations had occurred at Purdue, but they weren't a major part of the campus environment at this stable Indiana school. What did occur impacted and created concern for everyone. Now, after college graduation and after his first combat cruise tour, Cherrick was serving a second tour in the very same war zone. And, unlike the first cruise, this one was filled with combat action.

As the *Mason* was prepared to strike North Vietnam, south of Dong Hoi, Cherrick ordered the ship into position with the other strike force ships in the unit, the destroyers *Cochrane* (DDG-21) and *McCaffery* (DD-860).

Despite the length of the war and lack of cohesion in the United States, Cherrick's main thoughts were of the immediate action, and most important, not making a mistake. The ships were operating with only dim navigational lights, and at high speed in close proximity of each other. A wrong turn could mean a collision within seconds. Guns and missiles were going off all around these light naval units, which shook with every offensive shot. Cherrick figured the situation was thrust upon him, and he knew there was no upside to the situation. Operate perfectly and no one, outside the crew, will remember you. Make one mistake, and you could never erase it. With strong ties to his immediate crewmates, his family and friends back home, he would do anything to carry out his assigned job and live up to their expectations.

Fred Cherrick recalled being nervous during the first strike on this cruise, which had occurred ten days earlier, during Linebacker II. Those feelings had diminished after the second or third strike. One had to concentrate on the task at hand. He concentrated so hard on the turns and the formation, and the location of enemy counterbattery fire from the coastal defense sites, that everything else was pushed out of his mind. The war might be a mess, but he would do his job professionally. Cherrick thought, ultimately, that Nixon and Kissinger would straighten things out.

Suddenly, Cherrick saw flashes on land. Within seconds, the tactical radio circuit came alive. "Tin shop, this is Argentina. Commence firing!" With that radio chatter, the two double-mounts on the *Mason* roared in anger. Shots were on the way toward the southern area of North Vietnam.

Commander Warren, who Cherrick viewed as a highly capable officer and calm commander, looked over the radar screen. His face reflected concern as the silver-green traces also reflected upon his face from the radar screen. In the combat information center, enclosed behind the captain's bridge, similar screens were viewed intently by others, including Lt. j.g. Lou Hirsh. What they all saw was an active radar screen with many fired shells moving in all directions. Cherrick thought, despite the duration of this war, that the North Vietnamese were as game as ever to continue aggressively.

Zuni rockets were launched from the *Mason* with enormous roars. These rockets created chaff clouds and drew enemy fire at the chaff clouds. From a radar screen, it looked as if the three destroyers had grown into a small fleet.

As the ships turned parallel to the coast, south of Dong Hoi, enemy fire increased. Additional colors of flashes on the shore indicated the ships' firings were exploding, causing secondary explosions on impact.

After a few minutes, the three ships accelerated and turned to the open sea. Shells could be heard falling nearby into the sea, with a dull thud. Cherrick ordered a zigzagging course, as the ship formation broke to move out of gun range of the enemy coastal batteries.

Now, the men on *Mason* relaxed. The twenty-five-year-old ship with an aluminum superstructure and no defensive missiles had accomplished its mission. The ship had been called upon to exert the impact of America upon the enemy, and it responded.

At this point, Cherrick again wondered if this war would ever end. Wars, he thought, were between nations, not people. He recalled when the *Mason* crew had picked up a North Vietnamese fisherman after his boat had capsized. They had given him a pack of cigarettes. The man was so scared, he put a dozen cigarettes into his mouth at once. Cherrick thought: What very little people actually know of each other.

Cherrick relaxed and took off his sweat-filled helmet. After twenty of these strikes, he wondered how many more would occur. This strike had lasted less than a half hour, but the time was immeasurable while it occurred. There would be two more strikes this same evening, farther up along the coast.

A few days later, a lanky boatswain's mate by the name of Hobbs stopped Cherrick to talk to him. He thanked Cherrick for avoiding the incoming enemy rounds. Cherrick smiled and shook his head, but Cherrick never forgot what that younger man, Hobbs, had said.

Chapter 18

• • • • • • • •

Ceasefire

The North Vietnamese agreed to resume the Paris peace talks on January 8, 1973. At that time, the U.S. troop strength in RVN had dropped to twenty-four thousand personnel, mostly non-combatants. The combination of Linebacker II air attacks upon North Vietnam, counterattacks by the South Vietnamese during Lam Son 72 against the invading North Vietnamese Army in South Vietnam, and the extensive mining of the major ports and vital inland waterways of North Vietnam worked. It destroyed the will of the North Vietnamese to continue the fight with the Americans. This time, at Paris, the North Vietnamese were seriously ready to negotiate a settlement to get the Americans out of the battle with them.

While the negotiations resumed, we were allowed to bomb only south of the 20th parallel, but with the authority to chase MiGs north of that parallel, if attacked by MiGs. On January 12, 1973, we received a TG 70.8 message stating that navy pilot Lieutenant Kovaleski and his radar intercept officer, Lt. Jim Wise, from VF-161 flying an F-4 Phantom from the USS *Midway*, shot down a MiG over the Gulf of Tonkin. Ironically, this event would result in being the very last MiG shot down in the Vietnam War.

Back on June 17, 1965, two VF-21 F-4B Phantoms with aircrews (Cmdr. Louis C. Page and RIO Lt. Jack Baston and wingman team of pilot, Lt. John C. Smith, and RIO Lt. Cmdr. R. B. Doremud) shot down two MiG-17s with sparrow missiles while flying south of Hanoi.

On January 14, 1973, George Boaz, our staff TF 77 cognizant officer, received a TF 77 message reporting that a navy F-4 Phantom had been shot down by antiaircraft artillery over North Vietnam below the 20th parallel. The aircrew ejected and was picked up by a helicopter and returned to the USS *Midway*. The crew consisted of the pilot, Lieutenant Kovaleski, and his RIO, Ensign Dennis Plautz. Lieutenant Kovaleski, who may have been the last pilot to shoot down a MiG in this war, could possibly have been the very last U.S. pilot himself shot down in this unbelievably long and mismanaged war.

Everyone knew that this war was being conducted by one of the most powerful countries on earth against a third-world nation that did not manufacture guns, tanks, or aircraft. Yet, for years, Washington restrained the U.S. military from defeating North Vietnam. We had not responded adequately to defend an American ally. The Republic of Vietnam was invaded by the communist Democratic Republic of Vietnam (DRV). The DRV was a country capable only of manufacturing bicycles and not war weapons.

In the meantime, during January 1973 and prior to the signed Vietnam Accord in Paris, the Pentagon reported that 317 U.S. military were missing in Laos, in the secret war area.

The communist Pathet Lao spokesman Soth Petrasy reported that the Pathet Lao Army had a detailed list of U.S. prisoners and exact locations where they were being held in Laos. Soth Petrasy stated there would have to be separate truce negotiations between the United States and Laos for the release of the American POWs, but the Pathet Laos never were part of the Paris negotiations in the release of POWs.

The chief negotiator for the North Vietnamese, Bui Tin, had consistently told the American negotiators at the Paris talks that the United States would have to negotiate with the Pathet Lao separately for any Americans held in Laos.

President Nixon was now convinced that the North Vietnamese truly wanted an end to the bombings and the opening of their ports and sea lanes, particularly the Haiphong Channel and main supply routes, which were their lifelines to continued existence and economic survival. Apparently, Nixon believed the North Vietnamese were now seriously willing to negotiate an end to the conflict. Accordingly, Nixon suspended all bombing, mining, and shelling operations throughout all of North Vietnam, above and below the 20th parallel, by his directive on January 15, 1973.

Our ship had extended operating on the gunline for many extra weeks due to the feeling that maybe, now, the North Vietnamese might agree to end this war, but at this juncture, our ship's crew needed a well-earned rest.

Admiral Holloway stated to the skipper of our *Oklahoma City*, "Captain Kanakanui, now's as good a time as any to request a liberty run for the crew. I think we have things pretty much under control out here in the Gulf of Tonkin."

Captain Kanakanui answered, "Aye, aye, Admiral. My crew certainly needs some R&R after all these weeks of working around the clock. I'll request permission for a Hong Kong visit from January 21 through 28."

Within a few days, we sailed into Hong Kong Harbor, the busiest harbor in the world. The new hotels and gleaming white office buildings on Hong Kong Island were a very welcome sight for all hands on the *Ok City*.

Several of the staff wives, including my wife, Eleanor, flew down from Japan to meet us in Hong Kong. Unfortunately, due to our ongoing duties, we were allotted only two or three hours daily off the ship. Visiting with our wives for such brief times and not seeing our children (our wives hadn't brought them along) made us miss our children even more. We knew the children were safe, back in Yokosuka, Japan, with reliable babysitters, but longed to see them. Considering the gravity of our assigned jobs and circumstances, however, it was well worth it to see our wives, despite the limited time and the personal cost of airfare we paid to get them there. We staffers swapped covering for one another with the daily message actions and briefings in order to maximize what little free time we did have during that short trip.

The U.S. embassy in downtown Hong Kong had planned a dinner-dance reception for the commander of the Seventh Fleet, Admiral Holloway, his wife, Dabney, our staff, and the wives who had flown down from Japan. On the morning of the reception, though, it was cancelled, which was a great disappointment. Soon after, we were to learn the reason: former President Lyndon B. Johnson had died.

While we were still in port in Hong Kong, on January 23, 1973, President Nixon announced a ceasefire with North Vietnam, who had agreed to end all fighting in both the north and south and to release the prisoners of war. The United States agreed to the ceasefire and to clear the Vietnamese harbors of mines. Effective at 2400 Greenwich Mean Time, January 27, 1973, the agreement called for cessation of all military operations in both North and South Vietnam and was signed by both Dr. Henry Kissinger and Le Duc Tho.

As we departed from our wives and Hong Kong, all staff members knew we still had much work ahead. We would have to coordinate the mine sweeping operation, End Sweep, within the requirements of what the mine neutralization protocol would finally dictate within the peace accord. The signed mine sweeping protocol to the Paris agreement designated mine sweeping operations to commence at 2400 on D-Day, January 27, 1973. This designated beginning time for the mine clearing operation was the exact same time designated by the ceasefire accord to all hostile parties to stop military actions against one another. All hostilities were scheduled to end at the same time End Sweep was to begin.

We would also be ready to assist, where possible, in the return of our POWs from locations in North and South Vietnam.

On that supposedly last day of the war, January 27, 1973, aircraft from the carriers flew what they thought would be the last missions of the war. They flew attack sorties into South Vietnam. Commander Dennis Weichman, the commanding officer of VA-153, landed his F-8 Corsair II back aboard the carrier *Oriskany*. Weichman had completed his final combat mission of the war, his 625th, the greatest number of combat missions flown by any naval aviator in this long war.

The difference between the designated ceasefire agreement time of 2400 hours Greenwich Mean Time, January 27, 1973, and the time in Vietnam caused some confusion.

Ironically, at 0745 on January 28, 1973, the USS *Turner Joy* (DD-951) fired the last U.S. naval gunfire support mission in the Vietnam War. The *Turner Joy* had been involved in the famous Gulf of Tonkin Incident back in 1964, some nine years before their last shots rang out.

The morning after the January 28 ceasefire took effect, all the American advisers to the South Vietnamese were ordered back to the United States. Lieutenant Colonel Gerald H. Turley, assistant senior adviser with the naval advisory group, Vietnam, was among those ordered to return to the United States. Turley, who had been inspecting the Vietnamese Marine brigades and the 3d ARVN Division near the DMZ when the North Vietnamese slashed across with massive force and invaded South Vietnam on March 30, 1972, finally left Vietnam.

Although the peace agreement called for the hostilities to end on January 27, 1973, the NVA counterattacked in South Vietnam causing the VNMC to again seek to regain lost ground as they artillery dueled. Two days after the ceasefire, on January 30, 1973, the NVA surrounded, and then totally destroyed, a VNMC company-sized unit at an outpost on the Cau Viet River in South Vietnam.

On February 6, 1973, South Vietnam reported that fighting in the south had continued at low ebb. The Saigon military command claimed there had been 102 ceasefire violations during the twenty-four-hour period of this day. This was the lowest number of violations since the ceasefire went into effect on January 27, 1973.

Also, on February 6, 1973, the U.S. command announced that a total of 45,941 U.S. servicemen had died in action in Indochina from January 1, 1961, until the official ceasefire on January 27, 1973. The announcement listed 300,635 Americans wounded in action and 1,811 missing, captured, or interned during the twelve years of the war.

Article 20 of the peace agreement with the North Vietnamese states: "The United States anticipates that this agreement will usher in an era of reconciliation with the Democratic Republic of Vietnam as with all people in Indo-China. In pursuance of its traditional policy, the United States will contribute to healing the wounds of war and to post-war reconstruction."

On February 1, 1973, President Nixon, in a secret promise, pledged $4.5 billion in a personal letter to Prime Minister Pham Van Don of the Democratic Republic of Vietnam.

On February 21, 1973, the Laotian Provisional National Union Government signed a peace agreement with the communist Pathet Lao. Within the contents of that agreement, the Pathet Lao inserted comments regarding aid from the United States. It stated: "The Provisional National Union Government will hold discussions with the United States Government in connection with a contribution regarding Laos."

Chapter 19

• • • • • • • •

Operation End Sweep

The mine clearance, or neutralization, preparations that began in May 1972 were getting close to completion when, at Paris, an agreement was finally met for the wording of the mine sweeping protocol. D-Day for the commencement of the mine neutralization operations was designated for January 27, 1973, the same day the ceasefire was to take place.

On January 26, 1973, the day before this was to occur, a Marine helicopter from squadron HMH-463 completed its first practice flight of towing an MOP in Subic Bay, Philippines.

The next day, on January 27, the designated start date, four U.S. Navy mine sweeper MSOs — *Engage, Force, Fortify,* and *Impervious* — assembled off Haiphong Harbor.

On February 1, 1973, navy and Marine Corps helicopter units Alpha and Bravo embarked on the navy transport dock ships *Dubuque* and *Ogden* for more training in Subic Bay.

The Soviet Union's intelligence gathering ship, *Protractor*, arrived just off of Subic Bay to keep Task Force 78's mine sweep training under electronic surveillance.

While the mine sweep training was taking place in Subic Bay, logistics had to be discussed and prepared for. To properly execute Operation End Sweep, we needed the full cooperation of the North Vietnamese government and military.

On February 4, 1973, Rear Adm. Brian McCauley and his operations officer, Capt. Felix Vecchione of TF 78, Capt. Edward Briggs (plans officer C7F and representative to TF78), Marine Lieutenant Colonel Webb, and eleven others flew in a navy C-130 from NAS Cubi Point to Saigon. Representatives of North Vietnam met them upon their arrival. After discussions to assure that the North Vietnamese would not bother U.S. ships in the Haiphong area, the North Vietnamese agreed to have Admiral McCauley and his team fly to Haiphong from Saigon.

On February 5, 1973, Admiral McCauley and team flew into Gia Lam Airport, east of Hanoi in North Vietnam. The North Vietnamese then flew them in a Russian IL-4, twin-engine airplane to Khe Nan Haiphong Airport. They then were surface-transported to Cat Bi Airport near Haiphong City. At Cat Bi Airport, they were taken to the Duyen Hai Hotel. There they met with North Vietnamese Col. Hoang Huu Thai, the chief Democratic Republic of Vietnam representative and second-in-command of the North Vietnamese Navy. Admiral McCauley and his U.S. Navy–State Department team soon found out that Colonel Thai was an intelligent, military professional and tough negotiator.

Arrangements were agreed upon for the U.S. MSOs to begin sweeping the anchorage area off Haiphong Harbor entrance, allowing Task Force 78 ships to assemble to prepare for sweeping operations. Additionally, at the previous meeting in Saigon, agreements had been made to alternate meetings to be held in Haiphong, North Vietnam, and on board the Task Force 78 flagship USS *Worden* off the Haiphong Channel entry area. Subordinate committees were formed to work out technical details of coastal and inland waterways sweeping, Raydist transmitter installations ashore, and the use of Haiphong's Cat Bi Airfield for U.S. logistics support to the sweep effort. It turned out that Admiral McCauley and Colonel Thai met only about every tenth day during the progress of the sweep discussions while subcommittees met as often as necessary to meet the End Sweep requirements. Often, disputes originating at the subcommittee level were settled at the full committee level.

In addition to the technical items discussed, though, a key non-technical issue continued to keep our attention: "North Vietnam is to insure the safety of U.S. personnel for the duration of their mine-clearing activities."

Naturally, Jim Froid, Larry Emarine, and I had hoped to attend that first meeting in North Vietnam because the three of us were responsible for the assets involved and personally participated in much of the planning for Operation End Sweep, but at the time, we were on the *Oklahoma City*, back on the gunline off North Vietnam, when the TF 78 members flew into North Vietnam from Saigon after departing from Subic Bay in a C-130. There would be many other such meetings with the North Vietnamese. I hoped that I'd get to attend at least one of them before the execution of End Sweep in the Haiphong Channel.

The Joint Chiefs of Staff in Washington sent Cmdr. Billy Traweek to be the first JCS liaison officer to these meetings in North Vietnam. Commander Traweek remained in the Huyen Dai Hotel. Later, Captain Vecchione remained for some time at the hotel. After that, Captain R. E. Flynn and other staff officers remained for stays at the hotel so that we always had representation right at the Huyen Dai Hotel during all sweep negotiations and sweep periods.

Beside Admiral McCauley and his TF 78 team, our Seventh Fleet plans officer, Capt. Edward Briggs, flew from the *Oklahoma City* to attend some of the meetings. Captain Steven D. Marvin represented CINCPACFLT in Hawaii. U.S. foreign service officer, H. F. Colebaugh, served as interpreter during the meetings.

After several meetings with the North Vietnamese, Admiral McCauley briefed with the following firsthand view of the situation he encountered:

First of all, as I think most of you know, I was directed on the 4th of February to leave Subic and go to Saigon to attempt to meet with the North Vietnamese to get arrangements initially to start the MSOs up in the Haiphong area.

After considerable discussion it was agreed that my party and I would go up to Haiphong where we would meet first with the North Vietnamese to gain assurance that they would not molest the ships when they came into Haiphong.

We left Saigon on the 5th of February in a C-130 and flew directly into Gia Lam, which is the airport to Hanoi. The airport was almost totally destroyed. There was only one building standing, but the runway was in pretty good shape. We got out of the C-130 and were greeted by a North Vietnamese major who spoke English, and he greeted us politely and civilly. We were taken up to the one standing building where we were all given half a glass of warm beer and then were taken and loaded into a Russian IL-4, which was a pleasant twin-engine transport. The seats were larger than ours, and it was very clean and well kept up. I was quite impressed.

In the meantime, a communication jeep (MK 87 high-frequency radio), which I had with me, and all our luggage, was put into a Russian helo . . . an MI-6, which is a helo slightly larger than our CH-53, though not nearly so maneuverable.

We flew down from Gia Lam to Khe Nan, which is the airport outside of Haiphong. On the way down they specifically kept us away from the populous centers, but we did notice that every bridge that we saw had a span down; so the damage up there had been pretty great.

Khe Nan was a field that had been totally destroyed some years back. There was absolutely nothing standing. There was one patched-up runway that we landed on. We then shifted from the aircraft into two Russian sedans and four Chinese jeeps. We were taken then in a roundabout trip into Haiphong. The trip was purposely routed so we saw very little damage to the city. In fact, when you look at Haiphong itself there is almost no damage to the residential area. I would say that in about every two blocks there might be one house that had been destroyed.

We were taken into a small hotel where we were all put up for the night. The hotel was austere, but it was clean; and, like every other building in Haiphong, almost all of the windows had been broken out by the blast of the bombs.

On the way in, almost everywhere you looked there were bomb shelters, and they had been used. We found that our stay in the hotel had been relatively pleasant and we've had people over there every night. We're sort of kept prisoners there. We're not allowed outside of the building, and all the meetings have been held in the building.

We do fly back and forth to the ship by helo every day, and keep sort of a rotating party going.

One of the interesting things, the first morning at five o'clock we were awakened by loudspeakers all over town that started with martial music and exhorted the people to work harder for the fatherland, be more energetic, and all sorts of good things to do for North Vietnam. It would have sounded fine except five in the morning seems a little early to me.

In any event, the people in the hotel have been friendly, rather reserved; they were trying their best to make us as comfortable as they could within their limitations.

The negotiations have been going on for three weeks; they are very tough. The North Vietnamese, my opponent, is the number two in their navy. He's very intelligent, a fine-looking man who speaks French, Vietnamese, Chinese, German, and English, and his whole objective in life is to get us to do the sweeping faster, to do it earlier, to give him more forces, and to give them just practically everything in the world. My objective is to do the job as we're told to do it and no more.

It's a hard series of negotiations. Each one starts off as if any previous ones had never taken place. But about once a week we make a small step forward, and they're eager, of course, for us to get in sweeping.

Soon TF 78 assembled twenty ships in the Gulf of Tonkin to prepare for clearing the mines. This required much cooperation with the North Vietnamese coastal defense personnel in Haiphong. To prepare for setting up the Raydist electronic beacon equipment and towers required meetings with the North Vietnamese in the Huyen Dai Hotel at Khe Nan Haiphong Airport.

Several TF 78 officers took turns flying in from the USS *Worden* by helicopter to attend these sessions. On one occasion, there was a need for a yeoman, or clerk. This gave us an opportunity to send our Seventh Fleet staff chief yeoman, Petty Officer C. Horvath. Horvath was the first enlisted sailor in North Vietnam, while some hostilities continued in the south due to peace accord violations. An enlisted air force radio operator/technician from the U.S. Air Force mobile communications had been at the hotel grounds since day one to tend to the radio jeep set up on the hotel grounds.

Jim Froid went in on several occasions to participate in the technical sweep discussions. Later, I had the experience of going in with Captain Vecchione.

On February 7, the third day of meetings with the North Vietnamese, the USS *Worden* hosted the meeting. The *Worden* anchored as the MSOs swept the areas where the LPHs and LPDs would soon anchor to begin the sweep operations.

While the staffs carried on intense negotiations with the North Vietnamese and the MSOs continued sweeping the anchorage areas off North Vietnam, the airborne mine countermeasures units continued training in Subic Bay, flying over an electronic grid replicating the Haiphong Channel area.

Arguments at the meetings continued over the Raydist equipment installations, responsibilities for dud bombs, areas to be swept, and the speed of execution of the sweep.

On February 12, 1973, the first phase of release of the POWs began with the release of 116 Americans at Gia Lam Airfield in North Vietnam. We got the word of the release immediately and were elated.

On February 16, the now-trained Alpha unit boarded the USS *Dubuque* while Bravo unit boarded the USS *Ogden*, and they sailed from Subic Bay for the Haiphong Channel inlet anchorage area swept by the MSOs. We were all relieved that HMH-463, the Marine CH-53A helicopter squadron, was now fully trained. This was the squadron sent out by CINCPACFLT and FMFPAC in Hawaii to replace the HMM-165 composite squadron that was already partially trained at that juncture. We were fortunate that HMH-463 had time to train fully before we were obligated to execute the mine sweeping by the peace accord.

On February 19, Colonel Thai threatened that there would be a problem with the next release of POWs if we did not change our positions, particularly regarding the equipment we would provide for the inland waterways phase of the clearance operation.

Colonel Thai reminded Admiral McCauley's team of negotiators that Henry Kissinger had promised the North Vietnamese specific equipment that we weren't now agreeing to give them. Colonel Thai stated he was going to report this shortcoming to the Paris delegation.

We, on the Seventh Fleet staff and the TF 78 staff, were not in a logistical position to deliver what the North Vietnamese insisted on. They wanted the United States to provide trucks and towing gear to be able to pull our Mark 105s and Mark 104s (with MOPs trailing) along the inland rivers and smaller channels. They also wanted earthmoving equipment to dig up buried bombs. They demanded 150 bulldozers and felt that the wealthy Americans could easily afford to supply these bulldozers to them.

On February 21, I had the opportunity to attend one of the negotiating sessions in Haiphong. As we flew in a Marine CH-53 helicopter at a low altitude, we could see the large B-52 bomb craters and damage around military targets and power plants. As I gazed from the helicopter, I wondered where below some of our remaining POWs were still hanging on to the hope of a release from their cells to go home. Also, quite obvious, was the almost untouched civilian living areas of Haiphong City. We were not allowed to bring any weapons and cameras. The .50-caliber machine guns of the CH-53A helicopter that transported us were removed prior to launching from the LPH *New Orleans*.

As we approached Khe Nan airfield outside of Haiphong, we saw that it had been totally destroyed and only a damaged runway remained. The helicopter flew beyond the city and landed near a hotel. A U.S. MK-87 radio jeep was next to the hotel. We were parked in front of the Huyen Dai Hotel. The Democratic Republic of Vietnam personnel in the hotel offered tea, cigarettes, and candy; a peanut processing plant next door to the hotel provided the rather tasty peanut brittle. The meetings hosted by the DRV were held in a large room with a high ceiling. The negotiating table held nine people on each side. Memberships of the DRV negotiating team and our group varied for different meeting sessions. Sessions usually started at 0800 each morning and lasted three hours. Afternoon negotiating sessions commenced at 1400. Both sides taped most conversations.

During this session, Captain Vecchione explained to the DRV senior negotiator Colonel Thai that we needed permission from the DRV to land navy C-130 transports at Cat Bi Airport. We required this approval to bring in some bulldozers and Raydist equipment and aluminum towers to mount the transmitters on in various areas along the Haiphong Channel. The targeted date for installations of the towers and Raydist equipment was February 24. Captain Vecchione could not tell Colonel Thai exactly what these towers were to be used for because our mine sweeping technology was highly classified. Colonel Thai could not believe that he was being requested to start allowing American transports to fly in and out of Cat Bi Airport. He did not have the immediate authority to approve this and reported to us that the civilian communist commissar sitting next to him would have to go to Hanoi and request such permission and report back at the next session. The commissar was simply a messenger boy, with no decision-making authority.

On the 23rd, authority was granted to have navy C-130 aircraft land at Cat Bi Airport and bring in Raydist transmitters and towers for installation along the shore of the Haiphong Channel and elsewhere.

On the 24th, navy and Seabee teams went ashore at Do Son, Dinh Vu, and Cat Hai to install antennas and related equipment in North Vietnam. Marine helicopter squadron HMM-165 flew additional similar equipment to the Raydist sites in North Vietnam. One site selected for the Norway Isles (Grande Norway), located to the east of the entry to Haiphong Channel, was found to have unsuitable terrain. A decision was made to anchor the USS *Tawasa* (ATF-92) with a four-point moor 7.5 miles south of the Haiphong sea buoy and install a Raydist transmitter station aboard the anchored ship.

By February 25, all Raydist transmitters had been installed and the sweep activities were ready.

A Task Force 78 staff officer told me that when he was ashore, he saw something rather funny, so he reported it to intelligence. He had been out to several of the Raydist stations and had seen the North Vietnamese building wooden towers right next to our installed aluminum towers, which held the Raydist transmitters. He then observed the North Vietnamese installing seats at the top of their newly erected wooden towers. Obviously, the North Vietnamese wished to sit on those seats and observe our operation from next to our transmitters. This would allow them to gather intelligence on some of our airborne mine sweeping activities and possibly pass that knowledge on to their ally, the Soviet Union. The Soviet Union had many people in North Vietnam gathering all types of military intelligence—everything from this operation to the types of bombs we dropped to the types of electronic technologies we used during this confrontation with this communist country. There also had been some indications within intelligence communities that some American POWs had been interrogated by Soviet military while in the North Vietnam POW camps. Also, reports indicated that some Americans who had special, vital technology knowledge had been flown from North Vietnam to the Soviet Union for more in-depth interrogation and then apparently disappeared.

Airborne mine countermeasure helicopters began sweeping the main Haiphong Channel on February 27, but during the previous year's statements by President Nixon on May 16, 1972, Nixon had said that the United States would begin removing mines when the POWs were released.

On the morning of February 28, the U.S. government directed that sweep operations should cease because of problems with the North Vietnamese in arranging for POW returns. All TF 78 personnel who were ashore were called back to the *New Orleans*. The radio jeep and Raydist equipment remained ashore.

High-level negotiations took place in Saigon and Paris as TF 78 units remained in the Gulf of Tonkin. American negotiators in Paris used the mine sweep operation as a negotiating lever to force the North Vietnamese to comply with the POW return provisions in the agreement.

On March 3, TF 78 was directed to return to Haiphong. On March 3, agreement was reached to resume sweeping the next day, March 6. For the next six weeks, End Sweep operations continued in the northern ports of Haiphong, Hon Gai, and Cam Pha.

As a sweep in the main channel of Haiphong on March 9 was under way at 1240, a mine detonated when a MK 105 sled was being pulled. A photo had been taken of that explosion, and it hit the newspapers worldwide, including the *New York Times*. Most mines self-sterilized or self-destructed based upon the varied fuses set in the mines, as reflected in Lt. Cmdr. Larry Emarine's mapping charts.

On March 18 a Marine CH-53A, towing a MOP en route to Hon Gai sweeping, suffered a tail rotor failure and crashed. The crew survived and the ship, *Safeguard* (ARS-25), recovered the helicopter on March 24. It was soon realized that the Marine CH-53 helicopters had not towed equipment at such slow speeds for such long periods of flight, despite their towing training flights at Subic. It was surmised that the long towing flight hours at such a slow speed of 55 knots had resulted in the failure of the Marine CH-53A tail rotor link. The navy CH-53D helicopters had thicker links, and none of them failed during towing activities. As sweeping continued with the MSOs, the Marine helicopters were grounded until tail pitch control links were replaced on April 6. All sweep-towing flights resumed on April 6.

During End Sweep activities, it was felt that we had better devise some means of credibility to prove that the mines had indeed been swept and that no mines remained active and dangerous. This would assure the world that safe passage for vessels existed from the sea up the Haiphong Channel.

After some brainstorming, the navy came up with a feasible idea. The USS *Washtenaw County* (LST 1166) was scheduled to rotate back to the United States for decommissioning and then to be sold for scrap metal value. The ship had outlived its designed and planned life expectancy.

Instead, the landing ship would be decommissioned, undergo extensive modifications, and be recommissioned as a mine sweeper, USS *Washtenaw County* (MSS-2). The reborn *Washtenaw County* would be considered expendable, and a plan was formulated to use the ship as a tool to ensure that the clearance of the mines in Haiphong Channel was completed and the channel was safe for ships to traverse.

Neither Admiral Holloway nor the top-level naval commanders wanted to have an accidental sinking of an American active duty ship in Vietnam. We had not lost a ship during the entire long war; this was certainly not the time to risk losing one. The plan called for the removal of its designation prior to having it sail back to Subic Bay from the Gulf of Tonkin. Her name was removed from the U.S. naval active ship ledgers, and her crew was assigned elsewhere from the ship. If this ship were sunk by some freak mine circumstances we had not planned for, it would be a ship no longer carried on the active duty rolls of the U.S. Navy.

Once the *Washtenaw County* was in port at Subic Bay in the Philippines and all crewmembers removed, it was pumped full of foam, and special mine shock buffers were installed. Honeycombed paper padding was installed on the decks, overhead, and on the bulkheads, and a few shock-mitigating chairs were placed into the ship's control bridge. A remote control system was installed so that the ship could be operated from the bridge only, so no one had to be below in the engine room once the ship was set up in the

Haiphong harbor to run up the shipping lanes. The concept was to protect the ship from sinking in the event it would accidentally get hit by an exploded mine in the Haiphong Channel. The foam would assist in keeping the ship afloat. An all-volunteer crew led by Lt. Cmdr. James C. Kuntz operated the ship in Haiphong's main shipping channel.

The ship was also fitted with towing rings to enable a helicopter to tow it in the event it did get damaged by a mine and needed to be pulled out of the shipping lane. This led to many arguments on our staff, and TF 78 staff, regarding if in the event the ship were hit by a mine and slightly damaged, was it plausible that it could be pulled out of the shipping lanes by a CH-53 helicopter? After many discussions, I found a photo and study document written by the Marine Corps some years ago. Towing of a ship by a helicopter actually had been accomplished before. The Marine Corps had towed a ship during the evaluation tests of the CH-53A prior to the procurement of these large helicopters from Sikorsky Aircraft Corporation. Because the *Washtenaw County* was full of foam throughout the hull, I felt that a CH-53 helicopter could possibly tow the ship from the minefield area, if not too badly damaged. Not everybody agreed with me.

Once the ship and volunteer crew were ready for the task, the *Washtenaw County* sailed to the Gulf of Tonkin off the entry area to the Haiphong Channel. This would provide Task Force 78 a ship that could verify safe passage up the Haiphong Channel.

However, at the Haiphong meetings, the North Vietnamese wished to initiate some propaganda, so they insisted that the *Washtenaw County* fly a North Vietnamese flag during her transit runs up the channel. Admiral McCauley's negotiating staff refused, so then, the North Vietnamese demanded that no flag fly on the ship. On April 13, the American negotiating team insisted the ship fly the U.S. flag or there would be no demonstration check sweep by the ship. Late that evening of the 13th, the North Vietnamese agreed that *Washtenaw County* could fly the U.S. flag. The ship made six complete runs in the Haiphong Channel on April 14, 1973, flying the American colors, verifying that U.S. mines in that area were no longer a threat to shipping.

On April 17, during one of the meetings in the Huyen Dai Hotel, a young Marine who had been operating the MK-87 radio jeep outside the hotel had run into the meeting. The young Marine sergeant reported to Captain Vecchione that he had received a radio call directing all of us to return to our ships. I was to report back to an important meeting on the *Oklahoma City*. Captain Vecchione apologized to the DRV negotiators, then told them we had to leave because of a pressing meeting and that we would return Monday morning. We departed Haiphong.

Upon my return to the *Oklahoma City*, I went directly to the war room to see what kind of meeting was taking place. I expected to see a crowd of staff officers and the admiral in the war room. It was empty, except for a few watch officers and yeoman. I asked about the meeting. They responded with, "What meeting?"

I ran down the ladder to the admiral's quarters and asked Captain Briggs, now chief of staff, where the admiral was. He said that he was in his stateroom. I entered the admiral's stateroom and found Admiral Holloway sitting at his desk sipping tea. I asked the admiral what the meeting was all about, and did I miss anything?

Admiral Holloway answered, "The communists failed to adhere to the truce and ceasefire agreements in Laos and Cambodia. Kissinger has left the Paris meeting and is flying back to Washington. President Nixon has directed another squeeze be placed upon the North Vietnamese. It is possible he could even resume bombing North Vietnam. We had to get you all out of there immediately."

I shook my head in disbelief, as I imagined us still sitting at the conference table in Haiphong as tons of bombs rained down upon us. I said, "Admiral, do you realize I have to go back in there on Monday and face those people?"

The admiral laughed and said, "Better you than me. We received word that the mine sweep operation is being used again as a political weapon. All personnel from Task Force 78 ashore are being withdrawn. We'll keep the Raydist transmitting stations and inland waterway sweep equipment there in North Vietnam. Everybody and everything else will be withdrawn to a holding area in the Gulf of Tonkin."

On April 19, 1973, the Pentagon released the following statement: Mine clearing operations have been suspended because of the failure of the other side to abide by the agreements and assurances of Paris; because of continued ceasefire violations by the other side in South Vietnam and Laos; because of the other side's failure to respect the unilateral ceasefire declared by the government of Cambodia; and because of the continued flow of enemy supplies into South Vietnam.

Task Force 78 was held in the Gulf of Tonkin for six days. On April 23, higher authority directed us to move it back to Subic Bay. This gave TF 78 crews needed rest and the ships some needed repairs.

Upon TF 78 returning to Subic Bay, Admiral McCauley flew to Hawaii to confer with Admiral Clarey, commander in chief, Pacific Fleet. That same day, April 24, Lieutenant Commander Emarine, sitting next to me in our office, received a message that the *Force* had a fire in the aft engine room. Back on April 12 the *Force* had been detached from TF 78 in the Gulf of Tonkin to return to Guam for a regularly scheduled overhaul. After stopping to refuel at Subic Bay, the *Force* had continued on its way and was now 770 miles west of Guam.

Lieutenant Commander Emarine briefed Admiral Holloway about the fire. Seven hours later, Larry briefed that he had received a report that the *Force* sank at 1053 on April 24, 1973. A passing merchant ship rescued all hands that same day, and none of the sailors were reported seriously injured.

On June 13, 1973, with ceasefire violations continuing intermittently, the Democratic Republic of Vietnam (North Vietnam), National Liberation Front (Viet Cong), United States, and Republic of Vietnam (South Vietnam) signed a new pact that was to ensure the ceasefire agreement in Vietnam.

That same day, a joint communiqué was issued specifying that sweep operations would resume no later than June 18, 1973.

The TF 78 delegates arrived at Cat Bi Airfield on June 18 and quickly noticed that there were no anti-U.S. posters around the area like there had been during their previous landing. The Americans also did not experience any more rock-throwing incidents en route to the Huyen Dai Hotel. When Admiral McCauley and his TF 78 negotiating team arrived back at the familiar Huyen Dai Hotel in Haiphong, Colonel Thai did not criticize the American withdrawal from the sweep operation, but his deputy and the hotel staff did voice their displeasure.

There would be no sweeping the next day. North Vietnam had not directed their fishermen to stay clear of the sweep areas.

On June 20, sweeping resumed in the northern port areas. By June 26, sweeping of the northern ports was completed. TF 78 departed for an area off the North Vietnamese city of Vinh, where sweeping would continue along the coast. On June 28, the negotiating teams moved from the relatively luxurious Huyen Dai Hotel to a thatched-roof bamboo hut in Vinh. Major problems ensued over the wording of the U.S. mine clearance notifications and the DRV's continual requests for additional U.S. mine searching in the Haiphong Channel. Additionally, Hanoi demanded more equipment for their own inland sweeping activities. This remained a sensitive issue.

At Vinh, the DRV negotiators announced that the United States was not to sweep the Vinh River but only the seaward channel to the Vinh River. By July 1973, Airborne mine countermeasures unit Delta had completed the last sweep at Cua Sot.

Chapter 20

• • • • • • • •

Operation Homecoming

The deputy chief of operations of the Joint Chiefs of Staff in Washington established a special operations project for the eventual recovery of U.S. prisoners from Hanoi. This organization would be a joint armed forces unit. Marine Lt. Gen. Hugh J. Elwood, Deputy Chief of Staff for Plans and Programs at Headquarters Marine Corps, assigned Col. William J. Davis as the Marine Corps representative. Initially, this organization had developed plans to use U.S. Army and Marine Corps units to rescue prisoners from the Hanoi area POW camps; however, because the South Vietnamese counterattacks (Lam Son 72) to the 1972 NVA invasion were successful in stopping North Vietnam from taking South Vietnam, and the negotiations in Paris seemed to be heading for some sort of agreement, these rescue plans were shelved.

A Department of Defense prisoner task force was formed in August 1972, and Marine Maj. William B. Clark was assigned as an action officer involved with monitoring the status of captured Marines.

Dr. Roger E. Shields, a civilian in the office of the assistant secretary of defense for International Security Affairs, headed the task force on the prisoners of war and missing in action. Dr. Shields' efforts were coordinated with CINCPAC in Hawaii. A plan called egress recap was initiated and the name then changed to Operation Homecoming.

Operation Homecoming established three phases: Phase One was the airlift of the prisoners by the Thirteenth Air Force from Hanoi. Phase Two was the processing of the former POWs at an intermediate facility called the joint homecoming reception center, located at Clark Air Force Base in the Philippines. Phase Three was established as the return of the former POWs to the United States.

The ceasefire agreement in Paris had established a Four Party Joint Military Commission to coordinate the POW exchanges. The U.S. Military Advisory Command Vietnam in Saigon provided a two-man POW liaison team to the Operation Homecoming staff. Marine Maj. Gen. Michael P. Ryan had replaced Lt. Gen. Louis Metzger as the commanding general of III Marine Amphibious Force (CG III MAF) on Okinawa. General Ryan assigned Col. John W. Clayborne as his III MAF representative at the homecoming reception center at Clark Air Force Base, which included thirty-two Marine officers and twenty-eight enlisted men involved in the Marine processing team at Clark AFB.

Contingency plans also had U.S. Marine Brig. Gen. Paul G. Graham preparing the 9th MAB and 31st MAU afloat Task Force 76 amphibious ships to participate in Homecoming. Commander Jim Froid, cognizant officer of TF 76 on our Seventh Fleet staff, became involved in coordinating the TF 76 ships. Jim sent messages to TF 76 to ensure their ships would be available as backup transportation for the POWs from North Vietnam to Subic Bay in the Philippines if necessary rather than by air force airlifts. My own involvement was to send out a few messages to CG III MAF to assure that the 1st Marine Aircraft Wing had helicopters repositioned to partake in the Operation Homecoming activities at Clark AFB when needed.

A joint military facility was established at Clark AFB that offered medical, psychological, humanitarian, and financial support to the returning former POWs. At the joint homecoming reception center at Clark AFB, former POWs' records were audited, promotions and awards were presented to those who qualified, uniforms were provided, and their families were notified that they had arrived safely at Clark.

The first phase of the POW releases began on February 12, 1973, with the release of 116 U.S. prisoners at Gia Lam Airfield in North Vietnam and 19 prisoners in South Vietnam. After that first release, there were interruptions to the smooth flow of returning the POWs from North Vietnam due to snags in negotiations at the Paris talks and associated withdrawals of Task Force 78 End Sweep operations and renewed mine sweeping activities.

The POW releases were dependent upon the removal of the U.S. mines from North Vietnam's waterways, the withdrawal of the remaining U.S. forces from South Vietnam, and the exchange of 5,000 South Vietnamese and 26,508 communist prisoners.

The official ceasefire agreed upon in Paris was established to take place at 2400 hours GMT on January 27, 1973. This was 0800 Saigon time on January 28, 1973. The American POWs began departing North Vietnam on February 12, and within sixty days all POWs and remaining military forces were supposed to be out of Vietnam. The forces that had to withdraw from South Vietnam were 23,335 Americans, 35,396 South Koreans, and 113 other allies. From the first American POW departure that commenced on February 12, 1973, Marine Corps POWs were released on the days of March 5, 14, 16, 27, and 28, 1973.

Marine Gen. Louis H. Wilson Jr., commanding general, Fleet Marine Forces Pacific (CG FMFPAC), met the first POW returnees to Hawaii from Clark AFB. Lieutenant Colonel Halan P. Chapman was the first Marine to arrive in Hawaii. Chapman had been the longest held Marine POW. He had been captured on November 5, 1965. The last Marine POW to arrive in Hawaii was Capt. William K. Angus. He arrived on March 28, 1973.

One of the returnees, Chief Warrant Officer William E. Thomas Jr., returned to Camp Pendleton, California. Chief Warrant Officer Thomas, a thirty-six-year-old native of Pennsylvania, had been shot down near the DMZ in 1972. He was flying in the backseat of an OV-10A Bronco as an aerial observer and member of Sub Unit One, 1st ANGLICO. He had been controlling naval gunfire upon NVA positions when shot down. Both Thomas and Marine Corps Sgt. Jose Anzaldua arrived late in the United States, due to aircraft problems. Thomas, upon arrival at Naval Air Station Miramar, San Diego, was taken to the naval hospital at Camp Pendleton.

In 1975, two years after his return from POW camp, Bill Thomas flew as an aerial observer with me in OV-10 Broncos, when I was the commanding officer of Marine Observation Squadron Two (VMO-2) at Camp Pendleton. During our numerous flights together, and in discussions in the aircrew ready room, I got a better insight into what Bill Thomas endured as a POW during 1972 and 1973.

The first Marine who had been captured in Vietnam was Col. Donald G. Cook; he never returned. He had been a captain when captured in 1964 in South Vietnam by the Viet Cong. Soon after the POWs returned to the United States in 1973, the commandant of the Marine Corps, Gen. Robert E. Cushman Jr., received a letter from a POW returnee, Douglas K. Ramsey. Ramsey had been a civilian language officer. He was held as a POW from 1966 until his release during Operation Homecoming. Ramsey's letter revealed the story of Captain Cook. Captain Cook had been serving with the 4th Battalion of the Vietnamese Marines. On December 31, 1964, Captain Cook was wounded and captured during fighting against the Viet Cong near Binh Gia, Thy Province, South Vietnam. The Viet Cong held him prisoner until his death. Ramsey's letter detailed just what a real Marine Captain Cook was while a prisoner of war of the Viet Cong. Cook set the example for all the other POWs by his leadership, sharing his rations, attending to the injured and sick, organizing the prisoners, attempting to escape, and continuously resisting the Viet Cong. Captain Cook died in captivity in 1967 from malaria. The North Vietnamese did not notify the U.S. government about Captain Cook's death until 1973 during Operation Homecoming. As a result of returning POWs telling numerous stories of Captain Cook's highest Marine Corps standards while a prisoner of war, Donald G. Cook was promoted to colonel and posthumously awarded the Medal of Honor.

When the MACV Special Operations Group–Joint Personnel Recovery Center was deactivated in 1973, its functions were turned over to the joint casualty reporting center in Thailand, commanded by U.S. Army Brig. Gen. Robert C. Kingston in Thailand. There they continued to try to account for the 2,441 Americans missing in action in Southeast Asia.

Since 1973, 591 American servicemen's remains have been accounted for and returned to their respective families for proper burial. The search for more continues. The fifty-eight thousand names etched on the Vietnam Veterans Memorial wall properly portray a part of the Vietnam War story. There are more stories that we may or may never hear associated with those still missing in action.

As the last American POWs returned to the United States during Operation Homecoming on March 28, 1973, Operation End Sweep continued with mine sweep activities finally ending at the Sot River at Cua Sot on July 5, 1973. The day before, on July 4, the only fatality during Operation End Sweep occurred when a crewman aboard the LPD *Ogden* was accidentally caught in a closing stern ramp of a CH-53 helicopter.

Admiral McCauley presented the North Vietnamese with a written statement that mine countermeasures operations in those areas were completed.

At that same time, Admiral McCauley informed the North Vietnamese that they would be loaned additional U.S. equipment to support their own inland clearance operations. Two bulldozers, two trucks, five drone motor boats, and five mine detectors were loaned to the North Vietnamese. Admiral McCauley had informed the North Vietnamese the Americans were prepared to sweep two other port areas, Thanh Hoa and Dong Hoi, but further negotiations with the North Vietnamese were not successful. The U.S. delegation concluded that the North Vietnamese did not want an American presence in those areas for some unknown reason. The North Vietnamese contended that the southern ports were not swept as thoroughly as the northern ports. The U.S. delegation rejected that contention.

That wasn't the only point of disagreement. Lieutenant Commander Tom Tilt of Capt. R. E. Flynn's Mine Countermeasures Group (Task Group TG 78.4) described an impasse with the North Vietnamese over the bulldozers:

On the morning of July 12, two TD-6 bulldozers were delivered, and as was the custom U.S. and DRV representatives met that afternoon to inspect the machines. However, after a brief walk around, the DRV representative's senior army captain refused to accept custody of the bulldozers stating that they were in poor condition and also too small for the job. And that it was necessary for their technicians to make a more detailed inspection. That evening, CTG 78.4 (Capt. R. E. Flynn) requested a meeting the following day with Colonel Doan, DRV Senior Inland Waterway Representative; however, Colonel Doan refused to meet with Captain Flynn.

On the 13th, the U.S. Navy bulldozer technicians were made available to the DRV to answer any questions. The DRV continued the inspection, which included the spare parts pack-up. They asked numerous questions; however, they disputed many of the answers. The answers in most cases were facts extracted straight from the instruction manual, such as piston size and horsepower rating.

The following morning, CTG 78.4 (Captain Flynn) met with Colonel Doan and stated that if the DRV had not accepted the bulldozers by noon they would be flown out the following day, July 15.

At noon, the DRV presented a list of discrepancies and parts necessary to effect the repairs, stating that if they were repaired, they (DRV) would accept them.

On 15 July, both bulldozers and the USMC communications jeep were retrograded via C-130 to Subic Bay.

Later, Captain Flynn stated that the North Vietnamese just didn't believe that he would carry out his threat to retrograde the bulldozers and that they stood agape when the Americans loaded the C-130s with the bulldozers and took off.

On July 16 and 17, 1973, Captain Flynn negotiated the retrograde of the Raydist systems. On the 18th, Task Group 78.4 staff's Chief Electrician's Mate Davis dismantled the equipment in four hours. The Raydist equipment was then retrograded to Subic Bay.

DRV Col. Hoang Huu Thai and Rear Adm. Brian McCauley met for the last time in Haiphong. Unlike numerous other meetings, this was cordial, but no progress was made on any of the controversial subjects.

Admiral McCauley stated later that he felt Colonel Thai was a real professional who was under pressure from the political commissar-types in his delegation. He felt that Colonel Thai's personal stake in the U.S. sweeping was revealed to the admiral earlier in the negotiations when both had agreed they wanted to see a good job of sweeping accomplished. At that time, Colonel Thai stated to Admiral McCauley that he had to be sure that the sweeping was thorough because, after Task Force 78 had departed, he would still be there to answer if a mine exploded.

While the rest of Task Force 78 ships anchored off the North Vietnamese coastal city of Vinh, the USS *Inchon* remained in the Haiphong area ready to transport Admiral McCauley from North Vietnam.

The admiral had arranged his schedule so that he was to return aboard the *Inchon* via Marine CH-46 helicopter at 1300 on June 18, 1973, after his meeting with Colonel Thai. The admiral had scheduled the *Inchon* to sail out of North Vietnam at 1300. When 1300 passed and there was no arrival of the admiral, nor any word via radio transmissions from him, Captain Thomas, commanding officer of the *Inchon*, launched a helicopter. Captain Thomas instructed the helicopter pilot to climb to a high altitude to attempt to establish radio communications with the admiral's helicopter in Haiphong. No contact was established. Captain Thomas, well aware of the disagreements of both sides of the mine sweeping negotiations and concerned for Admiral McCauley's safety, actually considered sending a flash message advising all, including us on the Seventh Fleet staff, that Admiral McCauley, the U.S. negotiator, was being held in Haiphong. As Captain Thomas pondered that possibility, Admiral McCauley's helicopter pilot established radio contact with the *Inchon* and reported that he was inbound to the *Inchon* with Admiral McCauley aboard.

With Admiral McCauley aboard, the *Inchon* sailed from the Haiphong harbor area and joined the rest of the TF 78 ships off the city of Vinh. At sunset, at 2100 on the 18th, the *Inchon*, with the last U.S. ships, departed North Vietnamese waters.

Task Force 78 was disestablished on July 27, 1973, six months to the day after it had been formed by direction of Vice Adm. James L. Holloway III, commander, Seventh Fleet.

Chapter 21

• • • • • • • •

Back to the Real World

As the dust settled in Vietnam, and the United States ignored the communist takeovers of Cambodia and Laos resulting in the notorious "killing field" bloodbaths in Cambodia by the Khmer Rouge, *Oklahoma City* pulled off the gunline and headed for Taiwan.

Upon our arrival in Keelung Harbor, Taiwan, Admiral Holloway had been invited for an evening of dining by the CNO of Taiwan. Because Taiwan's CNO's invitation included the commandant of the Marine Corps of Taiwan, Admiral Holloway invited Col. Jim Dionisopoulos from our plans section and me from operations to attend the evening of dining out in Taipei.

Initially, the dinner discussions were dampened by the somber feelings expressed by both the Taiwanese CNO and CMC. They both expressed what all the people of Taiwan were concerned about: they worried about their future relationships with the United States. This was the result of what they had heard about Kissinger's secret meetings in Beijing, China. They knew there had been some agreements made with communist China that placed Taiwan in a weakened posture. These agreements that Kissinger had made with the Chinese leaders were paving the way for President Nixon to visit Red China now that the Vietnam War was over for the Americans. These agreements brought about a change of U.S. commitments to Taiwan. Henceforth, Taiwan could only receive defensive U.S. military weapons, not offensive weapons that could pose a danger to communist China.

After some somber expressions of this predicament, the CNO of Taiwan said, "There is nothing we military can do about the political situation thrust upon us by civilian leaders, so let's party."

And party we did. The CNO and CMC of Taiwan took us not only to one magnificent Chinese restaurant, but we went to three restaurants in a row and were given celebrity status at all three, in addition to the numerous delicious courses provided at each; we felt we had consumed enough food to last us the entire trip back to our homeport of Yokosuka, Japan.

Prior to our ship pulling out of Taiwan, I telephoned my Marine Corps assignments' monitor, Maj. D.E. P. Miller, at Headquarters Marine Corps in Washington. I had last flown with Major Miller in VMO-2 when we flew the very first combat introduction flights of the AH-1G Cobra attack helicopter into Vietnam in early 1969.

I asked Miller if he could help me with my next set of orders, which would have me depart the *Oklahoma City*. I asked him to send me from the staff job on the ship back to the 3d Marine Corps Aircraft Wing at El Toro, California. My wife and I owned a home in San Juan Capistrano, California, and I thought we could most easily move the family from Yokosuka back to San Juan Capistrano than be transferred elsewhere in the United States. Miller said that he would try his best as the monitor/detailer to assure that my orders would read to report to the 3d Marine Aircraft Wing at El Toro, California.

As our ship sailed from Taiwan en route to Yokosuka, Japan, I received my orders. They stated: "Report to the Marine Corps Air Facility, Jacksonville, North Carolina." Years before, in the fifties and sixties, I had served two tours of duty there. Enough said about friends in high places doing you a favor.

En route to Japan from Taiwan, Admiral Holloway expressed the following: "We have our government talking with the communist Chinese; now that we no longer have hostilities with the North Vietnamese, why don't we request a port visit to Vladivostok in the communist Soviet Union?"

All staff members thought that would be a good, after-war port visit. We all started imagining purchasing Russian amber and enamelware for our wives.

Admiral Holloway had Lt. Cmdr. Robert E. Waples, our staff schedules officer, send a message to CINCPACFLT requesting a port visit to Vladivostok in the Soviet Union for the *Oklahoma City*.

While still en route to Japan, Bob Waples received a message from CINCPACFLT that referenced a State Department response message stating that the time is not politically ripe to have an American ship, especially the flagship of the Seventh Fleet, make a port visit to the Soviet Union. That message ended those dreams of visting the Soviet Union.

This immediate after-war period also gave Admiral Holloway the time to talk future activities that concerned him. One of these concerns was the large power vacuum in the Indian Ocean, left there all these years since Great Britain vacated that area after World War II. During the entire Vietnam War, Soviet ships and submarines were coming and going from Vladivostok, sailing right past us to study our war activity. They then headed to Singapore. Then, after a port visit in Singapore, their ships headed through the Straight of Malacca into the Andaman Sea and Indian Ocean. In fact, during the Vietnam War, when our *Oklahoma City* was in a port visit to Singapore, our ship was tied up at a pier right next to a Soviet missile cruiser.

Admiral Holloway consistently stated that the back door to the Middle East oil was through the Indian Ocean, and so we had better have a naval presence in the Indian Ocean. The admiral stated that we really needed to negotiate with Great Britain for use of their isolated, small island of Diego Garcia in the Indian Ocean for some sort of base of operation, now that the Vietnam War was over for the Americans.

Admiral Holloway also expressed concern about the lack of postwar training areas in the Pacific. He immediately put our staff to work on finding proposals for postwar training areas. Most of the pre–Vietnam War training areas had become politically eroded during the long Vietnam War.

An example of such loss of U.S. military training areas was that our Marines could no longer live-fire their tanks while moving during training on Okinawa (Ryukan) Island. The Ryukan Communist Party, headquartered in Naha City on Okinawa, had held numerous, large-scale protest marches against U.S. tanks moving and firing on the island that our Marines and army units paid such a toll in blood to capture from the Japanese during World War II. These communist-led protests resulted in Jim Froid and me getting involved. Jim had to coordinate with Task Force 76 shipping schedules, and I had to coordinate with the staff of the III Marine Amphibious Force and the 3d Marine Division on Okinawa to establish training cycles for our tank crews to exercise the tanks on the island of Honshu, Japan. The 3d Marine Division's tanks had to be shipped from Okinawa to an offloading beach near Mount Fuji, Japan, not too far from Tokyo. On the slopes of the base of Mt. Fuji, the Marines still maintained a cold-weather training area that I had operated in and out of in 1958 as a helicopter pilot stationed at Oppama, Japan. This base consisted of several parts, including North and South Camp Fuji. After several cycles of our TF 76 ships taking our Marine tanks up there from Okinawa, it didn't take the local Japanese Communist Party long to begin large-scale protests at Kizarazu Beach, where our tanks would offload from Okinawa. This became disruptive for maintaining our tankers' combat readiness posture.

Another area of U.S. military training that eroded was due to the secret meetings of Kissinger with the People's Republic of China...communist China. These meetings, which set up President Nixon's visit to Red China, resulted in the United States no longer being authorized to fly attack bombing training flights, offensive-type flight training, on the seven-hundred-mile-long island of Taiwan. For decades, this U.S. aircrew training in Taiwan had been a routine. Now, only defensive-type U.S. F-4 fighter aircraft training missions could be scheduled in Taiwan due to agreements made by our government with communist China. Our government did not want to offend the People's Republic of China, as President Nixon wished to move forward to opening up dialogue with them.

Because our eroded training areas caused us to look all over the Pacific for amphibious training sites, we began studies of old World War II Marine Corps island-hopping areas for potential training zones. We began to look at islands such as the Gilbert, Marshall, Palau, Marianas—all bloody, hard-fought-for islands that Marines took back from the Japanese in 1944. Headquarters U.S. Marine Corps began studies at some of those sites to see if such areas might be feasible for proper joint navy and Marine Corps amphibious training in the near future. We probably should have looked at possibly using the famous Iwo Jima Island, maybe with the possibility of joint Japan's National Defense Force and U.S. Marine training. We didn't do that evaluation on my watch.

We did look toward Australia, and I participated in some initial planning with our staff plans division for the first post–Vietnam War amphibious operation to be held jointly with the Australians in Australia. The training operation was named Kangaroo One.

Commander William T. Majors from our N-6 plans section was lucky. Bill Majors made the trip to Australia for the first meeting with the Australians.

During 1972 and 1973, Bill Majors and I worked closely together on the Seventh Fleet staff, often discussing what our personal fates might have been earlier in that war.

Bill Majors had been shot down off the coast of Vinh, back in August 1964. Bill had been piloting a navy A-7 Corsair II attack bomber on a strike mission against a North Vietnamese patrol boat base. This attack was a result of the August 2, 1964, North Vietnamese PT gunboats' attack on the USS *Maddox* (DD-731) during the U.S. response to the notorious Gulf of Tonkin incident. Although under intense North Vietnamese fire, Bill Majors was rescued by a navy helicopter. The following year, in August 1965, I was shot down while piloting a Marine H-34 Sikorsky helicopter in support of the South Vietnamese. That incident happened just twenty miles west of Da Nang. When I got out of the disabled helicopter, my crew and I were completely surrounded by Viet Cong. Luckily, I got out of there because of my wingman diving down, picking us up, and flying rapidly away before obvious capture.

Bill and I discussed that if we had been captured during those long-ago incidents, it would have been unlikely that either of us would have survived in captivity until the POW exchange in 1973.

Another post–Vietnam War area of concern for us on the staff was Korea. Admiral Holloway dispatched me to fly to Iwakuni, Japan, to meet with 1st Marine Aircraft Wing operations training personnel to discuss possible training sites in Korea. Bombing training sites near Iwakuni, Japan, had disappeared during the Vietnam War, in part due to Japanese Communist Party pressures. Although our Marine fighter/bombers had been deployed in Vietnam and Thailand all those years, the Japanese people near the Iwakuni, Japan, bombing ranges had grown accustomed to not hearing bombing training in their area, and it became a volatile problem to attempt to resume the bombing in that area. After getting briefed by the 1st Marine

Aircraft Wing personnel about their plight of a lack of bombing areas for their Iwakuni-based fighter/attack bombers, I flew to Korea. In Korea, I did obtain scheduled monthly periods of bombing range availability from the U.S. Air Force in Korea. Our Marine Corps fighter/bombers would have to fly from Iwakuni, Japan, across the Strait of Korea, and check in with the air force range controllers in Korea to commence scheduled bombing practices.

During the final six months of the Vietnam War, Cmdr. Jack Beaver, a tall man with black, curly hair, who was our submarine warfare staff officer on the Seventh Fleet staff, had been hounding me for a ride in a Marine OV-10A Bronco, twin-engine, turboprop, armed reconnaissance airplane. This was the type of aircraft I had flown during my second combat tour in Vietnam as a forward air controller in 1969–70. I promised Jack that I would arrange a flight for him during one of *Oklahoma City's* port visits to Subic Bay. I scheduled OV-10A aircraft detachments to train in the Philippines, coming down from Okinawa on certain training periods. They had been doing this cyclical training down there anyway. All I had to do was match their schedules to meet at least one of our port visits and coordinate getting my friend Jack Beaver, the submariner, an airplane ride. Despite several attempts at scheduling and rescheduling, it never worked out. During that period of late 1972, our ship never made our scheduled repair visits to Subic Bay. This was due to events impacted upon us from the North Vietnamese invasion in 1972, followed by our authorized response raids into North Vietnam, which kept us busy on the gunline.

Jack had just about given up on his quest for an airplane ride. Jack would often say, "If you get me an airplane ride, I'll make sure I get you and Eleanor a ride in a submarine when the war is over." I believed him. Jack was a robust, joking, but extremely capable individual who always delivered. I kept trying to match our Marine squadron's schedule with our ship's schedule without success; on the last day of the bombings in Laos, though, after the end of hostilities of the Vietnam War, our ship pulled up beside the carrier *Enterprise* in the Gulf of Tonkin. Admiral Holloway wanted the *Oklahoma City's* crew to observe the return of the last attack bombers making arrested landings on the deck of the *Enterprise*. Admiral Holloway invited staff members to fly in his helicopter, Black Beard One, over to the *Enterprise*. There, he would personally congratulate the returning carrier aircrews for their last bombing raids in Laos.

Commander Jack Beaver chose to go with the admiral over to the *Enterprise*. Commander Ron Stoddart, our staff attack bomber specialist, began to brief the ship's crew over the loudspeaker about the carrier landings they were observing on the *Enterprise* as our *Oklahoma City* steamed alongside the carrier.

Now that the war was over and we could hang out on the deck, I chose to lay out and sunbathe. As I lay there soaking up the rays, I looked skyward and watched the attack bombers flying in from Laos and listened to Ron Stoddart briefing our ship's crew of the carrier landings over on the carrier.

While watching the numerous fighter/attack bombers circling above to land aboard the *Enterprise*, I could not miss the navy KA-6D fuel tanker flying above in an orbit at about eight thousand feet. The KA-6D tanker was refueling the returning navy fighter/attack bombers, who were extremely low on fuel due to the distance to and from their targets in Laos.

Later, at dinner in the *Oklahoma City*'s officers' wardroom, I observed Jack Beaver and several other officers who earlier had gone over to the *Enterprise* with Admiral Holloway. Jack spotted me dining and quickly walked over to me and said, "The hell with the OV-10A Bronco ride you promised. I got me a ride in a KA-6D refueler today from off the *Enterprise*." And Jack had indeed gotten a ride in the tanker that I saw flying directly overhead and refueling the returning bombing mission aircraft. Jack had talked himself aboard the KA-6D fuel tanker and was catapulted off the *Enterprise*.

I felt terrible. I had never delivered that ride to Jack. But, later, Jack delivered his promised submarine ride to my wife, Eleanor, and me.

Several months later, when our ship returned to our naval base in Yokosuka, Japan, Jack arranged with his friend, Cmdr. John D. Chamberlain, commanding officer of the special operations submarine, USS *Grayback* (LPSS-574), to give my wife and me a ride. Eleanor and I sat on folding chairs, like VIPs, on the deck of the surfaced sub. We enjoyed the salt-air breezes as we sailed from dockside at Yokosuka and out into the Tokyo Bay shipping lanes. Once clear of the shipping lanes that run up to Yokohama and

Tokyo, the sub went far out to sea. Well clear of all shipping lanes, sailors took our folding chairs down below, then we all went into the sub. The *Grayback* submerged for three hours, and we were shown a movie on how this special operations submarine discharges mini-subs carrying navy SEALS and Marine Corps reconnaissance personnel on special secret operations. After a dinner and some briefings, the sub surfaced, then entered the shipping lanes and Tokyo Bay.

When we returned to the dock at Yokosuka, Jack Beaver was smiling on the dock to welcome us back. Jack asked me, "Well, how was it? Did you like the submarine ride?"

I responded, "Jack, you'll never get me inside a submerged submarine again. It scared the hell out of me, so deep down underwater!"

With a chuckle, Jack answered, "I hate to admit it, but I didn't like that KA-6D aircraft ride over the Gulf of Tonkin. That pilot made a couple of sharp high-g turns, and although I was tightly strapped into the ejection seat, I thought I was going to fall the hell out through that plastic canopy!" Eleanor intervened into our conversation and announced she had thoroughly enjoyed the submerged submarine ride and was looking forward to any others she might be able to get.

A few days later, it was time for me to leave my job on the Seventh Fleet staff and move the family back to the United States. I felt like many a sailor must feel when departing a ship you spent two years aboard. The *Oklahoma City* was a fine ship with an excellent crew. In two years afloat that old World War II–type cruiser that had been converted into a guided-missile cruiser, I had gotten to know quite a few of the sailors and the Marine detachment running her. Additionally, it had been a special privilege serving with such intelligent navy officers on the Seventh Fleet. I particularly enjoyed working for Vice Adm. William Paden Mack during my first several months on the Seventh Fleet staff. Working for his replacement, Vice Adm. James L. Holloway III, was a once-in-a-lifetime opportunity for this career Marine Corps officer. Admiral Holloway was, indeed, the combination of gutsy Adm. William F. "Bull" Halsey of the South Pacific Command in 1943 and with the aggressive smarts of Admiral Spruance, Fifth Fleet Commander, who prepared the fleet for the great offensive against Imperial Japan during World War II.

Admiral Holloway just happened to be the Seventh Fleet commander during the wrong war. I also strongly felt I too was in the wrong part of the history book of the United States of America. I would much rather have served my nation during World War II than having spent from 1965 in and out of fighting in a war that Washington didn't understand, nor wish to win.

I left the Seventh Fleet staff and the *Oklahoma City* with very mixed emotions. I gathered the family of wife and three children, Monica, Bobby and Eddie, at Yokosuka Naval Base and shipped our household goods off to our assigned base in North Carolina.

As a sailor drove Eleanor, our children, and me from Yokosuka to Yokota Air Force Base for our departure from Japan, I could see Japan very well from the small bus. It had changed significantly since I had first been stationed there as a pilot back in 1958, thirteen years after the defeat of the Japanese during Word War II. During those fifteen years, since my first assignment there, Japan had risen rapidly from an occupied Japan of a decade of poverty after the devastation of World War II to rebuilding and becoming a leading-edge technological industrial nation, with associated wealth. Japan had grown economically as we Americans spent blood and millions of hard-earned dollars holding up a shield of defense against the aggressive military expansion of Communism in Asia during the Korean War and Vietnam War, right next-door to Japan. From 1946 until 1963, Japan had circulated their money only within Japan to build a very strong economy. They used very high tariffs to keep out any imports to prevent outflow of their money. In 1963, Japanese citizens, for the first time since World War II were allowed to take in excess of $700 worth of Yen outside their nation. That was when they immediately began purchasing hotels and other property in Hawaii. Now, in 1973, as I looked at their factories as we drove in the bus to Yokota AFB, Japan had already captured much of the world's commercial electronics business, particularly the manufacture and sale of televisions and VCRs.

I looked at Eleanor in the bus and saw, as she gazed over the countryside, that she had truly enjoyed her two years of living in Japan. Her association with the Seventh Fleet officers' wives and Yokosuka Naval Base officers' wives club had been good experiences for her. She had made some lifelong friends during her stay.

Later, after flying the family to Jacksonville, North Carolina, and checking into the Marine Air Group, my orders were modified by Headquarters Marine Corps. I was dispatched to become the executive officer of the Marine Air Reserve Training Detachment (MARTD) at Selfridge Air National Guard Base, north of Detroit, Michigan. We had three squadrons, and most of the pilots were commercial pilots (weekend warriors) in our reserve flying squadrons.

Then the turmoil of President Nixon's impending impeachment arose from Watergate. With the national disruption associated with Nixon's resignation as president, the recent war in Vietnam seemed distant.

In April 1975, the capital of Cambodia, Phnom Penh, was falling to a combination of communist military units from the Cambodian Khmer Rouge, thousands of North Vietnamese, and South Vietnamese Viet Cong. The United States sent an amphibious task force to locate south of Cambodia for evacuation of the U.S. embassy in Phnom Penh. Marine Lt. Col. James L. "Trapper" Bolton was the commanding officer of composite squadron HMH-462. HMH-463 was also dispatched to Southeast Asia from Hawaii. The operation for evacuation of the U.S. embassy in Phnom Penh was called Eagle Pull. Due to the distance from the sea to Phnom Penh, instead of using Lietuenant Colonel Bolton's helicopters, the air force used their helicopters from Thailand to evacuate the embassy grounds. Soon, after the evacuation, Eagle Pull, Phnom Penh fell to the communists.

Despite the signed ceasefire agreement of January 23, 1973, in which the United States agreed to withdraw all military from Vietnam except the U.S. embassy staff in Saigon, the North Vietnamese broke their part of the agreement not to invade South Vietnam again. In March 1975, two years after the ceasefire agreement and departure of Americans from South Vietnam, the communist government of the Democratic Republic of Vietnam launched another blitzkrieg attack from North Vietnam, Cambodia, and Laos into South Vietnam. The NVA swept southward down the coast of South Vietnam until Saigon and the Mekong Delta region was all that remained free. It was obvious that the South Vietnamese Air Force and ground units could not stem the communist tide of attacks throughout their country. By April 25, 1975, the communists took Hue, Da Nang,

Nha Trang, and other South Vietnamese cities as they continued southward toward Saigon.

As the defenses of Saigon began to fall, the U.S. leaders in Washington ordered the carriers *Midway* and *Enterprise* to return to the South China Sea. The carriers *Coral Sea* and *Hancock* were also sent to be available off of South Vietnam, if required. Ten air force helicopters were aboard the USS *Midway* (CVA 41) to prepare to join amphibious Marine helicopter squadrons for possible missions to evacuate Americans from the U.S. embassy in Saigon.

U.S. President Gerald Ford, who took office after President Nixon resigned, feared for the safety of the Americans and key South Vietnamese officials who faced certain death when the North Vietnamese Army would capture Saigon. President Ford ordered the Seventh Fleet to execute an evacuation order, Operation Frequent Wind.

On April 29, 1975, the Seventh Fleet executed Operation Frequent Wind, the evacuation of Americans and close Vietnamese allies from Saigon. At 1244 on April 29, 1975, Marine Corps helicopters from composite Marine Corps squadron HMH-462, commanded by Lt. Col. James L. Bolton, flew from the USS *Okinawa*. Composite squadron HMH-463, commanded by Lt. Col. Herbert M. Fix, flying off the USS *Hancock*, joined them. The combined Marine and air force helicopters flew to the U.S. Defense attaché office grounds in Saigon. Thousands of evacuees were helo-lifted to the ships at sea, and by 2100 the attaché's office landing site was emptied.

Carrier fighter/attack aircraft flew cover for the helicopters. Marine Corps AH-1J Cobra attack helicopters provided close-in escort protection for the Marine giant CH-53A Sea Stallion helicopters.

Nonstop helicopter evacuation flights continued throughout the day and night of April 29. That period became known as the Night of the Helicopters. Americans, their security units, and South Vietnamese employees who had been loyal to Americans and had worked at U.S. installations were flown out to the assembled ships, but the evacuations did not go smoothly.

Early on the morning of April 30, 1975, U.S. Ambassador Graham Martin, more than two thousand evacuees, and the embassy's Marine security troops were loaded on the Marine helicopters and flown out, amid frenzy at the embassy grounds. Thousands of panicking Vietnamese climbed over the fences and pressed the Marine security guards back as the Vietnamese tried to get into the Marine helicopters to get out of the falling city. On the egress, with Ambassador Martin aboard one of them, the helicopters had to evasively fly to avoid NVA ground fire.

Millions of Americans watched television reports of that frenzied Marine Corps helicopter evacuation of the U.S. embassy from Saigon just before the city fell to the advancing communists. Many Americans who saw those reports repeatedly on their TV screens still to this day erroneously think that this hurried departure from Vietnam by a small handful of Americans was actually when U.S. fighting forces left the country; in fact the massive quantities of American army and Marine Corps ground-fighting units had departed South Vietnam during 1971, under President Nixon's Vietnamization program and troop retrograde. That was one full year before the 1972 major communist Easter invasion into South Vietnam and four years before the U.S. ambassador and embassy support and security units were evacuated in 1975.

During April 29 and 30, 1975, at sea, the frenzy continued. In addition to the thousands evacuated by helicopters, from both the U.S. Defense attaché office site and the U.S. embassy grounds, who landed aboard the carrier decks, fleeing South Vietnamese aircrews flew out, many with their families aboard their own helicopters, and attempted to land on the ships. Many ditched beside the carriers, while forty-one South Vietnamese helicopters landed aboard ships and fifty-four South Vietnamese helicopters were pushed off the ship's decks by sailors due to lack of space.

On April 30, 1975, shortly after Ambassador Martin left the embassy in the evacuation helicopter, the North Vietnamese Army swept through all of Saigon City. The NVA then charged the gates of the Republic of Vietnam's presidential palace and the U.S. embassy in Saigon. The invading NVA quickly raised the Democratic Republic of Vietnam (North Vietnam) flag over Saigon. The Republic of Vietnam (RVN) ceased to exist, and North Vietnam had finally achieved their decades-long objective to conquer and occupy their southern neighbor's country. Communism now reigned.

After two days of tense efforts to save the evacuees from the North Vietnamese Army, which now fully occupied Saigon, the armada of ships departed on May 2, 1975.

The ships that carried eighty thousand American and South Vietnamese evacuees included U.S. Navy ships, the civilian operated military sealift command ships, South Vietnamese Navy ships, as well as South Vietnamese commercial fishing ships. They all departed from the South Vietnam coastline and headed for the Philippines and Guam. This was the U.S. Navy's last act in the American struggle to help the Republic of Vietnam save their independence from the communist army of the Democratic Republic of Vietnam.

The communists took South Vietnam and turned it into another failure of communist misconceptions of how people should live. Just as the captive people of eastern Europe lived, at that time, behind the Iron Curtain, the South Vietnamese captive people now were interned behind a Bamboo Curtain. These unfortunate people were militarily forced to join the peoples of China, North Korea, and Cuba, where all progressive life had ceased and dismal, poverty-accompanying communism cloaked them for decades. Only time will tell when Vietnam eventually becomes a free country and an open market nation.

Much later, a highly decorated North Vietnamese, Maj. Nguyen Than Xuan, a leader in the final attack upon Saigon, said, "We (NVA) completely surrounded Saigon and then held up the final assault. We did this to allow the final Americans to leave. We did not want them (Americans) to have an excuse to return, in force, to fight us again. We knew we had out-maneuvered this giant American country. As soon as we felt all Americans were gone from the U.S. embassy, our tanks and infantry swept in to take Saigon. We proudly renamed it Ho Chi Minh City."

In 1981, U.S. Army Col. Harry G. Summers presented a study, titled "On Strategy," to the U.S. Army War College at Carlisle Barracks, Pennsylvania. He stated that back in April 1975, the same month Saigon fell, he was in Hanoi. He had been discussing the fall of South Vietnam with a North Vietnamese colonel. Colonel Summers stated to the North Vietnamese colonel, "You (NVA) never defeated us on the battlefield."

The North Vietnamese colonel answered, "That may be so, but it is also irrelevant."

This was the longest war for the United States. It, like the Korean War, was an undeclared war.

In 1985, referring to the Vietnam War, an old communist North Vietnamese Army general stated to the press, "Lau Qua," the war that took "too long a time." The first U.S. serviceman to die was army Spc4 James Thomas Davis. Davis was killed in an ambush on December 22, 1961; he was twenty-five years old.

The last two U.S. servicemen killed by hostile fire in Vietnam were Marines. Corporal Charles McMahon Jr. and Cpl. Darwin Judge were security guards at Saigon's Tan Son Nhut Airport. On April 29, 1975, the day before the final evacuation of Americans from the embassy in Saigon, they died from a North Vietnamese rocket explosion. These were the last battle deaths recorded by the Pentagon. They were death casualties numbers 58,019 and 58,020.

The next day, April 30, 1975, a Marine helicopter crashed off the coast of South Vietnam on the final evacuation, Operation Frequent Wind. Two Marines, Capt. William Nystul, twenty-nine, from Coronado, California, and Lt. Michael Shea, twenty-five, from El Paso, Texas, died in their helicopter.

That U.S. Navy and Marine Corps evacuation of both Americans and many South Vietnamese ended the role of the U.S. Seventh Fleet in supporting the ill-fated South Vietnamese resistance to the onslaught of ruthless communism.

In 1976, Gen. Vo Nguyen Giap, the brilliant North Vietnamese military leader and strategist, had his memoirs published. In his book, *How We Won the War*, General Giap credited the American people for giving North Vietnam the will to hold on. General Giap wrote that the North Vietnamese knew they could never defeat the Americans on the battlefield, but they needed to continue to fight until the Americans became so disenchanted that the American people would force the withdrawal of U.S. troops.

The following quote from General Giap is documented in the Vietnam War Memorial in Hanoi:

What we still don't understand is why Americans stopped the bombing of Hanoi. You had us on the ropes. If you had pressed us a little harder, just for another day or two, we were ready to surrender!

It was the same of battles of Tet. You defeated us! We knew it, and we knew you knew, but we were elated to notice your media were definitely helping us. They were causing more disruption in America than we could in the battlefields. We were ready to surrender.

You had won!

Epilogue

• • • • • • • •

Twenty years after the capture of Saigon and fall of South Vietnam to the North Vietnamese invaders, in 1995, what had our national political leaders learned from the longest war in U.S. history?

In April 1995, U.S. policy makers finally had the U.S. Marines protect the withdrawal of the UN forces from a political-military failure in Somalia. Prior to that, the political leaders misused the U.S. military forces in areas such as Haiti and Rwanda. These misuses of military might for various international political encounters, without a full, thought-through scenario of what our national interests really are, continue decade after decade. Even in 2003, when the United States was planning to attack Iraq for the second time, many Americans questioned if U.S. interests were really being threatened by Saddam Hussein. Were there links between Saddam and Osama bin Laden's al-Qaeda?

Fortunately, using superior firepower, we had a fast victory in less than a month of fighting in Iraq to dispose of Saddam Hussein. Unfortunately, due to poor planning at the highest levels, and with total disregard of our highest military leaders' recommendations during planning for the attack upon Iraq, that quick victory was promptly followed by months of unexpected attacks by insurgents. These so-called insurgent attacks started first upon Americans and allies, and then upon U.S.-backed Iraqi forces. Deadly battles resulted, such as finally securing the Iraqi city of Fallujah in November 2004 with the killing of approximately 1,200 insurgents. These insurgents were former Saddam troops and supporters from the Sunni Muslim radical religious group who carried on a revolution. Their revolution was to attempt to grasp control of Iraq and establish a Sunni Muslim radical religious–controlled nation. Only then did tangible proof arise for a link between al-Qaeda and foreign insurgency leader, Jordanian-born Abu Musab al-Zarqawi. Al-Zarqawi had entered Iraq to exploit its instability for Osama bin Laden's international war to replace all free nations' governments with radical Muslim dictatorships.

The point is, our military leaders always add to their personal experiences by attending military schools, such as war college, amphibious warfare school, and a host of others. At these professional military schools/colleges, they review military history as related to international politics and associated past errors committed. As a result of the professional knowledge of these historical errors and lessons learned, our military leaders seldom repeat military tactical mistakes. Our civilian-elected national leaders—and some of their appointed friends serving in high national political offices—lack such schooling in former political blunders, however, and often repeat mistakes that history shows we have already paid such a high price for. The military, despite often being aware of these political errors, is then obligated to execute their assigned military tasks, which frequently are assigned by incompetent civilian leaders. The disregard of our highest military commanders' advice in 2003 on what was needed not only to defeat Saddam's army but also to successfully occupy Iraq resulted in needless carnage.

We often have heard American politicians rhetorically express some of those lessons that we have learned with our blood and substantial personal efforts. When did our political leaders act using the lessons learned in Vietnam as guidelines? Consider the following:

- Don't commit military forces unless there is a real threat to the security of the United States or it is obvious to our citizens to be in the best interest of the United States, and then, obtain congressional approval. If big enough of a military commitment is required, a congressional declaration of a state of war should be agreed upon. A nation is either at war, or it is not. Warfare is a deadly set of conditions and cannot be a halfway commitment.

- When military units are dispatched by our political leaders, we must ensure they are fully supported to finish the assigned mission.

- Use maximum force available for a final conquest of the foe until an unconditional surrender by the enemy is obtained, as during World War II. An example of not following this basic principle was when Saddam Hussein of Iraq was left free to continue to run Iraq after the allied forces had totally defeated Saddam's forces in the Gulf War, freeing Kuwait in 1992.

- If not willing to "go the distance" as discussed, don't engage our armed forces by placing them in harm's way in foreign nations, especially if they are ill-armed or restricted by cumbersome and dangerous rules of engagement from accomplishing the tasks they are so well trained to do.

- Have a specific plan for extricating from the conflict before committing the troops. This was not planned for prior to the 2003 attack of Iraq.

Our civilian leaders have not used the lessons learned from the Vietnam War.

During 1995, the twentieth anniversary of the reunification of North and South Vietnam by the communist invaders was celebrated, and the controversy of this long, misunderstood war continued then, and still continues.

Former U.S. Secretary of Defense Robert S. McNamara's book *In Retrospect: The Tragedy and Lessons of Vietnam* was released.

In that book, McNamara belatedly, three decades too late, admitted he concluded that during the mid-sixties, the war in Vietnam, as being directed by him, was unwinnable.

McNamara wrote in his book, "We were wrong, terribly wrong." McNamara was wrong, very wrong, in the way he personally applied well-armed and well-trained U.S. armed forces.

The vast majority of GIs, of all ranks, knew McNamara's war was the wrong way to fight against first the communist Viet Cong, and then the North Vietnamese invading army. We military who were there knew as early as 1965 that it was a stupid way to conduct warfare. We all complained about the rules of engagement limiting our capabilities to carry the war to North Vietnam from where the war against South Vietnam was directed and supplied.

The sad, immoral fact is that McNamara already knew in 1966 and 1967 that his strategy was wrong, yet he kept quiet. Instead, McNamara erroneously played guerrilla warfare, keeping his troops in South Vietnam with slow escalations. The enemy matched his slow escalations. McNamara never envisioned invading North Vietnam and then allowing South Vietnam's army to occupy the North. That is what military doctrine would call for with a well-organized, well-equipped army, navy, and marine corps. Of course, McNamara never attended any military tactics school, or war college, so how could he have known that?

During 1966–67, when McNamara already knew his strategies were wrong, approximately 6,000 Americans had been killed in Vietnam since 1965. By the time America ceased military action against North Vietnam with the ceasefire agreement of January 27, 1973, there were more than 58,000 Americans who had died. It was obvious to most Americans that the U.S. war actions were not run in a normal military manner. Only a fool would have thought that one of the most powerful military forces in the world could not destroy and enforce a military victory upon a third-world nation such as North Vietnam—a nation that did not produce handheld military weapons, antiaircraft weapons, tanks, or aircraft. The communist Hanoi government admitted it lost 1.1 million soldiers killed and 300,000 missing in action. Compared to 58,000 American military killed and 254,000 South Vietnamese, who do you think won the war's battles?

The war was not lost on the battlefield. The country of South Vietnam was lost to the communist North Vietnamese, as the communists predicted, in the American streets, college campuses led by leftist socialists, and the U.S. media.

An early strangulation of delivery to North Vietnam of weapons of war would have, in itself, achieved a military goal of denying the enemy the means to conduct warfare. McNamara never enacted that less aggressive strategy as a supplement to other means of military confrontation with the enemy. The Vietnam War was tactically conducted as if the United States had fought in Europe in World War II and planned to end all fighting against Nazi Germany only in France, without bombing and invading Germany itself, and then attempting to negotiate an end to the war with Hitler.

Immediately upon the release of McNamara's book in 1995, rage from Vietnam War veterans, especially those severely wounded, screamed across the nation with moral condemnation against the man who dictated the early phase of that ill-fated war. McNamara restricted the generals and admirals from professionally executing the war and established the modus operandi that resulted in the betrayal of the U.S. fighting men and women who served so honorably in that terrible, long war.

But we Vietnam veterans cannot lay the blame for that great debacle only on a few Americans. Much blame for the way the war was run can be directly laid upon the misguided American civilians who vigorously marched in mass demonstrations against our fighting the communists. It was their awesome and often violent pressures on our statesmen that influenced the course of actions in that war. The protestors carried the North Vietnamese and Viet Cong flags and shouted at our succeeding presidents, both Democrat and Republican. These American supporters of communism also shouted at and reviled even our young military men. The anti–Vietnam War protestors significantly influenced the outcome of that war, and the North Vietnamese utilized that to their advantage in conquering and turning South Vietnam into a communist police state.

Each Vietnam veteran quietly hopes that the blood of his comrades that was spilled in Vietnam remains on the hands of those Americans who not only supported the enemy, but also contributed to the communist invaders' final conquest of South Vietnam. It was they who forced the U.S. fighting forces from Vietnam, certainly not a superior enemy army.

Years later, on November 16, 2000, while the Democrats and Republicans were still competing for the critical vote counts in Florida over who really won the November 7, 2000, presidential election, a new chapter in U.S. international relations was written.

President William Jefferson Clinton, nearing the end of his second term as president, arrived in Hanoi, the capital of the Socialist Republic of Vietnam.

President Clinton's visit to Vietnam was almost twenty-eight years after the 1973 ceasefire agreement in Paris that ended the American fighting in Vietnam and released POWs returned home. It was also twenty-five years after North Vietnam brutally took

South Vietnam to absorb it into the communist state of the Socialist Republic of Vietnam.

President Clinton became the first U.S. president to visit Vietnam since the Vietnam War, and the first ever to visit Hanoi. President Lyndon B. Johnson and President Richard M. Nixon made short visits to the war zones, in what was then known as South Vietnam, to rally the U.S. troops during the Vietnam War.

En route to Vietnam, President Clinton expressed no intention to apologize in Vietnam for the war Americans fought there, and the war he personally, bitterly opposed.

Prior to Clinton's arrival in Vietnam, U.S. Ambassador to Vietnam Pete Peterson, a former POW in North Vietnam, stated, "I don't think anyone is looking for an apology."

Many of us Vietnam combat veterans wondered why anyone would even expect any U.S. president to apologize for our support in defending South Vietnam from North Vietnam's continual military invasions. It was North Vietnam that started the war, not the United States. It was North Vietnam that continued the war, after U.S. fighting units left Vietnam in 1973. And, it was North Vietnam that again invaded South Vietnam and conquered it in 1975.

Clinton's personal history as a Vietnam War protestor, and his avoiding the military draft, were unavoidable backdrops to his historic visit to Vietnam in 2000.

En route to Vietnam, President Clinton stated, "I now understand how difficult it had been for President Johnson and President Nixon. They did what they thought were the right things under very difficult circumstances."

In Hanoi, friendly Vietnamese greeted President Clinton. Banners were hung over the streets that read, in English:

WARM WELCOME H. E. MR. WILLIAM JEFFERSON CLINTON, PRESIDENT OF THE UNITED STATES OF AMERICA . . . AND SPOUSE ON AN OFFICIAL VISIT TO THE SOCIALIST REPUBLIC OF VIETNAM.

Ambassador Peterson said, "With eighty percent of the Vietnamese younger than forty years old, the average youngster knows as much about the war as our own high school students in America, which is probably nothing."

President Clinton's visit was, indeed, time for Americans and Vietnamese to seek closure to that bitter war, but the closure is complex and costly to the United States.

A quarter century after the Vietnam War, America's search for 1,992 unaccounted for servicemen went on with archaeological digs for bones and other clues of our missing in action. Some of this search effort is driven by rumors, persisting over decades, of live Americans left behind when the last known prisoners of war went home to the United States during the 1973 POW exchange.

During Clinton's visit to Vietnam, Robert Jones, the director of the Pentagon's POW/MIA office, stated, "We're not going to stop looking as long as we have leads to pursue."

At the time of Clinton's Vietnam visit, the Pentagon had already stopped pursuing 646 cases of the 1,992 MIA cases due to lack of leads.

During Clinton's eight years as president, 283 missing U.S. servicemen were accounted for in Southeast Asia. That was almost half of the total accounted for since the end of hostilities between the United States and North Vietnam in 1973, when U.S. support units withdrew and the last known POWs returned home.

The United States has been spending $6 million a year in remains-recovery operations in Southeast Asia, paying Vietnamese laborers to dig in search for fragments of bone, clothing, and aircraft debris. The recovery operations are conducted in Vietnam, Cambodia, and Laos.

Sandy Berger, President Clinton's national Security adviser, stated during Clinton's trip to Vietnam, "The cutting-edge of the remains recovery process from the very beginning has been, and remains today, achieving the fullest possible accounting for our POWs and MIAs."

The most difficult issue for both the Untied States and Vietnam is the suspicion by Americans that Americans remained captive after the last POWs returned home in 1973.

The Vietnamese have reiterated their position that all recovered remains of Americans have been turned over to U.S. authorities.

On November 18, 2000, President Clinton stood outside of Hanoi and watched Vietnamese and several Americans toiling, digging, and passing buckets of mud to a sieve at a possible MIA recovery site. Clinton said, "Until we bring every possible fallen hero home, the United States will not rest. Whether we are Americans or Vietnamese, I think we all want to know where our loved ones are buried. I think we all want to be able to honor them and be able to visit their gravesite."

Clinton was with his wife, Hillary, and their daughter, Chelsea, at the digging site. Beside Clinton stood Dan and David Evert of suburban Phoenix, Arizona. Their father, Air Force Capt. Lawrence G. Evert of Cody, Wyoming, had been shot down during a bombing run at a railroad site here.

Master Sergeant Gina Noland, at the possible remains recovery site, told President Clinton, "We feel confident we're at the correct site." Noland then showed Clinton a .38-caliber shell casing. Evert carried a .38-caliber survival pistol during his combat missions. Master Sergeant Noland added, "We do anticipate finding larger pieces. The wreckage is a lot older than many of us who are here digging in this field."

While in Hanoi, Clinton, standing in front of a large bust of former revolutionary leader Ho Chi Minh, encouraged Vietnam to become a more open society and said of the two nations' warring history: "We must not forget it, but we must not be controlled by it."

Vietnamese President Tran Duc Luong welcomed the prospect of "immense cooperation between the old enemies."

Clinton said that guaranteeing the right to religious worship and political dissent builds confidence in the fairness of institutions. National Security Adviser, Sandy Berger, reported that the Vietnamese officials did not agree with Clinton, saying the Vietnamese have different interpretations of human rights.

Clinton presented the Vietnamese with 350,000 pages of documents about battle dates and locations, along with medical records, to assist the Hanoi government in determining the fate of 300,000 missing Vietnamese.

Clinton praised the Vietnamese for their assistance in attempting to account for the remaining 1,992 missing Americans. Clinton said, "No two nations have ever before done the things we are doing together to find the missing from the Vietnam conflict."

Clinton then flew south from Hanoi to Ho Chi Minh City,

formerly called Saigon. Here, he was surrounded with emotionally charged throngs of excited onlookers, some of whom had fought alongside Americans against the communists from the North so long ago.

In Ho Chi Minh City, President Clinton again, as he did in Hanoi, insisted that the Vietnamese set aside their fears and join the global marketplace of trade and ideas.

Clinton said, "Imagine how much more you will achieve as even more young people gain more freedom to shape the decisions that affect their lives. The key to the future is entrepreneurship, innovation, and competition, as well as open exchange of ideas."

The crowds gathered around Clinton with spontaneous enthusiasm. This was something almost unheard of in Vietnam. This caused Le Kha Phieu, the Communist Party's general secretary to issue a verbal reminder that Vietnam had fought and sacrificed for its independence. Le Kha Phieu stated, "Where did the cause of our resistance war against invaders come from? Fundamentally, it came because imperialists invaded to get colonies."

The dueling statements were a public debate between two leaders. This event in Ho Chi Minh City took place four months after the Socialist Republic of Vietnam and the United States had signed a trade agreement paving the way for Clinton's visit. The trade agreement, if executed, would break down many of the protective barriers Vietnam has erected around its economy and society.

Clinton mentioned the previously signed trade treaty to Phieu and said, "The treaty will help develop a more open, sophisticated free market, based on international rules of law. The changes it will bring should be embraced, not feared."

Le Kha Phieu, former North Vietnamese Army general, retorted by saying, "Our economy has many sectors, in which the state sector plays the leading role. We have a private economy, but we do not privatize the economy. We respect the choice, the lifestyle, and political systems of other nations. We, in turn, demand that other nations respect our people's choices." Ho Chi Minh City's Mayor Thanh agreed with Phieu.

President Clinton further irritated his Vietnamese hosts when, in Ho Chi Minh City, he demonstrated his concern for religious freedom. He made a brief, unannounced visit to Pham Minh Man, the Roman Catholic archbishop of Ho Chi Minh City. Vietnam has about 10 percent of its population participating as Catholic Church members. Although all religious worship is permitted in Vietnam, churches of all faiths must submit to government regulations, as in communist China.

Those public exchanges between the leaders, during Clinton's visit, brought out the viewpoint of the Vietnamese that reflects their concern of the subversive effects of a free market on a controlled socialist society, referred to by communist Vietnam and communist China as peaceful evolution.

Both, Le Kha Phieu and President Clinton generally agreed on the effects of this process. And both were aware that with Clinton, it is not troops the United States was bringing to Vietnam but a free market. With that, the concerns of leaders like Le Kha Phieu are that the influence of a free market will diminish their own personal power.

News media covering Clinton's visit to Vietnam witnessed that most Vietnamese businessmen said they believe that an open market is inevitable and that President Clinton's vision for the future is a more likely scenario than that of Le Kha Phieu.

Soon after the Vietnam War ended for the Americans in 1973, President Nixon visited communist China. That historic visit began the slow evolution of opening the closed door of a communist nation. The evolution continued for decades, leading to open trade with China, even though China still remains a communist-controlled country.

Likewise, Clinton's historic visit to Vietnam was a simple but important foot in the door to get communist Vietnam to open the door to global trade for their own people's benefit.

Three years after President Clinton's visit to Vietnam and thirty years after the 1973 end of the Vietnam War, on November 10, 2003 (coincidentally, the 228th anniversary of the founding of the U.S. Marine Corps), under President George W. Bush's administration, a meeting between U.S. and Vietnamese officials was held in Washington, D.C.

U.S. Defense Secretary Donald H. Rumsfeld greeted Vietnam's defense minister, Pham Van Tra, on the steps of the Pentagon. It was another diplomatic move toward normalization. Agenda topics discussed included closer cooperative military ties and improving security in Asia against an existing terrorism problem.

Within nine days of the meeting, on November 19, 2003, the USS Vandegrift cruised up the Saigon River with U.S. and Vietnamese flags fluttering. The Yokosuka, Japan–based, U.S. Seventh Fleet frigate docked for a historic port call in Ho Chi Minh City. This was the first visit by a U.S. Navy ship since the Vietnam War. Some of the ship's crew consisted of sons and daughters of Vietnam War veterans. The objective of the port visit was to boost bilateral relations between the former foes and heal old wounds from the conflict that killed 58,000 Americans and 3 million Vietnamese.

One month before these historic activities, Vietnam had shown signs of growing prosperity. Vietnam began donating aid to a foreign country. Vietnam sent 1,500 tons of rice to Iraq through the United Nations. Only three years prior to that, Vietnam had been on the receiving end of a flood of aid.

On June 13, 2005, twenty-one Vietnam War orphans living since childhood in the United States flew from Atlanta, Georgia, to Vietnam to commemorate the thirtieth anniversary of "Operation Babylift," in which three thousand Vietnamese children were airlifted to the United States at the end of the Vietnam War. It was a happy/sad event for these adult Vietnamese who had lived thirty years as Americans and now visited their birthplace, Vietnam.

On June 21, 2005, President George W. Bush opened his Oval Office to the highest-ranking communist Vietnamese official since the end of the Vietnam War that had claimed more than 58,000 U.S. troops' lives. Prime Minister Phan Van Khai expressed his desire to have Vietnam join the World Trade Organization. Other topics discussed were security issues and the mutual desire to coordinate the war on terror.

Only the future can reveal when Vietnam will become an open, free society.

Appendix A
• • • • • • • •

Maps

Mainland Southeast Asia
kilometers 0 ——————— 300

Principal U.S. Airbases in Southeast Asia.

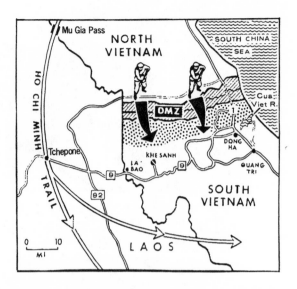

The "Easter Offensive": North Vietnamese invasion of South Vietnam, March 30, 1972 (detail along the DMZ).

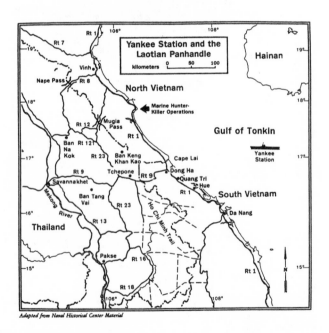

Marine Hunter-Killer Operations, June 22, 1972–January 26, 1973.

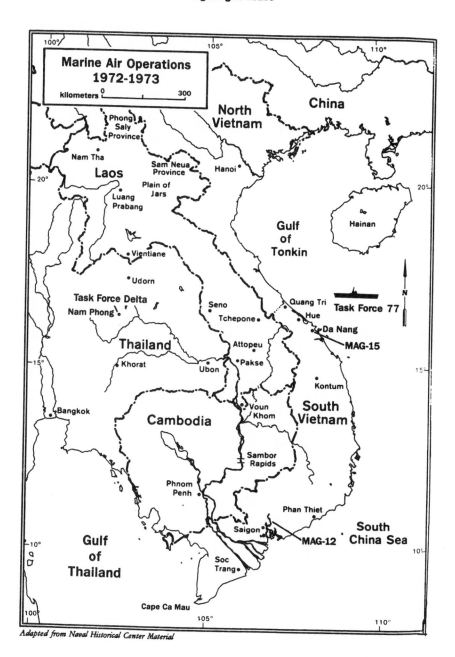

Marine Air Operations
1972-1973

kilometers 0 — 300

China

North
Vietnam

Phong
Saly
Province

Nam Tha

Laos

Sam Neua
Province

Hanoi

Plain of
Jars

Luang
Prabang

Gulf
of
Tonkin

Hainan

Vientiane

Udorn

Task Force Delta
Nam Phong

Seno

Tchepone

Quang Tri

Hue

Da Nang

MAG-15

Task Force 77

N

Thailand

Attopeu

Pakse

Khorat

Ubon

Kontum

Bangkok

Cambodia

Voun
Khom

South
Vietnam

Sambor
Rapids

Phnom
Penh

Phan Thiet

South
China Sea

Gulf
of
Thailand

Saigon

MAG-12

Soc
Trang

Cape Ca Mau

Adapted from Naval Historical Center Material

Organizational Charts

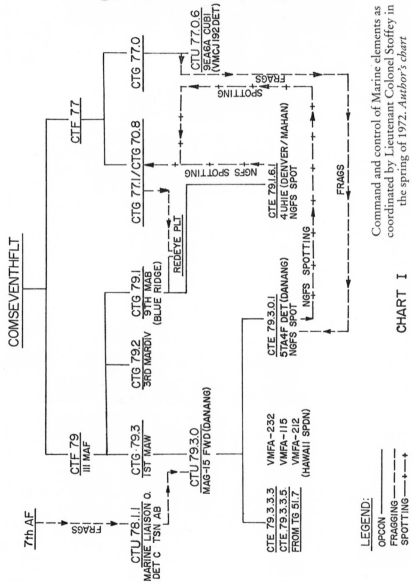

CHART I

Command and control of Marine elements as
coordinated by Lieutenant Colonel Stoffey in
the spring of 1972. *Author's chart*

LEGEND:

OPCON ————
FRAGGING — — —
SPOTTING — + — +

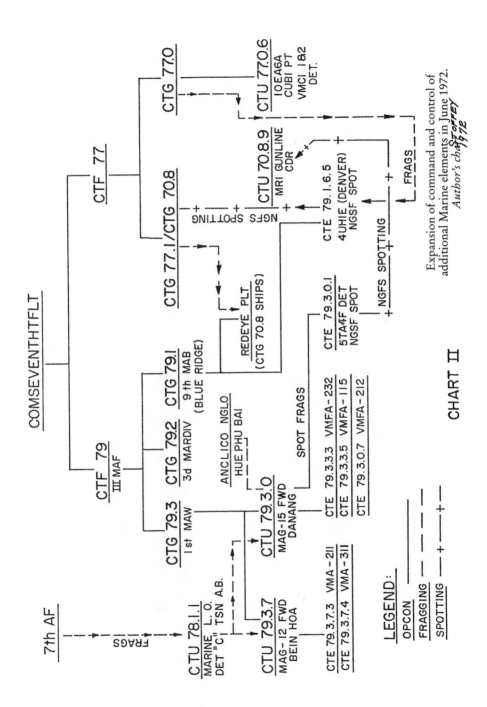

Expansion of command and control of
additional Marine elements in June 1972.
Author's chart

CHART II

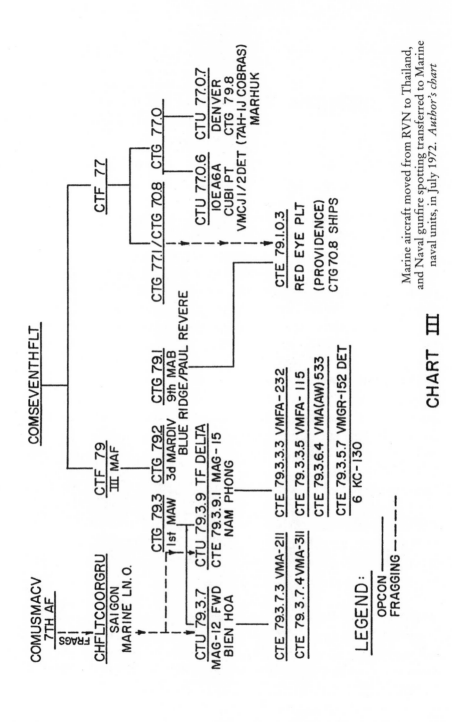

CHART III

Marine aircraft moved from RVN to Thailand, and Naval gunfire spotting transferred to Marine naval units, in July 1972. *Author's chart*

Appendix C

• • • • • • • •

Where Some of Them Are Now

Edward Ashman, a Marine A-6A radar-jamming pilot flew long, precarious missions to jam Hanoi and Haiphong area surface-to-air missile site systems in support of the air force B-52 raids in 1972 and early 1973. Ed resigned from the Marine Corps as a captain in 1980. Ashman was employed as the quality assurance manager for Hughes Aircraft Microcircuits Division in Newport Beach, California, while the author was the sales manager at the same plant. Ed resides with his wife, Pam, in El Toro, California.

John T. "Jack" Beaver was a navy commander serving on the Seventh Fleet staff as the submarine warfare officer during 1972 and 1973. Later, he served as naval attaché in Germany and was involved with damage assessment of an infamous spy. He retired from the navy as a captain and was employed, for years, with a navy support firm followed by working in the office of the national counterintelligence executive. Jack and his wife, Emily, live in Falls Church, Virginia.

George L. Boaz, a navy commander, served on the Seventh Fleet staff as the aircraft carrier operations officer during 1972 and 1973. He was promoted to captain, retired from the navy, and is living with his wife, Noel, in southern California.

James L. "Jim" Bolton was commanding officer of Marine Corps composite squadron HMH-462. Lieutenant Colonel Bolton led his squadron's helicopter flights in Operation Frequent Wind, the evacuation of the U.S. attaché office grounds and U.S. embassy site in Saigon, as North Vietnamese Army troops entered the city to capture it during the last few days of April 1975. Later, headquarters Marine Corps awarded Jim Bolton the award of the Marine Corps aviator of the year 1975. Jim retired as a colonel and lived with his wife, Margaret, in Vista, California, until her death in January 2005. Jim died in 2007.

Walter E. Boomer was a Marine major and adviser to the South Vietnamese Marines near the DMZ in March 1972 when the North Vietnamese launched the full-scale Easter Offensive invasion into South Vietnam and captured Quang Tri City. Somehow, Major Boomer survived that NVA three-division blitzkrieg attack and remained in the Marine Corps for a career. After earning notoriety during Desert Storm in 1991, as the commanding general (CG) of all Marines in Kuwait, he became the CG of the Combat Development Center at Quantico, Virginia. He then was promoted to four-star general and assigned as the assistant commandant of the Marine Corps in 1992, prior to his retiring. He then became the president and CEO of Rogers Corporation.

Edward Briggs, a navy captain, served as the plans officer, vice chief of staff, and chief of staff to Admiral Holloway, commander of the Seventh Fleet, on board the USS *Oklahoma City* during 1972–73. Ed Briggs went on to become a vice admiral, and his last assignment was as Commander Naval Surface Force, U.S. Atlantic Fleet, Norfolk, Virginia. In retirement, Admiral Briggs became an active volunteer in K–12 curricula and instructional development among local school districts, several veterans organizations, and the Surface Navy Association. Admiral Briggs lives in southern California with his wife, Nan.

Vernon A. Burkhart, a navy captain and physician, served as the Seventh Fleet staff surgeon during 1972–73 aboard the USS *Oklahoma City*. Dr. Burkhart assumed command of a naval hospital in the United States prior to his retirement from the military. "Doc" Burkhart passed away in 2000. His wife, Nancy, lives in North Carolina.

Fred H. Cherrick, lieutenant, junior grade, who at the age of twenty-three was officer of the deck aboard the USS *Leonard F. Mason* during two tours of combat in the Gulf of Tonkin during numerous ship raids into North Vietnam in 1972. An electrical engineer, he left the navy to receive an MBA from Harvard. He was the marketing director of Rockwell International Microelectronics and the boss of the author when the author was the national sales manager for Rockwell's microelectronics division. He is president and owner of Electric Stars, an electric solar company in Los Angeles, California.

Randall H. Cunningham, nicknamed the "Duke," was a lieutenant and naval aviator who with his backseat radar intercept officer, William P. Driscoll, shot down five North Vietnamese MiG fighters to become America's first Vietnam War ace. He then spent two tours of duty as a pilot instructor at the Miramar Naval Air Station Top Gun School in San Diego. He retired from the navy as a captain and became a U.S. congressman, representing a San Diego North County District. On November 28, 2005, Cunningham resigned from the House of Representatives and pleaded guilty to taking approximately $2.4 million in bribes.

James G. Dionisopoulos, was a Marine Corps colonel and the Seventh Fleet staff Marine officer in the plans section during 1972 and 1973 aboard the Seventh Fleet flagship, USS *Oklahoma City*. He retired in Carlsbad, California, where he died in 1987.

Andrew Dudley Jr., a young Marine lieutenant and fighter/attack pilot in 1972, flew the F-4 Phantom in VMFA-333 off the carrier USS *America*. Dudley remained in the Marine Corps and later served as the commanding officer of an F/A-18 fighter squadron, VMFA-451, and flew combat missions in Operation Desert Storm Southwest Asia in 1991. On July 17, 1992, as a colonel, he became the commanding officer of Marine Air Group 46, a Reserve Air Group at El Toro, California.

Larry L. Emarine, a lieutenant commander, served as the Seventh Fleet staff mine warfare officer during 1972 and 1973. Lieutenant Commander Emarine was instrumental in the mining and mine neutralization activities in North Vietnam's waterways. He left the USS *Oklahoma City* to teach NROTC at the University of New Mexico prior to retiring as a commander. Larry and his wife, Mary, lived in Albuquerque, New Mexico, where he teaches. His wife died several years ago.

James C. Froid, a navy commander, served on the Seventh Fleet staff as the amphibious warfare officer. After several Washington tours at the Office of the Chief of Naval Operations and the Naval Warfare Systems Command, he retired as a captain in Alexander, Virgina. Jim then spent fifteen years employed with the worldwide management consulting firm Booz-Allen & Hamilton, Inc., in projects related to navy command control and communications. He has since been involved in work at George Washington's Mount Vernon Estate. His wife, Marie, died in 1996.

General Vo Nguyen Giap, was born in 1912 in the village of An Xa, Quang Binh province. In 1939, when the French controlling Indochina cracked down on communists, Giap fled to China. He met Ho Chi Minh, a fellow Vietnamese, in China. He was with Ho when the Viet Minh was formed. Giap returned to Vietnam in 1941 and began organizing the Montagnards. Giap then built an army that changed Indochina. After Giap's defeats by the Americans in 1968, Tet, and again in his Phase III invasion into South Vietnam in 1972, he was replaced by General Dung. Giap became minister of defense. South Vietnam, including Saigon, fell to the North in 1975 under the command of Giap's replacement, General Dung. Giap retired in Hanoi.

Frank A. Hantz, a commander, served on the Seventh Fleet staff as the intelligence officer. He retired as a commander and settled down on a tranquil farm in Pennsylvania.

James L. Holloway III, a vice admiral, was the commander of the Seventh Fleet in 1972 and 1973. Later, he was promoted to admiral and became the Chief of Naval Operations and a member of the Joint Chiefs of Staff prior to his retirement. He and his wife, Dabney, reside in Annapolis, Maryland. For years in retirement, Admiral Holloway has continued to serve his nation in numerous responsible positions. He was chairman of the Commission on Naval Incidents at Sea, coordinating such incidents with the Soviet Union to avoid further conflicts at sea. He negotiated with the former Soviet Union and helped establish rules of handling naval encounters with the Soviet Union during the long years of the Cold War.

William A. Kanakanui Jr., served as the captain of the USS *Oklahoma City*, the flagship of the Seventh Fleet, during the North Vietnamese invasion into South Vietnam in 1972 and 1973. Captain Kanakanui retired in Pensacola, Florida, where he died in 1990.

Nguyen Cao Ky, was a flamboyant former South Vietnamese fighter pilot, VNAF chief of staff, and later premier and vice president of the Republic of Vietnam during the late years of the Vietnam War. Ky escaped from Saigon just prior to the NVA capture of it in 1975. An Air America (CIA) UH-1E Huey helicopter flew him out to the carrier USS *Midway*. Ky came to the United States and operated several businesses. On April 10, 1985, ten years after the fall of Saigon, Nguyen Cao Ky stated to the U.S. press, "I think the war was a waste for the sacrifice of 58,000 Americans. We could not win the war because we had so many limitations on the use of military power. I think the American officials at that time didn't have a winning policy." Ky recently stated, "Communism is dead in Vietnam."

Stuart D. Landersman was a navy commander and Seventh Fleet staff surface warfare officer during 1972–73 aboard the USS *Oklahoma City*. Stu went on to be promoted to captain and commanded Destroyer Squadron 23, the famous "Little Beaver" squadron. He then was Commander, Tactical Training Group Pacific and then a CNO Fellow with the first Strategic Studies Group at the Naval War College, retiring from the navy in 1982. He became a convoy commodore and holds a master's degree in international relations and a U.S. Coast Guard Masters license. For eighteen years, Stu worked as a fleet representative for the Johns Hopkins University Applied Physics Laboratory, advising surface navy staffs on operational matters, and retired in 2000. Stu is now a consultant and part-time teacher of maritime safety. Landersman has written and published numerous professional naval books and articles. Stu and his wife,

Martha, live in Coronado Cays, California, as a former career seagoing officer and licensed mariner. As expected, he has his own dock and boat next to his home.

William Paden Mack, vice admiral and commander of the Seventh Fleet in 1971 and 1972, he was an expert in amphibious warfare. He departed the Seventh Fleet on May 23, 1972, to assume the position of superintendent of the U.S. Naval Academy, Annapolis, Maryland, prior to retiring. Admiral Mack died at the age of eighty-seven on January 21, 2003. He had personally participated in much of U.S. history from World War II through the Vietnam War.

John S. McCain III, as a lieutenant commander and navy pilot, was shot down over North Vietnam on October 26, 1967. McCain somehow survived POW camp internment in North Vietnam including numerous tortures. He, along with the other American POWs, was released during the 1973 POW exchange, after the ceasefire agreement. Several years before the POW exchanges in 1973, McCain had refused to accept an early release offer by the North Vietnamese, who wished to propagandize his release due to his father, Adm. John S. McCain II, who was then commander of all Pacific forces. As a result of his refusal of release before other POWs, and other of his resistant activities, he was thrown into years of solitary confinement. He became well known as the senator from Arizona and then more famous as a presidential candidate for the Republican Party in 2008. He continues to serve his nation as of this writing.

Robert P. McKenzie, a captain, served on the Seventh Fleet staff as the operations officer in 1971 and 1972. Later, he was promoted to rear admiral and was assigned as the commanding officer of the Naval Air Station, North Island, San Diego, California, prior to his retirement.

Carl Miller was an air force colonel and commander of the U.S. Air Force 8th Tactical Fighter Wing that led the F-4 Phantom attack group that bombed the famous Paul Doumer Bridge in North Vietnam on May 10, 1972. Miller remained in the air force. Later, he was promoted to the rank of general. He was assigned as commander of the 21st NORAD of the U.S. Air Defense Command. He retired and became the national administrator of the Civil Air Patrol.

Thomas J. Murphy was a young Marine lance corporal who had volunteered to be a gunner in a Marine CH-46 helicopter during the South Vietnamese Lan Son 72 counteroffensive against the North Vietnamese 1972 Easter invasion of South Vietnam. In July 1972, Tom was severely wounded in the head. After medical discharge from the Marine Corps, Tom continued to pay an awesome price for being a good Marine and patriotic American. After Veterans Administration (VA) limited care, Tom's family found out that the VA does not have a long-term therapeutic rehabilitation system for veterans with traumatic head wounds. Private treatment centers like the Devereux Center for Head Trauma in Devon, Pennsylvania, do offer such rehabilitation therapy. There was, however, no federal funding for such treatment for veterans out of the VA system. Tom's brother, Gary, finally, after fifteen years of pressuring the U.S. government, obtained permission for private treatment at the Devereux Center for Tom. This was only temporary. The VA terminated the funding. The VA offered to put Tom Murphy, then forty, along with other similar brain-damaged soldiers, into VA psychiatric wards, but the VA would not provide ongoing rehabilitation therapy unless the Murphy family chose to pay for such treatments outside the VA, at a private facility.

Tom's brother, Gary, and Raymond Lynch, a former Marine, teamed up to fight the bureaucratic red tape. Finally, in November 1991, nineteen years after Tom had been severely wounded in action, Senator Frank Lautenberg (D-NJ) sponsored legislation that eventually had Congress provide $3.5 million funding for a one-year evaluation study for head injury rehabilitation through the Department of Defense. As of this writing, no long-term federal funding exists to provide rehabilitation for combat veterans suffering from traumatic head wounds of a piercing nature, not the blow on the head type of injuries. Rehabilitation doctors have documented proven improvement for Tom Murphy from the limited rehabilitation he has received, but the battle continues to attempt to get Congress to provide ongoing therapy for Tom Murphy and those who survived devastating head injuries while proudly and heroically serving their nation.

Le Kha Phieu was a general in the North Vietnamese Army during the Vietnam War. Le Kha Phieu is now the Vietnamese Communist

Party general secretary. Phieu met President William Jefferson Clinton during Clinton's visit to Hanoi in November 2000.

William M. Russell was a navy captain and the operations officer on the staff of the Seventh Fleet during 1972 and 1973. He retired as a captain and lives with his wife, Billie, in La Jolla, California.

Ray Smith was a Marine captain and adviser to the South Vietnamese in March 1972. He was up near the DMZ when the North Vietnamese overran his units during the 1972 Easter invasion into South Vietnam. He survived and remained in the Marine Corps. He became a brigadier general and served as J-5 of the Asian Pacific Division for the Joint Chiefs of Staff at the Pentagon.

Vo Vet Thahn was a North Vietnamese battalion commander who helped seize Saigon in 1975. Twenty-five years later, in November 2000, as the mayor of Ho Chi Minh City, he greeted President Clinton during his visit to the city, formerly called Saigon.

Felix Vecchione, a navy captain, served as a key staff officer on Rear Adm. Brian McCauley's Task Force 78 End Sweep. He conducted numerous meetings with the North Vietnamese negotiators in Haiphong, North Vietnam, and onboard the USS *New Orleans* (LPH-11) concerning the complex issues for sweeping the mines in the waterways of North Vietnam. Several years later, while still on active duty, Captain Vecchione and several of his staff personnel of his Charleston, South Carolina, mine sweeping unit were killed in a commercial aircraft accident while the aircraft was approaching Raleigh Airport in North Carolina.

John Vogt was the air force general and commander of the Seventh Air Force at Tan Son Nhut Air Base near Saigon in the former Republic of Vietnam. General Vogt directed all the air force raids upon North Vietnam during 1972 and until the Paris ceasefire agreement became effective at 2400 Greenwich Mean Time, January 27, 1973 (morning of January 28 in the Democratic Republic of Vietnam). Later, he became the commander of Allied Forces, Central Europe. General Vogt retired to Annapolis, Maryland, and continues to serve his country as a statesman and adviser to many national committees.

Nguyen Than Xuan served as a major in the North Vietnamese Army and was a leader in the final attack upon the U.S. embassy during the fall of Saigon in May 1975. On April 30, 1985, during the ten-year celebration of the fall of Saigon (renamed Ho Chi Minh City), Major Xuan, wearing his well-earned eighteen medals, paraded in his well-pressed uniform. Shortly after, Xuan retired and returned north to live near Haiphong City.

Appendix D

• • • • • • • •

Amphibious Squadron (PHIBRON) Ships of the Seventh Fleet, 1972–1973

Squadron	Ship
Task Force 76 Command	USS *Blue Ridge* (LCC-19)
	USS *Paul Revere* (LPA-248)
PHIBRON 5	USS *Tripoli* (LPH-10)
	USS *Duluth* (LPD-6)
	USS *Denver* (LPD-9)
	USS *Anchorage* (LSD-36)
	USS *Mobile* (LKA-115)
	USS *Tuscaloosa* (LST-1187)
	USS *Schenectady* (LST-1185)
PHIBRON 7	USS *Okinawa* (LPH-3)
	USS *Juneau* (LPD-10)
	USS *Point Defiance* (LSD-31)
	USS *Alamo* (LSD-33)
	USS *St. Louis* (LKA-116)
	USS *Manitowoc* (LST-1180)
	USS *Sumter* (LST-1181)
	USS *Cayuga* (LST-1186)
PHIBRON 3	USS *New Orleans* (LPH-11)
	USS *Juneau* (LPD-10)
	USS *Alamo* (LSD-33)
	USS *San Bernardino* (LST-1189)
	USS *Monticello* (LSD-35)
	USS *Ogden* (LPD-5)

PHIBRON 1

USS *Inchon* (LPH-12)
USS *Fresno* (LST-1182)
USS *Cleveland* (LPD-7)
USS *Tulare* (LKD-112)

Courtesy of Charles D. Melson, Chief Historian, Headquarters Marine Corps

Appendix E

Task Force 76 and 9th MAB Chronology, 1972–1973

Operation Name	Dates	Location	Units	Remarks	Losses
Air Support	12 Nov 71–17 Jul 72	USS *Coral Sea* (CVA-43)	VMA 224	Support TF 77	4 A6s
Air Support	3 Apr 72–18 Feb 73	Cubi Point/ Da Nang	VMCJ 1, 2	Support TF 77	1 EA6 2 KIAs
Air Support	6 Apr 72–21 Sep 73	Da Nang/ Nam Phong	MAG 15 VMFA 115, 232, 212 VMA 533	Support 7th Air Force SVN, NVN, Laos, Cambodia	1 TA4 4 F4s 3 A6
Heroic Action	11 May 72	Off NVN	31 MAU	Deception	-0-
Song Thanh 5-72	13 May 72	Quang Tri Province	9 MAB 31 MAU 1/4, 1/9 HMM164	Support VNMC Assault	1 HU1E 1 CH53

Air Support	17 May 72–3 Feb 73	Bien Hoa AB	MAG 12 VMA 211, 311	Support 7th Air Force SVN	3 KIA 1 MIA 11 WIA 3 A4s
Song Thanh 6-72	24 May 72	Quang Tri Province	9 MAB 31 MAU 1/4, 1/9 HMM164	Support VNMC Assualt	-0-
Air Support	5 Jun 72–24 Mar 73	USS *America* (CVA-66)	VMFA 333	Support TF 77	3 F4s
MARHUK	16 Jun 72–15 Jun 73	Vicinity of Hon La, NVN	9 MAB HMA 369	AH-1J Support TF 77	-0-
ReadyOp	27 Jun 72	DMZ	9 MAB 31, 33 MAU 1/9, 1/4 HMM 164, 165	Turnaway simulated landing	-0-
Lam Son 72 (I)	29 Jun 72	Vicinity of Quang Tri	9 MAB 31, 33 MAU 1/9, 1/4 HMM 164, 165	Support VNMC Assault	-0-
Lam Son 72 (II)	29 Jun 72	Vicinity of Quang Tri	9 MAB 33 MAU 1/4, 1/9 HMM 164, 165	Support VNMC Assault	3 KIA 2 WIA 1 CH53 2 CH46s

Operation Name	Dates	Location	Units	Remarks	Losses
Lam Son 72 (III)	22 Jul 72	Vicinity of Quang Tri	9 MAB 31 MAU 1/4 HMM 164	Support VNMC Assault	1 WIA
ReadyOp	9 Sep 72	Vicinity of Cau Viet River	9 MAB 33 MAU 2/4 HMM 165	Turnaway simulated landing	-0-
End Sweep	27 Jan 73–18 Jul 73	NVN	9 MAB HMM 164, 165 HMH 462, 463	Support TF 78 Mine Countermeasures	3 CH53s

Marine Corps casualties in Southeast Asia between April 3, 1972, and January 29, 1973, totaled seven KIA, fourteen WIA, and one POW. Total aircraft combat losses for the same period were twenty-four. *Marine Corps Command Center Chronologies, Courtesy of Charles D. Melson, Chief Historian, Headquarters Marine Corps*

Appendix F
• • • • • • •

U.S. Aircraft and Aircrew Losses in the Vietnam War

From 1962 until August 1973, 2,118 U.S. airmen were killed and 368 POWs were returned. There are still 586 missing in action. The United States expended 6.16 million tons of aviation munitions in Vietnam, compared to 2.15 million tons in World War II and 0.45 million tons during the Korean War.

The following table of U.S. aircraft losses is summarized from an October 1973 report by the Directorate for Information Operations, Department of Defense, and includes losses up to August 15, 1973, when all offensive operations ended in Southeast Asia in accordance with congressional mandate.

Selected Statistics of U.S. Aircraft Losses, 1962–1973

	Combat Losses	Operational Losses	Total Losses	Losses to SAMs	Losses to MiGs
1962–1971					
Fixed Wing	2,305	1,084	3,389		
Helicopter	2,452	2,229	4,681		
Total	4,757	3,313	8,790		

	Combat Losses	Operational Losses	Total Losses	Losses to SAMs	Losses to MiGs
1972–1973					
Fixed Wing	256	74	330	197*	
Helicopter	135	53	188	7	
Total	391	127	518	204	
1962–1973					
USN Aircraft					15
USAF Aircraft					63
USMC Aircraft					1 (1972)
Total	5,148	3,440	8,588	204	79

*USAF lost 16 B-52s in 1972 and 2 in 1973 to SAM missiles.

Appendix G
· · · · · · ·

Navy and Marine Corps
F-4 MiG Kills, 1972–1973

Date	MiG	Squadron	Carrier	Pilot	NFO
19 Jan 72	MiG-21	VF-96/64	*Constellation*	Lt. j.g. Randall H. Cunningham	Lt. j.g. William P. Driscoll
6 Mar 72	MiG-17	VF-111/ 43	*Coral Sea*	Lt. Garry Lee Weigand	Lt. j.g. William C. Freckleton
6 May 72	MiG-17	VF-51/ 43	*Coral Sea*	Lt. Cmdr. Jerry B. Houston	Lt. Kevin T. Moore
6 May 72	MiG-21	VF-114/63	*Kitty Hawk*	Lt. Robert G. Hughes	Lt. j.g. Adolph J. Cruz
6 May 72	MiG-21	VF-114/ 63	*Kitty Hawk*	Lt. Cmdr. Kenneth W. Pattigrew	Lt. j.g. Michael J. McCabe
8 May 72	MiG-17	VF-96/64	*Constellation*	Lt. Randall H. Cunningham	Lt. j.g. William P. Driscoll
10 May 72	MiG-21	VF-92/64	*Constellation*	Lt. Curt Dose	Lt. Cmdr. James McDevitt
10 May 72	MiG-17	VF-96/64	*Constellation*	Lt. Matthew J. Connelly III	Lt. Thomas J. J. Blonski
10 May 72	MiG-17	VF-96/64	*Constellation*	Lt. Randall H. Cunningham	Lt. j.g. William P. Driscoll
10 May 72	MiG-17	VF-96/64	*Constellation*	Lt. Randall H. Cunningham	Lt. j.g. William P. Driscoll

Date	MiG	Squadron	Carrier	Pilot	NFO
10 May 72	MiG-17	VF-96/64	Constellation	Lt. Randall H. Cunningham	Lt. j.g. William P. Driscoll
10 May 72	MiG-17	VF-96/64	Constellation	Lt. Steven C. Shoemaker	Lt. j.g. Keith Virgil Crenshaw
18 May 72	MiG-19	VF-161/41	Midway	Lt. Henry A. Bartholomay	Lt. Oran R. Brown
18 May 72	MiG-19	VF-161/41	Midway	Lt. Patrick E. Arwood	Lt. James M. Bell
23 May 72	MiG-17	VF-161/41	Midway	Lt. Cmdr. Ronald E. McKeown	Lt. John C. Ensch
23 May 72	MiG-17	VF-161/41	Midway	Lt. Cmdr. Ronald E. McKeown	Lt. John C. Ensch
11 Jun 72	MiG-17	VF-51/43	Coral Sea	Cmdr. Foster S. Teague	Lt. Ralph M. Howell
11 Jun 72	MiG-17	VF-51/43	Coral Sea	Lt. William W. Copeland	Lt. Donald R. Bouchoux
21 Jun 72	MiG-21	VF-31/60	Saratoga	Cmdr. Samuel C. Flynn Jr.	Lt. William H. John
10 Aug 72	MiG-21	VF-103/60	Saratoga	Lt. Cmdr. Robert E. Tucker Jr.	Lt. j.g. Samuel B. Edens
11 Sep 72	MiG-21	VMFA-333/66	America	Maj. Lee T. Lasseter	Capt. John D. Cummings
28 Dec 72	MiG-21	VF-142/65	Enterprise	Lt. j.g. Scott H. Davis	Lt. j.g. Geoffrey Hugh Ulrich
12 Jan 73	MiG 17	VF-161/41	Midway	Lt. Victor T. Kovaleski	Lt. James A. Wise

Courtesy of Edward J. Marolda, Head of Contemporary Branch, Naval Historical Center, and Charles D. Melson, Chief Historian, Marine Corps Historical Center

Appendix H
• • • • • • • •

Vietnam War Facts

- 58,148 U.S. military personnel were killed in Vietnam.
- 75,000 U.S. military personnel were severely disabled due to wounds.
- 23,214 U.S. military personnel remained 100 percent disabled veterans.
- 5,214 U.S. military personnel lost limbs.
- 1,081 U.S. military personnel sustained multiple amputations.
- Of those killed, 61 percent were younger than 21 years old.
- Of those killed, 11,465 were younger than 20 years old.
- Of those killed, 17,539 were married with an average age of 23.1 years.
- Five U.S. military personnel killed in Vietnam were only 16 years old.
- The oldest U.S. serviceman killed in Vietnam was 62 years old.
- 240 U.S. military personnel were awarded the Medal of Honor during the Vietnam War.

As of January 26, 2006, the Department of Defense listed 1,807 Americans missing and unaccounted for from the Vietnam War. The fate of the "last known alive," or LKA, remains the saddest for families. Live sightings occasionally stir hope for some families. The Department of Defense Prisoner of War/Missing Personnel Office (DPMO), as of 2006, has determined that of the 162 original LKAs, remains of 62 have been recovered (48 from Vietnam, 11 from Laos, and 3 from Cambodia). Declassified national intelligence estimates on Vietnam report unexplained reports that some POWs were sent to Russia.

Only one American emerged from the Vietnam War long after the war ended. Marine Private Robert Garwood was repatriated in 1979.

POW Escapees
Aiken, Larry Delarnard, E4, USA
Anderson, Roger Dale, E2, USA

Braswell, Donald Robert, E4, USA
Brewer, Lee, E5, USA

Camacho, Issac, E7, USA

Dengler, Dieter, 02, USN
Dierling, Edward A., E5, USA
Dodson, James, E5, USMC

Eckes, Walter W., E3, USMC

Graening, Bruce A., E3, USA

Guffy, Jerry, E4, USA

Hamilton, Walter D., E2, USMC
Hatch, Paul G., E3, USA
Hayhurst, Robert A., E5, USA

Iodice, Frank C., E4, USMC

Klusmann, Charles F., 03, USN

Martin, Donald Eugene, E5, USA

Nelson, Steven N., E3 USMC
North, Joseph, Jr., E2, USMC

Page, Jasper P., E6, USAF
Potter, Albert J., E5, USMC

Risner, Richard F., 04, USMC
Roha, Michael R., E1, USMC
Rowe, James Nicholas, 02, USA

Tallaferro, William P., E4, USMC
Taylor, William B., E5, USA

Vanputten, Thomas, E4, USA

Wright, Buddy, E5, USA

Courtesy of Richard Kutz, Veterans of Foreign Wars hospital contact representative

Bibliography
· · · · · · · · · · · ·

Many specific details and dates were from, and with the consent of, the following combat participants and authors:

Ethell, Jeffrey, and Alfred Price. *One Day in a Long War*. New York: Random House, 1989.
Kutz, Richard. Veterans of Foreign Wars Hosptital Representative: POW information.
Mardola, Edward J. *Carrier Operations*. New York: Bantam Books, 1987.
Melson, Charles D., and Curtis G. Arnold. *U.S. Marines in Vietnam: The War That Would Not End, 1971–1973*. Headquarters Marine Corps, History and Museums Division, Washington, D.C., n.d.
Sherwood, John, PhD. Historian at the Naval Historical Center, Washington, D.C.
Whitcomb, D. Darrel. *The Rescue of Bat 21*. Annapolis, Maryland: Naval Institute Press, 1998.

Personal Interviews
Edward Ashman (Vietnam War USMC pilot) on April 2, 1988.
Colonel Jim Bolton (USMC Retired) on March 14, 2001.
Fred Cherrick (Vietnam War USN officer) on December 2, 2000.
Captain Stuart D. Landersman (USN Retired) on March 22, 2001.

Miscellaneous
CINCPACAF 110033Z May 1972.
Messages CTG 77.4.
October 1973 report to Joint Chiefs of Staff by the Directorate for Information Operations, Office of the Assistant Secretary of Defense (Comptroller), Department of Defense.
Oprep-3, AR, NHC.
Records of the Chief of Naval Operations (00).
Summary of Air Operations in Southeast Asia, May 1972, CNA.
Toperczer, Istvan. *Air War Over North Vietnam*. Carrollton, TX: Squadron/Signal Publications, 1998.

Glossary

• • • • • • • •

AAA	antiaircraft artillery
AEW	airborne early warning aircraft
Arc Light	B-52 aircraft massive bombing raid
ALE-29	flare dispensers attached to aircraft used for evasive flight actions against heat-seeking missiles
ANGLICO	Air Naval Gunfire Liaison Company—a Marine supporting arms control unit
ARG	Amphibious Ready Group afloat navy ships
ARVN	Army of the Republic of Vietnam (South Vietnamese Army)
Bandit	enemy aircraft
BARCAP	Barrier Air Combat Patrol
Blue Chip	call sign for Seventh Air Force Command Headquarters located at Tan Son Nhut Air Force Base near Saigon
CAP	Combat Air Patrol
CAS	close air support—direct air support close to friendly troops
CASREP	casualty report
CIC	Combat Information Center
CTF	Commander Task Force
CVA	navy attack aircraft carrier
DMZ	demilitarized zone
ECM	electronic countermeasures
EOGB	electro-optical guided bomb
FAC	forward air controller
FAC(A)	forward air controller (airborne)
Fan Song	SA-2 missile fire-control built by the Soviet Union and named Fan Song by NATO
Flak	shrapnel of steel pieces from exploding ordnance
FMF	Fleet Marine Force
Formation	two or more aircraft flying together
Frag Order	fragmentation order, or an add-on order to an operation
GCI	ground control intercept
HMA	Marine Helicopter Attack Squadron
HMH	Marine heavy helicopter squadron
HMM	Marine medium helicopter squadron
Horsecollar	life preserver with sling dropped from helicopter for rescue
Iron Hand	flight operations against fire control radars

LGB	laser-guided bomb
Linebacker	operational name for attacks against North Vietnam in 1972
LPH	landing platform helicopters—navy amphibious ship
MEB	Marine Expeditionary Brigade
MEF	Marine Expeditionary Force
MIA	missing in action
OPCON	operational control
POL	petroleum, oil, and lubricants
POW	prisoner of war
Raydist	radio transmitter beacon device for ships or helicopters to track
RABFAC	backpack radio beacon used to direct aircraft to targets
Redeye	U.S. handheld surface-to-air antiaircraft missile system—has been replaced by Stinger system
SAR	Search and Rescue, or Sea-Air Rescue
Shrike	radiation-seeking missile
Sidewinder	AIM-9 heat-seeking missile
SITREP	situation report, or report of current happening
TACAIR	tactical aircraft
TF	Task Force
TFW	Tactical Fighter Wing
TG	Task Group
Tally ho	terminology used to express that target has been seen
Top Gun School	U.S. Navy fighter pilot's school in air-to-air combat maneuvering (ACM)
USS	United States ship
VA	Navy Attack Squadron
VF	Navy Fighter Squadron
VMA	Marine Attack Squadron
VMA(AW)	Marine All-Weather Attack Squadron
VMFA	Marine Fighter/Attack Squadron
VMO	Marine Observation Squadron
VNAF	Vietnamese Air Force
VNMC	Vietnamese Marine Corps
VNN	Vietnamese Navy
WBLC	water-borne logistics craft
WIA	wounded in action
Wild Weasel	tactical aircraft fitted with antiradiation missiles to seek and destroy enemy radar sites
Wonder Arches	large arched concrete domes built to protect parked aircraft from incoming mortars and rockets

Index

· · · · ·

Note: Traditional Vietnamese names give surname first; alphabetized by surname, "Bui The Lan," for example, is found under "Bui The Lan" not "Lan, Bui The," as would be expected of a Western name.

Johnson, Lyndon B., 18, 19, 34, 35, 104, 252, 296
Johnston, Kevin M., 178
Jones, George E., 162
Jones, William K., 102
Jones, Robert, 297
Joy, Jim, 38, 39, 44, 58
Judge, Darwin, 289

Kanakanui, William A., Jr., 98, 99, 186, 252, 313
Kennedy, Jack, 20
Kennedy, John F., 18, 19
Kingston, Robert C., 272
Kissinger, Henry, 9, 22, 73, 77, 92, 93, 137, 138, 165, 166, 215, 236, 248, 252, 260, 266, 276, 279
Kovaleski, Lieutenant, 250, 251
Kroesen, Frederick J., 48, 136
Krosnoff, Gregory, 115
Krulak, Victor, 225
Kulland, Bryon, 60
Kuntz, James C., 265
Kutz, Richard, 328

La Celle, Chuck, 62
Lan, Colonel, 132
Landersman, Stuart "Stu" D., 16, 75, 76, 84, 85, 87, 98, 99, 102, 104, 111, 130, 133, 134, 210, 313, 314
Landersman, Martha, 313, 314
Langan, William H., 128
Lansdale, Francis G., 17
Lapoint, John M., 56
Lasseter, Lee, 186–189
Lautenberg, Frank, 315
Lavelle, John D., 26
Le Ba Binh, 48, 49, 53
Le Duc Tho, 22, 92, 93, 165, 215, 252
Le Kha Phieu, 299, 300, 315, 316
Le Nguyen Khang, 52
Leavitt, Donovan R., 56
Littlewood, Lyle, 95, 98, 104, 108
Lively, Stephen, 159
Livingston, Lawrence H., 54, 56, 136, 160
Locher, Captain, 125
Lodge, Bob, 125
Long, C. W. "Woody," 103
Long, Robert L., 109
Luong, Lieutenant Colonel, 130
Lynch, Ramond, 315

Masstricht, W. H., 99
Mack, William P., 22, 26, 29, 30, 36, 52, 73–78, 80, 81, 84, 86, 88, 92, 95, 97, 101–103, 107–109, 111, 113, 126, 132, 133, 135, 283, 314
Majors, William T., 280
Maloney, William, 226, 227, 231, 232
Marshall, L. J., 74, 107, 138, 140, 166
Marshall, General, 69
Martin, Graham, 287
Marvin, Steven, 257
McCain, John S., II, 93, 126, 127, 314
McCain, John S., III, 93, 126, 127, 314
McCauley, Brian, 216, 217, 226, 255–260, 267, 273–275, 316
McDevitt, James, 125
McKenzie, Robert P., 74, 76, 77, 176, 314
McMahon, Charles, Jr., 289
McNamara, Robert S., 139, 171, 180, 293, 294
Melson, Charles, 15
Mentesana, Philip, 115
Metcalf, Donald J., 42, 48, 57, 58
Metzger, Louis, 159, 176, 178, 181, 199, 222–226, 232, 270
Milledge, Elvin, 124
Miller, Edward J., 103, 129, 132, 145, 151, 199, 216
Miller, Carl, 115–117, 314
Miller, D. E. P., 203, 204, 277
Moore, Ronald, 115
Moorer, Thomas H., 93, 126, 180
Morgan, Thomas,
Morgan, Barry, 114
Munsch, Al, 118
Murphy, Gary, 16, 315
Murphy, Thomas J., 16, 158, 159, 315
Murray, John D., 40–42

Ngo Quang Truong, 128–130, 145, 147
Ngo Van Dinh, 47, 48
Nguyen Cao Ky, 104, 313
Nguyen Dang Hoa, 160
Nguyen Do Ky, 132
Nguyen Nang Bao, 38, 39, 57
Nguyen Than Xuan, 288, 317
Nguyen Van Kiet, 69, 70, 72
Nielsen, Ben, 47, 62
Nimitz, Chester W., 137, 172
Nixon Doctrine of 1969, 19
Nixon, Richard M., 14, 19, 20, 22, 34, 35, 37, 73, 75, 76, 85, 88–91, 93, 94, 105–107, 109, 111, 113, 127, 137, 138, 156, 165, 167, 180, 189, 236, 237, 239, 243, 245, 248, 251, 252, 263, 266, 276, 279, 285–287, 296, 300

The Hub's Metropolis

Greater Boston's Development from Railroad Suburbs to Smart Growth

James C. O'Connell

The MIT Press   Cambridge, Massachusetts   London, England

MIT Press books may be purchased at special quantity discounts for business or sales promotional use. For information, please email special_sales@mitpress.mit.edu or write to Special Sales Department, The MIT Press, 55 Hayward Street, Cambridge, MA 02142.

This book was set in Garamond and Gotham by the MIT Press. Printed and bound in the United States of America.

Library of Congress Cataloging-in-Publication Data

The Hub's metropolis : Greater Boston's development from railroad suburbs to smart growth / James C. O'Connell.
    p.   cm.
Includes bibliographical references and index.
ISBN 978-0-262-01875-3 (alk. paper)
1. Boston Metropolitan Area (Mass.)—Economic conditions. 2. Cities and towns—Massachusetts—Boston Metropolitan Area—Growth. I. Title.
HC108.B65O26   2013
330.9744'61—dc23
2012029442

10 9 8 7 6 5 4 3 2 1